UNION HOUSE, UNION BAR

The History of the Hotel and Restaurant Employees

and Bartenders International Union, AFL-CIO

Union House Union Bar

THE HISTORY OF THE

HOTEL AND RESTAURANT

EMPLOYEES AND BARTENDERS

INTERNATIONAL UNION

AFL-CIO

by Matthew Josephson

RANDOM HOUSE, NEW YORK

FOREWORD

Wishing to do honor to our beloved General President Hugo Ernst, the 1953 convention of our International Union instructed me to arrange publication of a history of this great organization, to be written by a professional historian of standing in his craft. After careful thought we invited Mr. Matthew Josephson to undertake the work. Over a period of twenty-five years he has published numerous works of biography and history that have won him honors in his field and an international reputation. What is more, we felt that he would bring to this task a sympathetic understanding of the role of the trade union in society.

Although the convention's intent was to have the book between covers to place in President Ernst's hands in November, 1954, when he was to mark his fiftieth year as a member of this union, his untimely death in July of that year occurred while the manuscript was still in progress.

To the reader, especially the union member, who takes it up I commend this as a good book, accurate in its reporting of events and honest in its presentation of the life story of a social institution which mirrors the times through which it has grown to maturity.

The pageant of these years has been played by a million or more men and women in thousands of acts and scenes on many hundreds of stages. Handed the job of telling our story, a hundred writers would come up with as many different accounts, each accurate and true in its own way. But no one of them could hope to satisfy all the players in the pageant or leave all of them with the feeling that he had told the story just exactly as they might have liked it.

To attempt to mention by name all who participated in the events described here, or to have tried to do justice to all the local scenes involved in the story of our International Union, would have yielded not a single-volume history but an encyclopedia. Many will, inevitably, feel some measure of disappointment at finding no mention of their own town or local union. Others may, perhaps, differ with the author's interpretation at various points, or with the selection of the thread of events from which the story was to be woven. Yet selection there had to be, lest the account become—out of all proportion—overburdened with details.

The writing of any history covering over six decades and so many different places and people, the reading of thousands of letters, the interviewing of a myriad people in search of colorful eyewitness accounts of past events—all this might have engaged an author fruitfully for long years. Mr. Josephson had but fifteen months. In this time he performed prodigious labors, studying all convention proceedings, searching the files of our journals, collecting hundreds of letters and clippings, talking with hundreds of hotel and restaurant workers, union officers, and employers, in the course of seven thousand miles of travel, visiting local branches throughout the United States. He has come up with a well-knit and spirited account of the years of our union.

One of its chief purposes is to help later generations of union members gain some understanding of the early, difficult struggles required to forge this organization out of the experience of working cooks, waiters, bartenders, hotel service workers and others. It is hoped, as well, that this book will help our members and the general public to see how a great trade union, like any other social instrument, goes through a process of birth and growing pains before it arrives at a stage of maturity.

It was better, we believed, that such a history be written through the mind of a single personality than by the exertions of "too many cooks." Therefore we have not challenged Mr. Josephson's professional judgment, because we share his view that history should not be written to accommodate itself to the changing attitudes of different parties or factions. We think the story as it stands is a fair measure of our willingness to let the chips fall where they may.

Ed S. Miller

CINCINNATI, OHIO
July, 1955

Contents

Illustrations

INTRODUCTION

This is the history of an old labor union that is young in heart, for in the years of ripe age its growth and progress have been nothing less than spectacular. The Hotel and Restaurant Employees and Bartenders Union was born threescore and five years ago, not long after the founding of the AFL itself. But for a long period the union ranked low in the scale of organized labor. Its members composed but a small minority of the numerous men and women who worked at the catering and culinary trades, most of whom were semi-skilled or casual laborers. They were, in earlier years, truly downtrodden people, dependent for their poor existence upon an industry that was unstable and whose employing class consisted of tens of thousands of small restaurant and tavern proprietors and hotel men. (Even today there are about 300,000 restaurant and bar proprietors and some 21,000 hotel keepers, the large or "chain" concerns being the exception.) You might have said with justice that a union in this field might be "the hardest to organize" and "the least likely to succeed."

That the HRE has become in late years one of the ten biggest labor organizations of America, and as President Meany of the AFL-CIO has said, "one of the fastest growing," is in itself testimony to the validity and force of the trade-union idea. Compared with the average of all American unions, this International Union has expanded since 1933 at a rate that is twice as great as the others'.

Here it is plain that labor organization has provided the mass basis for self-help, for winning what the people need for their everyday existence. Sociologists have recently commented with interest upon the noticeable change in the spirit and manner of the service workers who nowadays feed about one-fourth of the U.S. population

—a change toward greater dignity and independence. With the social habits of Americans changing perceptibly, and the catering and hotel trades growing to the status of a fourteen-billion-dollar industry with a personnel of 1,800,000, the HRE has before it one of the widest fields of any union. The story of this union's trials and achievements foreshadows, no doubt, what may happen tomorrow among the unorganized masses of workers in the light industries and service trades, the "attendants," the retail clerks, even the salesmen and stenographers who are still without benefit of unions.

At various periods the HRE has suffered from almost all the ills that have beset our labor institutions in the United States; it was almost destroyed by the coming of Prohibition, which its members certainly never asked for. I have tried to write of the times of adversity, as well as of the days of good fortune, in a spirit of candor, while also paying respect to the courageous officers and members who reconstructed their union after the disasters of the Prohibition Era. It must be borne in mind that the fortunes of the labor movement, and its evolution, reflect the common cultural environment of America as a whole, including the existing standards of its local and national politics and, above all, those of its business community.

The late President Hugo Ernst used to call the people of his union "a regular League of Nations" because of the extraordinary number of different race and language groups they represented. He said also:

> How soon we are apt to forget the historic development of our organization. . . . We give too little thought to the changes in working conditions since the founding of our union. The memories live again for me of the days at the turn of the century when I first went to work as a bus-boy in a hotel at $4 a week, for fourteen hours a day, seven days a week. The waiter of today with his guaranteed wage, fixed working hours, security of his job from tyrannical employers—under union protection—has no idea of the conditions we "old-timers" worked under, or the wages we got—if any. Or the fear of being fired at a moment's notice. . . . Those days are gone forever.

Study of this giant union that has grown up in the restaurant and hotel trade would seem to offer all the greater interest for the very reason that it has confronted "a most difficult industry to organize," as George Meany said in an address before a recent convention of the HRE. He added: "You have come a long way. You have a long way to go."

The writer alone is responsible for the presentation of facts and events and for his interpretation of them. He is grateful to the general officers of the union and its headquarters staff at Cincinnati for their cooperation with him in gathering together records and documentary and pictorial material bearing on the union's history. President Ernst was frequently consulted up to the time of his death in July, 1954. He was not only a man of great character and stature but also, thanks to his rich experience, a fountain of knowledge of the labor movement. I wish to make acknowledgment also to President Ed S. Miller and to Secretary-Treasurer Jack Weinberger for the considerable help they each gave in bringing this work to fruition, so that there might be some adequate record of their union's history. W. R. Wasson and Director of Organization Charles Paulsen, at the union headquarters, also furnished the writer with much useful information and advice. Dr. Leonard Nierenberg, formerly of the HRE's Research Department, made available carefully prepared economic data concerning this industry. The unfailing friendliness and thoughtfulness of Frederick B. Sweet, the present editor of the HRE's official journal, is never to be forgotten.

John Bookjans, the union journal's former editor (now retired), a veteran of the struggles of half a century in the HRE, served as the writer's research assistant, and was an inspiring helpmate. Mr. Bookjans' vivid recollections of conditions and events of long years ago, happily recorded in diaries he kept, were drawn upon freely in the early part of this history.

The HRE is widely distributed in the geographical sense. There is endless fascination in the variety of scene and character one meets during a tour of the union's network of local branches that spread through forty-five states. In New England, in the Middle West, in the mining communities of the Rockies, and on the West Coast from Hollywood to Seattle, local officers and rank and file members received the writer with typical American and trade-union hospitality. They have all helped, more than they know, and more than can be told here.

Matthew Josephson

SHERMAN, CONNECTICUT
July, 1955

UNION HOUSE, UNION BAR

*The History of the Hotel and Restaurant Employees
and Bartenders International Union, AFL-CIO*

ONE

The Not-So-Gay Nineties

"If you get a picture of the restaurant business as it is today, you won't get a true picture at all. You should have seen it when the waiter was still mud under the feet."—AN OLD CHICAGO WAITER (quoted in W. F. Whyte: *Human Relations in the Restaurant Industry*).

The labor movement in America was young when the first local union of workers in the catering trade which we have record of was formed in Chicago almost ninety years ago, in 1866. It was called the "Bartenders and Waiters Union, Chicago," and was also known later as "Local 57," for it was affiliated with the city's trade assembly, and with the so-called National Labor Union, one of the early short-lived attempts at a federation of trade unions.

Labor unions in the nineteenth century were known generally as "benevolent" or "protective" associations and consisted usually of groups of craftsmen confined to a given locality or city. Some of these, to be sure, such as the printers and cordwainers, dated back to the days of George Washington. However, it was during the era of swift industrial expansion following the Civil War that we began to have numerous unions of nationwide scope, such as those of the iron molders, coopers, glass workers and locomotive engineers.

The Bartenders and Waiters Union of Chicago was, at any rate, an experiment in real trade unionism. "The oldest union in the

United States of amalgamated membership," it was called in an 1897 issue of the International Union's official journal. Its members, at the beginning, were all Germans who had absorbed lessons in unionism in Europe before they emigrated to this country.[1]

Previously, during the 1850's and 1860's, there had been only a few small "labor clubs" of immigrant German or French cooks and waiters who had come here to work in the culinary trade. But in the 1860's their industry, though ancient enough, was exceedingly small when compared with its present commanding size. With the exception of a few fashionable houses in our major cities, it was almost entirely made up of small eating establishments employing two or three workers. It was beginning to grow, however, and by the 1890's employed a labor force of approximately a quarter of a million persons.

Hotels and taverns have been supplying man's basic needs for food and shelter for some three thousand years. The first inn known to history is said to have provided lodgings and meals to travelers for a regular fee in Greece during the seventh century B.C. In the New World of the early American settlers, taverns and hostelries also flourished along the post roads, as in town and countryside of old Europe. Though they were intended mainly to accommodate transients, the old inns and taverns gradually developed into centers of informal social life for the local townsmen. Long before there were businessmen's conventions and church society meetings in hotels, human beings in groups found in the hostelries "dining rooms away from home" where they not only quenched hunger and thirst but drew an added nourishment of the soul from the sharing of food and drink with others, whether friends or strangers. But always at their side there were the waiter and the server of beverages, and there were the cook and the kitchen worker to whom life in the tavern meant not only the fellowship of men but an arduous and exacting labor.

In nineteenth-century America there had been only a few great "hotels"—the word in the original French means "mansion"—that could serve a crowd of two hundred or more diners and provide rooms for them as well, as did the old Tremont House in Boston or the Astor House in New York. The real boom in this traffic came during the "railroad age" after the Civil War. The railroads built hotels and the hotel men built or helped to build railroads. In the central quarters of our major cities large restaurants as well as hotels were erected that were now furnished with the most costly appointments. It was the age of plush that suited the tastes of the newly rich who had won fortunes overnight by packing pork, selling coal oil or building railroads.

Our nineteenth-century hotels had almost all been run according to the American Plan, with fixed meals served at stated times (usually without tips), after which the customer was refused service. But toward the end of the century epicurean repasts, formerly known only to Europe's aristocratic or wealthy classes, were being purveyed to prosperous Americans in restaurants and hotels of the "Continental" type. These were staffed by thousands of European-born and European-trained chefs, apprentice cooks, headwaiters and waiters who, in the late nineteenth century, introduced Americans to exotic foods and drinks of all sorts, guiding their tastes, and even acting, it has been said, as their "social arbiters."

The hotel and restaurant managers clamored for European craftsmen and apprentices—trained in trade schools or societies then unknown here—who could cook and bake, arrange food attractively upon a plate and serve it with skill. And so it came about that most of the catering workers, in that time of unrestricted immigration, were immigrants, or the sons of immigrants, coming largely from France, Germany, Switzerland, Italy and the Austro-Hungarian Empire. Often an American hotelier or restaurateur would go to Europe and there engage a skilled chef and with him a whole kitchen crew, or a headwaiter and his staff of waiters and busmen. Still others shipped as steerage passengers by the tens of thousands to serve in the gaslit hostelries of Boston, New York, Chicago, St. Louis and San Francisco.

In our big new cities, to the eyes of the immigrant all was noise and bustle. Wages were certainly higher than in old Europe, and each man had an equal chance to better his lot, which was why the immigrant had always come here. But employers had a sharp eye for profits and drove their workers hard.

In times of thriving trade the cooks and their helpers, still weary from their labors of the night before, rose before dawn, usually at 5 A.M., limped along through the dark, silent streets to the grimy back doors of their hotels or restaurants and started their fires. Day and night they toiled before great stoves in kitchens or cellars heated to the warmth of the nether regions.

The waiters, by custom, stood with their hands behind their backs, with a towel around one arm and bowing to the customers as they came in; or ran their feet off for fourteen or fifteen hours bearing trays of food and drink. Yet, though waiters' days were long and hard and their proprietors or managers traditionally exercised a stern discipline over them, all but a few eating establishments were small and "human." Life in America was more leisurely and spacious in that time. The streets of our cities were busy with horse-drawn carriages and buggies moving sedately at only eight or ten miles an hour. Meals were protracted affairs, with the hotels then serving four meals a day, including tea. But a substantial turkey dinner cost only twenty cents and a bottle of aged bourbon rated only seventy-five cents as late as 1900.

This tolerable state of affairs, however, could change overnight. At fairly regular intervals, after the years of plenty, a great panic and depression would suddenly burst upon the country. When business dwindled, the restaurant, tavern and hotel workers were the first to feel it, and many soon found themselves on the street. There was, of course, no Social Security of any kind. In bad times laborers from mills and factories besieged the restaurants for work at any pay, so that they might eat. The discharged waiters folded up their dress suits and hard shirt-fronts in a parcel and wandered from one town to another seeking work. News of a World's Fair and its expected tourist traffic would send crowds of traveling waiters to Chicago, as in 1893, or to St. Louis, later; rumors of a mining boom drew them to the new frontier cities of Colorado, with their free-drinking, free-spending, square-eating miners; or on to California and the small metropolis of San Francisco, beyond which lay the Pacific. Working in a tavern, a man could always eat. To find a job he had to apply at the back door of the restaurant or hotel, where the line-up customarily took place at the same hour, usually eleven-thirty in the morning. If there were too many ahead of him, and no job, it was too late to apply at another hotel until the next day; and so the idle waiter or cook would repair to some popular saloon where he might live for another day on beer and free lunch—provided he had the price of a beer.

The call of the road was strong for many waiters yesterday and today.

"We were young then and never worried about anything," one of the most venerable of their number said in reminiscence recently. "We could go off to some new place where we heard 'things were better.' In the morning you suddenly had a job and might, with good luck, earn as much as $1.25 a day; and you felt rich! A man could buy a meal for five cents, fifty years ago, or a glass of whisky for ten cents or less." [2]

When things went badly for workers, the more intelligent among them would say (as one was overheard saying only the other day):

"You can't get any place by yourself, but you have to get the guys together, and then maybe you can do something." [3]

The first impulse of workers who remind themselves of the hardships of their existence is to form a local union, as the bartenders and waiters of Chicago did in 1866. Then they seek to affiliate themselves with a national body embracing local groups in different cities or regions so that each can lend help to the other.

The 1870's and 1880's, the years of peace after the Civil War, saw great stirrings in the young American labor movement. There was, to be sure, much confusion of thought and loud controversy among those who tried to lead the workers: some were inspired by utopian ideas; others by the doctrine of socialism; and still others by the example of the British unions organized along economic lines by craft or trade. Eventually the native radical movement known as the Knights of Labor succeeded in uniting large numbers of mechanics and farmers for its "crusade of the plain people of America" against "wage slavery." By the 1880's the Knights had emerged as our most important national labor body with a membership of 700,000, at the peak.

With its mixed following, its quaint rites of initiation, its hope in cooperative ventures, and its opposition both to craft unions and to strikes, the Knights of Labor were wholly unlike our modern labor federations. Yet many local labor groups or trade assemblies were drawn into their ranks in all parts of the country. Their local assemblies and district assemblies did help to organize both the skilled and the unskilled in major industries; and, despite their avowed idealism, they did become involved in many industrial struggles or walkouts aimed at betterment of the workers' hours and wages. It is of special interest to us that the first known local union of bartenders and waiters, after having maintained its organization for about fourteen years, affiliated itself in 1886 with the Knights of Labor. It now assumed the title of District Assembly 7475, K. of L., with its membership made up mainly of waiters and "beer-slingers." Thus the catering trade workers were not far behind in the procession of America's early labor unions.

One of the founders of the present-day International Union, Jere L. Sullivan, has written of the first Chicago organization:

> In the few years of its existence, "old Seventy-Four, Seventy-Five," as it was lovingly called by its promoters and membership, blazed a trail the like of which no other labor organization had succeeded in doing up to that time. It was the original low entrance and high dues organization and the first labor organization in the

West that leased property and fitted up a meeting hall for labor, called Waiters' Assembly Cooperative Hall. . . . That hall, by the way, housed [District Assembly 24 and] several of the most famous labor unions of that period.

In his later reminiscences, Jere L. Sullivan, who as a young waiter worked with the Knights, conveys to us something of the humanitarian or "uplift" spirit that marked the early labor body. Meetings in the Knights' halls were conducted with great solemnity, and were begun usually with readings from the Scriptures and ardent sermons by the Master Workman who presided. And after such gatherings, as Sullivan relates:

> District Assembly 7475 sent forth into the highways and byways of the land men who had absorbed the teachings of Brotherhood and willingly surrendered time and money in endeavors to wake up the workers and induce them to organize.[4]

The Knights' missionaries must have traveled swiftly and far. In the same year that the Chicago group joined, some two thousand miles to the west, in San Francisco, a group of waiters and cooks formed District Assembly 58, Knights of Labor. Meanwhile, in Brooklyn, in 1882, a local group (which later was known as Local 2) was also affiliated with the Knights. What was to be Local 1, New York (in the present International) was formed not long afterward, in 1886, out of several labor clubs, named German Waiters Union No. 1, and was also affiliated for a time with the K. of L. Even earlier, a Marine Cooks and Pastry Cooks Association, with headquarters in Cincinnati, its workers drawn from the cooks on the Ohio and Mississippi river boats, had become active in these early movements toward a federation of local labor groups. Meanwhile Jere L. Sullivan himself, when only twenty-one years of age, on leaving Chicago for St. Louis in 1885, served as a missionary for the Knights of Labor and helped found a new Local Assembly of waiters (which later became Local 20).

How much the "great upheaval" of the 1880's affected the thoughtful members of the working class is shown by the experience of another itinerant waiter who was also to play a dominant role in the formative years of the catering-trades' union. He was W. C. Pomeroy, a tall and handsome youth to whom, as one of his contemporaries wrote, nature had been kind and generous:

> Born in Kentucky of old American stock, he had inherited the forceful eloquence of the Clays and Breckenridges. He was pos-

sessed of a keen and vigorous mind, a strong body, and unbounded cunning. . . .

In his early manhood Pomeroy had worked as a waiter on river boats plying between New Orleans and St. Louis. During one of his lay-over trips at St. Louis, he, with other waiters, went to a hall where they expected to dance. On this particular evening there was a mass meeting of wage earners. Peter McGuire was the speaker. It was the first time Pomeroy had heard his philosophy of trade unionism expounded and from its most able platform orator. That speech changed the course of his life and opened unto him a new field.

After this meeting Pomeroy went to Chicago, joined the Knights of Labor, assisted in organizing the catering crafts and soon became their outstanding leader.[5]

Peter C. McGuire's union, the Brotherhood of Carpenters and Joiners, like that of his friend Samuel Gompers, President of the International Cigarmakers, was then affiliated with the Knights of Labor. In good time both McGuire and Gompers, turning against the Knights, were to become the founders of the American Federation of Labor and leading exponents of craft unionism; but in the early 80's the Knights still appealed to trade union men as the best hope for a national federation.

In studying the early career of Jere L. Sullivan, who was also a much-traveled waiter and, like Pomeroy, was inspired by the teachings of the Knights to become a leader of his brother-workers, we receive authentic impressions of the hardships and hazards known to the men of his craft—though it was Sullivan's habit in later years to make light of his youthful experiences. We feel the strong currents sweeping through the rank and file of labor in the heyday of the Knights three-quarters of a century ago, and observe how the culinary workers, though low in the scale of labor then, were actually among the first to join the procession of our early unions into that federation.

"Shortly after Noah's ark arrived on Mount Ararat, I began working in a hotel . . . ," Jere L. Sullivan wrote long afterward, in his quizzical manner.

He was born in Willimansett, Massachusetts, not far from the city of Springfield, on January 3, 1863, the child of Irish immigrants. His father, according to his account, was a civil engineer, hence a man of some education, who was employed for a time in the paper industry. The young Sullivan attended the public grammar school of Willimansett and was for a year or two at a Catholic parochial school.

(However, in later years he ceased to be a practicing Catholic.) He was short and slight of figure, with sandy hair and blue eyes, which, in later life, had deep pouches around them. When still a boy of barely fifteen he left home and began to wander about, taking odd jobs of all sorts, including, finally, that of the waiter.

After working for brief periods in catering establishments in various New England towns, he journeyed on to the Middle West and resided more permanently in Chicago and St. Louis. As he describes his work in the small eating-places of the 1870's and 1880's, the duties of the waiter appear to have been much more varied than is the rule nowadays. He served, in fact, as "an all-around handyman, who occupied the position of cook, waiter, bartender and oysterman at one and the same time." What was more, he was sometimes obliged to fill in as a musical entertainer.

> The writer recalls a trip he made to New Haven, Connecticut, some years ago, and was offered a position on Chapel Street, where he had to take turns on the floor as a waiter, tend bar and do a singing stint each evening, alternating with others *who were forced* to show ability along the lines mentioned. (Italics added.)

Notice that, while making light of such experiences, he pictured the waiters as being "forced" to do turns of singing. Most waiters could not sing too well and felt humiliated by such demands on them. When they left their tables and appeared on a little platform, still wearing their aprons, as "singing waiters," some of the customers charitably threw them coins for their efforts; but the unruly ones who had eaten and drunk too well, though not too wisely, laughed and hooted at them. The old-time waiters disliked such chores and held that singing should be left to members of the Musicians Union.

Besides his other duties, culinary and musical, the waiter might be set to wielding the broom, washing floors, polishing silver and cleaning the windows, and doing the work of a cleaning woman. As one of the old-time, versatile breed of waiters, Jere Sullivan often prepared vegetables and "cleaned the overcoats off green corn," or presided over a steamtable in the dining room. Betimes he mixed an old-fashioned toddy or "early morning appetizer" at a sideboard in view of the guests. In Chicago he "killed fish," which was the term used then for opening and serving oysters. But when he first tried to gain admission into the cooks' union, he recalls, "they gave me the laugh, told me I was an oyster man, and belonged to the waiters."

Sullivan's object, in this jesting account of his early labors, was to emphasize what he came to believe in later years, the need for clearly defined craft or trade rules. "I organized a waiters' union," he concludes, "so as to be able to belong to *something*." That was the Local Assembly of Waiters of St. Louis, which, he adds, enjoyed fair success and even "had one strike of goodly proportions, which it won. . . ." [6]

By 1885 the Knights were at their zenith, following a victorious struggle against a lockout imposed on union workers along the Jay Gould railroads in the Southwest. For a brief season the urge to "join" was everywhere strong. But by 1886 the Knights of Labor's decline had set in, and men in the labor movement turned to other channels in their quest for unity and economic power. The extensive use of the boycott at this period ended by frightening people of property and political influence. A tragic episode for labor was the mysterious bomb explosion at the Haymarket in Chicago in May, 1886, following incidents arising from mass meetings of striking workers before the McCormick Harvester factory. A group of anarchists, who were not even affiliated with the Chicago unions directed by the Knights, was charged with being guilty of the bombing outrage; its leaders were tried, and four of them hanged. While laboring men throughout the world protested at what was widely believed then and now to be a "frame-up" or miscarriage of justice, a great hue-and-cry against all unions and especially the Knights' organization was set up in the press.

Meanwhile there was growing protest in the labor movement itself at the arbitrary leadership of the Knights of Labor, through the national council of Grand Master Workmen, which often overruled the wishes of local or district assemblies or constituent unions. The International Cigarmakers, led by the brilliant Gompers, had become embroiled in a bitter dispute with the K. of L. hierarchy, which had allowed the entrance of a dual union into the cigar trade. As a result Gompers, with McGuire and other strong craft union leaders, was busily promoting plans for a new nationwide labor body, the American Federation of Labor.

At about the same time the waiters' and bartenders' organization, Chicago's District Assembly 7475, also found itself involved in a serious dispute with the national leaders of the Knights, who had ordered them to exclude from their union members who handled intoxicating beverages—that is, the bartenders! The Chicago waiters, for a long period, stoutly resisted such orders, holding that the men who dispensed beer all day long were their hard-working brother wage earners, entitled to the full rights of unionism. Various local assemblies, including 7475, also protested at excessive assessments levied on their membership by the K. of L.'s high council, their protests being ignored. Ultimately, in 1889, the Chicago Assembly of waiters and bartenders had its charter revoked by the Knights of Labor; but that body was already a dying organization.

The wage earners, tired of ephemeral movements, were now pinning their hopes on the new AFL and the "practical idealist," Samuel Gompers, who was its architect. A Jewish immigrant from England, and originally a devoted socialist, Gompers had acquired in later life, through the successful struggles of the New York cigarmakers, deep convictions about the need for businesslike unions of skilled workers organized along economic lines, like the enduring craft unions of England. Above all, labor must avoid political agitation, unite its forces on the economic front, strengthen its weapons for collective bargaining and fight for "control of the job." Such were the ruling ideas of the new American Federation of Labor, whose small constituent convention held at Columbus in the dark days of December, 1886, was attended by several representatives of the first waiters' and cooks' unions.[7] With his stubborn drive for effective, "job-conscious" unions and a unified national body to lead them, Samuel Gompers in those earlier years proved to be the best organizer the restaurant and tavern workers had.

*

The arrival of that "young giant, the American Federation of Labor," as Jere L. Sullivan then called it, was actually a landmark in our history, though the press at the time gave only moderate attention to the gathering at Columbus, Ohio. Many new national and international unions had been launched in the 70's and 80's; many others were waiting to be born.

It is significant that several of the representatives of the scattered locals of waiters and bartenders from large Eastern cities, such as New York, Cincinnati and Boston, attended that first convention and earnestly considered how the new federation might serve to unite their separate groups so that they might be of help to each other. A certain Julius Weiner, spokesman for the German Waiters Union No. 1 of New York, was among those on hand in Columbus, in December, 1886. He presented a letter to the convention formally requesting that all its member trade unions help the waiters and other catering industry workers form a national trade union. These first local leaders in the movement were under pressure from their followers, who were keenly aware that they suffered from long hours, low pay and unusually evil conditions, even for those ruthless times. Here in short was a growing industry in search of a national union.

The old letters written by workers of that time trace for us a truly dark picture of conditions in the culinary trade. Thus the secretary of the Buffalo Waiters Alliance reports that as late as 1901 there were still places in that city where a waiter

> is compelled to work from five o'clock in the morning until nine and ten at night, seven days a week, for the munificent sum of $3 a week. Out of this they must buy jackets and aprons and wear clean linen. . . . The average hours for a day's work is 14, and the average wage $4 per week.[8]

An article in one of the earliest publications issued by a waiters' union, the *Kellnerzeitung* ("Waiters' Journal"), published for the German Waiters Association of New York in 1892, describes the unpleasant hiring methods in vogue at that period. Our "typical" migratory waiter of the not-so-gay nineties, when unemployed, often repaired to a saloon in the big cities and usually to one known to be frequented by people who worked in his own trade. It was not only for the beer and free lunch and fellowship that he came, but because it was usual that the bartender at such a place might know of a job to be had. Thus was developed a crude employment exchange, of which the writer relates:

> The Saloon Hiring System was the brain child of several New York City headwaiters. Since no legitimate employment agencies were in existence, the waiters hung around certain saloons. These saloon keepers, the bosses and the headwaiters worked together. A headwaiter or a boss would call one of these saloons for waiters. The saloonkeeper in no uncertain tones made it known that only his "good customers" would receive preference for a job. Hence a waiter in order to secure work and earn $2.00 was compelled to spend $1.50 in drinks. In addition, the headwaiter usually insisted on a kickback for the privilege of hiring him. The waiters referred to this hiring system as the "Vampire System." [9]

Another of the early waiters' union leaders of New York, named Julius Leckel, writing at the same period, laid stress upon the long hours and the "speed-up" methods used even then by restaurant proprietors:

> Traffic in black slaves was luckily abolished by the bloody Civil War, but, unfortunately, *white slavery* is still flourishing in various guises. . . . One class of wage-earners still suffering from such bondage is, without doubt, the waiters' profession . . . the general public is unaware of the fact that waiters are very often compelled to work fifteen hours, and even longer, day after day, with hardly

enough allowance of time to partake of the hastiest of meals. . . .
No man can work for fifteen or sixteen hours and do his work well.
The long, tedious days and nights make the waiters drowsy. . . .
To create incentive to remain keen and alert, a number of proprietors abolished the payment of regular wages and inaugurated
payment by percentage. This new method worked well at first, but
. . . as soon as the waiters, by increased activity, earned more
money than their former wages, the bosses cut down the remunera-
tion from 10 per cent to 5 per cent of their sales. . . . The majority only managed to earn about $4 a week, and being powerless to
help themselves, had to walk the streets. . . . [10]

Thus the leaders of the waiters' and cooks' locals who came to the
first AFL convention were full of the grievances of their people and
eager to apply for local charters from the Federation. The first of
these was granted to the New York Waiters Union in March, 1887,
under the title of Waiters Union, New York, No. 281. A bartenders'
union of New York was given a charter soon afterward, in May, 1887,
as Local 646, Bartenders, New York. In January, 1888, a bartenders'
union from Brooklyn was also chartered as Bartenders Local No. 643
(now Local 70); and in February, 1888, the bartenders of Boston
(later Local 77) were chartered. Next came the German Waiters
Union of St. Louis; and in 1890, when the AFL was growing rapidly,
there followed the American Waiters and Bartenders of St. Louis (now
Local 20), in which Jere Sullivan was a moving spirit; the Waiters
Union of St. Paul; then the Waiters League of Chicago (headed by
W. C. Pomeroy); and the Waiters Union of Brooklyn (now Local
2), all of whom were endowed, for the time being, with separate
"Federal" charters. After them, in 1891, came waiters' local organ-
izations from Indianapolis and Minneapolis; the first cooks' unions
from Denver, Colorado, and St. Louis; and the Bartenders Mutual
Aid of Logansport, Indiana.

Within four years after the start of the AFL, whose leaders, at the
beginning, moved slowly and prudently about their business, charters
had been granted to fourteen catering industry locals situated in different parts of the country. The strongest of these local groups, which
were working toward the objective of a national union for the catering trade laborers, were those of New York, Boston, Chicago and St.
Louis, where young Jere L. Sullivan showed much enterprise.

The movement of the old Chicago group can be traced from its
beginning in 1866, as an independent organization, to its entrance
into the Knights of Labor in 1880, and its transfer to the AFL in
1890, under a new name ("The Waiters League of Chicago"), at the

insistence of the ambitious Pomeroy. He had become their leader, saw the national union of the catering workers already taking shape, and now strove to gather its local branches together and assume command of the whole nationwide organization.

There was much busy correspondence between the other local leaders also. At the December, 1890, convention of the AFL in Detroit, a delegate for the Bakery Workers Union (which was eager to promote the use of its union label through allied labor organizations) announced preliminary plans for a "Waiters National Union," and called upon all other AFL unions for help.

Meanwhile, Julius Weiner, one of the leading spirits among the waiters of New York and Brooklyn, with the support of the locals in that area, called together several conferences of the representatives of waiters' and bartenders' groups and strongly urged that the proposed national union in their trade include the bartenders also, which was agreed upon. Finally, on April 23, 1891, a meeting of the same initiating groups from New York and New Jersey was held in New York City, and a provisional constitution for the new union was framed. That same day, the constitution, together with an application for a national charter, was submitted to President Gompers at AFL headquarters, then in New York; the application in the name of the "Waiters and Bartenders National Union" was approved by Gompers in behalf of the AFL Council, and granted on the following day, April 24, 1891, the birthday of the present union.*

Not long afterward, by a ruling of the AFL Council, affiliation with the new national organization was made compulsory for all waiters', cooks' and bartenders' locals; President Gompers, in fact, "ordered" all locals having AFL charters in the catering craft to enter it.[11]

*

The culinary workers and bartenders were now started on the road to a national union in which their forces might be combined. Zeal for the waiters' crusade was not wanting; and the bartenders too had a will to be organized. But the road to successful unionism was to be long and hard; many barriers were to be overcome. There was the difficulty, for instance, of having to conduct meetings in three or more languages, mainly English, German and French. Members from different nations did not understand each other well nor trust each

* The names of the original applicants for the National Union charter were: Julius Weiner, Harry Meisel, Louis Lange, all of New York; William Thiery of Hoboken, N. J.; and Fritz Junker of Brooklyn. Weiner was chosen by the others as the first Secretary of the new organization, whose affiliated locals were reported as having 450 members in all.

other readily. Before their first convention could be held, the weakness of their trade union principles was shown by a jurisdictional fight between two of the New York area locals which had provided the initiative for the national union. Local 1 had declared a strike against the "park" or beer garden run by a Mr. Brommer; but the bartenders of Local 2 who were employed there refused to come out with their brothers of Local 1, for the bartenders and waiters had not yet learned to love each other. The provisory National Board of the embryonic union could find no other way out of the dilemma than to suspend Local 2, of which Julius Weiner was a member. Thus he had to be replaced by a new National Secretary, Julius Leckel, waiter, of Local 1.

Leckel, the young firebrand who used to make such impassioned speeches on the wrongs suffered by the waiters, proceeded with a good deal of energy to organize the first national convention of the union, which was held on January 18 to January 20, 1892, at the meeting-rooms of the so-called Hotel and Restaurant Alliance of New York, at 132 West 27th Street. There were in all fifteen delegates present, representing, as the chairman reported, fourteen locals with an estimated membership of 1,014—much overestimated, according to some accounts. But in the case of most of those locals, there was just talk of affiliation. This was really a paper organization, with only a nucleus representing New York, Hoboken, New Jersey and Philadelphia. Pomeroy and the Chicago local held back. At the last minute, it was reported, the Waiters Alliance of Boston, a union claiming 1,600 members, had also decided not to send any delegates to this convention. There was even less chance, as yet, of having delegates from interested locals as far away as St. Louis and Denver, not to speak of San Francisco. In its first half year of existence the Waiters and Bartenders Union had raised only $440.45 in revenues and had a balance in the treasury of but $87.09. The old minutes relate: "The convention expressed regret at the inability of some affiliate locals in the Far West to attend the convention because of the expense involved."

National Secretary Leckel made the opening address for this first gathering, and Secretary Christian Evans and Treasurer John B. Lennon of the AFL also addressed the delegates, expounding the Federation's trade union principles governing the procedure of its affiliated bodies, which (unlike those of the Knights of Labor) stressed strict autonomy in the different trade groups. The new waiters' and bartenders' organization would need, first of all, a sound financial structure and a treasury, they urged.

The delegates deliberated over their constitution and bylaws and ratified them. But no clear rules were laid down for compelling local unions to pay their per capita tax promptly to the national union's treasury, which, as Leckel reported, already suffered from indefinite delays of payments. As for welding the different locals into a true union, there was also delay in several cases; the Philadelphia delegates, for example, stated that they were not authorized to act as yet, but would simply do their best to persuade their local union to ratify the convention decisions and combine forces with the others. (To the great joy of the delegates, news of the affiliation of the Philadelphia Alliance was received on the second day of the convention.) One article of the constitution agreed upon provided for Local Executive Boards in cities having more than one local union, the Local Boards being empowered to regulate wage scales and conditions in their areas. At that time one Local Executive Board was established to cover New York, Brooklyn (an independent city then) and Hudson County, New Jersey, including Hoboken and Jersey City. This was done with the thought of avoiding such quarrels as arose when, during a strike in New York City, members of the Hoboken local rode across the Hudson River by ferry to take the jobs of those who had walked out. The lessons of union brotherhood were not learned overnight.

It is noteworthy that among the delegates who participated in the founding convention were two colored men, Richard Ellis, of the Herbert Association of New York, and S. K. Govern, of their Philadelphia branch. The first convention of the Waiters and Bartenders showed more consideration for the lot of the colored brethren than was usual in 1892 by ruling that local unions of any color or nationality were to be acceptable to the national union; and that where there had been a strike of colored waiters, no white waiters were to apply for work for one year thereafter. In those early days of the labor movement not only were colored workers in segregated locals, but immigrant white workers of different racial stock often preferred to join segregated unions having members who were all Irish, German, Italian or Jewish.

The three-day convention at New York wound up its proceedings by changing the organization's name to "The Hotel and Restaurant Employees National Alliance." It also provided for a National Secretary to serve as a full-time paid officer, a Treasurer, and a National Executive Board of seven members who were all to be elected by convention vote. *The Waiters' Journal*, edited for Local 1 by Hugo Vogt, was adopted as the union's official journal.

These were humble beginnings (not unlike those of other new

unions of the time); yet high officials of the AFL watched closely over the birth of the new organization; and part of the New York press at least (notably the German-language daily *Staatszeitung*) reported its sittings as constituting "The Waiters Parliament."

To arouse enthusiasm for forthcoming organizing drives, a mass meeting of waiters was held at Clarendon Hall, at 13th Street and Third Avenue, New York, on the night of the convention's first day. There were, however, only a few score persons in attendance because —unfortunate augury—a fearful blizzard crippled all traffic in the city that night. While the snow fell outside, the speakers, headed by Chairman Max Becker, an officer of Local 1, warmed up the small audience with tirades upon the low earnings of waiters ($5 to $8 a week), the "kickback," and the "saloon-hiring" system. The Negro leader, S. K. Govern, in his talk, made the intelligent proposal that their new union try to establish a central employment bureau to control hiring.

One of the convention delegates, John Mee, a man sporting the full-blown walrus mustaches that were in fashion, and reckoned one of the ablest union organizers among them, spoke in practical spirit of the fine accomplishments of the Boston Waiters Alliance organized by himself (which later that year became affiliated with the national union). They had been able to reduce working hours of their members from fifteen to ten hours per day; wages in hotels had been increased from $22 to $30 a month. Holding up the strong Boston local as a model, Mee called for the building of powerful locals in other cities under the new national body as the one way out for the people of the catering trade.[12]

A leavening force at the start was certainly the group of socialists of the old style, typified by Hugo Vogt, editor of the *Waiters' Journal* and a leader of the Socialist Labor party. According to the recollections of Max Becker, of German Waiters Local No. 1, "The socialist spirit was unmistakably present. . . . Culinary workers who were socialists joined the unions as a matter of principle and did most of the organizing." Many of the immigrant workers in the trade had absorbed the teachings of the socialists in Europe, and earnestly believed, as one of the resolutions at the 1892 "mass meeting" in New York declared, "that all wealth is produced by the workers, and that the workingman does not get his share of the wealth he produces."

The closing day of the New York founding convention was celebrated by an enthusiastic banquet at which the delegates drank toasts to the health of the infant "National Alliance" and to the brotherhood of all culinary workers.

Chicago had been chosen as the site of the union's second convention, to be held in May, 1893, at the time of the opening of the World's Columbian Exposition. A convergence of the "traveling craftsmen" was naturally expected at the great fair which drew so many millions of tourists. The persuasive letters of W. C. Pomeroy, who was reported to have organized locals of bartenders, cooks and waiters in the Middle-Western metropolis, and the entrance of his large Chicago contingent into the "Alliance," also had much to do, no doubt, with the decision to meet in Chicago.

In 1892 and the early months of 1893—prior to the great panic and depression of that year—notable progress had been made in extending the organization. Ten new locals had been chartered. National Secretary Julius Leckel had shown great fire and helped to organize 1,800 waiters in two new locals, principally in the hotels of New York.

Though picketing was then forbidden by police regulations, and conviction therefor carried heavy fines and prison sentences, he led strikes against the old Holland House, Delmonico's Restaurant and other large establishments. Employing one ruse or another, he and other union officers would manage to get inside a hotel, jump on a bench, make fiery speeches to the "scabs" inside, and bring them out in the nick of time, before the police arrived.

The inspiring Julius Leckel, one of the early heroes of the waiters' union, who passed quickly into obscurity, was an ill and high-strung man. In a dispute with his fellow members of the first Executive Board, he suddenly, in September, 1892, resigned his office as National Secretary, though he continued his unremitting organizing labors for his local.

After 1893, in the days of depression, he was involved in a number of unsuccessful strikes, with the result that the two new locals he had organized, Nos. 8 and 9, within two years lost virtually all their membership. The unions had no funds and their members were blacklisted by every hotel in New York. One of his associates has related:

Julius Leckel brooded over the miseries of the workers. His health began to decline, and he went from one hospital to another, until he became insane and died in Central Islip Hospital, New York.[13]

But to return to Chicago where the second convention opened on May 22, 1893, with twenty-one delegates present, the new National Secretary, Theodore Birk, reported that twenty-four locals were now affiliated with the Hotel and Restaurant Employees Alliance. The large Boston union, Local 77, had come into the fold; St. Louis delegates also had come to Chicago; and there was a delegate from Denver, as well as one from Salt Lake City. What was more, Pomeroy, the big Kentuckian, brought in a group of four locals from Chicago, including the Western Colored Waiters Alliance, and a new Local 40, which claimed a numerous membership—though it was to be charged afterward that there were no records or other evidences of such members. A total of 3,533 workers was now claimed as enrolled in the National Union. This, too, was later considered a much inflated estimate.

At the Chicago gathering several of the delegates carried proxies for locals other than their own which had been unable to send a representative to the convention. The system by which a handful of men, wielding proxies for absent local delegates besides their own votes, could control these small conventions was thoroughly exploited by the forehanded Pomeroy, who easily dominated these gatherings. Moreover, he had his finger in more than one trade union pie at the time, it was noticed.[14]

Present for the first time as a convention delegate to the Hotel and Restaurant Employees Alliance was the lively little "globe trotter" Jere L. Sullivan, last residing in St. Louis, but now representing Local 6 of Salt Lake City, Utah. Sullivan in those days was inspired, as he said, with the gospel of brotherhood and unionism and was eager to play his part in promoting the new catering workers' organization. But from the beginning he found the "slick article" Pomeroy, who so fascinated his fellow workers, a lion in his path. Sullivan mistrusted the breezy Pomeroy; and the handsome Pomeroy in return characterized Jere L. Sullivan as a restless little "schemer" who smoked too many of those newfangled cigarettes and had a "yaller" complexion.[15]

There was a stubborn honesty in Jere L. Sullivan that led him to propose, before this convention, that inquiries be made into the alleged membership of Local 40, Chicago, organized but a few weeks earlier and headed by Pomeroy. Charges were filed against the local and a committee appointed to investigate its books; but access to any records was bluntly denied to it. Appealing to the convention, in a forceful speech, Pomeroy gained a sweeping vote of confidence, which ended all talk of inquiry for the time being.

John E. Mee, of Philadelphia, but then active in organizing New York, was elected President by acclamation. Woyt Losky, of Local 14, Denver, was chosen as Secretary. However, elections of members

of the Executive Board brought in three new officers who were associated with Pomeroy in Chicago, while Pomeroy was named as delegate to the AFL convention.

Changes in the union's laws were now made requiring prompt local
union tax payments (based on per capita of membership at five cents
per member) into the national treasury, on pain of suspension of the
delinquent local within ninety days. Publication of a new official journal named *The National Purveyor* was voted, and by resolution
headquarters of the Alliance were now shifted from New York to
Philadelphia. Another measure also authorized the issuance of
"special" charters as inducements to bartenders' locals, which were to
be affiliated under the separate heading of "National Bartenders
League, Connected with the Hotel and Restaurant Employees Alliance, AFL." For the English-speaking bartenders of 1893, in their
pride, were still hesitant to join forces with the (mostly) foreign-
born waiters and cooks.

"A determined effort was made at this convention," Sullivan wrote
afterward, "to get rid of the *barnacles*, but it was not to be. . . .
They remained to harass incoming officers and prevent progress." The
"barnacles" referred to by Jere Sullivan were the sort of convention
delegates who wielded proxies and through a clique of five or six men
dominated the lawmaking convention of twenty-five or more local
unions.

*

Things went badly for the new union during the terrible depression
of 1893 to 1895. Money was scarce, unemployment widespread, and
wages were cut. Strong unions that had taken part in the first push of
the AFL lost ground at this period, featured by heavy defeats of labor
in huge railway and steel strikes. In the case of the weak catering
workers' organization in New York, a veteran union officer recalls the
remaining members of a once-large local reduced to but eight in
number by 1895, meeting together and shedding tears at their reverses.[16]

The third convention of the Hotel and Restaurant Employees, duly
held in St. Louis in May, 1894, was a disheartening affair, with but
thirteen delegates representing, now, a smaller number of locals.
Secretary Losky reported that their treasury consisted of a deficit of
$584.88, incurred chiefly through advances to cover publication costs
of the official journal, *The Purveyor*, which appeared only at irregular
intervals. The time of the meetings was consumed chiefly by conflicts
over the opposing jurisdictional claims of the New York locals.

Jere Sullivan was on hand again, heading the St. Louis delegates on this occasion, and as persistent as ever in giving battle to the Chicago faction headed by Pomeroy. At his initiative a motion to eliminate the use of proxies at conventions was presented, but outvoted by the group that was armed with most of the proxies. Then Sullivan and his allies moved again to inquire into the affairs of Local 40, Chicago, which caused a tumultuous scene at the meeting, in the midst of which Pomeroy suddenly left the place on the pretext that an urgent "wire" had called him back to Chicago. His departure brought an end to the hostilities. Yet Pomeroy still kept his hand over the affairs of the small union.

The next two conventions again were also poorly attended, that of April, 1896, in Cincinnati, having only seven delegates, with Pomeroy and four of his associates in control. One henchman of Pomeroy was elected to the purely honorary office of President; Pomeroy himself was elected as Vice-President and Editor of the union's official journal; while the Secretary, Frank A. Egger, also a delegate from a Chicago local, was Pomeroy's chief lieutenant.

W. C. Pomeroy had begun his career in Chicago as an ardent trade union organizer, fluent of speech and with his pen. His book, *The Lords of Misrule*, written during the depression years, was a work of exposure and protest at the evils wrought by financial monopolists, a work that contemporaries said "might have come from the pen of a Bellamy or Ignatius Donnelly." [17]

But this able and eloquent man, driven by his ambitions, was caught up in the whirl of Chicago politics and, later, state and national affairs. The new trade union of catering industry workers seemed to him only a vehicle useful for political ends. By 1896 the Pomeroy faction ran the union, while the initiating groups in New York and elsewhere who were for "uplift" or socialism (such as the unfortunate Leckel), turned to other organizations or dropped out of the labor movement in disgust.

A contemporary's account relates that "in the exciting political campaign of 1896 Pomeroy became an ally of Mark Hanna (Chairman of the Republican party) and is said to have had charge of the distribution of immense sums of money to influence the votes of working men away from William Jennings Bryan." [18]

In St. Louis, however, the stubborn Jere Sullivan, who represented the decent element, clung to his position of influence in his local union, No. 20, though Pomeroy's influence was directed against him there, too. With increasing bitterness, Sullivan watched the behavior of his opponent, whom he regarded as a traitor to the working class, and waited for the good moment to attack him.

At the fifth convention, in Cincinnati, in 1896, as Sullivan (who was absent) learned: "The men from the Windy City had everything fixed many weeks in advance. On every proposition that came before them, it was fourteen to six, and though the opponents stood their ground, the Chicago gang was armed with sufficient proxy votes to overcome all opposition." [19]

Headquarters of the national union were now removed from Philadelphia to Chicago, under the wing of Pomeroy. His faction were determined to stay in office and ignored numerous protests and petitions sent by various locals to the Executive Board. The time and site of the next convention, in 1897, was to have been decided by referendum vote; but at the last hour, telegrams were sent to the locals that it would be postponed. It was, of course, a high-handed and unlawful action taken without sufficient notice and without the approval of the local unions.

"The feeling now grew," as Sullivan wrote, "that the real paying locals were being victimized; their officers, giving up hope in their national union, filed their complaints with President Gompers of the American Federation of Labor." [20]

The charges of the St. Louis group, headed by Sullivan, were serious ones: that unlawful actions had been taken in postponing a convention without the vote of the locals' members as required by the union's constitution; that funds of the national union were being wasted; that no adequate financial records were kept by the executive officers in charge; and that opponents of the "Pomeroy machine" were ousted from the Executive Board or even expelled from the national union. One major grievance was that when union workers from other cities came to Chicago and tried to deposit their union traveling cards with the Chicago locals, these cards were not honored and the men were refused work. The good folk in the New York, Boston and St. Louis locals, in short, were up in arms at the Pomeroy crowd, and determined to drive them out.

Pomeroy, with his "machine," reflected the low standards of big-city ward politics carried over into the labor movement. Sullivan, the former "traveling craftsman," represented the movement of reconstruction being directed by the pioneers of the AFL. He had pondered much and educated himself; at the age of thirty he showed brains and character and entertained serious views of his "mission" in the trade union field. As one eyewitness of the conflict relates:

At first Pomeroy tried to laugh Sullivan off, but Jere had a sense of humor and he refused to be whipped in that manner. The next attempt was to crush him. That ended in failure. Then they tried to buy him off, promising him influence, rank and position in the Union, but Jere remained obdurate and steadfast, rejected Pomeroy's bid for favor, and gave him battle to the end.[21]

While charges against the Pomeroy faction were being weighed by the AFL Executive Council, the spoilsmen went ahead and held their convention at Detroit in April, 1898 (later declared illegal), named their own slate of officers and passed new rules according to their pleasure. As in 1896, Sullivan did not attend these proceedings as a representative of his St. Louis local, No. 20. A new St. Louis local of mixed bartenders and waiters had been formed by a break-away group of Local 20, led by one of Pomeroy's henchmen; and it was this man who, with the connivance of Pomeroy, appeared at the Detroit convention instead of Sullivan as a St. Louis delegate. That year a number of New York local leaders turned up again at the Detroit gathering, among them William Lehman and Harry Meisel, officers of Local 1, who were both elected to the Executive Board. But when they discovered what was going on and refused to "play with the gang," they were suspended and replaced.

At the orders of Pomeroy, the Executive Board then moved against the leaders of the opposition. As the *National Purveyor* reported at the time:

> Acting under instruction of your laws your General Executive Board were compelled to expel ignominiously Jere L. Sullivan, Henry Newmark and W. F. Jones for crimes against the International Union too numerous to mention. . . . To the splendid and loyal membership we extend hearty greetings and thanks for their support. To schemers of the Newmark-Sullivan stripe, we say: Obey the laws, be honest or out you go! [22]

In the journal he edited, Pomeroy now wrote articles heaping ridicule upon "Cigarette Jerry" Sullivan of St. Louis. The cause of his expulsion is made clear in a satirical sketch describing "Yeller Jaundice" Jerry proceeding to AFL headquarters in Washington to bring complaints against his own union's executives:

> The "minister plenipotentiary" puffed three whiffs of stench into the face of President Gompers and the president fled from the city. The "special commissioner" then invaded the sanctum of Secretary Morrison and the atmosphere retreated into the inkwell, until Jerry departed for a scab joint to feast on a doughnut. . . . And Jerry returned to the arms of his anxious friends in St. Louis enshrouded in a glow of saturnine satisfaction and cigarette smoke. The National Capital was saved. . . . [23]

Jere Sullivan kept President Gompers closely informed of the instances of mismanagement and unlawful actions charged to the Alliance's executive officers. During the AFL convention of December, 1898, in Kansas City, he appeared again before Gompers and the Executive Council and, "armed with charges, backed with facts" that were "startling," renewed his appeals for disciplinary treatment. In an action unprecedented for that time, Gompers, in behalf of the AFL's Council, declared the latest convention of the Hotel and Restaurant Employees Union, in Detroit, April, 1898, to have been "an illegal gathering," its officers' actions irregular and unlawful, its decisions void. Pomeroy and his lieutenant, Eggers, were also on hand at the time in Kansas City, but failed in their efforts to have the blow softened. Yielding to pressure of the AFL leaders, Pomeroy now agreed to submit the matters in dispute between the two factions to a board of arbitration of five members, he to appoint two, Sullivan and his colleagues two others, and the fifth to be named by the AFL Council. This group, sitting as a high labor tribunal, was to examine the affairs of the Union, compose differences between the warring factions, lay down rules for proper conduct, and call for a new convention.

The five men who were chosen as members of the Arbitration Board were: Thomas L. Lewis, Ohio District Secretary of the United Mine Workers, and John F. O'Sullivan, Vice-President of the International Typographers, who both represented the Pomeroy faction; Owen Miller, Secretary (later President) of the Musicians' Union, and William E. McEwen, Secretary of the Minnesota Federation of Labor, both representing the Sullivan faction; while John C. Dernell, Auditor of the International Cigarmakers, represented the AFL and acted as chairman.

An informal conference was held at first in Kansas City between the Arbitration Board and the two opposing leaders, at which it was stipulated that the Board's members were to audit the union's treasury accounts and books; both sides were to cooperate with the Board and abide by its decisions; a call was to be issued for a special convention to be held in Chicago, in March, 1899; and the members of the Board were to sit in the convention.

To these demands Pomeroy had seemed to yield with good grace. However, he still had some last cards to throw in.

*

The arbitrators appear to have been a group of worthy AFL officials who acted with much prudence. "We were conscious that the ap-

pointment of this committee was a new departure in the American
Federation of Labor, and . . . that any action taken by us might
be construed as a precedent for violating trade autonomy for which
the AFL ever stands," they wrote in their report of the affair.

When they proceeded to investigate the financial accounts of the
union, they found that the Secretary, Frank Eggers, was out of town;
he did not even show up four months later at the special convention
in March, 1899. No minutes or records were made available to them.
They learned enough, however, to judge that the union's affairs had
been conducted "in an extremely loose and careless manner, but
there were no evidences of dishonesty on the part of those having
charge of the disbursement of money." This was a tolerably correct
conclusion, although many years later, one of the arbitrators, Mc-
Ewen, wrote that:

> The office work had been entrusted to an aged man, who held
> the office of treasurer. He was an honest German, too old to work
> at his trade, and in mortal fear of Pomeroy. He was the most out-
> standing example of a conquered man I had ever met.
>
> Thousands of dollars of the International Union's money had
> been wantonly dissipated. Pomeroy would frequently rush the aged
> treasurer, demand a sum of money and give him a slip of paper.
> . . . There were a few records and only a few memoranda to reveal
> what had been done with the union's money.

The union was small and its revenues were meager then, with from
one to two thousand members paying five cents a month. Jere L.
Sullivan himself stated that over several years of Pomeroy's leadership, up to 1899, its treasury had incurred a debt of approximately
$5,000, most of it owing to the AFL, and the rest, a few hundred
dollars, representing the "squandering" of funds, mainly for the
union's publications.

The arbitrators recommended changes in the union's laws, providing
for a committee of three auditors to examine financial accounts and
report publicly on them each year; the President was to be a responsible officer, appointing committees and regulating questions arising
between the local unions; the Executive Board was to be made up of
seven Vice-Presidents, elected at conventions, and commissioned as
general organizers. Finally, the Secretary-Treasurer was to keep minutes of convention proceedings and GEB meetings, maintain correspondence with the local unions, and make regular and detailed reports of the union's affairs each year.

> He shall receive and receipt for all moneys of the International
> Union; keep on file all itemized bills of expense, and record them

in a book kept for the purpose. . . . He shall not have more than $100 in his possession at any time. All moneys over this amount shall be deposited in some responsible bank. . . . He shall give bond in some security company in the sum of $2,000 for the faithful performance of his duties; prepare and submit to the local unions on or before the 15th day of each month an itemized statement of receipts and expenditures. . . . He shall furnish charters, blanks, supplies, etc., keep the seal of the International Union.

For all this he was to be paid the sum of $15 per week.

The arbitrators, as may be judged, worked to lay the foundations of a well-conducted labor organization, something that many of the members at that time knew little about. In preparing for the special convention which was to adopt these changes in the constitution, they also acted as a Committee on Credentials and a Committee on Rules who, as "silent spectators," supervised the convention proceedings. Their first step in issuing the call for the 1899 special convention at Bricklayers Hall, Chicago, was to forbid the use of proxies for locals unable to send delegates. The locals were to be entitled to one vote for every fifty members or fraction thereof.

The seventh convention opened on March 6, 1899, at Chicago. Despite "much bitterness between the factions" and the "arduous and disagreeable nature" of their assignment, the arbitrators saw their proposed changes in the laws adopted, and the International Union seemingly launched upon a steady course under new executive officers. They reported to the AFL that they were treated "with extreme courtesy and diffidence . . . by every delegate." [24]

This was a very broad understatement. The real story was quite different and far less peaceful.

Pomeroy's figurehead of a president and his secretary were absent, but he himself came down with a strong force of supporters and proceeded to "stampede" the delegates into his camp so that he obtained a majority of the Executive Board. Though some of the delegates had come with instructions to demand a "new deal," most of them were still dazzled by Pomeroy's "masterly moves on the chessboard of labor organization," as their effusions in early copies of the union's official journal show.[25] Sullivan and his friends were steam-rollered once more and looked on helplessly while Pomeroy's followers were elected to office: Joseph Michaels, of Syracuse, as President, and Fred E. Dresler, of Chicago, as Secretary-Treasurer.

The opposition delegates, as Sullivan said:

were treated in the most shameful manner . . . received neither justice nor courtesy at the hands of the Chicago aggregation, and many times during the week it looked as if the morgue might have some of the "outside" delegates as occupants. . . . Even the Board of Arbitration was abused and snubbed whenever the opportunity arose.[26]

Jere Sullivan, at least, had managed to be elected as Vice-President, thus one of the seven-man GEB, from which Pomeroy, this time, had chosen to withdraw while working behind the scenes.

When the tumult and the shouting of the Pomeroy crowd seemed to have gone too far, on the last day the Board of Arbitrators did take things into their own hands and lay down a series of firm rulings, which helped, as Sullivan recalled, "to revive the drooping spirits of those who had made a fight for better conditions."

The upshot was that, despite the intervention of the AFL's arbitrators, the Pomeroy crowd still controlled the national union— though by a narrower margin. During several months following the reorganizing convention everything went on as before: the Secretary-Treasurer issued no reports; he and Pomeroy paid no attention to the new rules laid down in the revised constitution.

But Jere L. Sullivan, in St. Louis, would not rest or sleep. It was he who persistently urged the President, Joseph R. Michaels, to call a meeting of the General Executive Board, which at length was scheduled for July 31, 1899, at the Chicago headquarters of the union. Sullivan was for forcing a showdown. Michaels, in the last resort, proved to be unwilling to submit to the orders of Pomeroy—who opposed holding such a Board meeting—in view of what he, Michaels, termed "the deplorable condition of the International" and the "criminal negligence of the Secretary-Treasurer, Dresler."

When a quorum of five members of the Board, Sullivan among them, arrived at the Chicago union headquarters for the meeting that was to open in the morning, Dresler, the Secretary-Treasurer, locked up his records and refused to issue any report to the Board. The Board members were also given to understand that unless they cleared out of the place "dire consequences" might follow. Whereupon the GEB moved over to a hotel, the Brevoort House, and resumed its meeting that same afternoon. With Pomeroy and his henchmen absent, the peppery little Jere L. Sullivan was able to outtalk and outargue the weaklings on the Board and win them over to support of drastic reform measures. Sullivan brought formal charges against the Secretary-Treasurer for criminal negligence: he had not even submitted copies of the new constitutional amendments to the union's locals during the past four months, nor reported on finances. The Board then passed measures providing for the suspension of that errant officer, and the written charges were delivered by messenger.

Pomeroy had tried to break into the meeting the first afternoon, saying he wished to report its proceedings in the union's journal. But as he was not a member of the Board he was ordered to leave by the President.

On the following day, August 1, 1899, when the meeting was resumed, Pomeroy burst in again, accompanied by Secretary Dresler and a whole band of his cronies, and addressed the Board

> in a most shameful and ungentlemanly manner, using the vilest and most filthy epithets, admonishing the Board to get out of town before they would land in the morgue, and acting like a maniac. . . .
> He continued this rowdyism for a full twenty minutes, and wound up by attempting a murderous attack, armed with a chair, on the members of the Board; he was prevented in this attempt at carnage by his followers who, by herculean efforts, made him desist. . . .
> As a fitting finale of this display Pomeroy declared he would "put our damned lights out before we left Chicago," meaning that he and his followers would attempt to . . . help the members of the Board off of Mother Earth via the shotgun route.

Sullivan, who was acting secretary of the meeting, and the chief target of Pomeroy's attack, though a small man, held his ground, undaunted. When order was restored, the Board members voted to oust Dresler from office and elected Jere L. Sullivan in his place as Secretary-Treasurer. Vice-President Browne, head of the Bartenders Local 68 of Cincinnati, then offered the union and its Secretary office space free of charge at the local's headquarters in Cincinnati.[27]

After a campaign of many years, Jere L. had bested the dishonest men who held power over the small union, and began his long career in office. He had caught the eye of President Gompers of the AFL; his election to what was then, in the hands of a strong man, the dominant office in the organization, received the approval of Gompers and of the AFL's Board of Arbitrators who still watched over the union's affairs.

The wrath of Pomeroy passed all bounds. He and his allies quickly organized a "rump convention," at Milwaukee, in September, elected new officers and Executive Board members and declared theirs to be the "real" International Union, demanding that the locals pay taxes to them alone. They also directed loud protests and petitions at the AFL Council. But the hard-headed Gompers had no doubts in his mind about which organization might best serve the wage-workers of the country's restaurants and taverns. The quarrelsome aggregation of waiters, cooks and bartenders had its important part to play in his plans for concerted economic action by wage-earners in the food, brewing and transport trades.

Almost a quarter of a century later, addressing a large convention of the International Union, Gompers, in reminiscent vein, described his own part in the Battle of 1899:

PRESIDENT GOMPERS: . . . I have known every president of your International Union from the time of its formation . . . and I think I knew Jere for a while. I think it was the day before yesterday?

SECRETARY SULLIVAN: Don't give away our ages.

PRESIDENT GOMPERS: Well . . . your organization got into the hands of those—well, those who did not regard your interests as the first interests to be considered. . . . But a movement that revolted against that mismanagement, if not corruption, which prevailed, arose and they selected a new Executive Board with Jere L. Sullivan as Secretary-Treasurer. And then when the new Executive Board came to demand the books and papers and other property of the International Union they were barred out. They were given nothing, not even a scrap of paper notifying them that they were not wanted.

The new Executive Board met and notified me that they were the duly elected Executive Board of the International Union. I received a communication from the Executive Board which had functioned before, claiming to be the re-elected Executive Board and consequently denying the validity of the other election or the new Executive Board. Money was continuing to be sent to that other group and very little, if any, to the group represented by Secretary Sullivan. He then wrote me about the condition, of this money being sent to a man who was not an officer of the organization and asked me whether I could assist him. I immediately wrote a circular letter to all local unions of the International, notifying them that the American Federation of Labor recognized the Executive Board of this International Union with Jere L. Sullivan as its secretary and no other. (Applause)

It was merely a stroke of the pen. But it starved those people out of the means of continuing to function.

I may say this, too. I saw Jere L. Sullivan and said to him: "I have staked a whole lot upon my action; I have placed the organization under the control of those with whom you are associated and under your leadership." It was the biggest thing of the kind I have ever done, and "Jere," I said, "I am relying on you to make good." (A Voice: "He has!") [28]

Jere L. Sullivan:
The Early Years

*"Organization only comes to men when they begin
to think."*—Anonymous Letter to the *Mixer &
Server*, March, 1901.

"At the opening of business, August 1, 1899, the International
Union's general headquarters were carried around in the vest pocket
of the writer," Sullivan reported some years later. "We did have hopes
that some day we would be able to pay off the outstanding bills.[1]

Those were dark days for the union of restaurant and tavern workers. Only eight years of age, it had compiled a record notable for
dissension and mismanagement when Jere L. Sullivan took over as
Secretary-Treasurer. He himself, in later, more fortunate years, rather
enjoyed recalling the low estate to which the union had fallen at the
time when he undertook its reorganization.

Its name had been changed once more (in April, 1898) to: "The
Hotel and Restaurant Employees International Alliance and Bartenders International League." The name of the union was long and
imposing, and the word "International" now provided for its expansion into the vast regions of Canada (which contributed three tiny
locals at this time). But it had not even an office of its own as yet.

Headquarters had been maintained lately in Chicago, under the
eye of Pomeroy. But the previous officials had simply barred the door

against Jere Sullivan, refusing to turn over to him cash, books, supplies or seal. The new Secretary-Treasurer was not even provided with a roll-top desk and, of course, he had no Treasury. He had a few dollars of his own which he was ready to advance by way of credit to the reorganized union.

Jere Sullivan knew, moreover, that three-quarters of the many locals chartered in recent years had passed out of existence. Out of two dozen local unions still affiliated with the International only fifteen were in good standing through regular payment of their per capita dues. The total membership, he estimated, in 1899, was 990.

What was worse, the International had lost its numerous members in Chicago who, during the recent period of dissension, had stayed in the locals controlled by Pomeroy and his cronies. Bartenders then wanted their own union and were reluctant to join forces with waiters and cooks, though their calling drew them together with the culinary workers in so many establishments. A report of the AFL's Executive Council, as of December, 1899, noted:

> We observe that the old element has taken advantage of a sentiment which exists in the allied crafts and that they have endeavored to call into existence a "Bartenders National League" separate and distinct from the International.

In New York City the International had also lost ground since 1895, when several hundred of its local union members broke away to join a separate, though small, labor body, called the Socialist Trade and Labor Alliance, which was opposed to the craft union policies of the AFL. This group included a German Waiters Union and the "Liberty Waiters," led by Hugo Vogt, former editor of the *Waiters' Journal*.[2] The ramshackle International Union whose command Jere L. Sullivan assumed in 1899 had but a scattering of small locals in New England, New York State and a few Middle-Western cities, not including Chicago.

Yet he had his "visions" of winning a membership of 10,000 some day and a treasury of "a thousand dollars"! The homeless Secretary had accepted the generous offer of Local 68, Cincinnati, of office space free of charge in its own quarters in the city's downtown district, until the organization could get on its feet. As he made ready to leave St. Louis, Sullivan's friends laughed at him and said he was balmy. But nonetheless he proceeded by train to Cincinnati, where he put up in a cheap furnished room, then went down the next morning to the office of Local 68 and hung up his hat.

The first thing he did, and it was very characteristic, was to purchase a twenty-five-cent receipt book in which to keep his accounts. There one may see how, in his firm, neat hand, he noted down all itemized receipts of various fees for the month of August, 1899, amounting to $33.15, and expenditures of only $24.80. He was bent on keeping the organization solvent, even if it meant paying himself no salary as yet and paying no rent.

Though the prospect seemed as dismal as any labor union had ever faced in its salad days, the truth was that there was tremendous need for a real nationwide union in the growing restaurant and tavern trade. Jere L. Sullivan, now thirty-six years of age, was a clever and resolute man; undoubtedly he had glimpses of the splendid opportunities beckoning the weak, disorganized "International" he now headed. There were thousands who had been organized in Chicago, St. Louis and elsewhere under the Knights of Labor; there were many thousands of others in various clubs, associations or independent unions in New York, in Philadelphia—even in far-off San Francisco. If they could only be brought together into a solid organization, if only their confidence could be regained, the Hotel and Restaurant Employees and Bartenders might go far.

He set to work writing circular letters to all the local unions throughout the country that had at some time been on the roster of the International. He exhorted, he inveighed; everywhere he expounded the principles of good trade unionism. In many letters and in articles in the monthly official journal, which he began to publish January 15, 1900, under the new name of *The Mixer & Server*, he also administered lessons to the members on how meetings of local unions should be conducted, how order should be preserved, how the members should be kept interested and work allotted to them in committees.

At first the still affiliated locals sent him angry complaints; their officers and members were suspicious. One protested that previous payments of per capita dues had never been acknowledged; another, that supplies of buttons and stamps ordered and paid for in advance had never been delivered. Secretary Sullivan continued, however, with infinite patience and stubbornness the unending task of correspondence; what was important was that each month he sent to all local unions a copy of his itemized statements of accounts, receipts and disbursements, small as they were. The several locals now began to show more interest in the reorganized International—which, moreover, had the support of Sam Gompers and the AFL.

In due course, and with careful regard to all the rules and provisions of the constitution, Secretary Sullivan sent forth his call for the annual convention of the International at Cleveland, in May, 1900, nine months after he had taken office. Thirty-one delegates arrived in behalf of nineteen locals, and Sullivan presided over this small gathering.

Most of the delegates now met for the first time the resourceful, keen-eyed little man who had assumed chief responsibility for their poor union. Though small of figure he bore himself proudly, as if conscious of his mental superiority over his bigger, duller-witted co-workers. It is significant that one of the articles he published in the union's journal, some years later, was entitled "Why Short Men Succeed." It made allusion to Napoleon Bonaparte and Admiral Nelson as men who, carrying less superfluous weight than others, worked with more drive and "heart-power." [3]

He was no orator for the masses; his speeches, sometimes long-winded and roundabout, wearied his hearers. On the platform he lacked, as he admitted, the gift of saying much in few words. But he could also show fire and imagination at times, especially in debate with those who challenged his policies. In explaining the reforms he was introducing into their organization, he would become, by turns, sarcastic and wrathful on the score of the misleaders of labor who had preceded him in office, the "wreckers" who, to his mind, were "guilty of a venality and corruption seldom seen in the world!" At this convention, Pomeroy and former Secretary Dresler were expelled from the International.

The union field in those days had many workers who were full of malarkey; and Jere L. could be exceedingly harsh and abrupt with those among them who thought they could pull his foot. From 1900 on he began to employ a few regular organizers who were paid a small salary and expense account and sent out on the road. One of them, a gay dog who usually wore a "rainbow hat" and striped walking stick, describes how, on coming to Cincinnati with a companion to see the Secretary, he found him at work in his office clipping his mail at 7:30 A.M. "And if he cut sandwiches, when in the business, as delicately and gracefully as he cut the ends of those letters, nobody in or out of this business has anything on him." The organizer relates that he tried to "warm him up" for a little advance of porter and cigar money, making various distress signals. But Secretary Sullivan was extremely dry of speech on such occasions. Taking out a document that was an insurance bond for his own good conduct, he waved it at his visitors to emphasize that he was being careful about advances and had no "candy money" for them. The other man recalled:

TO THE

American Federation of Labor

HEADQUARTERS: 21 CLINTON PLACE, NEW YORK CITY, N. Y.

SAMUEL GOMPERS, President.

Any number of Wage Workers, not less than seven, who are desirous of forming a Federal Labor Union, or of having their Local Union, National or International Union affiliated with the American Federation of Labor, must fill up this form and forward it, together with Five Dollars as Certificate of Affiliation Fee, to this office, as above, for approval.

(CITY AND DATE) *New York April 23* 18

We, the undersigned Wage Workers, believing it to be well calculated to improve our intellectual and social condition, and promote our industrial well-being and advancement, respectfully petition the American Federation of Labor to grant a Certificate of Affiliation to us as representatives of:

Name of Organization *Waiters & Bartenders National Union*

Holding Regular Meetings at No. *385 Bowery* Street

in the City of *New York* State of *New York*

We hereby pledge ourselves, individually and collectively, to be governed by the Constitution, Rules and Usages of the American Federation of Labor, with the reserved right to preserve the autonomy or self government of our own organization, subject to such rules and regulations as may be made, or are now established in our organization as above named.

Total number of members in Union *450*

Julius Wiener PRESIDENT

SECRETARY

ADDRESS OF SECRETARY *533 E. 83*

NAMES OF APPLICANTS.	ADDRESSES OF APPLICANTS.
Julius Wiener	*New York*
Harry Meisel	
Louis Lange	
Wr Thiery	*Hoboken*
Fritz Junker	*Brooklyn N. Y.*

Granted April 24

Application to the AFL for the first charter, 1891

Delegates to the Second Annual Convention, Chicago, May 22, 1893.
Seated: second from left, President John E. Mee; next to him, holding
framed charter of the union, Secretary Woyt Losky. Standing: first on the
left, Jere L. Sullivan; rear (tallest figure), William C. Pomeroy

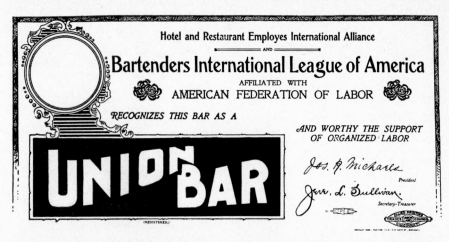

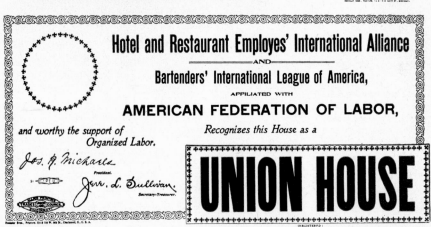

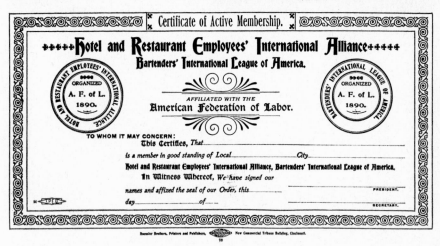

Union House and Union Bar cards used in earlier years

(left) Joseph R. Michaels, Syracuse, N.Y.; Third General President, 1898–1902
(right) Robert A. Callahan, Boston; Fourth General President, 1902–1904

(left) Jere L. Sullivan, St. Louis; General Secretary, 1899–1928
(right) Robert B. Hesketh, Seattle; General Secretary, 1929–1939

"This put a sort of damper on the amount we had made up our minds to ask for." Jere L. was saying to the two organizers, in effect: " 'Here's your hat—what's your hurry?' Quicker than it takes to write this we were hustled over to the fastest elevator I ever was on in all my life." [4]

The first International officers had been, with the exception of Pomeroy, a group of uneducated workers with but dim notions of how a union should be run. Some of the earliest unions among the bartenders, for example, such as the Bartenders Mutual and Benevolent Association of Boston, made it a point to state in their charters that they were organized not only to aid their fellow members but "for social pleasure and mutual advancement."

There was nothing wrong with that, but it represented no effective plan or program for advancing the labor power of the wage earners. What was more, some of the early local officers, as the late President Hugo Ernst used to say dryly, "did not know the difference between *mine* and *thine*." [5] Their gatherings were too often given over to horseplay and the setting off of "sky-rocket cigars" by practical jokers.

"It being my first attendance," wrote one of those who came to the convention of 1904, "I was under the impression that the principal business of the delegates was to have a good time; but I was speedily made aware of my mistake." The serious and efficient manner in which the Secretary and the President in the early years of the new regime conducted the proceedings and the absence of personal friction aroused favorable comment after 1900. [6]

Like a severe schoolmaster, Jere Sullivan labored to instruct his union brothers. In debate, he insisted, speakers were to be dignified and avoid "incriminating personalities." To everyone he expounded the practical businesslike trade union spirit that Gompers and his colleagues were bringing into play with such broad effect nowadays. Sullivan, a lifelong admirer of the AFL's shrewd strategist, said at this period: "A modern labor leader must be a financier, a general, an orator and a diplomat; it is the hardest job on earth." He himself was not all of these things, but certainly typified the new, hard-working administrators who headed the AFL's aggressive campaigns in the 1900's.

The delegates were so pleased with their new executive that they not only re-elected him unanimously but also increased his salary from $15 to $25 a week. At the same time they re-elected Joseph Michaels, of Syracuse, to the then unpaid office of President.

What the new Secretary-Treasurer had to report to the 1900 convention was a promising start for their union. He had been in communication with hundreds of groups throughout the country, and as a result had been able to issue forty-nine new charters—though sometimes to small locals having only ten members. There were by now ninety-four local unions that had become affiliated with the International which, he reported with evident pride, had all of 4,000 members and a balance of $282.94 in the bank.

The delegates at first refused to believe his report, for they had heard such fine things before from Pomeroy and company. But the Secretary spread out his receipts and his books; and the delegates, approaching his table, examined them with their own eyes and saw that everything was as he said.[7]

*

The International Union made a first approach at this time to the organization of women workers. At the next convention held in St. Louis in 1901 a first woman delegate, Sister Bertye Greene, representing Waitresses Local Union 249, of St. Louis, made her appearance and was given a hearty welcome. A year earlier, in Seattle, Washington, fifty waitresses had banded themselves together under the leadership of one of their number, Miss Alice Lord, to form the first waitresses' local, No. 240.

There was some talk, likewise, of organizing the colored workers who were then occasionally recruited in separate locals. Racial equality, practiced by few unions in America fifty years ago, was envisaged in a resolution providing for the transfer of Negro workers into white locals "at some time in the future" when the International Union deemed them "proficient and socially equal to the white crafts."

However, the overwhelming concern of Jere L. was to bring in masses of bartenders. The roster of 1901 shows that in Chicago, for example, where beer flowed in rivers, not one bartenders' local was left to the International—so much harm had the split with Pomeroy's faction wrought.

In seeking to build up the organization promptly, Sullivan, who had once organized a separate bartenders' local in St. Louis, pinned his hopes on the bartenders, holding that the men of this craft were easier to organize. They were chiefly of Irish, English and German stock then, and virtually all spoke English; whereas among the waiters and cooks there was a babel of German, French, Spanish, Italian, Jewish, Hungarian and a score of other races and tongues. The different racial groups among the cooks were also held to be very "clannish"; were divided from each other according to nationality; and, deeming themselves skilled and indispensable craftsmen who could deal with employers individually, resisted efforts to unionize them with waiters and bartenders.

With the sociable and political-minded bartenders it was otherwise. In Cleveland, where the International Union since 1897 had chartered three separate locals of waiters, cooks and bartenders, the waiters, after ten years, had no more than 300 members, the cooks only forty-one, while the bartenders expanded rapidly, organizing a great many small bars that employed no waiters or cooks, and reaching a membership of 500.[8]

In an effort to appeal to the bartenders, Secretary Sullivan, in 1901, encouraged the aspiration of Robert A. Callahan—a popular figure among the Irish barmen of Local 77, Boston—to be elected as President of the International Union. Callahan was a person of imposing physique and a fluent tongue, and, with the support of Jere Sullivan, conducted a most vigorous campaign prior to the convention of 1902, held in Louisville, Kentucky. The previous President, Michaels, seeing that his cause was hopeless, declined renomination. Another who was nominated, J. H. Sunthrop, of Local 51, St. Louis, also declined the honor in a very breezy way, saying in part that it was his intention to return home and build a wall around his home city, as had been declared a year ago by certain delegates who had come to the convention seeking what they did not get. In closing he said:

> In the present game I am up against the real thing: I know it; I have scanned over my hand and find that the best thing I can produce is three deuces and a pair of treys, while my worthy opponent is fully prepared with a Royal Flush; I therefore, Mr. President and delegates, move you that Brother Robert A. Callahan of Local 77, Boston, be elected by acclamation.[9]

In the years from 1902 to 1914 the union became predominantly a bartenders' organization, with the convivial Callahan playing a considerable part in this development. As soon as some funds had accumulated in the International's treasury, several General Organizers were engaged by Sullivan and sent traveling about the country talking to bartenders and tavern keepers with good effect. In many cities officers of existing locals held quiet sessions together and laid plans for membership campaigns, particularly in sections of their towns where union workers in other trades were congregated. The keepers of popular saloons who dispensed beer to the working class were generally not averse to having their employees become union men and having a "Union House" card posted over their bars. The cry was on for "union beer" both on behalf of the strong Brewery Workers Union and the bartenders.

In Boston union bartenders had been required some years before to wear a blue button that became the insigne of their trade. All other unionized workers in the city were instructed to "look for the blue button." Thus the local union of bartenders, No. 77, had grown rapidly, though its initiation fees were $25.00, a large sum for those days. Here as in other cities many bartenders joined the union for social reasons, to widen their circle of acquaintances at the bartenders' balls and picnics, and also with an eye to taking part in local politics.

The great bulk of the barmen's locals came into the International in the period between 1900 and 1904, when members of other AFL unions in large cities were urging bartenders to join or form locals. An old-time secretary of one of the bartenders' locals chartered over fifty years ago, Charles Ikenberry, has written reminiscences illustrating the manner in which many of these local organizations were started:

He had been working for $16 a week on the "six and twelve hour shift" at Sam Alexander's tavern at South Sixth Street, in downtown Minneapolis, for four years without a day off. He relates:

> Sam's place was a square bar where the customers could stand all around, with the bar boys and the booze inside the enclosure. Upstairs were the union halls, and these union men kept asking me: "Where is your union button?" So I said to Jack Hughes, Eddie Collins and two or three other bar boys, that we must start a bartenders' union. So we had a meeting in one of the small union halls upstairs, and just said: "Jack, you be president; Eddie, you be so-and-so"; and they said: "Charlie, you be secretary and get the necessary papers." So I wrote for the charter and "dope" from headquarters and Local No. 152 was started, with dues at $1.00 a month.[10]

At about the same period, Edward Flore, then twenty years of age, was working as a bartender for his father, who owned a downtown tavern in Buffalo, New York, that was frequented by many union men. There was then a small local union of bartenders in Buffalo, No. 175, whose secretary was Fred Seames, later (in 1902) an International Vice-President. At the friendly invitation of Seames, whom he knew well as a neighbor, Ed Flore became a member of the bartenders' local in February, 1900, though he was not actually a wageworker. He worked hard, but certainly did not need the union to win improved wages from his own father. He had then some vague notions of going into local politics and already belonged to several clubs.

Seames had called the young man's attention to the political advantages of joining the bartenders' organization, and Flore, after some reflection, decided to join. Thereafter he showed a genuine interest in his small union of fifty members, became its secretary, and was soon helping in his spare time to bring in more members.

Taking as his example the methods of the experienced Seames, Flore, in approaching his fellow bartenders, "laid emphasis on personal contact, good-fellowship, and friendliness." Often he would visit not only bartenders, but their employers, the tavern keepers, and convince them that it was better for their hired men to join the union, better socially and politically; and the employer would advise his bartender to do so. The saloon keepers had an association of their own and some of their members were active ward politicians. They looked with approval on the establishment of a small trade union body among their employees which might also have some political influence—especially in the days when the Prohibition movement was already gathering force.[11]

Jere Sullivan by now had become entirely convinced of the rightness of Samuel Gompers' teachings that the paramount thing for the American labor movement was to organize the steady workers and craftsmen. It was they who had shown themselves staunch in times of strikes. Without them (as before the days of the AFL), labor unions in America would "blow away" at the first chill winds of adversity, like the leaves on the trees in autumn. The country was being flooded with unskilled immigrant workers who were considered by the AFL leaders as poor union material (though this was later proved untrue). Before the immense task of unionizing these masses of the "unassimilated" and unskilled, most of the trade union officers of that day simply threw up their hands. Better to cleave to the steady craftsmen and fight to maintain the upgrading of wages for trained apprentices and master mechanics—which employers tried to reduce in sweatshops filled with foreign-born workers. In the catering trade, for example, the turnover of union members had been so great that in the International's first ten years Jere Sullivan had seen three-quarters of 191 locals that had been chartered disappear. It was in his eagerness to build a strong base for his union that he turned to the bartenders first of all; their wages were better and they enjoyed more "prestige" among workers than the waiters or pastry cooks.

This policy was noticeable from the early years of his administration. "I think there is a little friction between the two bodies, that is, restaurant employees and bartenders," wrote one delegate after the convention of 1904. "It cropped out on one or two occasions. I don't wish to be pessimistic, but I fear an open rupture in the near future." [12]

Divisions between the crafts were to plague the union for long years to come. The typical restaurant or hotel dining room is, in effect, a "shop" where food and drink is "processed for the public," with the traffic rising to a peak three times a day. Then everyone wants to be served at once and, in the rush-hour, each group of workers, cooks, waiters and bartenders, press or jostle against one another, tempers snapping. The waitress who marks too many of her orders for cocktails as "rush orders" may be rebuffed by the busy service bartender—and she may be seen sometimes bursting into tears of vexation. The cooks in the kitchen line up their work in methodical fashion and sometimes resist the urgent demands of nervous waiters for speed. The bartenders, in any case, used to take pride in the fact that they dealt directly with the public. They stood close to the cash box; had the responsibility of judging who might be served or refused, or trusted with credit; and they often became employers themselves. In former years the barmen tended to look down upon the "menials" who cooked and washed dishes, and upon the waiters as well.

The waiters, too, were at the public end of the "shop"; skill in pleasing the customer and knowing his tastes and habits could become an exacting art, and earnings from tips depended upon such skill. The waiters, however, suffered from the anxieties of a role in which they must strive to please two masters at the same time—management and consumer—whose interests did not always coincide. In any case there was (especially in past years) much friction and jealousy between the different crafts, manifested by loud bickering and swearing in the heated kitchens among the different groups stationed there: cooks, dishwashers, vegetable men, and the pantry-men at the dumbwaiters, who passed the waiters' orders and then the cooked dishes back and forth in an endless line.

The highly skilled craftsmen in this field were really the cooks. A restaurant might change its waiters or its barmen without ill results, but if it lost its good chef, it might lose all its trade. Often the cook's whole crew left with him.

In the unpublished papers of Jere L. Sullivan there is a letter from a skilled chef, dating from 1902, describing the problem of the cooks' trade at that time, a letter that Sullivan intended to use as material for an article in the official journal. It reads:

My dear boy, you will never live to see the day when the skilled workers of the American kitchens will lay aside their peculiar clannish ideas and wholeheartedly cooperate with one another . . . to reduce the obstacles that keep them separated.

The cooks worked fearfully long hours, so that it was said they literally only "worked and slept." That they were kept to this pace was due to the schemes of "dollar-seeking employers" who strove to keep crews of foreign-born kitchen workers divided according to nationality. The letter continued:

> Put a native of Italy in charge of a kitchen, and what is the result? That kitchen is a small portion of Italy set down in this country, and the workers of other nationalities have as little chance to secure employment there as they have of becoming the possessors of a million dollars overnight. The skilled cook of other nationalities may "break in" when the supply of Italians is insufficient, but when one of the nationality that predominates in that kitchen shows up, the non-Italian is quietly let out.
>
> What holds good with reference to the kitchen under Italian direction is equally true of those conducted under German, French, Hungarian, Spanish or any other chefs.[13]

Clannishness and suspicion among the different nationalities was fostered both by employers and by the craft clubs or societies in the trade here in the 1900's. When some of the cooks tried to organize a union, or better their conditions, the employer might turn to a crew of another race, thus pitting one nationality against the other.

On the other hand, the waiters, considered semi-skilled workers, were generally "progressive" and eager to enter unions. They learned much about the world by listening to what everyone was saying. The same anonymous writer remarks in his letter:

> Organizations come to men only when they begin to think, and the waiters especially have more time and reason to exercise their thinking apparatus. They may organize and encourage the cooks to do likewise. . . .

Yet the waiters also were relatively neglected by International Organizers in the early years.

In the 1900's large hotels and oversized restaurants were already becoming a feature of our big cities; the amount of service personnel in such units ran into the hundreds. Yet the men who were used to organizing bartenders (in small taverns with two or three employees) did little or knew little about recruiting hotel workers for the International Union. In January, 1901, out of 153 locals reported on the roster, 94 were exclusively bartenders', 30 were waiters' and waitresses', and only 6 were cooks' unions; the rest, "mixed" locals, were also largely made up of bartenders, who constituted about 70 to 75 per cent of the total membership. Within a few years (by 1904) a majority of the country's male bartenders, whose number had been reported at 21,000 in the 1900 census, were unionized. But out of more than 300,000 culinary and dining-room workers reported as employed in 1900, only about 3 per cent were enrolled in the union.

The methods pursued by Jere Sullivan and his colleagues have been criticized in later years as being based on too narrow craft union lines. They were, however, the methods pursued with success a half-century ago by most of the leading unions of the AFL, save for the miners and the brewery workers. The objective was to gather in, above all, the steady workers who would pay dues year in and year out, and fight for control of the job. The bartenders of the International Union were on the whole a "conservative" body of men—one seldom heard of their going on strike. But in the early days their swift mobilization made for the solid growth of a union that for long years had been a "chaotic" affair.

*

The period from 1899 to 1904, a time of business prosperity following the brief Spanish-American War, was one of spectacular advance for the American Federation of Labor. The AFL in its mighty youth grew from a total membership of 278,000 in 1898 to 1,676,000 in 1904, while the Railway Brotherhoods and other independent unions increased as rapidly. Almost overnight the country had begotten a real labor movement with more than 2,000,000 organized wage-workers. This swift expansion was accompanied with growing pains of all sorts, and encountered at times the most determined resistance by anti-union employers.

To slogans calling for the Union Shop and the Eight-Hour Day (which few labor organizations then enjoyed) the AFL campaigns swept through the main industrial centers of the East and Middle West. In the Far West the independent and extremely militant Western Federation of Miners, as in the 1890's, spearheaded the organizing battles of many different labor groups, including locals of cooks and waiters established in remote frontier mining towns and lumber camps.

It was a time of increasingly widespread and sometimes "general" strikes, such as the walkout of 147,000 anthracite coal miners in 1902; a time of great stir among the building trades, the streetcar men, the packing-house workers, and the teamsters. The promotion of the union label, the sympathetic strike and the boycott were highly effective also (in the days before repressive court decisions, as in the Danbury Hatters' Case in 1908, discouraged such methods). And one AFL union prodded the other: the Bakery Workers, Brewers and Teamsters called on bartenders and waiters to form local unions and support them or promote use of their union labels. The bartenders and the waiters, seeing that their brothers and their cousins and their uncles were joining unions of the barbers, the butchers and the bakers, also got themselves union cards. In Boston one saw the men with the blue buttons spreading the gospel of unionism. In Hartford, Connecticut, in 1901, placards were posted in all union halls announcing that a fine of $2 would be imposed on any union member caught drinking beer at a house without a union shop card. "It is not thought that many will want to pay $2.05 for a glass of beer," wrote an officer of the Hartford Bartenders.[14]

The news spread that the barmen of Boston had raised their wages from approximately $9 to $15 a week, reduced hours to sixty-three per week and were paying sickness and death benefits to their union members. Soon the bartenders and waiters of Local 1 in New York got busy and called on the proprietors of popular coffee houses and concert halls frequented by workers and by dint of much "moral suasion," as they reported, and some small strikes as well, won the ten-hour day and a fixed wage of $2.50 daily. Waiters' tips usually added up to as much as or more than the fixed wage.

Good tidings came from Cleveland also where the waiters of Local 106, in the summer of 1901, gained a wage scale of $9 a week and the ten-hour day. Within a little over a year a considerable recovery had also been made in the Chicago locals, which had been for a time extinct. Bartenders and waiters, waitresses, cooks and cooks' helpers were now gathered again in seven locals, of which two were for colored workers, and the total membership reported was 7,000 union members.[15]

It was a service trade union whose branches sprawled all over the map, and therefore faced problems entirely different in each section or state, in accordance with varying conditions of life, cost of living, geography and climate. From Chicago you could move on to Wisconsin and Minnesota and find small locals, mainly of bartenders, being formed in the big towns; then, leaving Minneapolis, you might cross 1,500 miles of sparsely populated territory before you came to a Hotel and Restaurant Employees local union once more in Seattle, Washington.

On reaching the Pacific you would find a young Scotsman named Robert Hesketh presiding over Local 33 of Seattle, chartered in April,

1900, and with a "mixed" membership of some 300. As he reported, the local "has so far progressed that it controls the cooks, waiters, hotel and restaurant employees of the city, and has assumed that name." Employers here accepted collective bargaining with the union.

Proceeding southward along the Pacific to San Francisco—formerly "too far away" for Pomeroy's men, but captured by Jere Sullivan's diligent correspondence—you would find in 1901 a thriving new branch of the International, called Waiters Local 30.

Thus instead of being able to unionize men who worked in groups of thousands concentrated in mine fields or huge factories, the early organizers and officers were forced to write many letters or travel far and wide to gather in their scattered union brothers employed in small eating establishments. And everywhere the contrast in conditions and the wage scales were baffling: in Philadelphia or Chicago a waiter might work twelve to fourteen hours a day for an extremely low fixed wage; but in San Francisco, four days' journey away, where labor was scarce, a kitchen or dining-room worker had the ten-hour day and a wage scale equal to that paid in the union houses of New York or higher.

Hope ran high in the opening years of the century among the new, inexperienced local officers and the ill-prepared organizers who carried on with the recruiting of members. The hardships endured by the early unions, their lack of means of any kind, are well illustrated in the reminiscences of the founding secretary of Bartenders Local 108, Cleveland:

> Many of the old timers can remember, when we first organized, how we had to get empty beer kegs and boards and pieces of lumber in order to make benches for the members to sit on; and when an empty dry goods box was used as a rostrum for our President, and no flooring but mud an inch deep; when we had no backing or support from anyone except those who believed that some day in the future our institution would amount to something.[16]

Many of the local headquarters in those days were grimy places, with a few broken chairs and a shabby desk. The International office at Cincinnati, toward 1900, was a one-room office at 528 Walnut Street, where Jere L. carried on with the help of one $6-a-week clerk.

Night and day Secretary Sullivan wrote letters by hand to local unions in thirty different states and in Canada; and his correspondents answered in letters or reports (published in the journal) describing—often in exaggerated terms—their bustle and derring-do, but with an optimism, a fine youthful ardor that still glows in the yellowed pages of the *Mixer & Server*.

From Boston the Secretary of Local 77 wrote in the autumn of 1901:

> Three years ago Local 77 . . . could lay claim to a membership of less than 275; it is today a lusty giant with a membership of 1,500. Our finances are in a flourishing condition, having over $5,000 to our credit. . . .[17]

At the other end of the continent, in San Francisco, the executive officer of the newly arisen Local 30 declared that he was doing a land-office business.

> One month after beginning the work of organizing we are able to report the existence of a local with 500 members, a paid business agent, and an employment office and headquarters located in one of the principal office buildings in the city. . . . Our membership is increasing at the rate of 100 a week.
>
> We have been so busy getting things into shape that I have hardly a moment to spare. *Our people are beginning to realize what can be done.* There are thirty eating-places friendly to us, patronized almost exclusively by union men; they will yield as soon as a slight pressure has been exerted. . . . Our men are growing enthusiastic, talking of a six-day week. I have discouraged this, however, as I am afraid the project is unrealizable." [18]

In the San Francisco local, then a mixed organization, the officers had to hold back the waiters and cooks from a premature struggle with their employers.

The note of high optimism also sounds from points in the middle of the country, such as Milwaukee, whose local secretary (for a cooks' union) writes at the same time:

> We enrolled 400 members at the start of the season. There is lots of timber to form a first class union from. It is pleasing to hear how eager every cook is to make this a success. The way they put it is: "We ought to have been organized long ago." [19]

But from St. Louis Local 20 comes a warning message written by one who signs himself merely "Umbrella Bill." The road ahead is still steep; he cautions:

> I have noted the glowing accounts of the wonderful progress of our sister locals. . . . My friends, kindly remember, our victories are not so easily won. Bear in mind that every advantage gained by wage earners has cost a struggle and the sacrifice of some of our brothers. Our fight is for freedom. We dare not for a moment relax. . . . We must not forget that we are industrial slaves.[20]

*

The momentum of organized labor's drive at the turn of the century soon provoked alarm and an increasing resistance on the part of employers throughout the country, a resistance that was to reach its climax in 1904-1907. Like other unions, the Hotel and Restaurant Employees' local branches were soon involved in costly industrial struggles: first in San Francisco, then in Chicago.

San Francisco, for special, geographic reasons, was then, as perhaps now, the country's strongest "union shop town." Here history was made swiftly and (for the labor movement also) was filled with episodes of romance, daring and violence worthy of a Bret Harte or Jack London. After the Gold Rush and the days of the Vigilantes (to paraphrase Mark Twain) came "civilization"; and after civilization came depressions, booms—and labor unions. As early as 1863 the cooks and waiters had their "Benevolent Society," a real union that conducted a strike. In the 1880's, following anti-Chinese riots provoked by the employers' wide use of low-paid Chinese labor gangs in competition with whites, a radical labor movement had sprung up that soon captured the major part of the city's wage-workers. A so-called White Cooks and Waiters Union affiliated itself with the Knights of Labor in 1880, helped to form the San Francisco Central Labor Council in 1886, and that same year, in sympathy with the Bakery Workers Union, conducted a strike against all of fifty restaurants.[21] It was this same militant group that, after some hesitation, obtained a charter in January, 1901, from the Hotel and Restaurant Employees and Bartenders, when it was seen that Jere L. Sullivan was seriously bent on bringing about reform.

Their local had mushroomed to a union of 2,462 members within four months. In the exuberant California manner, the secretary, Frank S. Hamilton, wrote to the *Mixer & Server:* "San Francisco trade unionists lead all others in the country. . . . The sentiment in favor of unionism here is so strong that hardly any business man cares to defy it."

After signing up 300 of the small, popular-priced restaurants in the center of town, along Market and Mission streets, the union members, in the spring of 1901, brought pressure upon the "big name" restaurants, famous to tens of thousands of travelers who came to the mountain-rimmed Pacific port from all the four quarters of the globe. Though having a population in 1900 of but 342,000, San Francisco's hotel and restaurant trade was always "outsized" in comparison with other cities.

On May 1, 1901, the cooks and waiters walked out on strike against the big "cash houses"—where waiters handled customers' payments—

about 2,000 workers being involved. It was the first large-scale labor struggle experienced by the International under the new regime.

The walkout of the culinary workers, following demands for a six-day week and pay raises, was actually a first, planned move in a larger conflict directed by the San Francisco Central Labor Council in 1901 to check a concerted anti-union campaign by the city's Employers Association. The employers in this region that yesterday had been frontier expressed great fear of unions and "socialism"; they were still quick to try strong-arm methods, and the police, too, fought hard for the employing class. But on the other hand, the wage-workers of San Francisco were highly independent in spirit and full of fight. What was more, they had made great strides in organizing themselves, with their different unions working together in closest cooperation through a powerful Central Labor Council. After the cooks and waiters struck, one by one, the bakers, the iron workers, the brewers, the longshoremen and finally the teamsters came out in strikes or lockout struggles that year.

The large restaurant proprietors were kept firmly in line by the Employers Association, which had recently accumulated a "war chest" for such conflicts. Wholesale dealers acted to cut off supplies of meat from restaurants that signed union shop agreements and displayed union house cards. But now the Bakery Workers of San Francisco staged a sympathetic strike, cutting off supplies of bread from the non-union restaurants. Then the Journeymen Butchers Union stepped in and called a short strike to force meat dealers to distribute beef to the unionized restaurants—for the culinary workers tried to keep open those establishments from whose owners they had gained union terms.

The summer wore on and Local 30's pickets did duty, it was reported, "from sunrise to sunrise, kept sober and orderly, and were a credit to the labor movement." After a three months' struggle their families were in want; but other San Francisco unions contributed generously to their relief, as did numerous Hotel and Restaurant Employees locals in the Eastern and Middle-Western cities. Even the ever-thrifty Secretary Sullivan, from Cincinnati headquarters, sent some $300 in behalf of the union's Executive Board.

Strikes spread in the other industries of San Francisco during the summer months, and violent clashes between police and pickets became daily occurrences. The "shooting and clubbing of strikers, the wholesale arrest of hundreds of inoffensive men, and the calling out of the National Guard," were to be remembered with bitterness by those who went to the election polls in November.[22] But by August the cooks and waiters had mostly drifted back to work, their strike a failure. "We have about 100 who sold their birthright and earned the despicable name of Scabs," the Secretary of Local 30 reported sadly in September. Another cause of their retreat was the fact that 8,000 teamsters had gone on strike and their union's financial support of the restaurant workers' strike was stopped.

"Guerrilla" tactics against single establishments were continued by the men of Local 30 well into the fall. By such intermittent pressure against individual restaurant keepers, some moderate improvement in wages and hours was brought about. Though the waiters and cooks had "lost the battle," as often happens in such industrial conflicts, they managed to "win the peace." The brilliant victory of the Teamsters Union that autumn, in which employers were forced to accept in full the terms offered them, gave new heart to the city's other labor organizations. Resentment against both ruling political parties, the Republicans and Democrats, ran so strong that year that a newly formed third party, called the Union Labor party, elected its candidate, Eugene E. Schmitz, of the Musicians Union, as Mayor of San Francisco.

The restaurant and tavern workers, though bearing many wounds, re-formed their ranks and steadily increased their membership in 1902. By the end of that year their numbers were large enough to permit them to divide their organization into four separate craft locals: Waiters, No. 30; Bartenders, No. 41; Cooks, No. 44; and Cooks' Helpers, No. 110. In addition, a Waitresses Local, No. 48, was inaugurated about three years later, in 1906.

The resistance and the vigilance of employers sometimes wanes in the periods that follow a costly struggle with their hired hands. But since the grievances of the workers continue, they do not tend to forget. They remembered "in their bones" that, as cooks, they were still made to work twelve hours and, as waiters, eleven hours a day, seven days a week. Early in 1902 a Local Joint Executive Board for the four culinary workers' unions was established to coordinate collective bargaining with employers. Then, after strikes against individual eating places during eighteen months, the Cooks Union, Local 44, reached an agreement with the San Francisco Restaurant Keepers Association providing for an eleven-hour day for cooks and, miraculously enough, at last, a six-day week, "the cooks' dream of the last century." This agreement, signed in the office of Mayor Schmitz, also provided for union control of jobs under an employment secretary who was to place all cooks arriving in the city in search of work.[23]

Further gains for the waiters also were established following the great earthquake and fire of San Francisco in 1906. The swift rebuilding of the city brought boom times. It was then they attained the ten-hour day and six-day week, conditions enjoyed by few workers in their field.

A half-century ago, the culinary workers of San Francisco, like men in their city's other trades, stood in advance of the rest of their fellows. They had a fighting tradition; and had begun to unionize *all* the crafts. The development of the International Union as a whole usually went forward at the local level and unevenly, under varying regional conditions, here favorable, there unfavorable. Under the system of local autonomy, control by International headquarters in Cincinnati was very slight. San Francisco was still far away. The example of special progress of such local groups was slow to take effect on the main army of culinary workers in America, who still labored from dawn to dark, under conditions which their spokesmen called "industrial slavery."

The "Western labor movement," not only on the Pacific Coast, but in the mountain states, was to play a notable part in later years in the development of the Hotel and Restaurant Employees, as of other unions. Its more militant and youthful leaders were refreshingly different from those of the old cities in the East, who too often resigned themselves to running AFL unions as social clubs or "burial societies," more or less. Fifty years ago the Rocky Mountain region was still frontier. As one labor historian has written:

> The hardy miner, self-assertive, daring, impatient under restraint, and . . . skeptical of property rights in a country where riches were often the result of mere luck, and not much given to respect for the social distinctions of a settled community, was inclined to follow leaders with radical programs.[24]

Such leaders arose in the 1890's to organize the insurgent movement of the Western Federation of Miners. Repudiating the AFL craft union program, the "class conscious" leaders of the Western Miners espoused the method of industrial unionism and pressed for the organization of the unskilled or neglected masses of workers. Though their movement grew up under conditions of violence often verging on civil war, the WFM made remarkable progress for a period of years in unionizing the men in mines and lumber camps, and migratory farm hands of the mountain states and the Northwest. In 1898 the so-called Western Labor Union was set up with headquarters at Butte, Montana, as a rival labor body in opposition to the

AFL. Before long it enrolled, in addition to miners and lumberjacks, large numbers of cooks and waiters of the Western states.[25]

Many locals of cooks and waiters formed in Colorado and Montana in the 1890's joined forces with the militant Western Federation of Miners, rather than with the International Union, then headed by Pomeroy and his associates. In the remote mining camps, worked by thousands of unmarried laborers, there were numerous cooks, but it had been noticed that in times of strikes the mine owners had tried to use the cooks and waiters as strike-breakers. As related by Richard Croskey, one of the old-time organizers in that region, the Western Miners handled this problem by taking the cooks and waiters into their camp. Thenceforth, no scabs, even when brought by force of arms into a strike-bound mine, would find anyone to feed them. Croskey, a young English immigrant who had worked as a chef in Colorado Springs, became, for several years, the organizer of a number of Western Labor Union locals in the boom towns of Colorado, whose night life was illuminated by "plenty of fireworks and firewater" and gambling dens that never closed.

As head of the independent organization of cooks' and waiters' locals, Croskey started off in the spring of 1901 provided with $100, but soon was reduced to sitting up all night in trains or sleeping in railway depots, to avoid the expenditure of fifty cents for bed and breakfast. To turn up hungry and broke in places like Leadville or Cripple Creek, he reflected, "would not have been in keeping with the dignity of our organization or its president." Yet, long afterward (in 1941), he wrote:

> But those were glorious days to organize. I wish we had some of the old spirit of the boys and girls then. How easy it was to talk to them and get them interested.[26]

Arriving in the mining town of Pueblo, where the people in his trade were working fourteen hours a day, Croskey soon had 300 workers organized in a new local union. In no time at all they were out on strike, had one of their pickets shot and killed and all the members of their local, men and women alike, thrown into jail. Yet the people in the Rockies persevered in their struggle for "One Day Off in Seven." In June, 1898, the cooks' local of Denver had wrested the six-day week from the owners of that city's large hostelries, then world famous for their extravagant clientele and luxurious cuisine.

In a series of strikes waged between 1899 and 1902—during which the partisans of both capital and labor distinguished themselves by their fierce combat spirit—the Western Miners imposed the nine-hour day for miners in Montana, Colorado and neighboring states. In Butte, the cooks' union sponsored by the Western Miners had gained the *eight-hour day* in 1899, approximately twenty or more years before it was won by their fellow workers in the Eastern cities. There, as in other frontier mining towns, the miners were almost all single men and ate in small hotels or boarding houses. At an early stage numerous young women were "imported" from the East to serve as waitresses in "wide-open" Butte, and like everyone else there they were organized in a union, this one being called the Women's Protective Association—a name that quite literally described the virtuous purpose for which they banded themselves together. They, too, won the eight-hour day in 1907.

By 1901 the unsleeping Jere L. Sullivan was in touch with the independent local unions of Colorado and other Rocky Mountain states, though at first they resisted his approaches. But a few years later, in 1905, the miners' organization suffered fearful setbacks in this region at the hands of mobs of Vigilantes. The Western Federation of Miners thereupon launched the new radical movement of the Industrial Workers of the World. But in the meantime some of the local unions of cooks and waiters had grown disorganized, their headquarters in Denver burned down by mobs and many of their members in jail. Convinced that "there is room for only one organization, and when there are two, the workers suffer," Richard Croskey then joined the organizing staff of the Hotel and Restaurant Employees and soon brought over the local unions of Denver (Nos. 14 and 18), and numerous other groups in the mountain states.

*

In the East the organizing movement was maintained at a more leisurely pace. The genial, fun-loving President Callahan journeyed through the towns of New England, presiding at barmen's picnics and dinner gatherings, where, he reported, he was received by the union brothers usually with "the best in the house" and sometimes, as Jere Sullivan said, with "a surfeit of wet goods." The barmen continued to flock to the union. But when the officers of Waiters Union No. 1 in New York at this period, 1901, appealed to Jere L. Sullivan for the help of a General Organizer, urging that there were opportunities to enlist some 30,000 waiters in their cause, the Secretary-Treasurer took no action, pleading lack of funds in the International's treasury. There was but one organizer then, paid $75 a month and very little, in addition, for expenses; so that his services had to be husbanded. Thrifty Jere L. managed affairs with the greatest parsimony, saving from a third to a half of the average $2,000 monthly receipts of 1901 and 1902, and disbursing only $35 to $100 a month on a few small organizing campaigns.

At the May, 1901, convention, held in Walhalla Hall, St. Louis, the number of delegates was still sixty-two, small enough to be accommodated in a single trolley-car of the new horseless type, which was engaged by their St. Louis hosts to carry them on a sightseeing tour of the city. The pleasures of union delegates in the era of the earlier Roosevelt would appear all too innocent by comparison with those of today: they included a visit to the cellars of the Anheuser-Busch brewery; a steamboat excursion on the Mississippi River, with dancing in the evening; a grand banquet served by the members of Local 20 at Schrapps' Café, with twelve courses, including champagne, a "Union Punch" ("For in Union there is strength"), and "Union Label" cigars; finally, on the last evening of the convention, a Grand Smoker, featured, as Jere Sullivan relates, "by many excellent hits and a set-to between two of the liveliest youngsters that ever put on a mitt." [27]

Membership of the International in 1901 rose to 9,552, with 180 locals affiliated. In 1902, at the tenth general convention, held in Louisville, Kentucky, the total of affiliated locals was up to 310, and membership to 18,268. It was at this gathering that provisions were made for death benefits to be paid to all members in good standing, and to be dispensed through the International's treasury. To this end per capita taxes against locals were raised from seven to twelve cents, the additional sum being used to defray the $50 burial payments.

Jere Sullivan wrote:

> In the old days it was no uncommon sight to see one or several men going from one catering establishment to another, pleading and begging for "two" or "four bits" to help defray the funeral expense of a bartender, cook or waiter; these self-appointed committee-men . . . recited the bare facts that John Doe was dead and that his body was laid out at some undertaker's and that it would be impossible to put his remains away decently unless the workers at the trade came across.
>
> We have made burial by strangers, so far as our membership is concerned, unnecessary. [28]

The International Union continued to increase at a rapid pace, so that by 1903 it embraced 528 locals and 38,571 members; and at the twelfth convention in Rochester, New York, in 1904, Jere L. Sullivan proudly reported membership at a peak of 50,430, and Treasury funds of more than $40,000—a twelve-fold increase in the number of workers organized in the trade within four years!

The union seemed to be growing almost in spite of itself, carried along by the tremendous momentum of the AFL as a whole, with one union opening the field for another. The great push of the Teamsters Union (which came from almost nowhere, in 1899, to 84,000 in 1904) and the spread of the big building trades unions in the cities were factors favoring unionizing of the catering-trade workers. They were further aided by the very marked growth of their industry itself. Between 1900 and 1910 the number of eating and drinking establishments and that of their wage-workers almost doubled.

The addition of new members at this prosperous period seemed to go on with little serious effort at planning by the union's Secretary-Treasurer or Executive Board members, but mainly through the activities of the locals themselves. In fact, internal dissension again broke out among the general officers, as in the 1890's. Secretary Sullivan, a difficult man at best, stuck to his office at Cincinnati, but had little to do with the person who happened to be the union's President. Moreover, the behavior of local union officers in a number of cases fell below standard. Sullivan, with his air of stiff-necked honesty, used to publish reports of mismanagement or dishonesty regularly in the official journal he edited, such as the following from a Western local:

> We regret to announce the very peculiar action taken by our ex-President, who fell from grace and as a consequence spent a vacation in the county jail for thirty days. Ex-President Dolan has been a member of this local for many years, and it was with heavy hearts that we undertook to punish him for misappropriation of our funds. To make matters worse he boasted that he had spent the money and would have taken more had there been opportunity.[29]

The cases of local secretaries absconding with a few hundred dollars were probably fewer than the number of such affairs occurring in business firms, and involved paltry sums—yet they constituted setbacks. Far more serious reverses, however, were suffered through the want of vision and the lack of talent for leadership in the executive officers of the International.

While the waiters, cooks and bartenders of San Francisco were in the vanguard of the Western labor movement, their brothers and sisters of Chicago were not far behind. The country's great railroad

center, scene of so many dramatic uprisings of the wage earners, was
now filling up with hotels and restaurants. Though the culinary
workers had become disaffected during the Pomeroy troubles, by 1903
the International's organizer, Fred Bauman, was able to report a
strong recovery of membership. The Chicago Waitresses Union reported: "Though but a few months old, we have over 2,000 members
and are growing at the rate of 50 to 75 new members at every meeting night." [30]

Chicago was now in a fever over the struggles of packing house
workers, teamsters and streetcar men who were fighting for a work-
day of nine or ten hours. But restaurant and hotel employees,
though no stronger than other laborers, were occupied for twelve or
more hours and for seven days a week. When the union men demanded one day off, "their employers told them they were crazy, for
who is going to cook the day the cook is off?" [31]

Feeling their strength, the waiters of the new Local 336 began
sporadic strikes, which soon involved all the other six locals, including the cooks, bartenders, colored waiters, waitresses and miscellaneous helpers. The colored waiters particularly were reported to be
in a state of extreme discontent. Another highly militant group, the
waitresses, was led by Elizabeth Maloney, one of the most famous
women labor leaders of the time in Chicago. Her girls were embittered (according to testimony she gave before a Federal Commission
not long afterward) at being paid fixed wages of $3 a week for a
seven-day week, and fed with wretched food that turned many of
them sick.[32]

In May, 1903, President "Bob" Callahan, now endowed with a
salary, turned up in Chicago at the first news of trouble brewing
there. He made inquiries, held conferences, then gave stringent
orders that the proposed strike action must be dropped as entirely
"unreasonable." Without attempting to do anything further about
the members' grievances, he then left for St. Louis where similar
trouble was brewing. On returning to Chicago five weeks later he
learned that the colored waiters of what was then Local 509 had got-
ten out of hand and walked out to the number of 500, without waiting for his authorization. His next step was to go into conference
with the head of the Chicago Restaurant Keepers Association and
the representatives of hotels that had been struck and arrange for
what he considered, in his own mind, improved wages and conditions. To his disappointment the agreement he worked out was rejected in behalf of all the seven locals by the Local Joint Board, which
then ordered a general strike of all their members.

In his own report of the affair, Callahan relates that he "became convinced that such conditions as expected by the members [of the Chicago locals] would be an absolute impossibility to obtain." Thereupon he left the scene again and proceeded to Cincinnati, where he called a meeting of the General Executive Board and persuaded its members to visit the strikers with a most drastic punishment, that of revocation of the charter of one of their waiters' locals, No. 509.[33]

What is plainly to be read between the lines of Callahan's highly partisan account is that the Chicago workers did not trust the President of their union, nor his associates, the other union officers in charge of Chicago. Among these were Organizer Fred Bauman and Ed Parlee, a former henchman of W. C. Pomeroy. Parlee, then business agent of Local 433 (white waiters), abandoned the International Union soon afterward and formed a large dual waiters' organization or "club" of his own, which he ran in such fashion that he gained the reputation of being the "Millionaire Waiter." Bauman, not long afterward, was expelled from the International for being a drunk and a "common thief." [34]

Meanwhile the rank and file, in desperation, carried on with their strike, which involved from 7,000 to 10,000 workers. That it was born of despair at brutalizing conditions (of "work and sleep, work and sleep") was shown by the fact that though the officers of the Chicago Federation of Labor made strenuous efforts to prevent it and, at first, refused to lend it support, they failed to halt the walkout. The Teamsters Union, in particular, refused to help by halting deliveries of food to the strike-bound eating places.

But at a meeting of delegates to the central labor body, Thomas Scanlon, a hitherto unknown member of the union of dishwashers and miscellaneous kitchen workers, managed to win a hearing for his people and spoke for hours on end of the degradation suffered by those who worked at the lowest level of the catering trade, of their wretched earnings, their long days without rest from a drudgery that deadened the brain, of the tyranny of headwaiters and managers. It was, according to an eyewitness, "the most stirring speech ever delivered up to that time before the central labor body of Chicago," and won the endorsement of the strike by nearly all the Chicago unions.[35]

The strike continued for about eight weeks, directed by a strike committee of twenty-one delegates from the several unions. According to one eyewitness: "A strong organization of dishwashers and miscellaneous kitchen employees" was the head and front of the movement, "and Scanlon was their brilliant leader." Under International Vice-President Tim Kinally, the bartenders gave solid support

to the strike, as did the cooks, waiters and waitresses. Leading restaurants and hotels were closed down, and a number of them after a
short time began to sign agreements with the union. "They are winning the strike in Chicago," ran the first reports in the labor press.[36]

The Teamsters' officers, usually staunch friends of the catering
workers, ordered deliveries of food continued. But the pickets for
the waiters and dishwashers threw lumps of coal at the wagons and
this gave their drivers sufficient excuse to return without delivering
their goods.

Then suddenly the fiery Scanlon, who out of the ranks of the poor
dishwashers, had risen to fame among Chicago's wage-workers, fell
sick and died, worn out by his own superhuman exertions and hardships. His union brothers mustered several bands and a procession of
800 mourners who paraded slowly in his funeral cortege through the
streets of Chicago to solemn music—"one of the most gorgeous fu-
nerals ever held in Chicago," it was said then, and "a rebuke to the
restaurant keepers." [37] But thereafter the spirits of the strikers sank
swiftly. Relief funds sent by the International Union were meager,
for President Callahan held that the Chicago workers were lacking
in the "conservative spirit." Jere L. Sullivan also was fearful of the
wave of strikes then spreading among catering workers of Kansas
City, St. Louis, Cleveland and Denver and a dozen other towns, until
25,000 were reckoned to have walked out. The "class struggle," Secretary Sullivan complained, was costing the International Union too
much money. Long-range vision and bold leadership on the part of
the union's top officers, together with generous financial support of
current strikes, might have gained far more union members and, in
the end, greater financial strength.

With the inspiring voice of Scanlon stilled, support of the other
Chicago unions dropped away; deliveries by wagon of food supplies
for strike-bound establishments were resumed in August. The police,
following numerous collisions with the strikers, arrested hundreds of
them. Firms that had signed union agreements repudiated them.
By the end of the summer the ill-organized, desperate movement of
the Chicago culinary workers had fallen apart. The members of the
newly formed locals drifted away. Unionization of culinary people in
the huge city of Chicago was set back for long years to come, their
numbers being reduced to between 1,000 and 1,500 members.

A few more years (at forty) and considerable success had made
Jere Sullivan, the former member of the Knights of Labor, more
wary and prudent. Despite setbacks in big cities such as Chicago and

New York, members were pouring into the Hotel and Restaurant Employees Union by the thousands during the wave of strikes "for recognition" that made 1903 and 1904 such memorable years. In those days many observers seriously predicted the coming of a "labor government" in America in the near future. The union's treasury funds surpassed $43,000 in 1904, and its current revenues and membership of over 50,000 made it one of the more important organizations affiliated with the AFL. Jere Sullivan's growing financial conservatism, though disappointing to many who hoped—in this fortunate season—for a more energetic program, undoubtedly contributed much to the staying power of the International in the darker times to come.

Meanwhile, in 1903 and 1904, years of boundless opportunity, his skeptical and conservative spirit was reflected in letters written to a long-time union associate, Thomas Farrell, Secretary of Waiters Local No. 106, of Cleveland. Sullivan bemoaned the expenditure of relatively small sums upon the big Chicago struggle, and put no faith in schemes to organize poor dishwashers or even cooks. Something must be done, he felt, to hold in check the people who ran to the union merely to go on strike, draw benefits and rush out as fast as they came in. He himself had voted with the other members of the General Executive Board to revoke the charter of the colored waiters' local in Chicago.

On the other hand he had noticed with growing displeasure the clumsy attempts of President Callahan to exercise leadership in his own right. Callahan drew a salary and traveled around in comfortable style nowadays, often intervening in affairs that he knew too little about.

In Chicago Callahan had permitted the rank and file to get away from him. He had alienated them by trying to "force" an agreement upon them, where a more skillful labor leader would have tried to attune his moderating efforts to the sentiment of his union members.

So to the great "melting pot" of New York which was most difficult to organize, Callahan came in the autumn of 1903 to perpetrate similar blunders. The two leading waiters' locals in New York were at loggerheads then, and competed with each other for jurisdiction over restaurants in the various zones of the city. After long and heated discussions with officers of Local 1 (some of whose rebellious members had publicly voiced complaints against both Callahan and Secretary Sullivan), the International President, in his brusque fashion, moved to suspend the local and placed its affairs in the hands of a committee of three. However, one member of the committee was Organizer Fred Bauman, who was as greatly disliked in New York as in Chicago. Bauman wrought no miracles for labor here. It was "impossible" to organize the culinary workers of New York, the President concluded.

In his report before the 1904 convention, Callahan dilated upon the improvements he had brought about in New York, boasting of having organized a new local of "3,000 cooks." As a matter of fact the local had at the time somewhat less than 1,800 members. It had formerly been an independent union of very progressive character, named the International Culinary Association, with a Paris-trained chef, César Lesino, as its Secretary. But a short time after joining the International Union, its officers and members found it so unrewarding to do business with President Callahan and Organizer Bauman that in December, 1904, they voted to withdraw from the Hotel and Restaurant Employees and resume their independence.

As Lesino recalled:

> President Callahan made a very poor impression upon us when we saw him occasionally in New York. We had a European, working-class background, and he did not understand us and was indifferent to our needs.[38]

With increasing anger, Jere L. Sullivan watched all the blundering of Callahan and said little. Sullivan had pinched everywhere, accumulated funds, built up the union, while "Bob" Callahan went about merely suspending locals and losing members. Callahan, as it appears, often rushed to the Secretary-Treasurer for expense money, but Sullivan stubbornly withstood his demands, saying pointedly on one occasion:

> The finances of this organization, so long as I am permitted to have any say on the premises, shall be used absolutely for the organization's benefit.[39]

Jere L. Sullivan was a good hater. That "Bob" Callahan was popular and that he was ambitious was borne in upon his mind. A tradition has come down that Callahan was "cynical" and "contemptuous of all who took trade unions seriously." Also that he was fairly indifferent to efforts being made to organize culinary workers, and preferred bartenders in the union. Jealousy between the bartenders, then a big majority of the membership, and the other crafts in those days always lay close beneath the surface, and some have said that there was much intriguing to remove Jere L. Sullivan from his office.[40]

On the other hand Callahan was known as a "regular guy." He

was very popular among the barmen, and had a decided aptitude for the rough and tumble politics of labor. One of his followers described him in terms of adulation:

President Callahan as chairman stands second to none; with a cool head, firm in his decisions, commanding at all times the respect of delegates. . . . I had no idea that a bartender had the ability of such a display of brilliant oratory.[41]

At the fairly triumphant convention of May, 1904, in Rochester, New York, Jere L. Sullivan was unanimously re-elected amid rousing ovations from the delegates who called him their "old war-horse" and the "master builder" who had saved the International Union and made it financially strong. But the cheering for Callahan, also re-elected, was even longer and louder.

Yet was it not Sullivan who had really been the "architect" of their union? On this score, Jere L. Sullivan left no doubts in the minds of his hearers at conventions. He often recalled, with emotion, how he had begun to work over their organization when it was without funds, without membership, without an office and laden with debts. And now "we are a great army of 50,000," he would cry. "The increase in local unions and membership," he acknowledged, "is the wonder of the world." [42]

And what was Callahan? he reflected bitterly. An interloper? His mind was inflamed against any man who would waste the moneys of the International treasury and threaten its security. One of his plainest allusions was a sardonic thrust at the Boston bartender as one of those men who "drew munificent salaries for the distribution of hot air, whose work as paid officials consists of one long list of dismal failures and an elongated expense account . . . busily engaged in trying to destroy that which they neither helped to create nor could conceive as possible until this organization burst upon them as a gigantic army of wage-workers." [43]

In awareness of the other man's growing threat, Sullivan had been saying before the General Executive Board, since early in 1904: *"This organization needs no master. You need none and I recognize none but the laws of the organization."*

The planful little Secretary smoked innumerable cigarettes and bided his time for two months after the Rochester convention of 1904. Then he struck swiftly and hard at his opponent.

THREE

Shake-Up

"Your Secretary-Treasurer's policies, with your consent, have become the policies of this organization."
—JERE L. SULLIVAN.

On July 5, 1904, the officers of Local 77, Boston, received from Jere L. Sullivan a notice warning them that their local was in arrears for over ninety days in payment of the per capita tax and was liable to suspension. This was the local headed by International President Robert A. Callahan. Sullivan added further: "There is also another matter that I believe you should get acquainted with, and that is the possibility of being compelled to declare the position of General President vacant." Since Brother Callahan was a member of the offending local, he, too, might be suspended. "Unless I am advised further by you, I shall use my own judgment within the premises within ten days from date."

Callahan was said to have exploded with wrath at the mere threat of suspension from office. It was a curious thing that the largest and richest local in the union should be in arrears for over three months, then, in August, 1904—after the axe had fallen—should pay all its debt in full. But at the time the chief officer of the local, Callahan, did not even deign to reply to the General Secretary-Treasurer.

Thereupon Sullivan wrote again, on July 15, 1904, to Local 77, Boston:

Inasmuch as this is the 15th day of July, making a total of 106 days that Local 77 is indebted to the International, and as we have

informed the secretary of that organization, as well as Mr. Callahan, we believe that we have taken all the steps necessary. . . .
According to the International Constitution, Article VI, a local
union being two months in arrears stands suspended forthwith.
. . . What comprises a local union? The membership of that
local; collective individuals. Consequently . . . no exception can
be taken for any purpose whatever, and this office contends that
Mr. Callahan is no longer the General President of this International.

We therefore inform you that from this day this office, in accordance with . . . Article X, Section 2, recognizes Mr. T. J. Sullivan,
555 Main Street, Hartford, Connecticut, as the General President
of this International Union.

> Yours fraternally,
> Jere L. Sullivan
> Secretary-Treasurer [1]

When news of this drastic step was made public in the official
journal, on August 15, 1904, union members all over the country were
astounded. Locals often fell into temporary difficulties and the general officers as often used discretion in punishing them. Many members wrote in protest at Jere Sullivan's action and called for a review
of the whole case by the General Executive Board.

But Sullivan imperiously brushed aside all complaints, declaring:
"The laws of the union are made for *all* members, without regard to
their official position." Making public his candid opinion of the deposed President, Sullivan described him, in an article in the union's
journal, as one who drew a salary and did nothing for it. "For what
were we paying that $200 a month?" he asked. The man had blun-
dered in Chicago and in New York. Callahan was nothing but "a
$200 luxury," Jere L. said contemptuously; and so, off with his head.[2]

In any case, the GEB, now made up of seven Vice-Presidents
elected at the last convention, included a majority of faithful adherents of Secretary Sullivan, among them the newly elected members,
Robert Hesketh, of Seattle, and Thomas S. Farrell, of Cleveland.
With but two votes in support of Callahan, the Board voted to sustain Secretary Sullivan's action.

With "Tim" Sullivan as President and Jere L. as Secretary, it was
for the time being an "all-Sullivan" team. Samuel Gompers in those
days used to speak of the union as "the Sullivan boys." In reality
no two men could be less alike. "Tim," the bartender from Hartford,
Connecticut, a former bricklayer, was a tall, paunchy man, well along
in years, with a bald head and handle-bar mustaches; he was, moreover, a genial and friendly soul, a good Catholic, and spoke with an

Irish brogue. Jere L., by contrast, was not disposed to encourage friendships indiscriminately. The fact that he was said to have given up professing his religion made him, naturally, the less loved by his Irish brethren, who were predominantly Catholic in faith. Compared with "Tim" he was all calculation and craft, and moreover gifted with a waspish tongue. Meanwhile "Tim" Sullivan, who thoroughly enjoyed the prestige of being a union President, tried to do as little as possible to cross the irascible Jere, through whose aid he had been raised to his high office. Nor did he venture far afield to organize the unorganized or expand the membership. In short, he was less energetic and more manageable than Callahan, while providing some help in conciliating the barmen's locals in New England, where Callahan had been popular.

The International Union now ploughed ahead again with little Jere L. Sullivan in the driver's seat.

At the thirteenth convention of the union, held in Kansas City, May 8 to 13, 1905, before a somewhat smaller gathering than the year before, Brother Callahan was on hand with a numerous group of supporters to give battle to Jere Sullivan. So tempestuous did the proceedings become that the convention was saved from breaking up in disorder only by the device of going into an Executive Session which, beginning in the morning of one day, ended only in the early moments of the following day, at 12:10 A.M.

In that heated session behind closed doors the Secretary used all the weapons in his mental arsenal with devastating effect upon the malcontents, so that his action in deposing Callahan was sustained. One of his most memorable pieces of sarcasm, that day, was a characterization of his opponents as resembling, taken all together, "a rotten mackerel in the hot sunshine—they shone while they stunk and they stunk while they shone." [3] When a fight like that was over, Jere L. used to strut about in triumph, looking at all the delegates with his sardonic smile, and say: "I've got my goat, but who's got yours?" [4]

At the 1905 proceedings the delegates voted to amend the International's constitution by holding conventions biennially thereafter, the resolution being subject to a referendum vote by all the members of the union. Because of delay in the referendum the next gathering of the delegates was not held until October, 1907, in Toledo, Ohio.

R. A. Callahan was not a man to give up the fight easily. Once more he and his clan, who called themselves "the Simon Pures," marched against Jere Sullivan at Toledo. But now they brought serious charges against the official conduct of the General Secretary. Three years earlier, as they alleged, he had unlawfully transferred sums of money which were supposed to be held separately and intact in the Death Benefit Fund in order to maintain certain organizers on the road.

This was a bad hour for Jere L., who prided himself upon the extreme probity with which he managed the union's finances. What was most painful to him was that the man who testified against him and exhibited their private correspondence was one of his oldest friends, W. F. Jones, a brother member of Local 20, in St. Louis, who, together with Jere L., had once been "expelled" during their common fight against Pomeroy. "Bill" Jones, though now an enemy, had been appointed to his office of General Organizer by Secretary Sullivan.

What was worse, while the charges against Jere L. were being weighed, the "Simon Pure" faction among the bartenders brought in a resolution to segregate the barmen from the other crafts. It was the most powerful effort yet made to split the International Union. The Boston locals, under Callahan's influence, showed themselves disaffected. A Chicago bartenders' local, evidently controlled by the expelled Pomeroy, had also been issuing circulars for years calling on the bartenders to secede from the Hotel and Restaurant Employees and Bartenders and form their own organization. As Jere Sullivan exclaimed at this time: "The wreckers never ceased to labor for that dissolution that they predicted [in 1899] when they were ousted from office."

The convention grew tumultuous and visitors were asked to leave the hall lest they witness fisticuffs between the delegates, who were in a continual uproar. Sullivan, engaged in one of the hardest fights of his career, with the support of his staunch lieutenants on the Executive Board, managed to defeat the secessionists' resolution by a vote of 239-⅓ to 169-⅔, which was uncomfortably close. It was resolved, then, that those advocating segregation would be expelled, unless they receded from their position, as "destroyers" who "were aiding the Anti-Saloon League in its campaign for the extermination of this Union." [5]

By 1907, the Anti-Saloon League, the dreaded enemy of bartenders and waiters, was making strong progress in establishing local option dry laws in many communities and states. To accuse a barman of helping the Drys was, of course, a deadly insult.

The opposition vote amounted to over 42 per cent of the convention. Only the stoutest sort of defense by Secretary Sullivan's "machine" prevented the International Union from being broken up.

Jere L. had gathered a solid phalanx of supporters around him by this time; they were the Vice-Presidents and members of the GEB whom he had selected or in whom he reposed confidence, such as Ed Horne, of St. Louis, Robert Hesketh, of Seattle, Fred Seames, of Buffalo, C. W. McCurdy, of Des Moines, and Thomas S. Farrell, of Cleveland. These men who were also heads of their locals were often engaged in organizing and trouble-shooting tasks in their districts, or had the privilege of recommending persons for the job of International Organizer. Through these lieutenants and by direct contact the Secretary-Treasurer also kept himself in close touch with well-established and active local leaders throughout the country—who supported his administration loyally in the stormy years of 1904 to 1907, when the International might have been rent asunder.*

With the secessionists beaten back, Secretary Sullivan on the fourth day addressed the convention, asked its indulgence and proposed that, before proceeding to the election of officers, the charges against himself be taken up in executive session, which was concurred in. The allegations against Jere L. were then laid before the convention by W. F. Jones, once a close associate of the Secretary, and now a delegate from Chicago's Local 285. With his own assent Secretary Sullivan's personal correspondence, dating from 1904, was read out. Then Sullivan replied.

As was his habit nowadays he began by recalling the unhappy past of their union, reminding the delegates how he had taken over a disrupted, insolvent organization, and struggled against danger, within and without, to bring the International to a peak of success in 1904, when it attained a membership of 50,000. Thereafter, it was true, much ground had been lost owing to factional strife. "We had grown too rapidly," he observed, "and after more or less shaking down our membership and our finances, showed quite a marked shrinkage a year later." But their Treasury had a larger fund than ever ($43,167.91). The thrifty Secretary-Treasurer had actually been

---

* Labor unions are essentially economic institutions functioning for the material improvement of the members' status. But since their officers are elected by popular vote, at the local level, and by representative vote of convention delegates at the "international" level, they tend to become *political* bodies also. And just as political parties seek to eliminate too much chance or hazard and function effectively, so do labor unions usually try to prepare or "organize" their action. Hence "machines" or "steam rollers" come into play in unions as in political parties, or New England town meetings, for that matter.

From his strategic post, employing the power of purse in good measure, Jere L. Sullivan, over the years, gave unflagging attention to the task of keeping the International Union *organized* politically.

saving money during a period of strikes and hard times. He continued:

In the period of time above quoted I have handled as receipts from our local unions the sum of $480,996.60; and have paid out $437,828.69. . . . *Every dollar of that immense amount of money has been properly accounted for.* Not one cent has been lost, strayed or stolen; it is in national banks, and the expert accountant and all of your International Auditing Committees have certified the facts time and time again. The writer has the distinction of carrying the largest individual bond written by any Bonding Company in the State of Ohio . . . and that distinction was not earned by association with . . . paid labor spies or union wreckers and paid secessionists; and while they are privileged to snarl and falsify (for I am free to admit a liking for that sort of enmity) the record is made, the money intact and all of their prevarication can't change what is.[6]

That Jere L. fairly reveled in opposition is plain enough in the acid speech with which he lashed at his slow-moving opponents.

The hearings of charges against him resulted in his complete exoneration; the report of the closed session reflecting

the general consensus of opinion . . . that reading of this correspondence [with W. F. Jones] was the dirtiest of politics; that the manhood of those who introduced it was decidedly questionable; and that the supporters of the proposition were unfit to be trade unionists. A vote of confidence was given to the General Secretary, which was unanimous.

When the election of general officers was called for, "Tim" was re-elected President by a thumping majority and Jere L. was unanimously re-elected as Secretary-Treasurer. In his speech of acknowledgment he spoke with unusual emotion:

Brothers and Sisters, few men have had crowded into one day the experience that has been allowed me. Early this morning, according to my accusers, I was on the threshold of the jail for alleged wrongdoing. In your executive session you washed the linen and discovered that it was not quite as dirty as my accusers intimated; you became cognizant of the fact that there are some beings in this world so unprincipled that they could be guilty of the most heinous of crimes—that of ingratitude. In your judgment my action was entitled to a vote of confidence. . . . Those who were the vehicles for this filthy task . . . are forgiven but not forgotten.

Your action in re-electing me to the position of Secretary-Treasurer, without a vote of dissent, fills my cup and in its overflow my generosity permeates to all alike in sincere thanks.

Here the usually tart man shed a tear, saying: "The transition from bitterness to joy is too much even for me. I would that I could more fully express my appreciation. . . ."

However, he soon collected himself and, resuming his customary tones of a severe schoolmaster, wound up:

But if you elected me to this position for the purpose of forgetting the International Union, you have made a serious mistake. What I did in the past I shall do in the future, if the interests of this Union command such action. I do not expect to do better work in the future than in the past.[7]

Thus the stubborn, hard-fighting Jere L. rode out the storm. The Toledo convention of 1907 "purged itself of a lot of bile," as he said. The Secretary-Treasurer also purged some of the men who had assailed his character—among them, "Bill" Jones, who had gone over to the enemy faction, and whose services as a General Organizer were now dispensed with. For, whatever Jere L. might say, he neither forgot nor forgave. The International Union was his creation; let anyone who dared challenge him take heed.

For five years after 1899 the restaurant and tavern workers' union had been increasing by leaps and bounds, and there was much talk of its reaching a membership of "one hundred thousand." As one enthusiastic local officer wrote in 1904:

We are all proud of our great Union. It is destined to become one of the greatest and most powerful labor organizations, if the rank and file will put their shoulder to the wheel.

But clouds gathered now. The "young giant," as the American Federation of Labor was then called, had moved forward so rapidly that the owners of large properties and industries were filled with alarm and disposed, after 1904, to extreme measures of self-defense. Banding themselves together in powerful employers' associations, sometimes under the banner of the so-called Citizens' Alliance, the country's biggest corporations sponsored a nation-wide propaganda for the "open shop," or, as they preferred to call it, "The American Plan." Thus the friends of organized industrial monopoly and enemies of organization by labor have always arrogated unto themselves a superior form of patriotism. A union shop under a collective bar-

A St. Louis hotel dining room of the time of the Exposition, 1904

Kramer's Restaurant, Pittsburgh, a famous landmark of 1901

Members of the Aberdeen, Washington, local in 1905, showing the different costumes of their crafts

In the wake of the San Francisco earthquake and fire of 1906; the temporary office of the HRE locals at Seventh and Mission streets is shown in the foreground

gaining agreement was held by them to be "un-American," or "Red"; but one where men were forced to sign the "Yellow Dog" contract, pledging themselves to avoid all unions (save the company-owned variety), was a "patriotic" or "American Plan" shop.

Not content with propaganda, the Citizens' Alliance element also used their own version of the boycott to cut off bank credit or supplies from firms signing agreements with labor unions—as reported by members of the San Francisco cooks and waiters' local in 1901, and in Chicago in 1903. The same local union officer who wrote of his high hopes for his union, also gave warning that:

> Conditions and problems are beginning to confront us which demand that we prepare to meet all emergencies. The gigantic trusts are baiting the smaller employers . . . to crush organized labor. We cannot expect that the smaller employers will not fall victim to the trust magnates who are instigating the war against organized labor. There is a saying: "In time of peace prepare for war." [8]

After 1904 business volume in the catering trade declined and membership in the International Union also dropped. The strife of factions led to some desertions by bartenders' locals, as in Chicago and elsewhere, and the establishment of several dual union groups. As late as 1911 and 1912 there was a so-called "Brotherhood of Bartenders" (the B.O.B.) offering competition to the official labor union.

From a peak of 50,430 members the year before, the International fell to 39,317 in 1905, and to 34,600 in 1906; then stabilized at 37,000 to 40,000 for several years.

Jere L. Sullivan observed that the organization had probably grown too fast and was benefiting from a "shaking-down" process. There was actually room for an immense expansion by the union, especially after the panic of 1907 had gone by. But with the years he had grown less venturesome and more conservative. A flood of immigrant workers poured into the country and great numbers of them were entering the hotel and restaurant trade, these "later immigrants" of 1900 to 1910 coming in overwhelming majority from Eastern and Southern Europe—whereas the "earlier immigrants" had been predominantly English-speaking or German and Scandinavian. The new influx of workers, arriving mostly by steerage, crowded into the New York and Chicago areas and those of other large Eastern cities, many of them joining waiters' or cooks' "benevolent associations" formed by their own language groups, such as the International Geneva Association. The majority of the newcomers among the catering-trade workers showed no desire to join what they called then the "Irish bartenders' union." [9]

The problem of organizing this great mass of the foreign-born was indeed difficult, though not insuperable (as was later seen). But Jere Sullivan shared the conviction of many AFL leaders of his era that the best recourse for their unions, in the face of such chaotic labor conditions, was to avoid the "drifters," stick to the steady craftsmen, and keep their organizations upon an even keel. Among the immigrants were many socialists and radicals of various sorts; from now on the Secretary "kept a sharp eye out for socialists," as his old friends recall.[10]

In 1907 and 1908 the United States Supreme Court handed down decisions that were disastrous for labor, one of them, in the Danbury Hatters' Case (February, 1908), invoking the full penalties of the Sherman Anti-Trust Act against members of a striking union. After a long legal contest AFL unions were compelled to raise $234,000 to pay the triple damages sustained by the ruined hat workers of Danbury. Henceforth the weapon of the court injunction against strikes was freely used by employers, and union men were in despair. Thus the Hotel and Restaurant Employees, like many other labor groups of that time, feared to resort to the strike.

*

Yet none could question Sullivan's untiring devotion to the organization's interests, as he conceived them. As its "permanent official"—though presidents might come and go—he carried on with the grind of paper work, almost alone in the Cincinnati headquarters, or with few assistants, since he exercised the most stringent economy. It was he who controlled the hiring and firing of International Organizers and planned their assignments in different sections of the country. According to his own statement the three different presidents who held office during the twelve years from 1899 to 1911 spent, all told, "less than 90 days in the headquarters of our International Union." [11]

It was at Jere Sullivan's initiative that, at the time of the earthquake and fire of San Francisco in 1906, Assistant-Secretary W. E. Horne was dispatched to the disaster area with a bag of $5,000 in gold, contributed by various HRE locals, for the relief of the union's members who had been rendered homeless and destitute. Horne, at that time, took eight days to get into San Francisco from St. Louis, and found a large number of the union's 3,000 local members living in tents, and lacking clothing as well as food. Remaining in California for several months, Horne raised and dispensed altogether more than $15,000 for the benefit of the stricken hotel and restaurant workers.

There was the other Sullivan, "Tim" the President. But it was not long before Jere L. found him sadly wanting even as a figurehead for the International. A bumbling speaker, he would give but a poor account of himself as presiding officer at conventions. In 1911, opening the biennial gathering of delegates at Faneuil Hall in Boston, "Tim" Sullivan read his report on the union's affairs to the convention in such fashion that a large number of the delegates—as if at a given signal—rose to their feet, with much scraping of chairs, and stomped out. Jere Sullivan, angered at the "dishonorable" conduct of those delegates, sprang up, and like an irascible schoolmaster, began to berate the members:

Delegates are elected by their local unions to come to conventions and properly represent such local unions. Being absent while the executive officers are reading their reports is not only unfair to their locals but to themselves. No man can properly appreciate what is contained in a report unless he hears or reads it himself, and few of the delegates are consistent enough to do such a thing as read the reports while in the convention city and during the week of the convention.

Yet in his outburst he could not refrain from making some reflections upon the poor performance of the titular leader—from whom he had been estranged for some time—and the other officers who were supposed to help lead their army:

Our membership could have done better work for the International since our last convention. . . . With anything like genuine cooperation there is no good reason why our organization should not be twice as powerful as it is now; the field is practically untouched, for out of hundreds of thousands who are engaged in our allied crafts we have but a miserably small percentage claiming allegiance to our Union.[12]

A part of this poor result was owing to the continued disaffection among the bartenders (especially in Boston) over the ousting of Callahan. But part of it could have been traced to the policies of Jere L. Sullivan himself, since he directed the union's efforts mainly to organizing barmen. Yet now he was filled with forebodings at the seemingly irresistible spread of the Anti-Saloon League movement, which, by 1912, had rendered nine states "bone-dry" while thirty-five others had many of their communities under local option laws prohibiting taverns or restaurants from dispensing alcoholic liquids. The specter of Prohibition inspired Jere L. Sullivan with dread and pessimism. However, instead of seeking new fields of enterprise, he cast about for some means of strengthening the union's hold on the dwindling force of bartenders.

For two years prior to the gathering in Boston in 1911, he had been looking seriously for a successor to the inadequate President Timothy Sullivan. For he, Jere L., had given the Hartford bartender his crown and he would take it away.

In 1905, Vice-President Fred Seames, of Buffalo, had decided to resign his office and enter business on his own. He then called the attention of Jere Sullivan, with whom he had been for some years intimately associated, to the sound abilities of young Edward Flore whom he, Seames, had inducted into Local 175, Buffalo, several years before and who had served as their business agent and secretary. Seames' recommendation was that Flore be named to succeed him as Vice-President.

*

Edward Flore, who had been moving up the ladder of the International rather quickly, was a man of a very different and rather finer mold than those who had been serving as its executive officers up to then. Born on December 5, 1877, in Buffalo, New York, he was the second son of George and Catherine Hassenfratz Flore, his father being the owner of a saloon and beer garden at 71 Clinton Street, in the downtown quarter of Buffalo. On his mother's side Edward Flore was German, on his father's he was the descendant of immigrants from Alsace who had come to America in 1840 from what was then part of France. The Flores were hard workers, thrifty, and very devout in their Roman Catholic faith. The father, George Flore, had worked for years in his parent's shop as a blacksmith, then had turned to tending bar and after a time accumulated enough money to purchase and renovate the old tavern at Clinton Street which, thereafter, bore the sign: "Flore's Lunch." Edward Flore, the third of nine children, was educated in a Buffalo grammar school until he was twelve, then went to a parochial school for two more years, and at the age of fourteen (like his father and two elder brothers) went to work behind the family's bar. There was no thought of further education; for his mother had just then died of her most recent childbirth, and there were numerous younger Flores to feed.

Flore's Lunch was the gathering place of workers, including railroad men who were staunch union members. In the early 90's there was a famous depression, followed by the great railway strike of 1894, which involved the switchmen of Buffalo's big railroad yards. In his youth Ed Flore heard much high argument, at his counter, over the rights of the working class and the wickedness of the bosses and the "trusts." President Grover Cleveland (the former Sheriff of Buffalo, who in earlier years used to imbibe freely at the local bars, including George Flore's) called out Federal troops to break the railway strike in Chicago that year—arousing the anger of union men everywhere. Quiet and deliberate in manner, even in youth, Ed Flore listened, smiled and said little. A bartender learns the way of the world. He saw men drinking when they were happy and had money jingling in their pockets, and saw them drink when they were bitter, in times of poverty and defeat.

When the discussions grew loud, the elder Flore, who was a large and solidly built man of moderate views, would calm the disputants by urging that each side give a little ground to the other so that they might "get together" and preserve the peace. His son adopted the same philosophy. As one of his lifelong friends has said, his father taught him from early years that "the best man behind the bar is the one who can maintain peace and order, and still do a profitable business, without resorting to force. Such a character was Ed Flore's father. Such a character was Ed Flore likewise." [13]

As a young man, with his serious and yet pleasing manner, Flore was well known and liked in his neighborhood. He took part in the social and charitable activities of his parish church. Bicycles were all the rage in the 90's, and from the age of eighteen, Ed Flore was an enthusiastic member of the Cycling Club of Buffalo. The Flore tavern, like most bars in populous quarters, was a rendezvous of ward politicians canvassing for supporters for the city's two party organizations. One local bigwig, Democratic Alderman Louis Fuhrman, who in later years was elected Mayor of Buffalo, liked to drop in at Flore's for a drink and became friendly with the sturdy young barman. On reaching the age of twenty-one, Ed registered as a Democrat and helped in electioneering for Mr. Fuhrman by talking to his customers at the bar or to friends at the Cycling Club.

It was not long after that, in 1899, that Fred Seames, an attractive-looking and well-spoken young bartender, who worked at some of the best taverns in Buffalo, had come in and invited Flore to join the local bartenders' union (as noted above in Chapter II). The fact that Flore was active in the local Democratic organization was known to Seames; he argued that by joining the union, Flore would not only be helping his fellow workers, but would broaden his acquaintanceship among people who were in good position to influence votes in their different quarters of the town.

At twenty-two, as at sixty-two, Flore was cautious and deliberate in action. He was then earning but $12 a week. The bartenders' local in Buffalo had made no great record as yet, and it was said that its members hardly knew what was done with the money they paid in per capita taxes to the Hotel and Restaurant Employees and Bartenders League. But Seames insisted that the International was now reorganized and in good hands. After thinking it over for several months, Flore decided to join. In February, 1900, he paid his $2 fee and became a member of Local Union No. 175.[14]

Fred Seames had wanted Flore as a helpmate in building up their small union. Ed would be serious about coming to union meetings regularly; with his standing in the local Democratic organization he could approach saloon keepers more easily than others and gain their consent to having their employees join the union.

The members were genial fellows, a few of whom met at regular intervals at a battered old union hall, drank beer together, talked and sang songs. There was little thought of doing anything about wages and hours, for their numbers were all too small. But soon Ed Flore found himself elected to the unpaid office of Financial Secretary, and in what little spare time he had, went pounding the streets to collect dues of seventy-five cents a month from members working in the side-street bars of Buffalo.

He had joined with a view to improving his situation socially and politically, and with little crusading zeal, much less knowledge of economic or labor questions. But his interest in the task quickened. Under Seames's tutelage, he became a good union officer, and even though his organizing was a casual and spare-time effort, the membership of Local 175 grew steadily until, by 1905, it stood at over 300, a fair size in those days.

Reports of the Buffalo waiters' and cooks' annual gatherings with the bartenders for buffet suppers or union balls fifty years ago mention the quiet, "ever-smiling Ed Flore" moving among them as one of "the shining stars of the fluid dispensers' union." [15]

When Seames, on withdrawing from the union in 1905, suggested that Flore be moved up to replace him as International Vice-President, Jere Sullivan said nothing at the time. But one day in the summer of 1905, he wrote Flore asking if he wished to stand for Vice-President. Flore answered in the affirmative; then several months passed before Secretary Sullivan wrote him again, as brief and curt a message as he had ever received, saying that he had been elected by the Board and notifying him when and where it would next meet. There was no salary with the office, only an allowance for railroad fare and a small per diem payment for time spent at Board meetings.

In May, 1905, Flore had gone with a friend in the union, Emmanuel Kovaleski, Secretary of Bartenders' Local 171, in Rochester, to Kansas City to attend his first convention as a delegate. It was the time of the confusing imbroglio between the deposed ex-President Callahan and Jere Sullivan; between sessions the leaders of both sides had buttonholed him and solicited his vote. Like his comrades, Seames and Kovaleski, he had gone along with the administration and voted for "Tim" Sullivan as President.

But the whole union seemed in poor shape after the business depression of 1904. As a Vice-President, Flore was occasionally assigned tasks of negotiation for the local unions in his district. One of these arose out of a threatened strike in a hotel in Buffalo, and was managed by him with such firmness and tact that a compromise was agreed upon and a strike avoided. In such affairs he was helped by having some standing in local politics as a lieutenant of Alderman Fuhrman—by whose influence Flore was appointed in 1908 to fill a vacant place on the County Board of Supervisors with a salary of $1,500 a year. The Supervisors not only directed the county's fiscal affairs but also controlled the issuance of liquor licenses. After that Flore had little trouble persuading Buffalo's restaurant and saloon keepers to let him organize their help. His union office was useful to him in local politics, and his public office helped him in his trade union activities—as was true of other men who rose to high posts in the International, such as Vice-President Robert Hesketh, a City Councilor of Seattle for many years. This was a period when Ed Flore was not clear in his mind as to what was to be his job in life: that of a trade union officer or a politician.

His friend Emmanuel Kovaleski, of Rochester, helped him to make up his mind. Kovaleski, who in his youth was an earnest worker in the labor union field, had recently been appointed an International Organizer, at the recommendation of Vice-President Flore. Journeying about a good deal thereafter through the towns of upstate New York and the Middle West, he was able to judge the condition and spirit of the branch unions, and found much was wanting. What was needed above all, he reported in a private talk with Jere L. Sullivan, early in 1909, was a man of character at the head of the union whom the members could respect. The well-liked and industrious Ed Flore of Buffalo was proposed by him as a replacement for the aging "Tim" Sullivan. Jere L. replied that he would think upon the matter. It was significant, however, that he assigned Kovaleski to organization work among the hotels of Minneapolis, in preparation for the forthcoming Hotel and Restaurant Employees' convention to be held there in May, 1909. While stationed there Kovaleski would be in a good position to use his spare time in lining up support for his presidential candidate among the Middle-Western locals.

When Kovaleski had first come to Flore to sound him out, and urged upon him the pressing need of the union for new leadership and the large opportunities before it, Flore, as was his wont, had been very silent and had in no sense leaped at the proposal. He was quite occupied, then, tending bar, acting as a County Supervisor and directing his local union. But on communicating with his fellow vice-presidents at the next Executive Board meeting, he gathered that there was much sentiment against re-electing "Tim" Sullivan, and talk of turning to some other man, such as Frank Hoffman, an able local officer of Minneapolis. Some of the Board members also encouraged Flore to stand for the presidency. It would thus be a three-cornered contest. Flore finally decided to throw his hat in the ring, and notified Kovaleski that he might get on with his canvassing of local officers for pledges. Fred Seames, though no longer active in the union, also came forward to help in the campaign.

That Secretary Sullivan covertly supported the first campaign for Flore is shown by an incident occurring a few months later, after the convention was over. President Tim, resentful at Kovaleski's busy electioneering, demanded that he be dropped from the payroll for neglect of his duties. To which Sullivan replied tartly:

> You forget that International Organizers are under *my* jurisdiction. Kovaleski is a competent organizer. What he does in his free time is his own business. As soon as he falls down on the job, I'll take him off the payroll and not before.[16]

At the Minneapolis convention, Tim Sullivan fought hard to stay in office for another term. A sizable contingent of "Callahan men" supported Flore on that occasion. But on the night before the election contest, a final survey indicated that Ed Flore would most likely be defeated, largely because of votes drawn by the third man, Hoffman. Tim Sullivan that night came to see Flore and appealed to him to withdraw and "trade" his delegates in return for the older man's promise to support Flore for the presidency in the next election, two years later. But Flore said firmly that it would be all or nothing for him; he would run in the face of expected defeat.

When the balloting was over, Tim Sullivan was re-elected, Flore ran a strong second and Hoffman a poor third. Flore's speech congratulating his victorious opponent was marked by good taste and manliness of spirit. He had lost, he said smilingly, but he would probably be back again at the next convention.

When nominations for vice-presidents were called for, however, Flore appeared on the rostrum again and took the unusual step of declining renomination, declaring that, as he had aimed at the presidency and lost, he would not at this time stand for the re-election to the Executive Board, but would be content to return to his lesser role as a bartender and secretary of his local, to await the will of the next convention in 1911.[17] Edward Flore in defeat made a fine impression on his fellow delegates and showed himself decidedly of presidential timber. He was then a personable young fellow of thirty-one. Jere L. Sullivan, who had helped him secretly while pretending in public to be impartial, thereupon decided to go all out in order to ensure the young man's election the next time.

*

In the merry month of May, 1911, the jovial clans of the bartenders were gathered again in general convention, 188 in number, at Faneuil Hall, Boston, the "cradle of liberty." (Actually they made up a party of 500, including wives and friends, as the Boston press reported.) The honorary chairman who welcomed the delegates was Richard W. Garrity, of Bartenders' Local 77, Boston, successor to Callahan. An elderly man, Garrity, to speak the truth, was no real "mixologist" but had formerly been a streetcar driver and an active and popular figure in Boston's labor movement. When the horse-drawn vehicles gave way to the new-fangled electric trolleys, Garrity quit his job in disgust—holding that a decent man could not abide driving anything but good horseflesh—and turned to tending bar. Thanks to his silver tongue, he had soon gained the leadership of Local 77, and in 1909 had been elected an International Vice-President. He had had the honor also of being President of Boston's Central Labor Union and a member of the Massachusetts State Legislature as well. It was rumored that, as an experienced politician of the labor movement, Garrity had joined the restaurant workers' and bartenders' organization with the ambition of becoming their president.

The residential headquarters of the delegates were at the old Revere House, whose lobbies and corridors and barrooms echoed and thundered for days and nights before the polling day with the electioneering of the rival factions. President Tim had sworn that his current term would be the last, but he wanted "one more" after all. The old disaffected Boston group, meanwhile, bustled about from room to room gathering pledges for the well-loved R. W. Garrity. And the Flore supporters were also there in force. Everyone seemed to be playing at union politics and few seemed to give thought to the weaknesses or needs of the union, save, perhaps, the long-enduring General Secretary, Jere Sullivan.

He looked on the presidents of the union with a jaundiced eye, as a sort of necessary evil. But a president there must be, and Jere L. had firmly made up his mind who it was to be. It was often said in those days that he usually managed to find out which small locals lacked funds for delegates' traveling expenses and helped them send someone to the convention.

For the union delegates it was a vacation, a spring holiday, and they made it a rousing convention—it was not very different from the legislative gatherings of other labor unions then, whether of mine workers, boilermakers or carpenters, which also flowed over with good spirits and beer. Garrity delivered himself of a windblown harangue in which the Boston Tea Party and the founding of the Republic were linked together in this historic meeting place, Faneuil Hall, with the destiny of "the world's greatest union." As guest speaker Garrity introduced his good friend, Mayor "Jimmie" Fitzgerald of Boston. The Mayor, after a brief welcoming speech that carefully avoided embarrassing issues of industrial relations, conceived the happy thought of leading the crowd in the singing of "Sweet Adeline," the great song hit of that era.

"Come on! Join in the chorus!" he cried. And everyone in that hilarious crowd threw back his head and sang until the rafters shook.[18]

John J. Kearney, later a Vice-President, but then a delegate for the first time for Local 80, Boston, has recalled:

> As I looked around me at the convention of 1911 I saw nothing but bartenders—probably 90 per cent of the delegates then were bartenders, though the culinary workers constituted more than three-quarters of the people in our trades.[19]

The delegates were in no mood to listen to the reading of lengthy business reports, and, as often before, the sharp-tongued Jere L. strode to the platform to apply the whip and bring them to order. As he passed from one end of the hall to the Secretary's table, he heard a delegate exclaim: "There goes Jere L. Sullivan, the *Czar of Cincinnati*, the maker and unmaker of presidents in this organization!"

The General Secretary thereupon began his admonitory speech by repeating the unwary remarks of that delegate as serving "to tear aside a veil," and giving a disconcerting view of the members' ideas about their organization. "The knack of saying much in little, unfortunately for you," he admitted, "is not one of my possessions." Everyone present gloomily agreed. But, he went on, the idea that he had engaged in any "pernicious activities," or had "bossed" the International Union must be denied, flattering though it might be to some. For the delegates to claim that he wielded such powers was to accuse themselves "of possessing a backbone of bilgewater and excelsior as a substitute for brains."

No, Jere L. Sullivan was in no sense the "Czar of Cincinnati," he maintained, and he scrupulously avoided "helping or harming the different candidates." To be sure the titular heads of the union had been indifferent, and he had been forced to "assume and shoulder executive responsibilities which others, for years, had abdicated." And so it happened that he "directed" the organization, and its policies were "your Secretary-Treasurer's policies." [20]

When nominations for president were called for, Kovaleski of Rochester led off with an enthusiastic address in behalf of Edward Flore:

> Brothers, President, and Delegates, I desire to place in nomination a brother who has been an officer of his local since 1900 and who has continuously and always taken an active interest in organized labor. . . . He has served on the Executive Board from 1905 to 1909. He is a young man—active, and one who will be in a position to visit the locals of our International Union irrespective of their location. . . . He is broad-minded, conservative and thoroughly conversant with our International laws . . . fully qualified to fill the position [for] which I am about to nominate him. Brother Chairman and Fellow Delegates, I take great honor and pleasure in behalf of my fellow delegates from the State of New York, in presenting the name of Edward Flore of Local 175, Buffalo, New York, for the office of General President of our International Union.

Jere Sullivan desired that sentiment for young Mr. Flore should appear to spring up from all parts of the country. Whatever his disclaimers, he had sent word to Hesketh of Seattle that someone from the Pacific slope should prepare a seconding speech in favor of Flore, and Delegate J. E. McCracken of Local 400, Spokane, Washington, delivered it.[21]

Following this, Tim Sullivan was renominated, being described as one who had grown to the stature of a "statesman of labor." Then that old worthy, Garrity of Boston, a colorful representative of the horse-car age, was given the honor of a nomination for the presidency, though everyone really knew what the outcome would be. The Boston bartenders and their friends, to be sure, made a tremendous commotion for the old horse-car driver, to the alarm of the other factions.

In those days, whenever the emotions of the delegates passed reasonable bounds, there was a steady group among them, a sort of Grenadier Guard who laughingly called themselves the "Knob Polishers." They were an informal club or clique of veteran local officers and members of the GEB, a "bunch of real good fellows who knew each other for that, and who, at conventions, would fight hard for what they believed was right. When passions had risen too high, the order 'Polish!' would be given and promptly obeyed." Among them at various times were Fred Seames, Tim Kinally, C. W. McCurdy, Ed Horne, John E. McCracken and others—all usually staunch allies of Jere L. Sullivan.[22]

The Knob Polishers, in 1911, answered the pro-Garrity delegation with long ovations for Flore. When the balloting was done, Flore had received 255-⅓ votes, Garrity, 111, and Tim Sullivan 94-⅔. Tim's sad, parting gesture was to move for the unanimous election of the victor, but the Boston group made an uproarious dissent, and needed to be gaveled down. The rift was still there.

In his acceptance speech, the smooth-shaven, thirty-three-year-old Ed Flore made an earnest plea for unity, saying:

> What we are all primarily interested in is the best way to improve the union and the welfare of its membership. Let us now forget whatever bitterness might have developed as a result of this campaign.

This was another of the old-time convention brawls. As one of the delegates recalled long afterward: "Those were the horse-and-buggy days for our International Union; it had a rather poor reputation in the AFL, and was looked down upon—until Ed Flore took over." In the end, as if in self-preservation, the union had turned to a young man of solid character and good sense, one who made clear his purpose of ending the petty squabbles of factions.

But the dominant figure of Jere L., as a sort of "gloomy Dean,"

busily manipulating and managing everything, while denying all—
and yet unconsciously, in flashes, revealing his pride in his power—
remained unforgettable. Would the great man of Cincinnati share
his authority with anyone?

The International was, indeed, at a crisis in its history, one that
demanded of every officer and member that he get on with the job
ahead. For by 1911 the enemy hosts of the Anti-Saloon League were
at the gates.

FOUR

The Dual Union Movement: 1912

*"The organized section of the industry . . . repre-
sented but an insignificant, small islet within an
ocean of unorganized territory."*—JOHN BOOKJANS.

In September, 1911, a few months after having been elected President of the International Union, Edward Flore was married to a
Buffalo girl named Mae Schneider, who was of French descent and
had worked as a dressmaker. Of a retiring, though very gracious, disposition, Mae Flore, by all accounts, was a devoted helpmate of her
husband throughout his life. The couple settled in a two-family frame
house at 469 Oak Street, Buffalo, Flore setting aside a room upstairs
to serve as his office. As his union work increased, Mrs. Flore added
to her homemaking activities the job of secretary, handling his correspondence and telephone calls for over twenty years, until the increase of his union's revenues permitted him a private secretary.

With his $200 a month as president of the union and $1,500 a year
as a County Supervisor, he was able to provide for a simple and
comfortable way of life for those days. For he was economical and
orderly in his affairs and very much the solid, unpretentious sort of
citizen who tended to avoid display or "flash." [1]

At union meetings, as in committees or conferences with employers, Flore made a pleasing impression, but also carried himself with

dignity. He was invariably a good listener who said little, his habitual reserve being perhaps due to his awareness of his lack of education.

"Ed Flore impressed you as a man who, when you asked him a question he didn't know about, would say nothing and wait until he could find the right answer." [2]

The son of a saloon proprietor, he had no working-class conscious-ness such as do those who must find a job or go hungry. He had never gone hungry and cold, and had been able to look forward to inherit-ing a share of his father's business with his brothers. Thus he had no particular philosophy of labor to begin with—at any rate, nothing beyond the current AFL doctrine of a "fair day's wage for a fair day's work."

His speech before union gatherings was labored and homely, but never resorted to the savage gibes or sarcasm of a Jere L. Sullivan. In judging between opponents in disputes within the union, his atti-tude was judicious and as far as possible he avoided offense to either party. A local officer, who, by chance, had made a blunder that cost the union some of its membership, might be forgiven with a kindly warning, because Flore had thought well of the man and was loyal to men he liked. Thus his influence as a moderator in an organization that had suffered greatly from the storms of internal dissension con-tributed in no small measure to its ability to endure adverse periods. It explains also his own long stay in office.

"It was Ed Flore who really made our union *respectable*," many old veterans remark.[3]

Rarely did he show anger or ever lose his temper. One instance, however, is recalled by John Bookjans, formerly editor of the union's official journal, and in earlier years a local union officer in Pittsburgh. In 1917 President Flore was called to Pittsburgh to help the waiters' and cooks' locals negotiate a settlement with an extremely stubborn restaurateur, a certain Mr. Hammel, weighing all of 400 pounds, whose employees had been partially organized. When a strike was called Mr. Hammel flatly refused to see any of the union representa-tives, declaring he had "the right to run his business as he pleased." Flore did manage to see the man and tried to convince him that the fair procedure would be to deal with his workers through their union; but every such proposal was met by the reply: "Mr. Flore, I'm run-ning my own business." This he repeated so many times that, at last, Flore became angered and turned to leave the man abruptly with the parting words: "Mr. Hammel, you just keep on running your own business and maybe you will run it into the ground!"

This was just what happened. Hammel's Restaurant was patronized by wealthy people who were accustomed to being waited upon by men who for long years had known their wants and habits. When these waiters struck and were replaced mostly by inexperienced workers, who were non-union, the regular customers became irritated and drifted away to other restaurants. Thus Hammel's Restaurant became unprofitable, closed its doors several years later, and Hammel became ill and died not long after that.[4]

At the start of his term as President, Ed Flore traveled about a bit to study conditions in the local branches of the International Union. In September, 1911, he visited New York City and held conferences with several of the local leaders there, and especially with the heads of the ancient Local 1, restored to good standing again since 1907. Returning to Buffalo, he then visited several nearby Canadian cities where some small locals (of bartenders, mainly) had been organized earlier. January, 1912, found him in Boston, addressing a meeting of Local 77, where he formally installed the recently elected officers. In Boston, too, he found—what was rare in those days—a thriving waiters' local, No. 80, with a young officer named John J. Kearney as its secretary. "Local 80 has a large organization and they are fortunate in having a man with the ability of Secretary Kearney. . . ." he reported.[5]

He expressed concern, however, about the morale of some of the branch unions; their quarters were dingy and depressing; their officers paid too little attention to ceremony and form.

> In my visits to some of our locals [Flore reported] I find that our ritual is not strictly adhered to. Plenty of time should be taken in the initiation of candidates, and the same should take place in the meeting-hall and not in the anteroom. . . . A great deal depends upon the impressiveness of the ceremony. Officers should commit their parts to memory, as it has a more commanding effect upon the candidate.[6]

What he saw in New York also troubled him a good deal. But writing of it to Jere Sullivan he expressed himself with reserve:

> Well, I do not know what to say about conditions in that city; they are very bad and there is no use trying to fool ourselves . . . New York is a great cosmopolitan city. There was a time when we had a membership there that was a credit to our International, but now—something has got to be done. I have a plan in mind to submit to the GEB.[7]

The monster city of four millions had only about 2,000 members in the Hotel and Restaurant Employees and Bartenders International at this period. In the country's greatest catering center, with a laboring population of over 75,000 workers, almost none of the cooks in the city were organized; and almost none of the hotel workers. Most of the workers were immigrants, and the more skilled or experienced, in great number, were members of the various "fraternal" societies or clubs, such as the Geneva Association, or the Chefs de Cuisine (which were in no sense trade unions). There were, however, several independent or dual unions at work among the foreign-born culinary workers, which were directed by leaders of a radical type. It was a confusing, a disheartening picture. Jere L. Sullivan used to say to his associates on the GEB: "You can't organize New York. . . ."

When the well-intentioned Flore pondered about what should be done, he soon realized that his role as President was more or less honorific. The General Secretary held the power of purse. Shut up in his headquarters in Cincinnati, with his several assistants, Sullivan guarded the treasury funds, collected local union taxes, issued charters and stamps and published regularly careful financial records of all transactions. More important still he hired and directed the staff of half a dozen General Organizers, and occasionally, also, several special organizers, who journeyed about the country recruiting members or "trouble-shooting." In addition to all that, he edited the union's official journal himself, with articles reflecting his own views, reports from local officers, and literary tidbits culled from a thousand different sources and reprinted without much rhyme or reason. But he seldom left his desk and seldom saw the President, who resided in Buffalo. After a while he had less and less first-hand knowledge of what was going on in the field—such as Flore tried to acquire.

Not long after Flore had been elected as International President in the autumn of 1911, he decided to pay a visit to Secretary Sullivan, journeyed to Cincinnati and walked into the "little chief's" office. Sullivan was busily dictating letters to a stenographer; he gave Flore a curt sign of welcome, and went on striding up and down, puffing at his cigarettes, and flailing his arms as he talked, as if addressing a great but invisible audience.

At length Flore, who had been sitting and waiting patiently, got the Secretary's ear and broached the problem that had been worrying him: that, as President, "he did not have enough to do!" Sullivan, at the time, avoided any direct answer, changed the topic of conversation, and "for two years thereafter ignored Flore's periodic suggestions that the International President be given a little more work." [8]

Nevertheless Flore persisted in his efforts to "do something," while avoiding as far as possible any conflict with the irascible little "Czar" in Cincinnati.

Meanwhile a period of crisis was at hand for the Hotel and Restaurant Employees and Bartenders. The labor movement after 1910 was in ferment, with most trade unions expanding, and both new opportunities and new dangers arising. Industry itself was changing under the feet of the labor leaders.

*

In the twenty years of the International Union's existence it had organized only a "nucleus" of the more experienced culinary workers in first-class restaurants of the larger towns. While people in other trades were improving their status and working conditions, as did those in mining and the building trades, the culinary workers had too small a part of the working force organized as yet. Compared with trades in which successful unions controlled a majority, or even 75 to 80 percent, of the labor force (as in coal mining), they had less than 10 percent organized up to World War I. Hence they remained an underpaid, sweated labor force. The threat of the strike weapon meant little, since employees could easily be replaced.*

From 1890 to 1912 there had been only a gradual and very moderate shortening of hours. Typical reports for kitchen workers and waiters in the big Eastern cities indicated eleven to twelve hours

---

* Though calling itself the "Hotel & Restaurant Employees International Alliance and Bartenders International League," people in the labor movement referred to it briefly as the "Bartenders Union," and with justice. A tabulation of the membership by crafts (as of January 1, 1910) shows that the mixers of drinks constituted about two-thirds of the total:

Bartenders	24,553
Cooks	2,004
Waiters	4,442
Waitresses	962
Mixed locals (part bartenders)	4,821
Miscellaneous	412
TOTAL	37,194

At this period, 1910, the U.S. Census report showed that there were 450,440 cooks and 188,293 waiters, or a grand total of 638,733 culinary workers in hotels and restaurants. To be sure, approximately 33 to 40 per cent of this number were self-employed, that is, in hole-in-the-wall establishments run by the labor of "Pop and Mom," hence not available for union membership. On the other hand, a respectable proportion, approaching 50 per cent, of the bartenders' craft were organized.

a day (instead of fourteen!) and the seven-day week as fairly prevalent.

Jere L. Sullivan's tendency to avoid centers like New York and Chicago is shown by the make-up of the Executive Board between 1910 and 1915, most of its International Vice-Presidents coming from locals in small cities, such as Des Moines, Iowa; Springfield, Illinois; Birmingham, Alabama; and San Antonio, Texas. In 1911, to be sure, Elizabeth Maloney, of Chicago, was elected as vice-president-at-large representing women workers. But up to 1923 there was no member of the GEB representing New York.

There, "In America's largest city, the organized section of the industry represented but an insignificant, small islet within an ocean of unorganized territory," John Bookjans has written.[9]

The day of the "skyscraper" hotel had come to America's cities in the first decade of the twentieth century. The twenty- or thirty-story hostelry, with 1,000 rooms and upwards of a thousand workers to serve its guests and "process" meals for them, was run at an entirely different tempo from that of the small inn where the proprietor often worked alongside his helpers. It was in effect a "factory" serving food and shelter on a big scale; and now whole battalions worked in these "factories" from dawn to dark. These were, in overwhelming majority, foreign-born, especially in the big cities of the East and Middle West. But virtually none of them were members of the Hotel and Restaurant Employees Union.

New York had the well-established Waiters Local 1, then of 660 to 1,000 members, but it followed the "closed book" policy after its reorganization in 1909. Holding jurisdiction over various downtown and East Side restaurants (that were patronized by many union men) and over the outside catering and banquet trade, it was a "job trust," restricting its membership by charging high initiation fees of $65. Its officers never seriously tried to organize the "luxury" hotel industry, now growing by leaps and bounds, whose mass of unorganized workers constantly tended to undermine union standards. As Bookjans has written:

> In the course of years, an almost impenetrable barrier grew up between the workers in the small organized sections of New York and those employed in the large hotels. The two didn't seem to speak the same language. Many hotel waiters and cooks in those days held membership in such organizations as the Geneva Association, the Deutscher Kellner Bund [German Waiters Association], and other such "social clubs" as they were known, the leaders of which, more often than not, were steeped in anti-union prejudice.

"You can't organize New York" was often the frustrating comment when the union question was raised. . . . Meanwhile, the big hotels exploited the helplessness of their kitchen and dining room employees by stretching hours and shaving down wages.[10]

In these "palace" hotels, some of which were already being combined as chains, the managers laughed at efforts of union agents to organize their personnel by methods used in gathering in workers of small taverns or bars. The hotel managers often recruited and trained their own personnel, most of them drawn from the foreign-language, or "Continental," clubs or agencies. "Formerly the owner of a small inn had known all his employees by their first names. But now in the large hotels *the waiters were known only by a number they wore on their badges.*" [11]

At places like the fashionable Belmont Hotel in New York (now dismantled) discipline over waiters was extremely severe. The headwaiter would hold a line-up of his workers each morning and inspect them before they marched into the dining room. Here a man who joined a union could do so provided he kept his ideas about the value of unions for the working man to himself. But if he talked union to his fellows, woe unto him, for he would soon find himself outside, looking for another job. As a rule he would not be told why he was suddenly discharged, except that it was for the "good of the business." In many instances the blacklist stopped him from finding work in the same town and he would have to move on to another city.

In the same luxurious Hotel Belmont (as in many others) a system of fines caused intense irritation among all the hired help. A waiter receiving $25 a month, with meals and tips, would be fined twenty-five cents for dropping a piece of silver, or being late on the job, or talking too much to customers, or not standing at his station. One waiter was known to have been fined $2.00 for drinking leftover coffee and two others were fined $1.00 each just for looking on, seeing what he was doing, but not reporting it to the management.[12]

Although the labor of bartenders, waiters and cooks and cooks' assistants traditionally ranks low in prestige compared with that of heavy industry, the truth is that it is labor performed under great tension and nervous strain, with every step in the process highly interrelated and organized. In a busy restaurant or hotel dining room the appearance of a waiter or waitress with a tray of food is actually the final step in a long and complicated process of production and service. William Foote Whyte, a professor of sociology who made careful studies of the craft (during a year of employment as a waiter in a Chicago restaurant), has written with a fine understanding of the "nerve strain" suffered by waiter, waitress and kitchen employee. The customers must be served—and always at the same time, at a "peak-traffic" hour arriving three or four times a day.[18] The waiter hurries his orders to the kitchen staff and the rush is on to meet the demands of a hundred or a thousand different persons ordering a variety of different foods all of which are to be served in a matter of minutes. The rush hours for breakfast, lunch and dinner, and in some places late supper, reach their climax amid conditions often suggesting a grand turmoil, yet the job is carried off by the experienced workers with great order and concentrated effort. Then there is the break in traffic; the workers relax from tension, before preparing for the next rush.

Most arduous and exacting of all is the labor of the men with the white caps during the rush hours. One of the most gifted of modern novelists, the late George Orwell, who once worked as a *plongeur* (dishwasher) in an old-fashioned hotel in Paris, has left us in his autobiographical writings word-paintings of great realism representing the locale and atmosphere of the hotel, or restaurant, kitchen— as it was in America also—thirty to forty years ago:

. . . A stifling, low-ceilinged inferno of a cellar, redlit from the fires, and deafening with oaths and the clanging of pots and pans. It was so hot that all the metal-work except the stoves had to be covered with cloth. In the middle were furnaces where twelve cooks skipped to and fro, their faces dripping sweat in spite of their white caps. Round that were counters where a mob of waiters and *plongeurs* clamoured with trays. Scullions, naked to the waist, were stoking the fires and scouring huge copper saucepans with sand. Everyone seemed to be in a hurry and a rage. The head cook, a fine, scarlet man with big moustachios, stood in the middle booming continuously . . .

At a quarter to five we went back to the hotel. Till half-past six there were no orders, and we used this time to polish silver, clean out the coffee-urns and do other odd jobs. Then the grand turmoil of the day started—the dinner hour. I wish I could be Zola for a little while, just to describe that dinner hour. The essence of the situation was that a hundred or two hundred people were demanding individually different meals of five or six courses, and that fifty or sixty people had to cook and serve them and clean up the mess afterwards. . . . And at this time when the work was doubled, the whole staff was tired out, and a number of them were drunk. I could write pages about the scene without giving a true idea of it. The chargings to and fro in the narrow passages, the collisions, the yells, the strugglings with crates and trays and blocks of ice, the heat, the darkness, the furious festering quarrels which there was no time to fight out—they pass description. Anyone coming into the basement for the first time would have thought himself in a den of maniacs. It was only later, when I understood the working of a hotel, that I saw order in all this chaos.

At half-past eight the work stopped suddenly. We . . . used to throw ourselves full length on the floor, and lie there resting our legs, too lazy even to go to the ice cupboard for a drink.

One had to walk and run fifteen miles during the day, Orwell relates. "One had to leap to and fro between a multitude of jobs," but he insists, "the strain of the work was more *mental than physical.*"

And there was the heat (nowadays mitigated somewhat by ventilators).

Our murky cellar was lighted by one dim electric bulb, and four or five gas fires that sent out a fierce red breath. There was a thermometer there and the temperature never fell below 110 degrees Fahrenheit—it neared 130 at some times of the day.[14]

César Lesino, a venerable chef and union officer who had been trained in Paris, has described the wretchedness of the foreign-born kitchen armies in New York's de luxe hotels in similar terms. For second cooks the wages were $40 a month and meals; the hours, forty years ago, were still twelve a day, or more. He says:

You could tell a poor assistant cook or dishwasher a mile off coming down the street at six in the morning on his tired legs, because he looked so terrible usually. They would work until they could not stand up any longer, then go home, get drunk, sleep, fight with their wives, have kids and get drunk again. It was all work and sleep, drink and fight.

César Lesino also relates that at the hotel when the fires were stoked high during the rush hour and one of the cooks fainted, one of a line of unemployed cooks sitting on a bench in the back of the kitchen would be called in to take his place without a minute's delay, while the unconscious man was being carried out.

Relations between New York's big hotel managers and the personnel were far from friendly then. Lesino, hired toward 1907, as *chef de garde manger* at a great Fifth Avenue hostelry, was given stern orders: "See that none of your crew steals any of the food, or this hotel will spend $50,000 to catch him and put him in jail!"

LESINO (proudly): "None of my men steal. They are all good union men."

THE MANAGER: "But X— stole enough to build up a whole Hotel St. Regis!"

LESINO: "I knew him—he was not in the union, I can prove it to you!"

On another occasion, at this period, the same union officer called upon the manager in his office with a committee to lay the grievances of their members before him. The manager, though formerly a waiter, remained seated as they came in and stood before him. Thereupon Lesino sat down in a chair, and his comrades did likewise.

"What do you mean, how dare you sit down in my office!"

"Well, we saw you sitting there so we sat down too." [15]

Bartenders, once considered the "aristocrats" of the catering trade, almost universally complain of the nervous tension under which they work. "A bartender must get to know people well," many of them have said. He becomes, at best, a figure of paternal authority in the neighborhood. He must know who can be served and not served. He helps the local politician, or conciliates the husband and wife who quarrel; or disposes of the people who want to stay up all night. "He knows everybody's troubles, yet must keep a civil tongue in his head and help them all." But when his children are asked by others what trade their father works at, they notice that his labors are not regarded with as much social esteem as is given to men employed in far less trying and exhausting occupations. And life insurance companies often require bartenders to pay rates as high as those for coal miners or sandhogs.[16]

The problems of the waiter are particular because he serves "two bosses," the customer on the one hand, and his supervisor or head-waiter on the other—who often do not have the same interests. A typical complaint of waiters and waitresses runs:

"The trouble is, when the guests get nasty with you, you can't tell them off. You have to keep it all inside you. That's what makes it so nerve-wracking." Or another says, "You can't talk back to people. I learned that it pays to keep quiet and just not say anything when a customer gets excited." [17]

The tipping system adds to this calling the play of chance or risk and tended in former years, it has been said, to cut down wages. America used to be tipless. It was only toward the end of the nineteenth century that tipping as an established European practice was introduced in this country in fine restaurants and hotels, then spread later to popular-priced places. As one old-time waiter observed:

Wages of waiters in luxurious hotels and restaurants in America, where the tipping system generally prevailed, were often less than half of those paid in cheaper eating-places patronized by the common run of people who did not tip. The employers soon learned to exploit the tipping system for their own advantage by whittling down wages of waiters and waitresses. . . . It also operated to lengthen the hours of work.[18]

"This tipping business is a great evil," many waiters say. "It gives the waiter an inferiority complex—makes him feel he is at the mercy of the customer all the time. I wish they would have the 10 per cent [service charge] system everywhere." [19] Our best clubs use this method.

Others, however, are accustomed to the speculative excitement of their daily occupation—the chances of $100 tips from men who are no "stiffs" and have just found a gold mine—much as they enjoy going to the races. John Nolan, the fictive waiter-hero of A Tree Grows in Brooklyn, in his unfailing hope for lucky winnings at the races or at his dining-room tables, is typical of many waiters of yesterday and today.

John Bookjans, for many years editor of his union's official journal, arrived in America from Germany in 1897, as a young immigrant, and found employment, not long afterward, as a waiter in New York, Toledo, and then Cleveland, Ohio. Becoming a member of Waiters Local 106 of Cleveland, he showed himself an ardent trade unionist who devoted his spare time to advancing the interests of his local, as well as to his own self-education. From an early period, almost a half-century ago, he kept a diary noting down in objective terms his observations in his trade. Employers in those days showed a remarkable disregard for the health and life of their personnel (as in most other industries). A chef was expected to hold food costs down, especially in serving food to waiters and kitchen help. A universal complaint before World War I was the poor, even decomposed quality of food served employees. I cite:

> *Cleveland, O., August 19, 1909*
> I have learned that a waiter at the Euclid may have something edible for breakfast and dinner only if he tips the cook a dime. It would not cost me much more to get a good meal in a restaurant, but I am not permitted to leave the house during working hours. Yet I seldom eat more than one meal, for even if one pays the cook one does not get good food.

Cleveland, O., August 23, 1909

No matter whether it is the long day or the short day, when going home in the evening my feet feel very tired. This is caused by walking many hours on the hard floor in the Grill Room. It is seldom that a waiter in the Euclid is allowed to sit down. Every man invents some excuse occasionally for going downstairs, so that he may give his feet a rest for five or ten minutes.

Cleveland, O., August 24, 1909

Peterson failed to report for duty yesterday, and for that offense was discharged this morning.

The headwaiter seems to be aware that the discouragement born from continually standing upon one's feet for eight and a half to fifteen and a half hours a day has a connection with failure of waiters to appear for duty. . . . In the afternoon, when no guests are present, a few of the waiters will frequently be found in one of the booths, where they make a pretense of folding napkins, so as to allow their feet rest for a few minutes. There is hardly a waiter who does not complain of the long working hours.

That year Bookjans decided to travel to other cities and deliberately seek out establishments with the worst reputation for ill-treatment of their employees, in order to study and compile a record of labor conditions there. In Chicago he sought work at one luxurious hotel known as "a veritable hell for waiters." The hours of work were twelve a day, but he was detained for a half-hour or longer after that without pay. For his meals he would sometimes be given meat that was plainly inedible and that fellow workers threw away with cries: "It smells!"

Similar unsanitary conditions were endured by the waitresses of Chicago, according to International Vice-President Elizabeth Maloney; and they were soon engaged in a number of strikes. Testifying before the U.S. Industrial Commission in Washington, in 1914, Miss Maloney declared that, prior to the passage of an Illinois ten-hour law for women, girls had been working as waitresses twelve to fourteen hours a day for seven days a week, for wages of $3.50 to $5 a week and small tips. In the big hotels of Chicago chambermaids earned but $14 to $15 and board a month:

I investigated the case of girls where they were poisoned on food that was spoiled, and I went into quite a thorough investigation of that and found out from those girls that they received food that was . . . in a decomposed state. These girls were poisoned through eating spoiled roast pork. . . . I went to the room of the girls because they were in bed from those attacks of ptomaine poisoning and found on their window sills boxes of crackers and bottles of milk. I said, "What does this mean? Don't you get your board at the hotel?" "Yes, but it is not fit to eat half the time and whatever tips I get I use to buy things to eat." [20]

Bookjans, in his diary, also reports one incident of several bellboys in a big hotel throwing the lobby into a commotion because of their wild anger at having received for their dinner food unfit for a human being to eat. "One bellboy swore that if he had the money he would join the union, while another spoke quite favorably of socialism." The status of restaurant and hotel workers was far below that of most other labor in America. But the official labor union in the field was doing all too little for them. In the fierce heat of the kitchens their tempers were snapping; the nerve-wracked waiters in bustling dining rooms were on the verge of rebellion. In their despair they were beginning to fight back, almost blindly.

It used to be said in the days when the luxury hotels were being established in New York, Chicago and other big cities, at the turn of the century: "You cannot get an American-born boy to work before a kitchen range for years as an apprentice and learn to be an expert cook." The vast majority of the culinary workers, as we have noted, were then foreign-born—often the chefs made their individual bargains with employers, and managed their kitchen gang as a small corner of Germany, Hungary, Austria, France or Italy. For union agents these people were not easy of approach.

Under Jere L. Sullivan, however, the International's organizers had made no special efforts to master the difficult problems presented here. On the contrary, Secretary Sullivan himself showed an instinctive distaste for dealing with the foreign-born mass of hotel workers in New York. These ill-used laborers were often the targets of his most abusive articles and speeches:

> . . . For years the agents of the Hotel Barons of Greater New York systematically scoured the Hell Pots, Cess Pools, alleged Catering Schools and Padrone Agencies of continental Europe for foreign lackeys to displace their competent, though somewhat independent English and American-speaking employees. . . . Inside of a few years' time the Mastodon caravanseries of Gotham became the asylum of as craven a bunch of scalawags as were ever seduced or driven from their native slums. The wage system was supplanted by an insidious and crafty cooperation between employer and employee. Every effort was made to impress on those "continentals" that they were superior to the home-grown bartender, cook, waiter . . . and to remain aloof from these workers and congregate in

social clubs which had an exclusive foreign membership and directorate. . . .[21]

The truth was that much ill-will had grown up between the members and officers of the International's locals and the foreign-born craftsmen who were gathered in small independent unions or in "clubs." The AFL organizers usually committed the error of trying to unionize the workers from the "top down" instead of trying to "reach the men first" and then proceed to enforce improved conditions.[22]

Organizers, then, were accustomed to seeking union members mainly in small privately owned saloons and eating places, by approaching the employer first. A talking point often used was that the union would make common cause with the tavern proprietors in the fight against Prohibition. As one of the early reformers in the union wrote in 1915:

> . . . The officers of the union presented the agreement, the employer signed (if it were not a mere verbal understanding), and directly or indirectly imparted to the men and women in his employ the information that henceforth their job would depend on their joining the union. The workers in such a restaurant were thus led to look upon the affair as a sort of conspiracy between the boss and the union business agent to levy upon them a tribute for the privilege of working.[23]

Thus many members in the older job-controlling locals of New York, Boston and Cleveland regarded the union as something "forced upon them" and not something they had worked to build up themselves.

Since the 1890's the American Federation of Labor and its typical craft unions had been subjected to constant and severe criticism by radical or reformist labor leaders. The main ground of their opponents' argument was that by dividing the workers into crafts, by discriminating between the skilled and the unskilled, the AFL encouraged the establishment of labor "aristocrats," while neglecting the categories of workers who were poorest or most sweated—these often being the "later immigrants" belonging to minority racial groups. The fact that one craft might be called out on strike, while other workers in the same shop continued on the job, often led, it was argued, to one union "scabbing" against the other. Finally the industrial system itself was changing: whereas the Gompers strategy of unionizing the skilled craftsmen gave strength to the labor movement in earlier years, it now appeared that the huge newer industries such as steel and automobiles were introducing mass-production methods and would use less and less skilled labor.

As examples of a superior form of unionism the successful records of the United Mine Workers and Brewery Workers, both "industrial unions" within the AFL, were cited (for the AFL was not of one mind). These had organized all the workers of the different crafts within any industry, "vertically," into "one big union." Similar tactics, pursued with extreme militancy, were used by the unions in the new federation called "The Industrial Workers of the World," organized in Chicago in 1905 (under the sponsorship of the Western Federation of Miners), and thereafter spreading eastward to penetrate many fields of industry which the AFL unions had either neglected or found beyond their ability to organize.

Although the IWW's, the native "Reds" of forty to fifty years ago, were widely condemned for their radical, or "subversive" tendencies, as we say nowadays, they administered some useful lessons to the official labor movement in America which were afterward taken to heart by many conservative union groups. They demonstrated clearly the failure of the narrow-minded, bureaucratic officers sometimes directing such unions as the Hotel and Restaurant Employees. For here the union's leadership and organizing staff (as it was seen even then, forty years ago) had signally failed; they failed to realize that their old methods could not work in big modern chain hotels. They failed also to grasp the meaning of changes that had developed in worker-owner relations in those new large hotels—where the waiter, as Bookjans has said, was but "a number on a badge." That the workers were growing steadily more alienated, that their grievances were piling up intolerably, was not clearly grasped by anyone—or at least nothing was done about it—and thus precious opportunities were lost. The International Union might have gathered in whole armies of discontented workers into its camp, instead of losing them to less responsible and less moderate leadership.*

* Many severe criticisms were made in later years of the type of General Organizers kept on the payroll of the International Union in its earlier phase. Though most of them were decent fellows, it was said, "they lacked the will to organize. . . . They were not crusaders. They lacked the impelling force of idealism, which I consider indispensable in this work. But in order to stay on the payroll these organizers had to show something. By approaching small proprietors and tavern keepers, they managed to get just barely enough applications to make possible the issuance of a charter. Then a set of officers were elected and installed, and after being provided with a few superficial instructions, left to paddle their own canoe. The result often and again was that these locals with their inexperienced officers threw up the sponge within a short time." (Editorial in the CIE, February 17, 1953.) The lapsation of membership was always high in this trade filled with casual workers; but the turnover in whole local unions was also high.

In the autumn of 1911 Waiters Local 1 of New York, which was the International's strongest unit there, undertook at last to organize the neglected hotel workers by setting up an affiliated union, Local 5, for cooks, and a Branch A of this local that was to bring in miscellaneous hotel workers. Joseph Elster, an eloquent speaker and tireless organizer, was engaged to head the hotel workers' drive.

Flore, who had been earnestly hoping to expand the union membership in New York, despite Jere L. Sullivan's doubts and misgivings, then appointed a special commission made up of himself, as chairman, Secretary Sullivan and three other members of the General Executive Board, who were to visit New York, study conditions there at first hand, and map out an ambitious unionizing drive. In the whole city the International had less than 2,400 members at this period.

Early in 1912 the commission came to New York for a visit of several weeks. There was intense unrest among the catering trade workers and much talk of an independent or rival union that was being organized for the hotel workers. The International's commission hoped, however, that the new Local 5 would cover the cooks and hotel workers, become a large unit, and offer them "better protection" than had been the case hitherto. High initiation fees (from $15 up to $65), which had been a stumbling block, were to be reduced now to $5 during the new drive. The existing craft locals were urged to lower the "fences" they had built around their memberships.

The strategy mapped out in the summer of 1912 was to divide the whole city into districts, concentrate on the weakest hotels and restaurants to begin with, then, these having been won, tackle the big establishments employing large bodies of workers. New York, as Flore remarked later, might be "a hard nut to crack," but the commission was hopeful now that "they had a solution for the defects that have existed. . . ." [24]

However, jealous quarrels over jurisdiction soon broke out between the several established locals, with Waiters Local 1, under Secretary William Lehman, following their own views, and the others clashing with them.

In truth, the International's commission members and the kind of paid organizers they sent in knew very little about the difficult job of organizing the hotel trade, now expanding at great speed. What they knew were the small taverns. Sullivan repeatedly said that the whole problem of chain hotels, their finances, their methods of doing business, was too complicated even for him. Moreover, he always remained skeptical about taking in the "miscellaneous workers" in hotels and restaurants, with their low cash wages of as little as $25 a month. But even he could see that when the experienced waiters and cooks alone walked out on a strike against a big hotel the un-skilled bus boys and kitchen assistants, *who had been left out of the union*, were always used to fill in for them as "scabs" and break the strike.

In the spring of 1912, Joseph Elster, who headed the organizing job for the new Local 5, after many differences with the officers of other Hotel and Restaurant Employees locals in New York, suddenly walked out, taking several hundred new union members to the rival labor union for hotel workers being set up in New York. Local 5 became defunct—but by now, May, 1912, it was too little and too late anyway. Thousands of hotel workers of New York seemed to be in a state of violent eruption, and were moving out into the streets *en masse*.

*

At noon on May 7, 1912, a well-dressed young man was seen strid-ing briskly into the spacious dining room of the Hotel Belmont, on 42nd Street, directly opposite the Grand Central Terminal in New York. He halted, took a whistle from his pocket and blew it shrilly. At the signal 150 waiters promptly took off their white aprons and marched out of the dining room and out of the hotel; then bus boys, cooks, dishwashers and even bellhops and chambermaids followed them to the street. On the sidewalk pickets lined up and unfurled placards that announced their demands in bold letters: *"One Day Off in Seven,"* and, *"Ten Dollars a Week for Waiters—Seven Dol-lars a Week for Bus-Boys"*; or, *"We Want Sanitary Lockers."* One poster even proclaimed that the pickets were bent on improving *"The Worst Trade in the World."*

Similar walkouts took place all that day at the ornate, old Waldorf-Astoria (then at Fifth Avenue and Thirty-Fourth Street), at the Plaza, the old Holland House, the Knickerbocker and at the world-famous mid-town restaurants, such as Churchill's, Delmonico's and Sherry's.

Instead of dining at leisure and with decorum, men and women of wealth and station found themselves in the streets outside their fa-vorite rendezvous, immersed in riotous crowds of workers who, at-tacked by guards and detectives, shouted: "Hotel workers unite!—Don't be slaves!"

This unprecedented and spontaneous strike movement spread

rapidly: there were 3,000 out on the first day; 8,000 within the week; and a few days later, all of 18,000.

For New Yorkers it was a most novel sight. All the "slaveys" at the fashionable hotels and restaurants seemed to be up in arms, as the New York press reported—even the women service workers, the house-keepers and charwomen. The spark that ignited this conflagration was said to have been the tyrannical behavior of a headwaiter at the Belmont who had suddenly discharged three waiters who were ac-cused of having marched in the recent May Day Parade in New York. Others, however, ascribed it to an accumulation of long-smol-dering resentments and grievances, which the newspapers reported with some sympathy and also with some attempts at humor. Indeed, as the newspapers played up the sudden, picturesque "uprising" of the people with white hats and the dining-room "flunkeys" in black coats, more and more hotel workers read of it and walked out all over the city. It was the first "general strike" against the hotel trade of New York, or at least the first widely effective one—although there had been some partial movements against several big hotels twenty years earlier and in 1907, in which several HRE locals participated for a while.

For years the International Union's officers had puzzled over the problem of organizing New York; and now overnight an apparently spontaneous mass movement had erupted whose force and breadth astonished them. What was more, the strike at the start seemed to have great "punch"; for "everyone under the roof" seemed to come out of those hotels, no matter how high or low his station or craft might be.

Who had done it? Who had brought on this veritable explosion? After a few days it was clear that the Industrial Workers of the World were at the bottom of the affair. At the crowded and hectic mass meetings held by the strikers, the banner of the new "Hotel Workers Industrial Union" was held up to public view. A strange assortment of orators addressed these great crowds: on the one hand the IWW firebrands, such as Arturo Giovanitti and Joseph Ettore, and on the other, "parlor socialists" or feminists out of the upper crust of New York society, such as Rose Pastor Stokes and Inez Haynes Millholland.

But behind the new dual organization, there were also two ener-getic and experienced leaders of the culinary workers, Jacob Bloech-linger and Joseph Elster, who had done some organizing for the HRE's new hotel local in New York, then broken away, in the spring of 1912, to lead the rival union movement. Exploited by the hotel owners and the "vampire employment agencies," neglected by the AFL union, the workers had responded to new efforts to organize them with much élan, had gathered regularly in small union halls, since the autumn of 1911, and quietly laid their plans. A number of the small, independent, or Socialist Labor groups in New York had joined forces with the IWW's Hotel Workers Industrial Union.

The IWW movement had a powerful appeal for underprivileged and migratory workers in mining and lumber camps and on the big farms of the West. Although their membership was never really numerous—it was estimated at 60,000 to 100,000 at the peak, during World War I—their leaders held great sway for a few years, especially among the unorganized immigrant workers.

It is noteworthy that, as friends of the immigrant workers particularly, the IWW organizers made special efforts to reach foreign-language groups by circulating pamphlet literature printed in Italian, Polish, Hungarian, Russian, Finnish, Bohemian and even Chinese. They also used spectacular methods of "mass action" in leading unorganized groups in sudden, wildcat strikes. They ignored grades of skill or wages, or lines of craft, and organized "everyone from the roof to the cellar."

To the hotel and culinary workers, they said: "We are going to get down in the gutter to get at the mass of the workers and bring them up to a decent plane of living!" Their crusading leaders preached the "class struggle"; vowed that they would abolish "wage slavery"; and repeatedly, when engaged in strikes, rejected all proposals of compromise. Though their strikes were called without preparation, and often without hope of success, the IWW men, when defeated, moved from one "class-war" front to another, as if reckless of the consequences, either for the lives or pocketbooks of the workers.

The Hotel Workers Industrial Union strike, like many IWW affairs, was carried on with tremendous zeal for several weeks, despite numerous scuffles and arrests, and despite the lack of funds for strike relief or organizers. A few establishments, such as the Hotel Plaza and Churchill's Restaurant, early in the course of the strike, granted the demands of their workers; but most of the hotel keepers declared that they intended to run their business as they pleased, and were able to engage non-union help sent in by various "benevolent societies" for cooks and waiters. The strikers grew hungry; moreover, they had no training or discipline as trade unionists, and when they saw there would be no easy settlement, became discouraged and drifted back to work.

(top) Edward Flore, as Secretary of Local 175, Buffalo, in 1901
(bottom) Edward Flore, Sixth General President, 1911–1945

Members of Waiters Local 30, San Francisco, 1907

Carrie A. Nation, sworn foe of tavernkeepers and
bartenders, going into action, 1907

Float entered by the Billings, Montana, bartenders local in a patriotic
parade, April 10, 1917 (World War I)

Bartenders Local 108, Cleveland, in 1913 Labor Day Parade

After seven weeks, on June 26, 1912, the great spontaneous "uprising" of the hotel workers was over, when 2,800 union members who were still out voted to return to work. Those who had made themselves known as more militant than the others, or as leaders, were blacklisted and forced to leave town.[25]

They were defeated. But the hotel keepers eased up conditions for their help and paid somewhat higher wages. Thus, in the long run, no strike is ever really lost.

The IWW cohorts scattered far and wide and turned up to compete with (and also to stimulate) the Hotel and Restaurant Employees' craft locals, in Boston, Albany, Pittsburgh, Cleveland and Chicago. Charles Sands, a veteran official of the HRE, declared: "The Hotel Workers Industrial Union did a good job for our own International and our craft." And others supported the view that the very existence of the HWIU spurred the progress of the International Union in the field in subsequent years.[26]

In Boston, in June, 1912, the IWW organized several large hotels and called a strike involving about 1,000 hotel workers. The strike was lost, but a goodly number of those involved, 497 in all, wound up in a new hotel workers' local chartered by the International Union and later merged with the present Local 34, Boston. Thus the AFL's established catering trades union was gradually brought into the hotel field, almost untouched before that time.[27]

In Albany, New York, the IWW men suddenly appeared in the summer of 1912 and soon had organized the largest hotel in town, the Ten Eyck, and called a strike. The Hotel and Restaurant Employees' local in Albany, which was also trying to organize the hotel workers, avoided a clash with the rival labor group. As Charles Sands declared later, the HRE's members in the same hotel were convinced that "it was not the part of good unionists to break a strike against the employers started by another labor group." Instead, through the exercise of diplomacy, the membership of the Industrial Workers' local was eventually brought into the AFL's local. Like the dual union or secessionist campaigns of the CIO, twenty years later, the result was generally a powerful stimulus to improvement and reform among the "official" trade unions of the AFL.

The IWW organizations, to be sure, showed very serious weaknesses and, after a time, suffered from internal dissension. They created much ferment for a season, jumped into strikes without preparation or financial means, refused to sign agreements with employers, then, defeated, the "revolutionary" leaders moved on to stir up another strike somewhere else. The tactics of sabotage attributed to some of their firebrands also aroused intense fear and antagonism, not only in the employing class, but among great numbers of workers who desired permanent unions of the industrial type that maintained responsible contractual relations with employers.

The onset of the industrial union movement greatly alarmed President Gompers of the AFL and brought from him the most sweeping denunciations of the radicals. His declared policy, carried out with the support of most AFL unions, was to exterminate all the dual labor organizations, while vehemently reaffirming the conservative ideals of the AFL's affiliates.

Exactly on New Year's Eve of 1912 the HWIU once more called a strike of hotel workers in New York, with the idea of providing the utmost vexation for the restaurant keepers. The IWW's fire-breathing orator Joseph Ettore, on January 10, 1913, addressed a strike meeting of the hotel "slaves" as follows:

> Remember, if you are compelled to go back under unsatisfactory conditions, go back with a determination to stick together until you get what you want.
> Go back with your minds made up that *it is the unsafest thing in the world for the capitalist to eat food prepared by members of your union!* [28]

This ill-concealed invitation to his followers to use tactics bound to alienate or exasperate many real or potential friends of labor was considered then, as now, to be self-defeating. The strike of 1913 was also lost.

Jere L. Sullivan, like Gompers, was quick to denounce the leaders of the rival union in his most wrathful terms as "loud-mouthed demagogues," who, proceeding without financial backing, without knowledge, without reason, were doomed everywhere to "dark dismal failure." "Amid much noise and excitement, parades and other obsolete methods, including sabotage, viciously employed," he held, they led their followers from disaster to disaster, and victimized thousands, who forfeited their jobs.

> They [the IWW's] then sought to secure converts in other cities, going so far as to disrupt locals of this International in their mad scramble for power. . . . The "Wandering Willies" are reported to have landed in crowds in Chicago and are trying to rouse up the cooks and waiters of the Windy City. Their gall is peerless.[29]

The Industrial Workers had been strongly entrenched in Chicago for several years and had organized both a Bartenders and Waiters

Local and Hotel and Restaurant Workers Local. (In 1918 they were to conduct a strike involving 10,000 people against Chicago's hotels and restaurants.) They were strong also on the Pacific Slope, with branches in Seattle and Spokane, as well as in the mining country of Colorado and Montana. But where the AFL local leadership was alert and aggressive, where differences over crafts and jurisdictions were subjected to the common good, as was true, for example, in San Francisco, the "Wobblies" failed to make headway against the going unions.

In the summer of 1912 they had come also to Cleveland, where the Hotel and Restaurant Employees locals were established in some strength, under the leadership of Thomas Farrell. Here the better restaurants were operating under union agreements, and the three leading hotels were partially organized so far as their waiters and cooks were concerned. Then the Statler "chain system" opened up one of its new, machinelike skyscraper hotels, and would have nothing to do with Brother Farrell and his union members, but chose instead to import crews of trained cooks and waiters from New York, who seemed eager for work. These included a sizable admixture of the IWW men who had found it healthier to leave New York after the recent unpleasantness. Thus, about two weeks after the new Statler opened its doors in Cleveland, it had a serious strike on its hands. The same Joseph Elster who had been a leader in the New York upheaval reappeared at the head of the Cleveland workers.

Farrell, who was then chief of the HRE's Waiters Local 106, promptly informed Secretary Jere L. Sullivan of what was going on and asked him for instructions as to the proper attitude toward the insurgent union. Sullivan replied that the IWW union was "illegitimate" and the AFL unions might therefore do as they pleased about reaching a union agreement with Statler's.

In his emergency the manager at Statler's had, of course, appealed to Farrell for assistance in signing up waiters, cooks and bartenders; and Farrell was able to obtain a union shop agreement for the AFL locals exclusively covering the dining-room personnel of the new hotel—whereby the IWW's were shut out, and their strike was broken.

At the time when Farrell submitted the agreement to his membership at Local 106, a number of those who constituted a sort of "loyal opposition" within the organization raised strenuous objections to making a deal "behind the backs" of other workers. One of those who protested was John Bookjans, who was later elected Secretary of Local 106. Within a year, he predicted, the Statler management, having got rid of the "revolutionaries," would also repudiate the union shop contract with the "regular" Hotel and Restaurant Employees. The employer, he argued, was merely taking advantage of the conflict between the two labor unions.

Farrell, however, in good-humored fashion rejected Bookjans' counsel, saying: "Bookjans, you would be a fine fellow if only you weren't so much of a socialist!" The union members gave their chief officer a sustaining vote. But in the summer of 1913, when the one-year union contract was up for renewal, surely enough, Farrell was bluntly informed that his union members could continue working at the Statler only under the "open shop" plan. Thus the AFL locals, which had helped the Statler against the trouble-making IWW group, now had a strike or lockout on their hands.

Farrell and the other officers of the three Cleveland locals were fairly gloomy about such a contest and strove to dissuade their union members from such action "with winter approaching," but the members would not be held back and voted to strike. Whereupon Farrell and his fellow officers loyally assumed command and did a fine job. The walkout lasted about eight weeks, but had the cooperation of all the principal AFL unions of Cleveland, including the Teamsters, Brewery Workers and Engineers. Thus the hotel workers were able to reach a compromise settlement providing for modest wage increases and better accommodations and food, which marked, at any rate, a step forward in the fight for union conditions in Cleveland's hotels. Two other large downtown hotels had been struck at the same time, and they too came to terms with the union. In this case, as in many others, the ferment created by the rival unionists, misguided or deluded though they might be, actually redounded to the advantage of the "regular" trade unionists in the field.[30]

It was the time when the Hotel and Restaurant Employees and Bartenders, during the advancing phase of the entire labor movement, approached its pre-World War I peak of membership (65,000). Workers were literally pouring into the unions again. In Chicago a powerful movement to organize women workers, led by Vice-President Elizabeth Maloney, and supported by the Women's Trade Union League, brought an influx of waitresses to the International's Local 484. By January, 1914, numerous downtown lunchrooms and restaurants, including one chain system with twenty units, were being picketed by their girl workers, who demanded but $8 a week as fixed wages and one day of rest. Though union shop agreements were won in a number of cases, the Chicago Restaurant Keepers Association intervened and forced their repudiation. Thus the waitresses' strikes dragged on throughout the rude winter season in Chicago, until May. Court injunctions followed, and numerous arrests were instituted by the rough-handed Chicago police. In moving testimony given that year before a Federal Commission at Washington, Miss Maloney spoke of "two-hundred-pound cops using their brute strength upon frail girls, twisting their arms, bruising their bodies. . . . In taking the girls into the police wagons they treated them very badly, though they gave no resistance. . . ." [31] The beginning of the waitresses' movement was no afternoon tea affair!

The International's waitresses' local in Chicago, No. 484, was small as yet, having but 600 members in 1914; yet its people showed no less courage than any of the thousands of brawny men who marched out on strike up and down the land in the turbulent year that brought the opening of World War I in Europe. Slowly the wage level for women workers was forced upward and the six-day week won at last, so that the small waitresses' union, even in 1914, set the wage standard for thousands of non-union people working in the popular restaurants of the Loop District.

*

Edward Flore, who was slowly learning about his job as President of the International, observed all the unrest and commotion caused by the dual union movement in the catering trade with deep concern. In dealing with this problem, we must note, the local unions exercised a great deal of autonomy, according to AFL practice. In New York, the officers of the International's small locals, observing how the great mass of unorganized hotel workers had been swept overnight into the rival camp, made a number of overtures, following the strike of 1912, with a view to bringing over first their leaders and then their followers into the Hotel and Restaurant Employees Union. Thus Local 1, then headed by Secretary William Lehman, a veteran of New York labor politics, called back the rival union's dynamic leader, Joseph Elster, in 1913, and reappointed him as a business agent of their organization. He had an enthusiastic following among the hotel workers, and now seemed eager to help them build a stable organization. "We thought it would be good tactics to deprive the opposition of the services of this man," said those who defended Elster's reinstatement.

Flore appeared agreeable to almost any moves that would have pacified the quarrels of the New York factions. But Jere L. Sullivan showed an unrelenting hostility to all who had been associated with the IWW movement. He was able to bring Flore over to his way of thinking; and he persuaded the convention at Denver to pass a resolution by which all who held membership in "craft or industrial organizations that are not affiliated with this International Union" were to be expelled. He also put the greatest pressure upon Secretary Lehman of Local 1 to have Elster dismissed, which was done. Then when the same man turned up again as an organizer for Local 109, Newark, N. J., Secretary Sullivan moved heaven and earth to have him expelled from the union by a vote of the 1913 convention. On that occasion Sullivan's faithful lieutenants, Kovaleski and Thomas Farrell, assailed Elster as a "renegade" who had caused untold damage to their organization in New York and Cleveland, and his expulsion was voted.[32]

The plans for organizing the New York center under the banner of the AFL's Hotel and Restaurant Employees thus foundered quickly. Flore made overtures to the people in the rival camp, advising them to disband their locals and come into the International Union individually. Instead, many of those who had worked for the dual union and become disappointed with the IWW leadership, broke away in 1916 and formed still another organization of hotel waiters, cooks and miscellaneous unskilled workers which they named the International Federation of Workers in the Hotel and Restaurant Industry. (Under different names, the same industrial union group persisted in New York for almost twenty years longer before it was to be merged eventually with the HRE.) The "Federation," made up of socialists and former followers of the IWW, organized itself on industrial lines, ignoring craft distinctions, but (unlike the IWW) pursued businesslike methods, accumulated a treasury, and employed paid officials. As one writer on the labor movement commented (in 1928):

> Its leaders demonstrated a fundamental knowledge of practical trade union tactics. Avoiding the general strike with all its complex problems they deliberately concentrate on individual establishments where their prospects are best. By striking at strategic times they generally secure concessions at least and are gradually winning a foothold.[33]

By 1919, the Federation had a building of their own as headquarters and called out 24,000 workers in the big hotel strike of that year. "We could have taken over the dual union organization as a whole," Charles Sands, the International's veteran legislative representative in Washington, wrote long afterward, in recollection of these events.

*

At the 1913 convention of the International Union in Denver there was much discussion of the dual union movement and of the admittedly difficult problem of organizing the armies of service trade workers. The young President had been doing a heap of thinking about the business of organizing campaigns and making them more energetic. Why should the International not have twice as many members, at least "a hundred thousand," the great goal of that pre-war era? Flore, therefore, prepared a report (published in the union's journal prior to the Denver convention), in which he ventured some criticisms of the International's organizers and made the proposal that they be placed under control of the General President, instead of the Secretary-Treasurer, as heretofore. The Secretary was too busily occupied with administrative work at the Cincinnati office and seldom able to observe conditions in the field. Since the President traveled about a great deal and met and conferred often with the different local officers, he was presumably the logical officer to direct the organizing staff.

On learning of this proposal, Jere L. Sullivan flew into a great rage, then proceeded to write a supplementary report fiercely assailing the new President for his suggestions. The job done by the organizers, he maintained, had been "successful," despite the handicaps they faced. He, Secretary Sullivan, had directed them so that "they would care for as much territory as possible with a limited number of men," and as usual had saved much money.

But what he most feared was the possibility that the new President, having got control of the organizing staff, would make its members his own political lieutenants, with a view to gaining the dominant position in the International. "Czar" Sullivan knew well that, only two years before, he had encouraged his organizers to campaign for the defeat of the previous President and the election of Flore. What if Flore were to use the traveling organizers to undermine Sullivan's long-established power? An agonizing thought that caused him to direct words of harsh rebuke at the President:

> Organizers are the servants of the International Union; *they are not the "political fence-builders or repairers"* of any officer or set of officers; their appointments are made on account of presumed

ability to deliver results . . . and not as alleged payment for pre-
sumed services in behalf of any officer or aspirant for office. . . .

It was Flore's first run-in with the "little chief" and he was startled
by the man's ferocity. Jere L., it was plain, would tolerate no General
President save one who would take his orders. He was forever on
guard against real or fancied schemes to remove him from office, and
had the convention delegates well drilled to check any moves Flore
might attempt in opposition to himself.

The mild-mannered Flore yielded and kept the peace. More than a
decade was to pass before he challenged Jere L. again. With the aid
of many of the delegates from small town locals, and of Executive
Board members long associated with him, Sullivan maintained his
ascendancy, while Flore, disliking strife and wanting, perhaps, in
ardor for his own cause, reconciled himself to the role of junior or
silent partner in the concern.

At the 1913 convention Flore was re-elected without opposition,
and Sullivan also was re-elected, as he records it, amid "a tremendous
ovation." However, a "progressive" faction showed itself at this convention, when one delegate from San Francisco, and Charles Sands,
from New York State, asked to be recorded as opposed to Secretary
Sullivan's unanimous re-election. One promising young union officer,
A. J. Cozzolino, of Local 109, Newark, was nominated for the office
of Fifth Vice-President, and though without Sullivan's blessings,
made a strong race, being defeated by the narrow margin of some 50
votes out of 483 cast.

One of the International's veterans, Emmanuel Kovaleski, who
served for forty years as a General Organizer under both Sullivan and
Flore, said: "If Jere L. Sullivan had a fault it was that he was too
jealous of the union. He thought it was his own."

In the end Jere L. Sullivan had ridden rough-shod over those who
urged that more should be done to "organize the unorganized." Their
union must continue to follow conservative policies. In his speech
closing the convention, as was customary, the Secretary strutted and
mocked and denounced his opponents, delivering his strongest bursts
of sarcasm against the "Bummery" and their leaders who deluded so
many poor workers with promises of "pie in the sky." As for his own
critics within the organization, he was undismayed by their resentments, but was willing to admit that since many local officers came
to him for help in the way of relief funds or for strikes, and he often
had to refuse them, "nobody likes a fellow who does that." He added

sadly and thoughtfully: "It is the lot of some men to be misunderstood. . . ."

Then came the characteristic flash of arrogance:

But, let me say, if you elected me with the expectation that I would change my methods of trying to handle your affairs at headquarters you are going to be sadly disappointed.[34]

FIVE

The "Western Movement"

"In those days every American had the right to join a union and every employer had the right to fire him for doing so."—AN OLD WAITER.

In the spring of 1915 many local officers of the Hotel and Restaurant Employees Union prepared to cross the continent in order to attend the eighteenth convention, scheduled to open in mid-June in San Francisco. Nothing illustrated better the difficulties in the way of organizing a union whose membership was scattered so far and wide. Once having reached the beautiful, mountain-rimmed harbor, the Eastern delegates were to meet the members of the largest and most successful branch of the International, who had developed their unions under an economic and geographical climate quite different from that of the east.

San Francisco alone, with roughly a tenth of the population of New York, had 5,022 members in its restaurant workers' and bartenders' locals; the neighboring cities of the Bay had 2,000 more members, whereas all of Greater New York had but 2,400 members. The San Francisco culinary workers, moreover, enjoyed a higher scale of earnings than others, with second cooks receiving $3.00 a day and meals, and waiters $2.00 a day (not counting tips and meals). Part of this good fortune was due to the building boom that had followed the earthquake and fire of 1906, during which $500,000,000 had been expended for reconstruction and labor had become scarce. A part was undoubtedly due to the more aggressive labor union tradition that had made San Francisco America's union-shop town.

One would have thought, therefore, that Jere L. Sullivan and his associates in the International's high councils would have looked forward to gaining both pleasure and instruction from their visit among the San Francisco brothers. On the contrary, Jere L. anticipated nothing but trouble as he journeyed westward. He did not care for the sort of men who headed the San Francisco locals, and they seldom heeded his counsels. "In those days," one of the San Francisco leaders has said, "we just sent our per capita tax to Cincinnati and paid no further attention to the people who ran the International office." [1]

What was worse, there had been rumblings of revolt from San Francisco for two years. In publications and pamphlets issued since 1913, the California local leaders ridiculed the "Czar" of Cincinnati, assailed his rulings, and even threatened to secede from the International. In bringing the convention to San Francisco, Jere L. was really turning to deal with those who had declared themselves his opponents; he was moving to quell an incipient revolt.

The industrial union movement, conceived in the mines and forests of the Rockies and the northwest states, had spread rapidly among the migratory workers of California and left a deep impact upon many union men, including those of San Francisco's catering trade. Though the extremists of the IWW had failed to capture the strong, well-conducted AFL locals, their idea of concentrating on the "organization of the unorganized" had taken hold. The locals here were separate craft locals for waiters, cooks, bartenders and waitresses; but they also worked together to unionize the underprivileged and unskilled or "miscellaneous" workers, the bus boys and dishwashers who at length were grouped in Local 110. As a whole they constituted a highly progressive labor group, standing squarely in opposition to the conservative craft-union policies of Jere L. Sullivan. At the head and front of this opposition movement was Hugo Ernst, Secretary of Waiters Local 30, San Francisco.

*

In November, 1904, Ernst, a slender, dark-haired young man, with gray eyes and a very expressive and lively face, had turned up in San Francisco, taken out a card as a member of Waiters Local 30, and soon become one of its leading spirits.

Hugo Ernst had wandered a long way from his native land, for he was born on December 11, 1876, in the small town of Varazdin, in what was then Austria-Hungary's territory, but now in Croatia, a part of the Jugoslav Republic. He was the second of six sons born to Rabbi Ignatz Ernst, one of the most prominent men of the town and a leader of the Jewish community of about 1,800 persons. That his parents were in comfortable, middle-class circumstances is shown by the fact that Hugo Ernst was given the advantage of a high school education, not at all common in the Croatia of those days. The high school (called *gymnasium*) was, in fact, a thoroughgoing affair, requiring eight years of study, and corresponding in scope of instruction to our college, or junior college. At eleven Hugo Ernst studied Latin, and at thirteen the classical Greek, as well as modern languages and the sciences. Forty years later he could still recite from memory and with relish the opening six pages of Homer's *Iliad* in Greek before a learned friend in San Francisco.[2]

At sixteen, however, he left the high school, two years before he would have been graduated, and, at the wish of his father, became a clerk and bookkeeper to a grain merchant in the town. But he was a restless, high-spirited young fellow whom his parents found hard to manage. In less than a year the keeping of account ledgers palled upon him, and he threw up his job and traveled off to Budapest, Vienna, and Northern Italy. "I was the family's black sheep then," he said afterward. His father had hoped he would become a solid man of business. For many months he eked out a meager living by writing articles for his home-town newspaper in Croatian, for he had the idea of becoming a journalist. He loved travel, and it broadened his outlook; moreover, he became fluent in German, French and Italian. On returning to Varazdin he joined a patriotic youth organization that was agitating for Croatia's independence from Austro-Hungarian rule. The Jugoslavs generally were harshly exploited by the Hungarians, who, according to Ernst, kept the Croatian farm hands toiling at the wages of coolies.

A Jew, and no less subject to oppression than the others, young Ernst began to take an active part in what was then a forbidden labor movement of the Jugoslav people and soon found himself an object of interest to the Hungarian police. Life under the Hungarian regime, with its menace of prison for rebellious patriots, had grown hazardous as well as oppressive. In 1900, Hugo Ernst, twenty-four years of age, joined the great tide of European immigrants flowing westward toward America and all its freedoms.[3]

Arriving in New York with $2 in his pocket, he found a first job writing articles for a Croatian nationalist weekly at a salary of no more than $4 a week. Being hungry much of the time, he asked for a raise, but was fired. Thereafter he found work as a bus boy in the restaurant of the St. George Hotel in Brooklyn, at $20 a month and meals. "But I never saw all that money, as I had to pay a kickback to the headwaiter for the right to hold my job. A bus boy then was supposed to live on tips." After a few months he was promoted to the job of a waiter and ran about with trays of food for twelve or more hours a day. From Brooklyn he went to the old Holland House in Manhattan, and thereafter he waited in the large, ornate Luchow's Restaurant, on Fourteenth Street, still one of the landmarks of old New York. However, there would be long periods of layoff. In 1904, with the wanderlust still strong in him, he made his way to the St. Louis World's Fair and there helped open the new Jefferson Hotel. It was the summer of 1904, a Democratic convention was in progress, and Ernst waited upon the fabulous William Randolph Hearst, who with his staff had taken two upper floors of the Jefferson and directed a fruitless campaign to win the presidential nomination for himself.

What were the characteristic features of a waiter's life, Ernst was asked in later years. "To be broke," he would reply. But he was young and loved the freedom of life in the New World. Being broke was always a good reason to return to the waiter's trade in some other town. Then having found work, as he would say gaily, "After eleven or twelve hours I would be rich! With $1.25 in my possession. In those days five cents was a decent tip; and $5 a month was enough for an attic bedroom."

After the St. Louis Fair, he joined other itinerant waiters and journeyed on to San Francisco. Practicing his trade again at some of the local "hashhouses" and in cafés of the "Barbary Coast," such as the famous Black Cat, Ernst eventually became a waiter practiced enough to win a place on the permanent staff of the nobby St. Francis Hotel. Amid these marble halls reflecting the grandeur of bonanza days in California, Hugo Ernst for years served many of the financial nabobs and mining kings of the locality. But his happiest memories were of the days when he worked for the more flashy or Bohemian patrons of the Black Cat cabaret, among them the famous editors Lincoln Steffens and Fremont Older, and the hard-drinking novelist Jack London, all of whom became his friends.

At last the rolling stone stopped rolling. Life in San Francisco was good: it was "cosmopolitan," it was gay; few who came to live here cared to run off to New York or even Paris. Among the many colorful characters of the town none was more remarkable than Hugo Ernst, the immigrant waiter who could quote from Latin literature to his patrons or converse with them on history or political science.

In his leisure hours he would dress immaculately, with colored vest, spats, a carnation in his lapel, and go sauntering about with a walking stick in hand, until he became a sort of landmark of the town—a dandy, who was, nevertheless, strong for the rights of the laboring man and headed picket lines of the waiters during strikes.

Some of his brother waiters and bartenders found him at first hard to digest. He used to sit in a coffee-house or tavern and talk much of the need for improving their unions and weeding out doubtful characters among their officers. On one occasion a worker of native American stock took offense at his remarks and burst out at him: "Why you —— —— greenhorn, how do you come to tell us all this! You can't even speak English—we can't understand what you're saying." Ernst answered the rough-spoken man deliberately: "That's all right; some day you will pay good money to hear me speak." [4]

There was a period of several years following the earthquake and fire of 1906, when the city was filled with the scandal of political corruption. Some of the labor organizations also grew lax, and according to Ernst, crooked waiters who appeared among them were given jobs in all-night cafés of the Barbary Coast. There, in the times of roaring trade and wide-open vice traffic that followed the Great Fire, they would feed customers Mickey Finns and "roll" them. These people, Ernst has said, were placed in their jobs at the word of local political bosses, who had accomplices among the officers of the waiters' union. A rank and file movement soon arose in Waiters Local 30, in opposition to the clique of "bosses," and in 1910 Hugo Ernst, chosen to head their ticket, was elected as Secretary. He went to work at once cleaning house and replaced the reputedly crooked waiters with decent folks. At the Local Joint Executive Board of the five San Francisco locals of restaurant workers and bartenders, Ernst, thereafter, played a leading part. He represented his union also in the city's Central Labor Council, where he became an associate and friend of the inspiring George Kidwell, head of the Bakery Wagon Drivers Union; and of Tom Mooney, leader of the Molders Union, hero of many a hard-fought industrial conflict. These were devoted trade unionists of unusual caliber, the real heads of San Francisco's powerful labor body, from whom Ernst learned a great deal about the job of the labor leader. In his own union, according to its severe by-laws, he would be rotated in office every six months, serving now as paid Secretary, and now as (unpaid) President, who resumed work at the trade of the waiter.

Among the members of Local 30 and of the Cooks Local, No. 44, were many alert and forward-looking men. The meetings of their

Joint Board, at which concerted action by the combined locals was discussed and voted, were nothing if not animated. During the long sessions, Ernst, who often presided, would fold his arms and listen patiently until all the others were done. Then he would sum up the discussion and present his own views with clarity and force, and his counsels, it was said, usually prevailed.

The members respected his native intelligence, in which there was a fund of prudence and shrewd realism. "What are we going to use for money, if we pull a strike," he would say warningly. In relations with his fellow workers, he had a light touch and a genial spirit. With a salty story or a jest he often would make light of difficulties that others feared too much. After a sharp contest in which high words had been exchanged, he would be found generally tolerant and magnanimous toward those who had opposed him.

"I as a Jew suffered often from the intolerance of people, and so I taught myself to be tolerant of the intolerant," he used to say. But when tough characters tried to threaten or bully Ernst, they found him a cool fighter. There were times, in the rough-and-tumble of union gatherings, or of strikes, when he, a man of slight figure, received a beating at the hands of some individual who preferred to settle an argument with his weight and muscle. Ernst would pick himself up, arrange his clothing, and say with a laugh: "Well, it's all in the game."

The genial, philosophical Ernst, with his old head and his Old-World courtesy, might have risen farther and faster in the labor movement in early years if not for his foreign birth and his marked European accent. "I was unambitious," he used to say. Wherever possible he encouraged others among his union associates to seek high office in city or state labor bodies, which for his own part he tended to avoid.

In 1911, Jack Weinberger, whose wandering life as a waiter duplicated that of Hugo Ernst and many others of his calling, arrived in San Francisco and became a member of Local 30. A native of Hungary and a son of well-to-do farmers and cattle-dealers, he had run off to America in 1901, when he was not yet twenty, cabling to his parents: "Don't worry about me. If I can do nothing else I can always become a waiter." And, after working his way up and down the East Coast, he had indeed become a highly skilled waiter who took pride in his craft. In San Francisco he was employed for many years at the luxurious and fashionable Palace Hotel. In this long, thin man, who was long-headed as well, Ernst soon found an extremely loyal and enthusiastic union associate. Several years after joining the union, in 1916, Weinberger replaced Ernst as Secretary, and there-after the two alternated in the office of president or secretary. While Ernst tended to be indifferent to detail, Weinberger was a tireless worker who took infinite pains with any task assigned to him. The two men, so different in temperament—Ernst keeping everyone in good spirits, and Weinberger doing everybody's worrying for him—made a remarkable team.

Another striking figure among the officers of the Hotel and Restaurant Employees locals of this period in San Francisco was John St. Peter, of No. 44, a cook, who was a native of Wisconsin. He, too, had wandered up and down the country, had taken part in the struggles of the Industrial Workers and, arriving in San Francisco in 1913, was to devote a lifetime of service to the men who labored before the flaming kitchen ranges.

In the five years after Hugo Ernst took charge of Local 30 its membership doubled, so that it became the largest local in the International Union. Moreover, its members believed, as Ernst said, in helping the other crafts and the unskilled people to organize themselves, so that the cooks', waitresses', bartenders' and miscellaneous workers' locals also expanded in size, until, as a group, they were the second largest labor organization in the city with 1,800 members. "One of the strongest units in the San Francisco Labor Council is Waiters Union No. 30," the city's leading newspaper reported at this period.[5]

*

They had organized the city's big "name" restaurants and most of the popular-priced eating places. Now they were tired of working ten hours a day, and were eager to get on with the job and unionize all the hotels. In the increasingly important hotel trade, however, only a few of the dining-room waiters were as yet organized, and fewer still of the cooks. But if the hotels, with their growing armies of semi-skilled culinary workers, maids and housekeepers remained non-union, then in the long run the hold of the unions on the restaurants also would be imperiled, for strike-breakers could always be sent over to restaurants from the hotels. Moreover, you could not organize the hotels unless you brought in all their semi-skilled people, their dishwashers and chambermaids, as well as their craftsmen, and formed them into something equivalent to "one big union," in which every craft or group pulled together with all the others.

When the waiters became engaged, as on one recent occasion, in a serious dispute with the management of an important hotel, they were simply locked out, while the non-union bus boys (who were their apprentices) and dishwashers and housemaids were all pressed into service to wait at table on the guests. Yet Jere L. Sullivan still ridiculed the idea of unionizing these unskilled, ill-paid workers. But for the waiters and cooks it was a real problem that had to be faced sooner or later.

Without necessarily eliminating craft lines, Ernst and his associates hoped to weld the different locals together firmly under their Joint Board, and complete the job of bringing in the unorganized.

Hugo Ernst posed the problem very clearly in a speech he made in 1917 before an audience of University of California students at Berkeley, in which he pointed out that the employers in San Francisco were solidly and "cooperatively" organized around their Merchants and Manufacturers Association and their new Law and Order Committee, which aimed to put down strikes of all kinds. The workers, however, were still aligned in old-fashioned craft unions, their different groups competing with or in friction with each other. Hence the series of defeats suffered by the longshoremen and others recently.

> Labor is learning also from its defeats. . . . That there must be an improvement in the methods of organization is apparent to all. Gradually the old lines of craft organization must give way to a wider form of industrial unionism in which a given industry will strike as a whole and in which one part of organized labor will not be in the position to aid the employers of another group of strikers. Every convention of organized labor shows a conviction on the part of the workers that in order to cope with the enormous power of capital it will be necessary to follow the example of the ruling class in its solidarity and class-consciousness.[6]

Against such ideas, supported by the whole San Francisco group, Secretary Sullivan set his face like flint. In a serious talk Sullivan held with Ernst some years later (when they were on a friendly footing), Sullivan said that he did not wish to see their union imposing through mere numbers or mass, but hoped it would excel through the experience and skill of its members. "You seem to care only for quantity, and are sidetracking quality altogether," he argued. "Inducement to join our International ought to be good craftsmanship." The two men simply did not speak the same language; but Sullivan often seemed to be living mentally in the more leisurely nineteenth century, unaware of the changes sweeping over their industry in the Machine Age, with its one-arm cafeterias and drug store lunches.[7]

The International sent no organizers to complete the job in San Francisco or anywhere else because, as the Secretary said, "our revenues do not warrant the employment of large corps of organizers and it would be unwise to exhaust our funds." He saw the San Francisco union men as "hotheads," ever eager to go on strike, and made equally sour comments to the effect that "too many members think they are born generals." Talk of the eight-hour day in their trade (already won in many industries) was in his opinion "premature," and those who went on strike with such demands would have little assurance of help from the International treasury.

Meanwhile Jere L. gave his nights and days and much of the union's money to the defensive struggle against the growing threat of Prohibition. Legislative representatives for the union worked in Washington and in various state capitals together with representatives of the liquor-dealers' associations to stem the advance of the Anti-Saloon League. The *Mixer & Server*, the union's official journal, at this period carried news of virtually nothing else. Yet year by year larger areas of the country went dry, and the outlook for the bartenders grew more dismal. Theirs was a losing struggle that was to be ended suddenly within four years.

The California leaders protested repeatedly, after 1913, against all the attention given exclusively to the affairs of a dwindling group of bartenders, while opportunities to organize several hundred thousand culinary workers were neglected. At the Denver convention of 1913, delegates from San Francisco had entered earnest petitions that something be done to improve the condition of the growing army of dining-room and kitchen workers who dragged down the standards of the craftsmen in the trade. Their pleas went unheeded. Shortly after this convention, a group of seven members of Waiters Union Local 30 began to issue a monthly publication of their own called *The Culinary Crafts*, copies of which were distributed freely among the different locals of the International Union. What the dissident group proposed was the drastic move of segregating the culinary workers from the bartenders and having the bartenders join with the Brewery Workers Union in one AFL International, while the waiters and cooks and hotel employees, under a charter and program suited to their own needs, would be able the better to work out their destiny. It is interesting to note that, as often before, many bartenders favored the plan of segregation, and of joining forces with the old Brewery Workers Union—then engaged in the common life-or-death struggle against Prohibition.*

* The Board of Editors, who signed the editorials of *Culinary Crafts*, were Hugo Ernst, Jack Weinberger, James Karsten, Theodore Johnson, A. C. Rose, J. D. Kirkpatrick and Dan Regan, who was head of the Bartenders Local Union, No. 41.

To Jere L. the whole idea was nothing short of treason. As usual he saw in it also a scheme to oust him from office. The San Francisco group were, to be sure, thoroughly fed up with the policies of the "little chief" in Cincinnati. Hugo Ernst said: "Jere L. Sullivan's idea was simply *not* to organize the unorganized."

Weinberger strongly believed in the importance of organizing the workers "from below," and then, by their united action, imposing better conditions on their employers. But too many of the bartenders (who were still in a majority in the union), were "forced" into the union by arrangement with the saloon keepers' associations, or at the order of their employers. They showed a considerable indifference to the idea of spending money to unionize culinary workers, waitresses, dishwashers and bus boys, and the like. The hope of the California insurgents, then, was "to build a fire under the administration of Jere L. Sullivan," as Weinberger has said, and stimulate it to do something for other crafts besides the bartenders. "The International had almost totally ignored the culinary workers." [8]

Several months prior to the 1915 convention in San Francisco a resolution in favor of the segregation plan was sent to the General Secretary by registered mail with a view to its publication in the official journal. Its authors heard nothing more and it was never printed, though it should have been published like other resolutions announced in advance.

Sullivan did, however, publish fierce denunciation of those who had been editing the *Culinary Crafts* and signed the resolution, calling them "The Seven Slimy Scribes of Seventh Street"—a reference to the address of Local 30's office, then at Seventh and Market streets, San Francisco. Taking up his wrathful pen he described them as "a ruthless and conscienceless bunch of fabricators," whose "puny brain drips" were combined in order to produce "an insinuating and prevaricating drivel" about himself as an alleged obstacle to the union's progress.

The Seven Scribes of San Francisco replied in kind, with sharp thrusts at "our Big Little Chief," at the size of his salary ($225 a month) and his expenditure of many thousands of dollars a year for the services of a lobbyist in Washington. They also belabored the band of eleven General Organizers surrounding the chief, all "hirelings selected by him and also provided with salaries so that they might eat at the pie counter." These "plunderers," it was alleged, had always fought against the rank and file of the International's membership, and promised to do so again at the forthcoming convention in San Francisco:

For many small locals, unable to bear the financial burden of sending delegates, are induced to issue credentials to these hirelings,
as the general membership foots the bill. . . . Never before has
such a formidable army been organized by the Little Chief or such
activity been displayed.[9]

The convention held in San Francisco in June, 1915, according to
many old-timers, marked the real beginning of the "modern" International Union, amid a controversy in which the proposals of the
dissident faction were thoroughly ventilated. The California block
appeared in force, under Hugo Ernst, since they were in home territory. But the rest of the 213 delegates, though representing only
124 out of 577 locals in affiliation, could easily bring to bear a superior voting power in support of Secretary Sullivan. Though they
were prepared to put up a determined fight, the segregationists sent
word to Sullivan that they regarded themselves as a loyal opposition,
held him to be an honest and capable officer, and had no wish to
remove him from office. He, however, disdained their peaceful overtures and sought to prevent their resolution from reaching the floor
of the convention.

His opponents, however, succeeded in laying their proposal before
the delegates—for the calm and judicious Flore was in the chair—
and also in bringing charges against the General Secretary for having
"refrained from publishing" the copy of their resolution mailed to
him in good time. Flore admitted ignorance of why the Secretary had
acted in what his opponents termed a "high-handed, tyrannical and
unlawful" manner. Sullivan wasted no time either in self-defense or
explanations, but vigorously assailed the whole plan to segregate the
bartenders as "a union-wrecking proposition that strikes at the very
foundations of our International Union." Since it was ruled that the
measure involved a question of law, it required a two-thirds vote of
the convention for passage, and was easily defeated. This was hardly
surprising. In 1915 the bartenders numbered about 37,000 out of a
total of 61,000 members, but were said to command 90 per cent of
the convention delegates.

At a caucus held the night before the vote was taken, a group of
"progressive" New York delegates, who had joined forces with the
Californians, had expressed doubts that the segregation measure
would pass, and, at an early stage of the proceedings, one of the New
Yorkers made a motion that they adjourn and go home. To the New
York delegates' surprise Hugo Ernst seconded the motion, which
was carried. When he was asked afterward why he had suddenly
changed his mind about fighting on for the resolution, he expressed

discouragement, then laughed and remarked with his characteristic good humor: "Well the big steam roller is running things and we only have a little steam roller as yet." [10]

Ernst for his part came to the conclusion that the segregation move, in the long run, might not have turned out to be a good idea:

> I am glad that the matter did not come to fruition, but at the time we felt that too much attention was being paid to the bartenders, what with the threat of Prohibition . . . and that the culinary workers did not have enough representation on the Executive Board and in conventions, since both were composed mainly of bartenders.[11]

What Ernst resented most deeply was the accusation of "union wrecker" hurled at him, for he believed all his life in abiding by the rules or the majority vote of any organization of which he was a member. There was for years thereafter much ill-will shown by Sullivan against Ernst.

In the heat of that fray Jere L. Sullivan had leveled the most fearful charge of all against Ernst: namely, that he was a "dry." It was true that Hugo Ernst, as a result of some childhood experience, never drank intoxicating beverages throughout his life, a rare thing for a waiter; but he was always agreeable to having other people drink all they liked.

*

For years the little "boss" in Cincinnati observed with extreme suspicion and dislike the activities of opposition groups in the union that favored various reforms he disapproved of. What he desired was that the International continue as before to pursue the policies he had shaped for it and which were supported by the more conservative bartenders' officers who had formed the original nucleus of the organization twenty years before. When local leaders agitated for more organizing of the culinary workers or of the unskilled groups in their trade, he attributed their ideas to the reputedly "evil" doctrines of socialism, or to their being secretly in sympathy with the industrial union schemes of the IWW's. Wherever possible, here and there, he exerted his influence discreetly to have the would-be reformers removed from their local offices.

Yet this was the heyday of Wilsonian liberalism; thanks to the agitation of reformers the Clayton Anti-Trust Act, with its provisions (as it was then believed) guaranteeing the rights of labor unions, had been enacted in 1914. Almost a million Americans voted regularly for the Socialist party in this decade; approximately one-third of the delegates to the 1912 convention of the American Federation of Labor voted for the moderate socialist, Max Hayes, as candidate for president, and against Samuel Gompers. (No one dreamed then that America was to become in future years the "citadel of conservatism.")

But the aging Jere L. Sullivan had moved a long way from the dreams of brotherhood for all workers that he had entertained as a member of the Knights of Labor. His vigilant hostility was directed not only against the would-be insurgents in California, but even against minor officials of liberal views, such as John Bookjans, who served as Secretary-Treasurer of Waiters Local No. 106, in Cleveland, from 1914 to 1915.

The forthright Bookjans worked with great enthusiasm to organize the unorganized culinary people of Cleveland, and with much the same spirit as shown by the San Francisco local leaders. Thus (as noted earlier) he had experienced serious differences with Tom Farrell, the powerful local leader in Cleveland, and a close associate of both Gompers and Jere Sullivan. Farrell has been described as an amiable opportunist and an active figure in Cleveland's local politics. Bookjans, meanwhile, had grown to be highly popular with the rank and file of his union's membership. But when election time came for Local 106, in the summer of 1915, all of Farrell's influence was thrown into the balance to bring about the defeat of the young reformer. That Farrell, though outwardly still friendly, employed most ruthless measures to discourage members from voting for Bookjans became known afterward.

It was not known, however, that, at the time, Secretary Jere L. Sullivan was kept closely informed about the affair which, like many other local contests, he watched over carefully. In a letter in which he promises that later, when he was to come to Cincinnati, the "whole story" would be told in person Farrell writes:

> Cleveland, O.
> August 18, 1915
>
> Mr. Jere L. Sullivan,
> Cincinnati, O.
> My dear Jere:
> In reply to your favor of the 1st Inst., which was in reply to my telegram informing you as to the outcome of the election in Local 106, I have been going to write you at some length. . . .
> I might impart the news, however, that ex-Sec. Bookjans is seeking a new field of activity and I sincerely hope that it will be large

enough for him to show some results in the way of organizing the downtrodden and oppressed culinary workers.

The latest information I have received is to the effect that he has adopted the Smoky City for his new home.

Fraternally yours,
Thomas S. Farrell
Secretary of the Cleveland
Federation of Labor

Thus these gentlemen seemed to make mock of the misfortunes of one who overly concerned himself, as they felt, with the lot of the "downtrodden culinary workers." Though he was much attached to Cleveland and grieved at leaving the place, Bookjans that summer moved to Pittsburgh. But soon he was busily engaged in helping the Cooks and Waiters Local 209 (later called Local 237) organize its field. In time, to the surprise of Farrell and others, he was to reappear again as Secretary of his Pittsburgh local (which became one of the largest in the system) and pursued vigorous campaigns aimed at unionizing Pittsburgh's big hotels. Thus the movement of the waiters and cooks, spurred by the hard conditions they endured, rolled on.

Meanwhile, in the year that followed the 1915 convention the San Francisco locals became involved in a desperate struggle with employers in their trade. But in view of their officers' strained relations, at this time, with the old "Czar" in Cincinnati, little financial help was to be expected from the International Union.

During the winter of 1914-1915, following the outbreak of World War I in Europe, there was depression and unemployment in America and hunger-marchers were seen in California as well as in New York. But by the summer of 1915 war orders for munitions and raw materials were pouring in from the Allies, campaigns for Preparedness were under way, and labor grew scarce, with immigration from Europe entirely halted.

The San Francisco waiters and cooks were determined to win for themselves that "better way of life" which all good Americans believed was their right. The railroad workers, the machinists and other groups were fighting for, and winning, the eight-hour day. What of the waiters? They were organized in San Francisco. In no other city, prior to 1930, was there any branch of the Hotel and Restaurant Employees equipped as they were to carry out a "general" or city-wide strike as part of an aggressive, planned effort for the betterment of their condition. In the East, large-scale conflicts hitherto had been but spontaneous uprisings of mobs, led chiefly by the rival Hotel Workers Industrial Union.

The San Francisco waiters and cooks had had no formal pay raise since 1906. But now (for the first time in the history of this union) they were determined to set the eight-hour day as their basic demand, instead of seeking more wages. The spirit of local employers, meanwhile, during a period of renewed labor strife, had hardened again. With the support of the local Chamber of Commerce a special Law and Order Committee had been established in 1914 with the purpose of doing all that was possible to curb the growing power of labor in Northern California. When the restaurant keepers' counterproposal (during negotiations in the summer of 1916) of a nine-hour day was rejected by a solid vote of the workers and a strike was authorized, the new Law and Order Committee actively intervened in the affair.

The walkouts, authorized by the San Francisco Labor Council, and also by the International's GEB, began on August 1, and closed up seventeen restaurants and cafeterias in the downtown section. But within ten days 3,000 workers were on strike (with one report fixing the number at about 4,000 all told), a very large stoppage for this trade in 1916.

The directors of the Restaurant Keepers Association had noticed that the union had lately followed the tactics of harassing small groups of restaurants, or one or two individual places at a time, while avoiding a large-scale attack. Now, therefore, small proprietors were forced to line up with the "Class A" houses and pledge themselves to lock out or discharge union men whenever they made the demand for the eight-hour day. Thus, as the head of the Association reported to the Law and Order Committee, "the union will not be able to boycott a single signatory (of the agreement) without having a general strike in the restaurant business on their hands. . . ." The pressure of wholesale merchants was also applied to force weak restaurants in line, while credit was maintained for open-shop firms and denied to union houses. Strike-breakers were brought in from points as far off as Chicago, though many were also supplied by "benevolent" societies of cooks and waiters, such as the Pacific Coast Waiters Association. Finally, energetic measures were taken to stop all picketing by means of court injunctions under local laws.[12]

Hugo Ernst always maintained that the San Francisco union men learned their business by hard fighting. In this strike they showed themselves uncommonly sharp-witted and resourceful. On one day in August pickets posted before the Hofbrau Restaurant were faced with a temporary restraining order issued by a local court. On the next day the union men brought out great crowds before the same place, and ran pickets in relays, who passed their placards from one to another and slipped away through the crowd before they could be caught. Yet the police worked hard to obtain evidence and numerous pickets were arrested, including the picket captain for Local 30, A. C. Armstrong. According to the veteran labor lawyer Henry B. Lister, who was retained by the Joint Board, a total of 216 court injunctions "rained" upon the union men.

Ernst, Weinberger and St. Peter used their wits to devise many ingenious schemes to defeat the effect of the injunctions issued by a judge who heard only the petition of one side, then assumed power to punish for contempt—and without jury trial—those against whom evidence had been furnished by the Law and Order Committee sleuths.

One day San Francisco saw with surprise a small herd of long-eared burros stationed in front of a large restaurant that was on strike. On the donkeys' backs were hung banners with the legend that the restaurant was unfair to organized labor. When the owner tried to have the animals pushed or dragged away, they proved, in keeping with their "asinine" character, stubborn and hard to budge. Injunctions were then issued in this case also and all the unlawful "pickets" were ordered brought to court.

"But, your Honor," protested Attorney Lister for the union, "I doubt that they will be permitted to come up the elevator into this building; they are long-haired, dirty, ill-smelling, wild—in fact, 'begging pardon of the court,' they are *asses!*"

The strike wore on until the November city elections, when the employers' group, amid a great scare campaign, succeeded in having a most drastic anti-picketing ordinance passed in San Francisco by referendum vote—though only by a narrow margin. At this stage a stratagem new to San Francisco labor disputes was introduced; it is said to have been an invention of the new Secretary of Local 30, Jack Weinberger. Numerous union members, though being absolutely prohibited from normal picketing, posted themselves as usual before restaurants that were struck and shouted, "Extra!" as they hawked what appeared to be special editions of a San Francisco weekly labor newspaper, the *Labor Clarion*. On its front page were huge headlines reporting that such and such a restaurant (before which the "news vendor" stood) was unfair and locked out its employees.[13]

More than four months were consumed by this wasting struggle, and many cooks and waiters were finally forced by hunger to return to work in the non-union establishments. There had been collisions between pickets and police and numerous union members had suffered injury. Although other San Francisco trade unions gave generous financial aid to the culinary workers, they received almost no support from their own International Union, a source of much bitterness. A reduced force of about a third of the original army were still out on December 15, 1916, when the Central Labor Council, representing all AFL unions in San Francisco, voted to terminate the strike. Waiters Local 30, by then, was down from a membership of 1,800 to 460; and Cooks Local 44 had also lost about 60 per cent of its force, the high-paid Class "A" cooks showing extreme disappointment at the heavy costs of the long stoppage.

*

It was a defeat, but not a disaster. For no well-fought strike is ever really "lost." Ernst and Weinberger, the leaders of Local 30, for example, retained the confidence of their rank-and-file membership and soon began rebuilding the organization, favored by the wartime prosperity of 1917-1918. Within a little over a year, Secretary Weinberger—for Ernst was then President—was able to report membership back to 1,665, a remarkable recovery. What was more, the nine-hour day, at any rate, was quietly introduced in the popular-priced establishments and wage increases were also granted.*

Taking advantage of the Government's more enlightened wartime labor policies, the union leaders in San Francisco then made quite a push at organizing the kitchens and dining rooms of the three leading hotels in the city. In 1918 a small secret committee of union men used to meet at night at Weinberger's apartment, where they consumed quantities of coffee and sandwiches while plotting out their campaign.

In the three hotels singled out for treatment strike committees were quietly formed, Weinberger acting as spokesman for the workers in the Palace Hotel where he was then employed. The management would rather have fired him than talked with him, but in

---

* In his report for 1919 Jack Weinberger wrote: "Our theory of rebuilding the organization was and still is—reach the men first, educate them to a certain standard, then proceed to enforce conditions, rather than . . . asking the employer to force his men to join the union. Our method is based on a sounder theory and better tactics, and of course, in the judgment of the writer, is the reason for the success of the reorganization campaign commenced in the spring of 1918. . . ." *Mixer & Server*, February 15, 1920.

September, 1918, under wartime rules (imposed by the War Labor Board) he was permitted to make his proposals, which were at first refused. The sittings of a large and tense strike committee throughout the night that followed, and the authorization of a prompt walkout, persuaded the Palace Hotel management to grant the union demands for recognition and the nine-hour day. The two other hotels that were under pressure followed suit, and thus the union at last had a big foothold in the city's first-class hotels.[14]

The cost of living by 1918 was rising very rapidly in a cycle of unrestrained inflation. There had been a time, after the lost battle of 1916, when several hundred disgruntled waiters and cooks of Locals 30 and 44 applied to Secretary Jere L. Sullivan for a separate local charter, declaring they were desirous of forming an organization of their own. But to Sullivan's credit, it must be recorded that he firmly rejected this "union-splitting" proposal, despite his resentment at Hugo Ernst and company. The workers meanwhile had learned that the union's demands for the nine-hour day and wage increases had first been refused then accepted. The San Francisco newspapers reported in July, 1919:

NINE-HOUR DAY AND SIX-DAY WEEK GIVEN COOKS AND PANTRY-MEN [15]

Now the workers, who had deserted the organization for a period, streamed back into their old unions.

The skilled cooks had generally been more difficult to organize than were the waiters. But during the war period very able leaders appeared among them, particularly John A. St. Peter who as Secretary of Local 44 was to be one of the leading spirits of the HRE's Joint Board in San Francisco and who saw his local become one of the strongest in the International. At a period when skilled craftsmen were scarce, the cooks were able to win sharp wage increases up to $45 a week for first cooks and $35 for second cooks, and reduction of hours to "nine hours straight" or to "eight-hours-within-twelve."

Another innovation was the establishment of the union shop in the many popular-priced Greek restaurants of the town. The Greek workers had formerly been very clannish and much prejudiced against the "bartenders union." But thanks to the patient "Trojan Horse" strategy of James G. Manus, a member of and special organizer for Local 30 (and of Greek nationality himself), about 500 Greek culinary workers were led, first into a "Hellenic Association" of their own, then to initiation en masse as members of Waiters Local No. 30 and Cooks Local 44. The San Francisco branch emerged from the war period to face the readjustments of peace in stronger force than ever before.

One singular and little-noticed episode that grew out of the San Francisco culinary workers' strike of 1916 might have taught men much about the latent resources even a small labor group can summon up during an emergency.

That seemingly unimportant strike of 1916 took place during the national election contest between the party of the liberal President Wilson and the party of the conservative Republican, Governor Charles E. Hughes of New York. With America's possible involvement in the European war as a burning issue in the electoral struggle, the outcome appeared highly uncertain and it was anticipated that California's vote might play a decisive role in the final result. Hughes' subsequent defeat in November, 1916, by the very narrow margin of his loss of California, has usually been attributed to his political blunder, during his visit to California, in avoiding a meeting with the popular Progressive Republican, Senator Hiram Johnson—who, thereafter, gave Hughes no support. The real story behind the loss of California's electorate, and by only 2,000 votes, is something quite different and constitutes a corrective footnote to history conceived by a couple of union waiters.

On August 16, 1916, Governor Hughes arrived in San Francisco to speak at a luncheon of the Chamber of Commerce at the Commercial Club. There was a great longshoremen's strike raging at the city's docks, and the strike of the city's waiters and cooks was approaching its climax—but the restaurant at which Mr. Hughes was to address a large body of California's citizens was one that displayed an open-shop sign in its window.

A few days before the luncheon meeting was to take place, Hugo Ernst (possibly at the suggestion of Jack Weinberger) determined that if Mr. Hughes spoke at that restaurant a picket line would be thrown about it. As President of the striking local union, he therefore sent an open letter to the newspapers protesting against "this placing of Mr. Hughes in the position of endorsing the open-shop policy." Surely some other arrangement could be made, he suggested, to entertain the Republican presidential candidate in a place and in a way that would not "constitute an affront to organized labor in San Francisco."

The reply from the Republican party official in charge of the arrangements stated that nothing could be done at this late date, and that everything had been fixed by Mr. Hughes' advisers in New York long before the labor troubles had arisen in San Francisco. But later researches have shown this to have been an evasive answer; it was customary to have the state Republican leaders select the site and guests for such a political address, especially where the situation was as "delicate" as in California. The probabilities are that they knew all about the plan to have the "open-shop" placard prominently displayed at this banquet.[16]

On being rebuffed, Hugo Ernst came before the city's Central Labor Council, charged that the Republican State Committee was deliberately using the incident as a provocative, anti-labor demonstration, and urged that a great hue and cry be raised by all labor groups in California. Come what may, his union's pickets would be posted outside the restaurant and that banquet would be served only by non-union waiters and "scab" cooks. In response the labor press and all AFL unions in California circulated reports of the affair, bitterly assailing the Republicans and their candidate.

In due course, Governor Hughes arrived at the luncheon meeting at noon, August 16, walked through the Local 30 picket line, and, as the California labor press described it, sat down to a feast served by "scabs." "Thus within forty-eight hours the Republican candidate had managed to incur the enmity of both San Francisco labor and the middle-class progressives" (who were Senator Johnson's admirers). Although the general newspapers ignored the incident, or censored news of it, thousands of union members learned of it; and that alone "insured a solid union labor vote for President Wilson," as another commentator has written. "In my opinion Wilson's meager majority came from union labor in San Francisco. Page Hugo Ernst!" [17]

The vote in California was so close that it was not known for forty-eight hours after Election Day that President Wilson had been re-elected. The impassioned protest of Hugo Ernst may well have been the finishing blow for Mr. Hughes.

Ernst had become an American citizen in 1910 and very proud he was of his rights and prerogatives as such. But why did not others exercise their democratic privileges to the full, he asked, in the light of the Hughes affair of 1916? Labor must participate more and more actively in our political life, he said at the time:

> Organized labor is learning that it must use, not one, but all the weapons at its command to fight its enemies. The anti-picketing ordinance in San Francisco shows that the employers are using political action, legislation, to take from the workers their economic weapons. It is up to the trade union movement to realize that they also must use their ballots. . . .[18]

The close of the war in Europe saw the organized labor movement in America rising again with a well-nigh irresistible momentum that touched even the most backward or ill-used sections of the working class and reached even the small towns. In 1919-1920 many trade unions doubled in size, and one organization helped the other. The service workers in hotels and restaurants were ready to fight for unions not only in San Francisco, New York, Pittsburgh and Chicago, but in small places like Bellingham, Washington. In this remote region of the Northwest, whose main industry was logging, the loggers and pile-drivers who had gone into unions "helped talk up the union idea wherever they went—they helped plant signs and literature." Thus the hundreds of cooks and waiters in the logging camps were organized in 1919 by a devoted woman labor leader, Mrs. Ida Peterson, and Local 529 was born deep in the timberlands of Washington State, with 500 members and firm union shop contracts.[19]

One would have thought that the executive officers and General Organizers of the Hotel and Restaurant Employees would have found inspiration in the initiative of local unions in San Francisco or Bellingham or Pittsburgh, where local members were also struggling to organize the hotels. In these and other localities the officers in the field already pointed the way to an immense future expansion for the International Union. Yet the union as a whole did not go forward, but shrank in size, though nearly all others were growing rapidly then. In those days, when the dreaded Eighteenth Amendment overhung them, Secretary Sullivan and President Flore could think of nothing else; they seemed paralyzed by fear of the impending disaster that no exertions on their part could help to avert.

SIX

The "Great Drouth"

*"In many respects our union occupies the least se-
cure of any field in the economic world. . . ."*—
JERE L. SULLIVAN, in 1917.

The United States as a whole had prospered greatly between 1915
and 1920, and labor, too, had bettered its condition, if not by an
advance of "real wages" (which were diminished by the higher cost
of living) then in the shortening of hours. However, the Hotel and
Restaurant Employees, after having reached a peak membership of
65,938 in January, 1917, showed a loss two years later, to 60,679—at a
time when most other trade unions were undergoing a mushroom
growth. By 1925 a third of the remaining members—almost the entire
contingent of bartenders—were gone, so that total membership stood
at less than 40,000.

A strange catastrophe had engulfed not only the bartenders but also
the brewery workers, the coopers and the bottlers, as well as the eating-
places and hotels that depended on the sale of alcoholic beverages
for their existence. Since 1907 they had watched the "prohibited territory" constantly spreading over the map of the United States, until,
by 1917, as we entered the war in Europe, twenty-six states and three
territories were dry; three more states were to follow suit that year,
and the end was in sight. Indeed, only a few large metropolitan centers in the East and Middle West and along the Pacific Coast were
truly "wet" still.

At the 1917 convention in St. Louis, Jere L. Sullivan spoke of the
onset of Prohibition in tones of despair. After twenty-five years their

union had somehow failed to organize more than a small part of its industry. This disappointing result was to be attributed to the fact that "our International Union occupies the least secure of any field in the economic world, and occupies that place exclusively. Our employers are equally menaced."

At the end of 1917, Congress was to pass a resolution providing for submission of the Prohibition amendment to our Constitution to all the states, and within a year three-fourths of their legislatures had voted approval. A billion-dollar industry was doomed, as Jere L. foresaw. All the pleasant haunts of men, the taverns and beer gardens were soon to be closed as so many "dens of vice." Americans, on the average, did not consume more alcoholic liquors than Europeans. In fact, prior to the World War many millions of citizens, especially in rural communities or small towns, still clung to their old ideals of sobriety and quiet religious observance which had given us so many Sunday "blue" laws. For them the saloons of the big cities had become a sinful spectacle; the organized liquor industry was also feared and detested in the same quarters because of its supposedly sinister political power. Now they were bent on imposing their moral standards on the others by statute.

Part of the success of the temperance movement, according to Jere L. Sullivan, was to be laid to the greed and stupidity of those tavern keepers who had not known how to make their places respectable. He said in 1917:

> Legitimate business does not flaunt in the faces of its patrons that which will cause organized opposition. . . . Yet the catering industry is honeycombed with investors whose moral ideas are on about a par with a digger Indian's. . . . Immodest pictures may have a reason for existence, but there is none for their exhibition in connection with the vending of beer, wines and liquors. . . . The "nude in art" . . . the so-called "works of art," paintings and statuary which strike a coarse, sensual note, which appeal to the lasciviousness and excite sexual desire, are useful to the antagonists of the catering industry. . . .
>
> Another of these cankerous worms is that other license holder, who endeavors to hide behind an honorable calling, yet in heart and mind is a moral pervert, a serpent whose prey is ushered into private rooms, boys and girls of early adolescence, permitted to partake of intoxicants, to enjoy secretly such privileges which bring shame and disgrace in their path.[1]

Edward Flore, at the same 1917 convention, made the prophetic statement that better public morals would not follow the introduc-

The soldiers returning from France in 1919 voice their sentiments

The Cleveland lockout, 1930

(opposite) 1919, popular demonstration against the Eighteenth
Amendment

The "circle," or moving line of pickets

tion of prohibitory laws; that in every state or locality where they had already been tried "a debauch of political and private immorality had followed in their wake."

Flore had gone to Washington for the "eve of war" conference of AFL International presidents called by Gompers in March, 1917, and tried to warn other labor leaders, whose members would be affected, of the efforts being made by the Anti-Saloon League to have its dry program rushed through as a wartime emergency measure. But other organized labor groups, aside from the Brewery Workers and Teamsters, were scarcely energetic in opposing Prohibition. It happened also that a number of labor's strong friends in Congress were ardent "drys." And not only did fanatical churchmen and (as Flore called them) "political purifiers" of all sorts join in this strange moral crusade, but the leaders of industry, the exponents of a soulless efficiency for labor, donated large funds to the propagandists of the Anti-Saloon League and the Women's Christian Temperance Union. It was widely believed before 1919 that the worker, once deprived of his liquor and beer, would toil harder, produce more, earn more, and that the whole country would become more prosperous.*

However, the union's experience in Canada several years earlier had given it a foretaste of what was to happen in the United States. Canadian locals had been chartered by the HRE since 1899, when the movement of Canadian workers toward affiliation with AFL unions was well under way. The first comer among the Canadian locals was No. 197, Bartenders, of Hamilton, Ontario; then came two locals in Vancouver, B.C., these being virtually neighbors of the HRE locals in the Seattle-Tacoma region below the border. To be sure, progress in organizing the Canadian catering workers was slow, owing to the sparse population of the Provinces and the vast distances between their cities. But the enactment of Prohibition in most Canadian Provinces as early as 1916 proved to be practically a death sentence for the HRE bartenders' locals, of which all but one were disbanded. This was Local 676, of Vancouver, which survived as a small Beverage Dispensers' union, thanks to the efforts of its Secretary, Tim Hannafin.

---

* In 1928, at the time of the Great Drouth, the writer had the experience of hearing a leading industrialist, Louis Swift, of pork-packing fame, discourse upon the advantages of total abstinence for the laborer—while holding a glass of the forbidden liquid in his own hand. "It used to be that many of the men never got down to the plant at all on Monday, or had hangovers on Tuesday. But now, under Prohibition, only a few are absent on Monday, and by Tuesday all are going in full swing." (Cited in "Chicago," by Matthew Josephson, *The Outlook*, April 17, 1929.) See also Mark Sullivan: *Our Times*, Vol. IV, pp. 22-27, 131-32.

Elsewhere, in the large cities of Eastern Canada, the union's following among culinary workers had always been very small. With the elimination of the barmen in 1916 the Canadian branch of the HRE became almost extinct.

Eight months after the war had ended, the Eighteenth Amendment was ratified to take effect in the United States on January 16, 1920.

Nearly 6,000 members of the Hotel and Restaurant Employees Union had joined the colors during the war. Bartenders fought and died on foreign soil in the service of their nation, and many were sorely wounded. When they came home the taverns or first-class restaurants that had taprooms and served liquors and wines were closing down. Their jobs at the bar were gone; and thousands of the cooks and waiters who had worked in such establishments were discharged also.

In the "dry decade" of the 20's, Edward Flore's predictions were borne out: the dispensing of liquor continued (as in the communities that in earlier years had local option dry laws), but in the hands of lawless individuals and gangs. Illicit beer and liquor running, or "bootlegging," became one of America's major industries—an empire of organized crime.

Meanwhile, about 20,000 union members who had been barmen gave up their cards; locals that had been in existence for thirty years lost their charters. In a few instances the bartenders' locals survived by holding together a minimum of ten members and continuing to pay their per capita dues, in the hope that the nightmare of Prohibition would some day be ended. To earn their bread many of the displaced barmen were forced to dispense the forbidden beverages in thousands of "blind pigs" or "speakeasies" that soon flourished everywhere during the 1920's—with the support of the public.

After three years had passed, Jere L. Sullivan said in 1923:

> The coming of the Federal Amendment disclosed to the astonished gaze . . . that bartenders' unions remained in existence and that these wage earners continued to pay their dues. It also gave us all the pleasure and privilege of retaining the bartenders of the United States as our co-workers, as loyal members as the sun ever shone on, to whom we gladly bow and salute.

The number of illegal dispensaries operating in the large cities, he estimated, generally surpassed that of the number of regularly licensed taverns as of 1917. In Boston, according to John J. Kearney, there had been about 700 licensed liquor distributing places before Prohibition; but afterward there were 2,000 speakeasies!

At first men had thought only of how sober the factory workers would be and how much wealth would be gained as a result of Prohibition, writes Frederick Lewis Allen in *Only Yesterday*, a history of this period. If you had informed the average citizen that Prohibition was destined to furnish "the most violently explosive issue of the nineteen-twenties he would probably have told you you were crazy." And if one could have sketched for him the picture of actual conditions as they were soon to be, he would have been goggle-eyed with disbelief:

> Rum-ships rolling in the sea outside the twelve-mile limit and transferring their cargoes by night to fast cabin cruisers, beer-running trucks being hijacked on the interurban boulevards by bandits with submachine guns, illicit stills turning out alcohol by the carload, the fashionable dinner party beginning with the contraband cocktail as a matter of course, ladies and gentlemen undergoing scrutiny from behind the curtained grill of the speakeasy, and Alphonse Capone, multi-millionaire master of the Chicago bootleggers, driving through the streets in an armor-plated car with bullet-proof windows.

*

With the passing of the old barroom, the Hotel and Restaurant Employees had, nevertheless, new fields of conquest open to them— as inveterate critics of the leadership, such as Hugo Ernst, had been saying for years. The old-fashioned, mahogany-paneled restaurants, with their white tablecloths, their potted palms and their luxurious *à la carte* service were also disappearing in great number, since their profit margin was sharply reduced by the loss of their liquor and beer trade. In their place the self-service "cafeterias" appeared in force at about the time of World War I. Out of the old ice-cream soda fountain in pharmacists' shops the drug-store lunch also evolved at the same period and drew its millions of customers. The self-service cafeterias, by exhibiting attractively prepared foods on their counters, and by abolishing tipping, won over the public in ever larger numbers. With their lightning-fast meals or cold lunches, self-service cafeteria and drug store alike embodied the mass-production system adapted to the ancient catering craft of hand workers. Hundreds of people trooped into these latter-day feeding stations—in one fairly mechanized type they would simply drop nickels in slots—gulped down their meals and made way for others, who entered and left as on an endless belt-line. They were served in the post-war era by hard-driven crews of men and women catering workers who possessed little skill, or relatively little, in comparison with the long-trained craftsmen attending the wants of discriminating patrons of the old carriage-days.

So much change in the industry brought new headaches as well as opportunities for new departures. The Parisian or Viennese chefs, the skilled waiters, the former barmen in the International Union disliked the new order of things, and sometimes exhibited a professional hostility to the new thousands of city laborers who worked at the cafeteria or drug-store counters. In 1920 the U. S. Census reported 627,000 persons employed in the catering trade, now a rapidly growing industry spurred by the swift growth of cities and the changing habits of an expanding population.

Edward Flore, as early as 1919, proposed to his union members who had lost their jobs in taverns that they try to adjust themselves to the new order:

> We are endeavoring to encourage our present local unions . . . to take up the work of organizing the soft-drink dispensers and soda-fountain employees, for if we are to remain a country divested of all alcoholic drink or beverages, then we must meet that condition.[2]

Yet the change-over was not an easy process; as one observer noted:

> To ask an expert bartender, used to waiting on "men with hair on their chests," to serve old ladies and schoolgirls marshmallow sundaes set off with maraschino cherries was just a little too much. Some bartenders made the heroic effort, passed out banana splits to giggling schoolgirls, and then disgustedly took off their aprons and sought work as teamsters or pick and shovel men. . . .[3]

The bartenders, for the most part, who had known no other trade, acted as if their whole world had simply come to an end. As for the old-time waiters, many of them resented not only the cafeterias but the unskilled or semi-trained people who worked in them, as "interlopers" who were destroying the livelihood of craftsmen. Reflecting this "craft pride," many of the International's local unions made no effort to organize the self-service cafeterias and refused to accept their employees as bonafide waiters or cooks who could become members of their organizations. Jere L. Sullivan used to wring his hands in despair at the radical changes produced in the industry by "one-armed lunchrooms" and self-service places. And their employers advertised for help in the following terms: *"Experience unnecessary."* How could such personnel be initiated into a dignified old craft union?

But when the growth and popularity of the cafeterias resulted in much business being lost by hotel dining rooms and first-class restaurants, their proprietors cut wages and increased hours during the anti-union drive of the 20's. Thus failure to organize the new armies of cafeteria workers did injury, in turn, to the skilled craftsmen in the trade. Many hotels, meanwhile, were being combined into chain systems of large financial resources. To organize them and their 200,000 workers seemed a task beyond the capacity of the HRE's general officers and its dozen organizers, most of whom were former bartenders.

As Jere L. Sullivan remarked at this period: "The problem is one of immense proportions . . . hardly susceptible of solution without much preparation and the expenditure of greater sums than have been available during our time." Sensibly enough, he added the reflection that exact research into the complex business of modern hotel management would be required as a preliminary step; but no research was undertaken, though other unions, such as the Railway Brotherhoods and the Amalgamated Clothing Workers, were already making serious studies of changing economic conditions in their fields.

*

The year 1919 saw widespread industrial warfare throughout the United States, during which organized labor, at the height of its power, gained many notable victories. Strikes had been spurred by the inflationary rise in the cost of living during the war, at the end of which the index of food prices, for example, had soared from the 1914 average of 135.6 to 288.1 at the beginning of 1920. The cost of meals in restaurants and hotels doubled generally in this period, while wages lagged behind.

The labor movement, with 5,000,000 organized, a peak never attained again until fifteen years later, was in a state of extreme unrest, attributed then to a rising tide of liberalism and radicalism. With wartime controls ended, more than 4,160,000 workers were involved in strikes and lockouts in 1919—whereupon the middle-class, fearful of the growing power of labor and "Bolshevism," underwent an attack of anti-Red hysteria that is a recurrent phenomenon of American political life. Eugene Debs, the Socialist party's perpetual candidate for President, was convicted and imprisoned on charges of "espionage" in 1919; many raids were instituted by Federal authorities upon immigrant workers; numerous members of the IWW were arrested and imprisoned under new "criminal syndicalist" laws; and hundreds of accused radicals were deported to Europe. Although the "Bolshevists" proved to be few indeed, the ranks of the AFL's solid trade unionists were also to suffer severe losses in legitimate strikes for wages—as a consequence of the emotionalism engendered in the public by self-appointed "patriots" and "hundred-percent Americans."

In the autumn of 1920 came the post-war reckoning for our over-speculative businessmen: a steep financial crash, followed by unemployment that reached a total of about 4,000,000. Where management, during the wartime labor scarcity, had been disposed to sit down at the conference table with labor, it now instituted wage cuts which were timed with a powerful campaign against legitimate trade unions. But instead of appearing to deny the wage-workers all right to organization (such as capital freely used in its own interest), efforts were made to supplant the workers' own unions with "company unions," controlled by the employers.

In the catering and hotel trade with its many small, weak establishments vulnerable to the collapse of speculative prices, and also suffering the effects of Prohibition, pressure for wage-cutting was intense and serious efforts were made to break up or lock out the HRE local unions, wherever they existed in some strength, or to repudiate agreements with them.

The accumulated difficulties of this "reconstruction era" imposed upon Sullivan and Flore, as well as upon the local officers, the heaviest burdens they had yet borne. Around this time, Edward Flore gave up his salaried political office as a member of the Board of County Supervisors in Buffalo, in order to devote all his days to the struggle to save the International Union.

Hugo Ernst, during a trip across the country in the spring of 1923, happened to visit many different locals, and was able to observe the heavy losses they had borne in strikes or lockout struggles of 1919-1920, the effects of which were evident three or four years later. Where the union organizations were solid, as in San Francisco and Cleveland, they were able to resist or, at least, moderate demands for extreme wage cuts. Restaurants all over the country felt the downswing in business volume, and many operated in the red or went into receivership.

In Cleveland, for example, the waiters' and cooks' locals had agreed to accept wage reductions of 10 per cent, but held their union ranks together. In San Francisco the Hotel Association had confronted the waiters and cooks in 1921 with stern demands for a full 33-⅓ per cent wage cut. But Ernst had made himself "hard to find," and the union members refused to consider even a small reduction. As Weinberger said then, accepting the employers' demands "would have meant surrendering the gains of the last three or four years and perhaps killing the local union." At length a compromise bargain was struck providing for a 7 per cent general reduction in wages for steady employees, with no change in working conditions.[4]

Elsewhere the union restaurant workers faced opposition that was too strong for them. During his trip eastward across the country from San Francisco in May, 1923, Ernst stopped first in Denver where there had long been two flourishing locals of the HRE. Here he was able to measure the heavy toll taken by the 1919 "industrial war" between the Western Federation of Miners and employers. The destructive attacks upon the alleged "syndicalists" in the mine fields by Colorado Vigilantes had spread to include the AFL's politically "moderate" restaurant and barmen's unions. Ernst reported from Denver:

> Picketing of any kind is strictly prohibited. Even handbills with "unfair" are illegal. . . . They have a Ranger Law in Colorado now, a Ranger being a sort of constabulary with unlimited powers, practically speaking above the law. This constabulary can break up meetings, arrest you, throw you into jail, or make you leave town at will.

In St. Louis where Ernst next stopped, the problem was different. The Hotel and Restaurant Employees' locals had been strongly entrenched here for thirty years, Waiters Local 20 having been organized by Jere L. Sullivan himself in the days of the Knights of Labor. There was also a waitresses' union here, Local 249, whose members earning $12 a week in fixed wages in 1920, had demanded an increase of $3. A hotel and restaurant owners' association that had been newly organized thereupon ordered its members to reject these demands and suddenly the union girls were locked out.[5]

A long contest followed in which the police of St. Louis, then under a corrupt city administration, handled the waiters' union pickets with the utmost brutality, so that only the line of women pickets was left to carry on the fight, the chivalrous St. Louis policemen sparing their persons. Many waitresses, however, were arrested for alleged "disorderly conduct." As Mrs. Kitty Amsler, their veteran Secretary, has related: "A goodly number of the pickets had little to eat. That year, almost from the time the strike started in late autumn, the city was swept by snow and sleet. Day after day passers-by saw the waitresses in their threadbare coats, sloshing along. We had to beg for money from all sorts of unions and other organizations," Mrs. Amsler recalls. Secretary Sullivan, for the International Union, sent some small sums, for defense funds were much reduced. But some other St. Louis unions assessed themselves to help the strikers, the AFL's streetcar workers' local giving the finest display of solidarity. One of their officers had seen how the waitresses continued their picketing during a blizzard, when the trolley-cars themselves were stalled. Soon he came from his union meeting to their headquarters and, with the gruff words: "Get the girls some shoes and something to eat!" handed Mrs. Amsler a check for $1,000.[6]

After a four-month endurance test the girls returned to work in the restaurants in February, 1921, at the same wages they had earned before. At least the lockout had been broken, which was all-important.

Hugo Ernst, reviewing the case in 1923, judged that

> The strike should have been avoided. . . . The leaders evidently overestimated their own organizations and underestimated the other side, and so found themselves confronted with a combined Restaurant Association, with the result that they lost out completely.

Local 20, formerly with a membership of nearly 500, was soon down to 75; the cooks were virtually wiped out; and the waitresses' local lost the majority of its members.

These unions were completely shut out of the St. Louis hotels for the next seventeen years—which speaks for the effectiveness of the anti-labor drive in those days.

In Chicago, as in New York, Ernst found that the dual union originally set up by IWW leaders, but now under new management and a new name, controlled the majority of the organized culinary workers. A great strike of nearly 20,000 persons had been directed by the independent union here in 1920, and its defeat had wrought injury to the Hotel and Restaurant Employees' locals, too. Chicago had boasted a large cooks' union for the HRE, of some 2,000 members, and a local of 600 waitresses. But during the 1920 strike, its waitresses' local was lost; and the independent union, then called the Amalgamated Food Workers

> captured the [AFL] organization lock, stock and barrel, one night, at a meeting that was ostensibly called for the purpose of discussing new wage scales. There were about 350 members of the cooks union present out of a total membership of over 2,000. No wage scales were discussed at all, but a motion was made unexpectedly to secede from our International. That motion carried, the charter was torn up, the green books were returned. . . . The property of

the union was removed; $1,600 of furniture was sold for $5, a brand-new typewriter also for $5, and the secretary was voted the sum of $900 for services rendered.[7]

In Buffalo, where the San Francisco officer was received as the guest of President and Mrs. Flore, he also found an organization somewhat reduced in size since a strike it had lost in 1919. Repeatedly Ernst observed that inability to compromise between the terms of the union and those of the employers led to a fight to the finish. "After the smoke of battle had cleared away, the union was crippled and they accepted the bosses' offer, but the bosses refused to sign any agreement," he remarks. Everywhere the affairs of the International Union offered a picture of discouragement and recession —though it was true all but a few of the strongest labor organizations in America lost membership heavily during the 1920's.

In those days the American worker, as one historian of labor, Professor Selig Perlman, has said, "seemed very much on the fence." On the one hand the employer offered him the company union through which he could "protect" his rights by permission of the management, but might be given the advantage of some profit-sharing or incentive-bonus plans. On the other hand were the free and legitimate trade unions with representatives of the workers' own choosing, but to join them often meant the loss of one's job. "What can the union do for me?" was the question many workers raised.

*

Hugo Ernst, as it happened, wrote a most detailed and searching report of his cross-country tour that was published at the time in the union's official journal. It serves as an honest review of the "state of the union" at a period of difficulty and change. What is more it is a document of much historical value, giving us first-hand impressions of the labor movement in its post-war transition.

At the beginning of 1923 he had been appointed a member of the three-man Board of Auditors who visited the general office in Cincinnati annually to inspect the records and financial accounts kept there. It occurred to him that while taking this long journey across the country (for the first time since he had settled in California almost twenty years earlier) he would have an opportunity to see for himself the way the other local unions in the Middle West and the East managed their affairs. The members of Local 30, San Francisco, authorized him to extend his trip to New York and, upon his return, to make a full report to them of what he had learned.

He had become a man of mark in the California labor movement. At the time of the trial and conviction of Tom Mooney and Warren K. Billings on charges of having plotted the bomb explosion that came during the Preparedness Day parade of July 22, 1916, Ernst, like all who knew Mooney well, became convinced of the accused men's innocence. As Secretary of the Molders Union in San Francisco, Mooney had been for years the most aggressive labor leader in the city. Ernst, together with George Kidwell and Paul Scharrenberg, played a leading part in the San Francisco labor committee that originally began to agitate for his pardon. The Mooney Case (which had all the earmarks of a veritable frame-up) became the *cause célèbre* of the entire labor movement in America—though twenty-one years were to pass before Mooney was pardoned by a governor of California.

In 1922, Ernst who "knew everyone in San Francisco from the Mayor down," as he said, ran for Congress on the Socialist party ticket against a reactionary Republican politician, with the support of the AFL labor bodies in California. There was no Democrat in the race. Though defeated, Ernst had the satisfaction of rolling up a very large protest vote against the Republican candidate.

His appointment as one of his union's Board of Auditors in 1923 reflected the better feeling between himself and Jere L. Sullivan, following their clash in 1915. By now the bartenders had been thoroughly "segregated," in any case, by Federal law, and the union was forced to look to the waiters and cooks for all possible support. Though the "little chief" in Cincinnati still felt that Ernst and Weinberger were not as conservative as they ought to be, they headed the largest waiters' local in the system, Waiters Union Local 30. With bartender locals all but vanished, the real strength of the International Union—a fourth of its membership—lay in California, with its 9,000 organized catering-trade workers, most of them in the San Francisco Bay area, whose chief spokesman was Hugo Ernst.

On learning of Ernst's plan to visit many different locals and give a report of them, Jere Sullivan had written him most courteously, offering to publish his findings in full in the *Mixer & Server*. Ernst (while en route) replied, that in view of the frank criticism he might feel obliged to make, he believed it might be unwise to publish his report in its entirety. But the Secretary declared that the International Union now courted intelligent criticism, "let the chips fall where they may." [8]

Like a Diogenes, Hugo Ernst, leaving California on May 7, 1923, journeyed everywhere seeking the truth about the condition of his union. He had no family, no wife. He had lived only in the California labor movement for twenty years, and had his own philosophy of labor, at any rate a more liberal and progressive one than that of the International's leaders. Now he sought answers to the question: what should be done? How could the union organize one hundred or even two hundred thousand of the unorganized and "backward" restaurant workers and win decisive labor power in its industry? His fifty-seven-page report contained suggestions and ideas that were to serve as a rough blueprint for the rebuilding of the HRE in future years.

After his visit to Denver (cited above), he came to Kansas City and found conditions "none too good" as a result of a lost strike several years earlier.

The main support of the boys in Kansas City is the club. Steady men working there make $200 a month, and the two-meal men, about $35 a week. . . . Wages in the clubs are $60 a month for two-meal men and $80 for three-meal men, with two days off per month with pay. In addition thereto ten cents tip per check is given to the men by the house.

The Muehlebach Hotel [leading house in the city] pays $50 a month, less $4 for uniforms. Extra men are paid $2 for lunch and $2.50 for dinner. . . . The steady men are getting $18 per week of six days, ten hours.

Cooks have headquarters with the waiters and cooperate fairly well. The cooks' helpers belong to the cooks union but are poorly organized. . . . Waitresses have a membership of 175. (The total membership of the three locals in Kansas City was about 500 then.)

The police commissioner is busy in the performance of Carrie Nation stuff, the "axe squad" trying to enforce the Eighteenth Amendment and purify the city of gamblers. The headquarters of the waiters' union has been invaded several times, so there is nothing now except pool on baseball games. . . ."

In St. Louis he noted especially that there was no cooperation between the waiters and waitresses, such as had existed in San Francisco for many years:

They seem to have inaugurated a system of catch-as-catch-can, and when the girls organize a house the boys try to take it away from them, and vice-versa. The consequence is that no one has anything.

Here also there was one of the new "monster" hotels belonging to the Statler Corporation, and it was significant that it employed mainly non-union Negro and Mexican workers and girls, as did the other large hotels in St. Louis. Only a few Negro workers who labored on the river boats in the summer and for catering establishments in the winter were organized in a segregated local of the HRE.

Cincinnati, the headquarters of his organization, he described as most "miserable" from a trade union point of view. The whole waiters' union had but 276 members and had unionized only four sizable restaurants where waiters were paid $2 for a nine-hour day (aside from tips), and $90 a month in clubs.

> There is no Union House card in Cincinnati. The waiters . . . are continually fighting with the cooks. Girls are absolutely unorganized. The cafeteria girls get $10 a week and three meals. . . . At the Sinton Hotel, with 22 cooks employed, the cooks walked out on strike, the waiters stayed in. The waiters are still in and the cooks still out.

In Washington, with its immense hotel industry, he found only 375 members in the union, with none of the women organized and none of the cooks. Most of the hotels employed non-union Negro workers and paid them but $40 a month. In the hotel trade was a vast market for the International Union and yet it had less than a hundred members in the important centers such as Baltimore, Philadelphia, and Atlantic City.

Arriving in New York at last, Ernst reported:

> New York strange as it may seem *has no union*. They have a "job trust" which they call Waiters Union Local 1 and with over 1,800 members. They could if they wished have more members, but that would endanger the complete control of the jobs. . . .

This old union demanded extremely high initiation fees, and held absolute control over the East Side's "kosher" (Jewish) restaurants and some of the financial district's eating-places, with whose owners, organized into a Restaurant Men's Association, it had established firm contractual relations. No union member, after working for a week, could be discharged without approval of the union. One clause of the agreement provided that a restaurant proprietor might be "tried" and fined if found guilty of insulting or striking a member of the union. Workmen's compensation for injuries while on the job was also provided for; finally each employer was required to come to union headquarters to sign his agreement, and pay $5 for the privilege of doing so! It was a "classic" agreement, as Ernst said, and provided job security for its select group of members in the old craft-union style.

In those days many of the tidy little locals in the East seemed more like "employment bureaus" than real labor union branches.

Local 1 had a well-heeled secretary, the veteran "Bill" Lehman, whose salary ($4,500 a year) almost equaled that of President Flore; also a capable assistant-secretary, Louis Finkelstein, and three business agents. Its financial reports were audited by an outside accountant and made public. But aside from this old "craft" local, which included only 200 waitresses in an auxiliary unit, there were virtually no other culinary workers recruited for the International out of the 75,000 people now said to be employed in New York's multitude of restaurants and hotels.

In Brooklyn there was also an old local, No. 2, much like Local 1 in composition, but the waiters' organizations of the two boroughs of Manhattan and Brooklyn were engaged in ceaseless war with each other, much like their professional baseball teams, the Dodgers and the Giants. Local 1, from Manhattan, claimed jurisdiction over Brooklyn's beach resort of Coney Island, and Local 2 clamored to heaven because the place was within the geographical boundaries of Brooklyn.* To make peace, the mild, patient President Flore was called down from Buffalo, and, like a Solomon, administered even-handed justice by dividing the union business of the beach resort into two equal parts, more or less.

But during these petty squabbles the independent or dual union group made hay and organized along industrial union lines the cooks and cafeteria workers who had been neglected by the AFL's union. Though he was an officer of the "enemy" union, Hugo Ernst paid a diplomatic call at the rival headquarters and wrote:

> The Amalgamated Food Workers have a very strong organization of cooks, some bakers and some waiters. They are building their own home on 51st Street and are able to control the larger

* That Hugo Ernst's account was in no sense exaggerated is shown by the statement of Organizer Tony Schwartz, made before the 1923 convention, to the effect that there were many hundreds of suspended members of the various sister locals of the International Union working at good jobs in New York who might be of much help to the organization. "But when we ask them to reaffiliate, they call our attention to the demands made upon them by the last union they were attached to—demands running from the unreasonable to the positively tyrannical. The worst feature in connection with such demands being that the unions making them are seeking to get their pound of flesh no matter what the consequences. New York is not going to be organized until a more liberal and cooperative spirit takes hold of those local unions referred to." (1923 Convention Proceedings, pp. 177-178.)

hotels owing to the scarcity of cooks, but they have no signed agreement of any kind. Nevertheless in almost all the big hotels their members are employed. During my stay in New York they pulled a little strike at the Plaza Hotel, calling out fifty-two cooks, and I understand after a four-day struggle they were able to gain most of their points. Several attempts have been made to get the Amalgamated into our International; at one time they were ready to join as a body but our International objected to some of their members, expelled from our organization, formerly, and on the other hand a few extremists in the Amalgamated objected strenuously to any alliance or compromise. The whole thing fell flat.

Journeying westward again in July, Ernst halted at Cleveland, which he described as one of the union's "bright spots." Under the shrewd Farrell, who was a local Republican politician and official of the city government nowadays, the cooks', waiters' and waitresses' locals maintained signed agreements with the hotels and Class A restaurants, at any rate, and imposed union shop standards. Dues were moderate and sick benefits of $10 a week for cooks and waiters represented progress along human welfare lines. Detroit, next on Ernst's itinerary, was then a strongly anti-union town, dominated by the influence of the great "Flivver King," Henry Ford. Yet Secretary Louis Koenig of Local 705, formerly a New York waiter, appeared to be an aggressive and enterprising officer who was building up a loyal group of union waiters. When a new restaurant downtown had tried recently to open up with a crew of non-union waiters and cooks sent over from Chicago by the (anti-union) Geneva Association, Koenig dealt promptly with the situation. "He immediately formed a strong reception committee," as Ernst wrote, "and when the train pulled into Detroit there were about 200 waiters at the depot ready to use persuasion and other methods to stop this crew."

In New York, Washington and Philadelphia, Ernst observed with his own eyes how the sway of the racketeer and bootlegger, during the years of Prohibition, debauched an industry and many of its workers. The HRE's Washington local had no clubroom, he related, because "the clubrooms they used were raided by the police on account of gambling and bootlegging." At the Philadelphia local's headquarters, a gang of "gamblers and booze-fighters" had driven out the better class of members and obtained control of the local union for their own purposes. Operated ostensibly as locals or clubs for workers, with a bar-concessionaire dispensing costly booze, such places were more immune to raids by the authorities enforcing the Volstead Act than were the speakeasies. Thus in New York, the almost extinct Local 5 kept its charter for several years on the pretext of being a bona fide union of cooks and hotel workers, but was actually run as a speakeasy in the convenient Broadway theatre district.

Ernst, among others, warned Secretary Sullivan of what was going on. Some months later, Jere L., accompanied by another International officer, as he related,

> visited the alleged headquarters of Local 5 rather early one morning and observed more than ample to satisfy him that the only purpose . . . was to enable a few of its alleged members (who we doubt were waiters) to conduct a gambling establishment which, while parading as a labor union, seemed less likely to be molested by police authorities.

Not long after this Local 5 was suspended.

In Chicago, also, Ernst had a good look at the new breed of racketeers who had thrust themselves into the union "game," and noted the swift deterioration of what had once been a large local organization. In his report he described a "slight case of murder" at the headquarters of Local 7, supposed to be an organization of culinary workers.

> You are all acquainted with the unfortunate affair of the shooting up of the headquarters and the killing of President Regan. The whole trouble started over the gambling and booze concession. Regan and his partner were defeated at a regular election for the club concession. They claimed fraud and maneuvered for a new election in which they won out by one vote. On the night they were to take over, the other gang came to the headquarters to stop Regan from taking the concession. Regan and his gang, sensing trouble, had a policeman in the headquarters, but unfortunately this policeman wore no uniform. . . . Then the fun began; Regan was killed, the police officer was shot; the man who did the actual shooting got away; and they have one man in jail as the goat.

Secretary Sullivan later made some personal investigations of Local 7 and its concession, and concluded that "the moral atmosphere surrounding the headquarters of Local 7 is wholly repugnant to decent men. . . ." Moreover, within two years, following the homicide affair Ernst had reported, it lost three-quarters of its membership. Soon its charter also was revoked.[9]

Ernst's summary of conditions in the International Union in the early 20's shows it moving at a very labored pace through the doldrums. In addition to the reverses that almost all trade unions experienced in the years after World War I it suffered the chaotic and demoralizing effects of Prohibition. No thoroughgoing effort to get on with the job of organizing the unorganized in the catering trade was being undertaken, save in California, and particularly the San Francisco Bay area. Women workers, Ernst pointed out, now approximately a third of the industry's labor force, and the colored laborers were virtually excluded, and thus, inevitably, lowered the standards of union people. Finally he laid great stress upon the lack of cooperation between the cooks and waiters, and the failure to organize but a few thousand of the nearly 400,000 cooks and kitchen helpers reported in the U. S. Census for 1920.

We must be frank to admit that the cooks are the backbone of our organization, their skill making it possible for them and for us to get what little we have. It is equally true that the waiter is the fighter and the cooks will do well not to forget that skill alone without fighting ability avails nothing, and that we must have both together in a solid organization. . . .

He also made the keen observation that Chicago, a busy point of migration for workers, remained disorganized because so many waiters came there from other towns where the union was weak.

The unorganized condition of the surrounding territories naturally reacts upon the main arteries, and it seems to me that something ought to be done to start a campaign for *regional organization*. By that I mean that certain large towns and surrounding territories ought to be selected for intensive organizing campaigns, because as long as the immediate vicinity of a town remains unorganized, as long as one city is able to draw upon another for unorganized workers, so long will it be hard or impossible to unionize our industry.

*

The full-length report of Ernst's tour of observation was published by Jere L. Sullivan in the July 15, 1923, issue of the union's official journal. "Somebody may feel hurt," Ernst had warned him; but the aging General Secretary was seriously troubled now over the straits into which the International seemed to have fallen, and was willing to have the members waked up.

This was on the eve of the 1923 convention that met in Chicago in the first week of August, and all the delegates read Ernst's "Travelogue" with mixed feelings. While many honored him for his courage in telling the painful truth, more than one assailed him for "supplying our opponents with ammunition that will be used to our injury for years to come."

On his arrival in Chicago, the night before the convention, Ernst stopped at the Hotel Morrison and there, in the café, met John Swinehart, an officer of Local 865. Swinehart, a man of great girth, expressed his disapproval of Ernst's published opinions of the Chicago branch by smashing in his bowler hat and roughing him up. Nothing daunted, Hugo Ernst turned up at the convention's session the next morning and proceeded to play an active role in its debates.

Secretary Sullivan, on hearing of the brawl, gallantly came to Ernst's defense and assumed full responsibility for having published the article:

> I desire to express my utter opposition to what occurred in this city when a member of one of our local unions imagined that if he could injure Brother Ernst he would offer ample response to criticisms of this city and its local unions. I have assured Brother Ernst that neither myself nor my associates on the GEB approve roughneck tactics and . . . that it was a noticeable thing that the man who had assaulted him made it a practice to pick out men of about half his size. Now as to printing Brother Ernst's survey . . . as long as I can remember, the AF of L has advocated free speech and a free press, and my conception of both is to allow men to talk and write and print their viewpoints. . . .[10]

The delegates now were reduced to the number of 152; there were but 290 locals in affiliation and 37,743 members, a loss of 27,000 since 1917. Some former union strongholds, such as Boston, seemed unable to recover from the misfortunes that befell them in 1919-1920. Local 34, of Boston, which, under "Jack" Kearney, had been one of the largest, saw its membership reduced at this period from 2,800 to about 900 members.

The convention delegates had Hugo Ernst's report before them; they could judge in some measure what was wrong and what must be done. Yet this gathering behaved much like those that had gone before. The venerable Samuel Gompers, president of the AFL, was guest of honor and set the keynote for the meetings. What concerned him was the fierce anti-labor campaign now being waged all over the country by great corporations and in the press, and he preached, above all, conservative tactics which might tend to calm the opposition.

Gompers himself had actually been accused, in some of the particularly wild propaganda that was then circulated, of plotting to "arm labor"! That such things should be said of Sam Gompers of all people passed all human understanding. For forty years he had urged —as he did again before the Hotel and Restaurant Employees' convention in Chicago, on August 13, 1923—that the American labor movement "is evolutionary rather than revolutionary." He declared now:

> I say to our organization, as I say to the organizations of all wage earners: Never leap, never jump, for those who leap forward usually lose by overrunning.

Gompers was now a tired old man of seventy-two, and indulged in rambling reminiscences of the old days in which he had first met and reposed his confidence in Jere L. Sullivan, to whom he paid his compliments. But perhaps because of failing memory, he finished up with a most tactless statement before this convention:

> We have by our movement reduced the hours of toil so that few, comparatively few, are now working more than eight hours a day.[11]

The truth was that with the exception of one or two local unions of the Hotel and Restaurant Employees in the Rocky Mountain states, such as Butte, Montana, none worked as little as eight hours a day in this trade and the majority worked nine or ten hours. Indeed, just before Gompers had spoken, Secretary Sullivan in his biennial report had expressed the gravest doubts that shorter hours could be attained by their union in the foreseeable future:

> There are several hundred thousand catering industry employees who never have been affiliated with our union. Is it within the realm of possibility for us, who are but a small percentage of the whole wage-earning aggregation to put into effect an eight-hour day? The author of this message does not hesitate to assure you that . . . any such general drive will result in failure for any number of reasons. We have neither the numerical strength nor financial strength to make such a drive even partially successful.[12]

In mellower vein, Jere L. showed a marked disposition nowadays to conciliate the progressives in the union, such as Hugo Ernst. Yet his characteristic pessimism prevailed to the end.

One of the "burning issues" discussed at the 1923, as at the 1921, convention by some of the delegates was the emergence of chains of huge corporation-owned hotels, such as the powerful Statler company, which posed a nationwide problem for the union. A resolution was brought in authorizing special preparations for a contest with the non-union Statler chain. "The control of the hotel industry is being rapidly absorbed by gigantic corporations, whose tendrils are reaching into all sections of the United States and Canada," the resolution stated. It was proposed that the job be tackled nationally or "collectively" by the union's Executive Board instead of locally, since the company operated in many different cities now, and that efforts be made to work out a standardized wage scale.

DELEGATE WHISSEMORE, Local 106: I think it is about time we got ready to go to bat with the Statler Hotels. All of you who have had any experience with them know that the local managers prefer the non-citizen and non-union catering industry worker to the unionized and citizen worker. In some towns where they have their employment bureaus working, a union member has about as much chance to get on their payroll as we have of becoming millionaires overnight.[13]

But as always, Jere L. Sullivan opposed such moves, and declared that an attack on the Statler "trust" was virtually doomed to failure:

I can assure this gathering that if I had the ability to perform what these proposals urge us to accomplish, you would not be able to retain me in your service for the salary you pay me. Investigators are specialists . . . must be expert accountants, before they can begin examining the returns made by innumerable catering establishments with one general head or manager. Do you imagine such a task can be taken in hand by any of your present Board Members? Speaking for myself, all that I know of chain houses is what you in this room know, and that, if you will pardon me, is mighty little. . . . If we desired to get inside information we would not know how to take the first step to acquire it. . . . Let us employ a little common sense and not exact impossible things from our official family. The only thing that is possible is for us to try and organize the several hotels and chain lunchrooms which are under centralized control. . . .[14]

His counsel in short was to "go slow." It was better not to inform the Statler Corporation that "we are out to fight it." "Do not overlook the fact that the corporation and its resources are large." They were training their own bus boys and "ham" waiters and cooks in the thousands. And "Where is the coin coming from?" he wound up. Whissemore replied: "Where is the coin? We have been in more than one scrap without a great deal of money. The Statler Company is now fighting us everywhere." Jere L.'s counsels of caution prevailed, but the resolution was introduced again in 1925.

Let us use the old, tried and tested methods, Sullivan urged. Let the union members overcome their apathy, and go ward by ward and street by street to organize the many eating establishments. As he had said to Ernst during their recent meeting in Cincinnati, he still hoped that the International would remain an organization of "quality" and craftsmen, primarily, rather than of great numbers. One of the AFL spokesmen at this convention even made a virtue of small unions and went so far as to attack those who desired to form "mass organizations," by taking in the great unwashed, unskilled and unorganized workers:

> Strength does not lie in bulk. Bulk sometimes represents merely fat. The Spanish with a few hundred conquered Mexico and Peru. . . . Look around you at any trade union movement and what do you find. That progress has been made through great numbers? No. The greatest progress has been made through small groups.

On the third day of the convention, usually set aside for the election of general officers, Flore, Sullivan and the Executive Board's Vice-Presidents (most of them of Sullivan's choosing) were re-elected. They were the people from small locals, usually, whom he had long preferred as his associates. On behalf of the big California contingent, a San Francisco delegate, on this occasion, nominated Hugo Ernst for Vice-President as a candidate possessing "ability, education and courage." Many were convinced that Ernst, leader of the union's biggest local, was one of the ablest officers in the International and that his presence on the GEB was badly needed. But one Al B. Hassel, who headed the small former bartenders' Local 284 of Los Angeles, with only seventeen members, was re-elected. The administration, though it respected the San Francisco leader, was not ready to lend him support. Ernst, and Jack Weinberger also, in those years, represented the "militants" or "loyal opposition" whose tendency was toward a gradual adaptation of industrial union tactics within the Hotel and Restaurant Employees International. The 1923 convention did, however, make one concession to realities by electing William Lehman, Secretary of Local 1, Vice-President, thus, after some twenty years, giving representation on the Board to the workers in the largest catering center in America.

In the intermittent tilts that went on in those days between the "progressives" and the conservatives, Hugo Ernst sounded a note of optimism, calling attention to the enterprising and aggressive methods used by his California branch. They had gathered in all the apprentices, the "miscellaneous workers," the pantrymen, cooks' helpers and vegetable men and poor dishwashers in a single strong local, No. 110, San Francisco, having about 1,000 members. He said:

> Your Secretary-Treasurer directed your attention to the lassitude or indifference that has taken hold of too many. . . . Merely talking about a bad situation isn't going to cure it.
>
> As to the appropriate time to begin work, may I say that waiting for a suitable time to organize our industry has set us back too far. In my judgment *the time to organize is now*—every hour of the day and every day of the week. We of California did not learn the trick overnight, I can assure you, but we did not sit back and bemoan our fate. . . .[15]

SEVEN

The Passing of Jere Sullivan

"The more we looked the more our wonder grew.
That one small head sufficed to carry all he knew!"
—JAMES DUNCAN, at 1925 Convention.

One cause of the union's failure to make headway during the 1920's was the continuing friction between the different craft locals within a given area. Not only in New York but even in San Francisco, where the union members had more economic power to impose wages and conditions, there was as yet too little harmony between cooks and waiters.

Even as Hugo Ernst spoke before the 1925 Convention at Montreal, declaring that the time to organize was now, his "fighting waiters" of Local 30, in San Francisco, jumped off to a strike against three leading hotels in the town. They took action, however, without waiting for the formal approval of the Local Joint Board or of the International GEB, though in accordance with the local union's by-laws.

They had been negotiating, for many months, for an increase in the wage scale, from $3 to $3.50 for a day of nine hours, while the hotel men and restaurant keepers used the tactics of delay. The last straw was the sudden discharge of thirty union waiters from the Palace Hotel and their replacement by forty non-union waitresses. Some ill-feeling had shown itself at this period not only between the cooks and the waiters, but between the waiters and waitresses, whose local unions in former years developed all too slowly. The women workers were given lower pay and were expected to care for fewer tables than men. The men feared and resented their periodic replacement by women, especially non-union women.

This time only about 300 waiters were called out; but when the waiters tried to persuade the cooks to join them in their strike, they met with a firm refusal from the members of Local 44. Had the cooks walked out, the hotels that were affected would have been quickly starved into submission; but without them it was hard.

The waiters and cooks, hitherto, had kept each other closely informed of all agreements they entered into with employers. But the recent arrangement made by the cooks' union was a separate agreement which Jack Weinberger, heading Local 30 then, held was contrary to all previous understandings with the waiters.

The men of Local 30 fought hard; they assessed their employed members heavily and provided approximately $10 a week in strike relief, which was liberal for that period. The International Union also contributed $10,000 this time. But the hotel managers, aided by the city's so-called Law and Order Committee, an aggressive strike-breaking organization, brought in out-of-town workers, obtained police protection for them, and sent letters all over San Francisco calling on the public to patronize the struck hotels.

After several weeks some of the strikers began to drift back to work. At this point, the union with the approval of Ernst, who had just returned from Montreal, decided to call off the strike. On this occasion the hotel proprietors, who had a healthy respect for the union, were glad to dismiss their strike-breaking crews and take back their old hands at the same wages as before. Thus the union was not weakened by the conflict and, in fact, continued to grow in numbers. A year later, after peaceful negotiations, the employers granted the wage scale their waiters had fought for in 1925—thus demonstrating the soundness of Local 30's tactics of unremitting pressure.[1]

"The great lesson learned from this strike," Jack Weinberger wrote afterward, "was that no local union was strong enough to go it alone." The all-important thing was to work out complete cooperation between the different crafts so that they would move as a solid phalanx under their Local Joint Board. But for more than a year after the strike of 1925 the San Francisco Local Joint Board, in which five culinary unions were represented proportionately, was the scene of raging conflict, the two largest locals, the waiters' and cooks', showing intense ill-feeling toward each other. The cooks were then much afraid of being dominated by the greater numbers of the waiters.[2]

It needed statesmanship to compose the quarrel based on quite serious difficulties inherent in the trade then. Ernst had no authority over the cooks, and besides, he was a waiter. Secretary Sullivan was far away in Cincinnati, busy at his desk work, and the International Union's organizers who were sometimes stationed in California were of no help. By the beginning of 1927 things had reached such a pass that Ernst and Weinberger insistently demanded that President Flore come to San Francisco to settle the disagreement in the Local Joint Board. At the time, February, 1927, the cooks were planning a strike, but would not come to an understanding with the waiters of Local 30 that no agreement terminating the strike was to be signed without the approval of the other local. The imperative thing was to end all such dissension.

President Flore arrived from Buffalo and stayed in San Francisco for more than a month. He conferred at length with Ernst, Weinberger and August Van Bebber, business agent of the cooks' local, who showed himself most cooperative and, by persuading his members to make concessions to the waiters' point of view, helped to bring about a lasting accord. Rules were set up that made the Local Joint Board in San Francisco so much a unit, dependent always on concerted action, that henceforth no strikes would ever be run by a single local in that city. Out of the experiences gained in this affair were developed the new International Union by-laws regulating the procedure of city Joint Boards everywhere in the organization to the end of labor solidarity.

During his visit to San Francisco, Edward Flore also exerted himself to interview the heads of the two leading hotels, the St. Francis and Palace, and as a result gained concessions for the waiters' local that strengthened the union's position. For a whole decade that followed there was no more industrial war in San Francisco's catering trade.

In these negotiations Ed Flore was at his best, showing the qualities of moderation and tact that made many in the union admire him and urge that he assume its full leadership. "I want to add a word of praise for the General President," Ernst said with much feeling, a few months later, before the International's convention held in Portland, Oregon, in 1927. "I would be derelict in my duty if I did not explain what transpired in San Francisco. The President had to handle a very difficult situation. . . . The task required extraordinary diplomacy and courage, and the General President acquitted himself wonderfully." [3]

The ice was now broken between the reserved Flore and the leaders of the "Western Movement." In his talks with Ernst, Weinberger and Van Bebber he learned much that strengthened his belief that the organizing staff of the International must somehow be rebuilt from top to bottom. It was high time, in fact, that the General President assume a more decisive role than that of "nominal" head of the union; for Jere L. Sullivan, remarkable figure though he was, was growing old and declining in health.

*

From about 1925 on, attacks upon Secretary Jere Sullivan by local officers and convention delegates grew steadily in frequency and vigor. They were aimed at his policies, at his methods of operation, and at his editing of the union's official journal, though his personal honesty and integrity were never brought into question. He, for his part, withstood the periodic bombardments with relative composure or even indifference. The International Union was a tolerably democratic organization and dissatisfied members had a right to throw verbal custard pies at their officers if they chose to.

But even so, there was no doubt that he was still their crusty "little chief." His salary (though not excessive) surpassed President Flore's by $25 a month. As before, the Executive Board guided itself by his counsels.

The 1925 convention at Montreal devoted one whole session to celebrating Jere L. Sullivan's twenty-fifth anniversary as Secretary, with one speaker after another paying him homage, while President Flore, presiding over it all, was almost forgotten.

A guest of honor, President James Duncan of the Granite Cutters Union, and a Vice-President of the AFL, exclaimed:

> Presidents may come and Presidents may go, but Secretaries go on forever! To mention your organization to the older and newer members of the American labor movement means no one but Jere L. Sullivan!

Sullivan acknowledged the ovations in honor of his long ministry in his rather heavy style of oratory. He strutted and pontificated and exhorted the members to new effort by the old tried and true methods. But it was nonetheless the beginning of the end—the last act of his play. Two years later, at the convention in Portland, Oregon, his back was to the wall; he was fighting for his very life, as it were, while the excited delegates roared for his removal from office.

The composition of the union itself had changed perceptibly; it was no longer made up of barmen, but of waiters, cooks and other culinary workers, and Sullivan at sixty-five was not a man to change his ways, as he used to boast. He was, moreover, increasingly difficult to work with, habitually wary and suspicious of everyone. "He used to burn up all his records and correspondence, saying 'There are always spies around.' " [4] Many of the union officers, aside from any personal ambition they may have felt, were convinced that, for the good of the organization, he must be supplanted or reduced in power.

The complaints against him, often expressed in letters circulated among the convention delegates, were many and diverse. A local in Los Angeles might appeal to the GEB for $1,000 from the International for organizing purposes. Jere L. would send $100.

A typical instance of his treatment of such complaints shows him answering the petitioner simply by appealing to the convention for a vote of confidence:

> SECRETARY SULLIVAN: Mr. President, there has been laid on this table what purports to be a resolution, a portion of which charges the General Secretary with neglect of duty and refusing to aid a local union in alleged distress.
>
> DELEGATE KLOTER, Local 326 (Pittsburgh): I am the delegate responsible for the resolution which the Secretary finds fault with. . . . The only object I had was to secure the services of an organizer to help us in combating sinister influences that have surrounded our membership. These opponents seek to destroy our union.[5]

By such parsimony, it was charged, Sullivan accumulated large funds in the union's treasury (used mainly for death benefits) and failed to help it gain membership. The California contingent was especially vehement in opposition to Sullivan, one delegate, Rudolf Wartenberg, of Los Angeles, declaring at the 1927 gathering in Portland:

> We do not believe that the Secretary-Treasurer's office has been conducted as fully in cooperation with the local secretaries as it should be. . . . We do hope that the Secretary-Treasurer, after what has been said on the floor and the letters he has received, will realize that we are opposed to him and some of the other worthy officers, and . . . if re-elected in the convention, we hope he will eliminate some of the sarcasm he bestows upon the locals. Some have seen this organization grow since it was small, in a cigarbox so to speak, up to three hundred thousand dollars in the treasury. I believe that had the Secretary shown a large increase in the membership that the money in the treasury would be still more.[6]

Another of the Westerners, John St. Peter, of Local 44, San Francisco, brought forth a resolution at Portland severely censuring the existing method of apportioning votes at conventions, as not being fairly representative of the numerical size of the local unions or of their per capita tax payments. Thus "Brother Hassel had one vote for his nineteen members while Brother Ernst had only three for a thousand that he represented." Another example was that of one local having nine votes for 426 members, while St. Peter's Local 44 had only eighteen votes for four times as many members.

The strongest criticisms, however, were directed at the Secretary's handling of the general and local special organizers. Thus Martin Spiegel, of Local 106, Cleveland, urged removal of the organizing staff from the Secretary's control:

> I do not believe the membership is willing to let things continue as they have in the past. I believe that our General President is handicapped and that he is really the nominal or figure head of this International Union. The General President has traveled the country over and knows of conditions and understands the situation better than anyone in the International. I believe he should have the power to place organizers where they will do the most good.
>
> We would be hypocrites to sit here and not say a word as to this report.
>
> Things might have been satisfactory twenty years ago; but times are changing. I do not think the organizers today are doing any good.[7]

Never before had the aging Jere L.—though he had rather courted controversy or thrived on it—been subjected to such a pounding as he received in 1927. Flore now openly headed the opposition movement, though his own language was as restrained and courteous as ever.

The union of which he was the titular head seemed—when one recalled its promise of large growth in the 1900's—to have missed the bus. For fifteen years, Ed Flore, as the younger, less experienced man, had deferred to the veteran Jere Sullivan. But now he was no longer young, he was fifty. During the crisis-years following Prohibition he had traveled much, worked over many troublespots, learned much. What he had learned finally was that he must "do something," that he must wrest the leadership of the organization from Jere L. before it was too late. At one recent Executive Board meeting the dispute between Flore and Sullivan had grown so warm that the little Secretary, beside himself with emotion, "picked up his papers, jumped to his feet and ran from the council-room." [8]

Now Flore had the support of the GEB members, especially the most experienced among them, Vice-President Robert Hesketh of Seattle, who was determined to run against Sullivan himself unless changes were promptly introduced that would permit the union to expand again. Flore had therefore prepared an amendment to the Constitution that was more important than any legislative change proposed since 1899. It provided that Section 112 which read formerly:

> The General Secretary-Treasurer, with the approval of the Executive Board, shall appoint a number of organizers who shall be assigned to duty in different portions of the United States and Canada. . . .

should be changed so that the words "General Secretary-Treasurer" were stricken out and the words "General President" put in their place.

Flore's contention was that organizing work had not kept pace with the needs of the union, and, as he tactfully phrased it, the Secretary-Treasurer was unable to supervise it adequately inasmuch as he was generally confined to his headquarters in Cincinnati. Whereas the President, who traveled about the country frequently, would be in a better position to direct the organizers in the field. If he could, as President, select and appoint people, subject to the GEB's approval, and follow their work, they would be more responsive to his direction. Flore had tried to take the organizers from Jere L.'s control fourteen years earlier, and failed. This time he meant business.

Sullivan fought bitterly against this resolution in the preliminary stages before the convention opened. But when Flore showed him that he had the backing of the Committee on Law and of enough pledged delegates to have the resolution passed, Sullivan suddenly gave way. The control of the organizing staff, in his own hands for twenty-eight years, now passed into those of Flore. In this sprawling union structure, based on widely scattered and autonomous local units, he who controlled the organizers controlled a good deal of the engine power.

The convention at Portland, attended by a more numerous body of younger and more progressive delegates than in the past, prominent among them the men of the growing Pacific Coast branches, held animated debate over the reform of the organizing staff. Everybody was aware that this was a turning-point in the union's history. The convention's Law Committee had reported in favor of leaving "direction" in the hands of the President but "appointment" of organizers to the members of the Executive Board. There were some who held this to be an awkward example of divided power.

DELEGATE B. F. DODGE, Local 44: We should retain the power [to appoint and direct, both] or consolidate it in the hands of one man. Give him the responsibility and make him live up to it.

DELEGATE BOOKJANS, Local 237: We are a democratic organization . . . but we are democratic in proportion to the results obtained. I believe the best results are accomplished if you make one man responsible and give him the power equal to his responsibility, so that he cannot pass the buck.

But Hugo Ernst argued:

In spite of the great confidence I have in the General President I am opposed to giving any one man such power. Even the President of the United States has to go before the Senate to have his appointees approved. . . . Only along democratic lines can this organization amount to anything. I have never seen an organization whose sole power was vested in one person amount to anything. (Applause) [9]

The resolution adopted in 1927, at first as a halfway step, transferring control of the organizers to the President, was still subject to the GEB's power of appointment. (Soon afterward it was to be amended, as was foreseen, so that he would have both full appointive power and responsibility.) After the vote had been taken, Jere Sullivan strode across the platform to shake hands with Ed Flore and wish him success. He was quite satisfied, he declared, as "he had long wanted to get rid of the job and put it on the shoulders of someone else." But the finishing touch for Jere L. during the proceedings was the passage of a measure raising the President's salary to a level with that paid the Secretary-Treasurer.

The reform spirit was rife among the delegates at this convention. Women leaders appeared among them now in goodly number. The courageous Elizabeth Maloney was no longer there—she was to die two years later—but Kitty Donnelly of Cleveland, Alice Lord of Seattle, and Kitty Amsler of St. Louis spoke fervently and well in behalf of a resolution to establish equal rights and equal pay for women workers. Action upon this extremely important question was, however, deferred for further study. The adoption of a policy of equal wage rates for women was to wait ten years more, until the New Deal had come for labor in 1937.

No less pressing was the problem of honoring traveling cards presented by migrant cooks and waiters who had left their home locals to seek work in other towns. Some local officers were notorious for their use of every possible means to deny or delay the admission of traveling members to full rights in the unions to which they applied, or to the assignment of "extra" work as it became available. At the Portland convention a law was passed that was aimed at overcoming the evil of the "closed book" tactics of certain locals. It prohibited all discrimination against members arriving from another city who were in good standing with their home locals.

The election of Hugo Ernst as a Vice-President, which his Western followers had so long urged, was one of the major events of the 1927 convention, and gave formal recognition to the local officer who by then enjoyed more real prestige among his union brothers than any other.

Dan Regan, of Local 30, nominated Ernst as head of the "largest local union in this International," whose work "shows for itself." John St. Peter of the San Francisco cooks' local, No. 44, seconded the nomination, declaring that Ernst spoke for the rank and file, and was of "the finest caliber of manhood. We differ with him upon occasion but respect him for his fine judgment." St. Peter then hinted at what many already knew, that Ernst was expected at some time in the future to replace the incumbent Secretary-Treasurer.

> I am afraid some day that the State of California will lose the services of this, one of our greatest members. We dread that day, and yet we feel that if he should take it upon himself to go out of our great state we should send our congratulations to those organizations that should get him. . . .[10]

No one being nominated in opposition to Ernst, he was elected unanimously, and, in his forthright manner, acknowledged the honor in behalf of the San Francisco branch with which he had been associated for almost a quarter of a century. He said:

> The labor movement is my fetish. I work, eat, sleep only in the labor movement. . . . I have always tried to be fair and impartial and have made enemies, as you do in order to be fair and impartial. I expect to make enemies on the Board. I promise that if any-

thing happens that merits my censure I will say so. I hope I may be of assistance in carrying on the great work of our International.

*

The entrance of Ernst into the GEB signalized the beginning of change in its composition, by his representation of the "Western Movement"—which Jere L. Sullivan had once fought so bitterly—and of a more modern, less craft-minded philosophy of labor. The previous incumbent in the California district since 1925 had been one Frank Johnston of Local 17, Los Angeles (then a very small organization). But Johnston had the fancy to run for Secretary-Treasurer and had started to campaign a bit. Whereupon, as Hugo Ernst recalled the incident, "Johnston became *persona non grata* with Jere L. and Jere suggested to me that I run for Vice-President in that district." [11] *

Flore had been re-elected, and Sullivan, too, without opposition. Jere L., who suddenly looked rather tired and old, gallantly saluted the parting delegates with some last words in which he implied that he held no grievances against those who had assailed him, at the same time denying that he had ever taken it upon himself "to be the whole works." As a humorous parable he related a story concerning an accomplished colored waiter who years before had worked at a luxurious summer resort where he regularly served a certain, once famous tycoon, John W. ("Bet-You-A-Million") Gates. The man worked smoothly and well, and Mr. Gates, as was his custom, rewarded him with lavish tips of $20. But one day the affluent customer noticed that his regular waiter was stationed at another table in the hotel while a new man waited upon him. When he called the one who had formerly served him so well and asked him why he had changed his table, the other replied sadly: "Mr. Gates, I done *lost* you last night." The other waiters had challenged him to shoot dice for the right to serve the various guests; he had thrown his dice and lost to one of his fellow waiters the valuable privilege of serving the great man. And so Jere L. Sullivan summed up his own feeling about the action at this convention through which the delegates had reduced his power: "I some-

---

* The GEB of 1927-1929 consisted of Edward S. Flore, President; Jere L. Sullivan, Secretary-Treasurer; and Vice-Presidents R. B. Hesketh, of Seattle; Frank Hoffman, Minneapolis; Carl T. Frederick, Portland, Oregon; Kitty Donnelly, Cleveland, Ohio; John C. Staggenberg, Chicago; J. M. Osborn, Denver, Colorado; William Lehman, New York; and Hugo Ernst, San Francisco. It now contained three Pacific Coast members. After the death of Hoffman, in January, 1929, John J. Kearney of Boston was chosen to replace him, thus giving a fair representation to the largest city groups in the union.

how carried the impression that perhaps someone had placed Jere L. 'in the game' and they were 'shooting for him' for all they were worth."

This was his last talk before a convention of the International Union. In the months that followed he appeared depressed and ill, and seemed to grieve over the defeat he had suffered. He had the habit, according to Assistant-Secretary Ed Horne, of taking a rather violent form of exercise each day, chinning up and down a bar he had set up above the doorway of his office. Perhaps owing to such unwise exertions, he was suddenly taken ill and died of a heart-stroke on September 27, 1928, at the age of sixty-six.

Edward Flore, like almost everyone else, in his memorial speech for Sullivan voiced the deep and abiding respect in which the Secretary had been held by the members, and attributed to him exclusively the credit for having laid the solid economic foundations of the Hotel and Restaurant Employees and Bartenders Union, without which it could not have endured.

He was to be known always as their union's "master builder." Thus the contribution of this able and colorful, if rather sardonic and crusty, man strikingly paralleled that of Samuel Gompers on the greater stage of the American Federation of Labor. Sullivan had been a lifelong admirer of the tough-minded Gompers and had embraced his practical and sometimes opportunistic philosophy of the labor movement. Like Gompers he had brought order and a degree of economic strength where, in earlier years, there had been principally confusion and weakness; and like him also, in his later years, Jere L. Sullivan was reluctant to change old usages and policies adapted to the circumstances of an earlier era, although new industrial methods were changing everything under the very feet of the trade unionists.

EIGHT

The Great Depression

*"I would never live through the depression again. I
would shoot myself rather than take again what we
had then!"*—A CHICAGO WAITER (quoted in W. F.
Whyte: *Human Relations in the Restaurant Industry*).

On the death of Jere L. Sullivan, President Flore promptly called a
meeting of the General Executive Board, which was empowered to
elect a new Secretary-Treasurer in his place.

Vice-President Robert B. Hesketh and Vice-President Hugo Ernst
were both nominated at the Board meeting in Cincinnati in October,
1928; the eight members were evenly divided in their choice and for
a time there was a deadlock.

Hesketh, a sort of elder statesman of the International Union and
a member of the GEB for twenty-four years, had built up in Seattle
one of the strongest local organizations in the union. Like other local
leaders he had combined a political career with trade unionism, having served for many years as a member of the Seattle City Council. A
jovial and keen Scotsman, Hesketh, at this period, had the reputation
of being a staunch trade-unionist who had done much to help all
union labor in Seattle. Possibly he had "stayed in politics too long,"
as his friends said later; for the decade of the 20's in Seattle was not
distinguished for virtue in public office. In any case he was now eager
to leave his home city, assume a high office in the union he had long
served and settle down in Cincinnati. There had been reports that he

was even planning to run against Flore for the presidency at about the time when Sullivan died and the Secretary's office became vacant.

Ernst, though representing a much larger local unit and considered the more inspiring personality of the two, was certainly less middle-of-the-road than "Bob" Hesketh. In the end, the prudent Flore, presiding over the GEB, cast the deciding vote for Hesketh. Ernst, then fifty and in the prime and vigor of life, might have made a most forward-looking Secretary. His progress up the trade union ladder was long retarded, however, by associates who never doubted that he had brains and character. Flore in later years would regret his choice of Hesketh. In defending his decision in a letter written at the time to one who had urged the selection of Ernst, he said he had decided not to vote for him "because of his long and close personal friendship with Hesketh." Actually they had not been on very close terms.[1]

Ed Flore had been looking over the field for a long time. Now his hands were free and he made ready to overhaul the International's structure and launch a series of organizing drives. His first move was to bring into play some of the San Francisco talent he had found on his trip to California in 1927. In December, 1928, August J. Van Bebber, business agent of Local 44, was named an International organizer and set to work first in New York and later in the Chicago area, which had given the President so many headaches. In 1928 Ernst's old colleague, Jack Weinberger, of Local 30, was named an International Organizer in charge of the Northwestern states, his territory spanning the vast, sparsely populated region, 1,700 miles in breadth, between Portland and Seattle on the Pacific Coast and Minnesota. Weinberger's work as a local secretary showed outstanding business ability and a highly analytical mind. His was now a grueling task, involving constant travel by train to recruit small groups of culinary workers in hundreds of widely scattered communities. "I threw up my job three times in three months, but somehow I hung on," Weinberger recalled afterward. In truth no one else hung on so well, for during a period of several years, in the 1930's, he was to be retained as the union's only full-time organizer.

Under the late Jere L. Sullivan the International Union had moved so slowly that for a decade after the Eighteenth Amendment had been enacted, it still retained as part of its old name the words "Bartenders International Alliance"—which was unlawful. At the convention held in Kansas City, August 12-17, 1929, President Flore proposed that the organization, by an amendment to its constitution, change its name to *Restaurant Employees and Beverage Dispensers International Al-*

liance. The members, he argued, might as well reconcile themselves to the facts of life and recognize that the country was going to stay dry for a long time. The change in name would also keep the union in line with restrictive laws then prevailing in Canada also.

"An optimist is a bartender who pays his union dues," was one of Ed Flore's humorous quips on this occasion.

"Beverage Dispensers!" Forsooth! This measure was not passed without heated debate; many a manly bartender's breast burned with anger and shame at the thought of abandoning all hope of winning Repeal, or at least of continuing the fight for wine and beer. As one veteran mixologist cried out:

> You are about to close a chapter in the history of our great International.
> You are proposing to change the name we have had for the past twenty-five years. . . . But to change the title is to show a weakness on our part.

The learned delegate J. William Knispel, a waiter who affected a ribboned pince-nez and looked very much like an old-time gentleman and scholar of the labor movement, made reply by citing Shakespeare and argued, that "a rose by any other name would smell as sweet." And Vice-President John Kearney, the leader of Boston's old bartending battalions, sadly proclaimed: "The saloon will never be brought back!" (Actually, the return of the lawful saloon lay only four years in the future.)

Flore had good reason to raise his sights everywhere in 1928-1929. The country was in a boom, and no industry boomed and "busted" more than the hotel and restaurant industry. In 1919 the Pennsylvania Hotel opened in New York, with 2,200 rooms and about 2,000 employees, as "the world's largest hotel." In Chicago, by 1928, the mammoth Stevens, with its almost 3,000 rooms, dwarfed the Pennsylvania. Everywhere skyscraper hotels were rising in our urban centers. The growing restaurant trade, featured by "automatic" or self-service cafeterias and lunch-counters, was also thriving and recruited new legions of workers. Americans were spending money freely in eating and drinking establishments, the U. S. census report for 1929 showing a sales volume of more than $2,124,000,000. Thus catering had become a giant industry. To be sure the big units in the restaurant field were still the exception rather than the rule, and the business itself was notably competitive and risky. Yet the marked growth of the trade gave the union leaders much ground for hope of expansion.

In his good-humored memoirs, *Hotel Splendide*, Ludwig Bemelmans, the waiter turned author and artist, has pictured the mood of fine, careless rapture that possessed not only the well-heeled clients of our de luxe hotels but even the service workers who waited upon them during the bonanza days of the late 20's. Everyone, literally, was making money quickly by gambling in the stock market, which did nothing but soar continually toward the stratosphere. In the "Hotel Splendide" (pseudonym of the Fifth Avenue hostelry he worked in) there was, and doubtless still is, on one of the upper floors a dining room for private parties which, with the aid of removable partitions and folding doors, could accommodate a banquet of sixty persons or a gay and intimate little party of four.

Men important in business or with positions of responsibility in Washington met here, and in the course of one evening a violent change would come over them. They arrived with dignity and they looked important and like the photographs of them published in the newspapers, but in the late hours they became "Joe" or "Stew" or "Lucius." Sometimes they fell on their faces and sang into the carpet. Leaders of the nation, savants and unhappy millionaires suffered fits of laughter, babbled nonsense and spilled ashes and wine down their shirt fronts. Some of them became ill. Others swam in a happy haze and loved all the world.

On such a party, a drunken financier would throw one arm about a senator and hang the other arm around a judge's neck. Then the three would back onto a soft sofa. The financier would shout: "Waiter! Hey, waiter! Pencil and paper. Oh, where is that goddamned waiter?"

The waiter was nearly always ready with a pencil and pad such as he used for orders, and with a carbon sheet tucked inside the pad. After the guest had written his note and torn it off the pad, the waiter would ask for the pad again and go off behind a screen to study the meaning of the message written upon it in duplicate. "The tender plant of morality does not thrive in a grand hotel," Bemelmans explains, "and withers altogether in its private rooms." Sometimes the information thus obtained was of no value; sometimes, by means of the carbon paper in the pad the ever hopeful waiter had information for which big bankers and statesmen might have given their eyeteeth. But if the guests got drunk enough, one didn't even need a pad of paper.

There was always one who, at the high point of the proceedings, backed the maître d'hôtel, a favorite waiter, or the wine steward against the bar and said: "Ambrose, I am going to make you rich!

. . . Now listen, Ambrose" he said and both his hands came down upon Ambrose's shoulders like two hammers. Ambrose's knees gave way and he was pinned against the bar. . . . Slowly, thoroughly, as if for an idiot, it was explained to him what stock to buy and when to sell. . . .[2]

In this fashion, Bemelmans tells us, he, like other banquet waiters, "became rich several times." It was not unusual, after a gay dinner party of this type, for a bus boy or a waiter to make a thousand or five hundred dollars overnight. Information gained in this way usually leaked out through the grapevine from the banquet department until it was shared by all the staff of the hotel, from basement to roof. Thus the "Wall Street fever" hit the hotel workers and waiters so that it was sometimes hard to keep them working steadily during the market boom. Many of the roving waiters who migrated from New York to Saratoga and to Palm Beach in the winter had always loved to play the horses; but in 1929 they played Cities Service and Radio and General Motors.

Doubtless these stock-gambling banquet waiters were but few in number compared with the great majority who earned only $2.75 a day and their tips, and had to support a family. But they were symptomatic of the extravagant mood that gripped the moneyed classes frequenting the "grand hotels."

No one has ever succeeded in giving us a reliable estimate of the sums spent by the public in speakeasies and illicit night clubs during the bootleg era. Many of these establishments by 1929 were also able to serve good food at reasonable prices because of their profits on liquor and beer, whereas the law-abiding "dry" restaurants lost business. Hence great numbers of first-class cooks and waiters accepted employment in blind pigs—with an effect that made the problem of union organization more baffling than ever.

Many bartenders, with the coming of Prohibition, had unhesitatingly gone to work in the speakeasies, as we have noted, believing that the general public supported their view of the case. Some of these, at any rate, maintained membership in their old local unions, though the union could do nothing for them now in the matter of wages and conditions.

How could one negotiate a labor agreement with people who flouted all laws and all contracts? How could one present the grievances of the workers or call a strike against employers who glared at you through a peephole, gun in hand?

In Chicago, where rum- and beer-running had become an efficiently managed business, controlled by a select group of gangster overlords, the workers in speakeasies and usually their local unions, too, came under the sway of the racketeers. Hugo Ernst had found much cause for complaint against one Chicago local in 1923. In May, 1928, he joined Vice-Presidents Hesketh and Lehman in Chicago, where, as a committee for the GEB, they swooped down upon Waiters Local 7, Chicago. After looking the place over, they firmly recommended that the charter be immediately revoked, that a new charter be issued to Chicago waiters, and that their members be examined carefully so that "undesirables" might be kept out. The new local (called No. 25) was forbidden to keep its headquarters in a building where booze was dispensed or games of chance were played.

On the strict understanding that "no liquor was to be sold or gambling tolerated in its premises," another new local made up of speakeasy bartenders was also given a charter in December, 1928, thanks to the organizing efforts of George B. McLane, a veteran Chicago union member. Although McLane himself was reported now to be the owner of a profitable speakeasy, he, at first, seemed to confine the small new Bartenders Local 278 (with but 137 members in 1929) to legitimate union business.[3]

According to one account:

> The gangsters who supplied the speakeasies naturally learned of the loyalty most bartenders had for their union. If that loyalty could be utilized to push their particular bootleg product it would eliminate much of the selling problem; and so they deliberately set out to capture bartenders' locals and use their membership.[4]

But this curious development really took place some years later toward the end of the Prohibition era, or shortly after Repeal (in 1933). In the meantime the local of Chicago speakeasy bartenders remained quite small; the new waiters' local, No. 25, had scarcely 400 members on its roster in 1929. This was also the case in New York, where the recently chartered Captains and Waiters Local, No. 16, whose members worked in the illicit night clubs of the Times Square theatre district, after four years of organizing effort had no more than 182 members. The union could really do nothing for its members in this industry of outlaws, except by permission of the racketeers.

The obstacles in the way of unionizing the speakeasies are shown by one incident that took place in Detroit at about this period. In the huge city of motor factories, a few minutes' journey from the Canadian border, the liquor trade was in flourishing condition and boasted the best whisky and beer in the United States, most of it being smuggled from Canada. To earn their bread the cooks and waiters had, for the most part, gone to work in downtown Detroit's (estimated) 1,500 blind pigs. Yet, though they earned a living of sorts, the workers were unhappy; they were forced to toil long hours under unsanitary conditions, but dared not speak of their grievances before the rough-handed employers. According to Louis Koenig, the veteran secretary of Waiters and Waitresses Local 705, Detroit, the speakeasy restaurant proprietors "did not pay any wages to their waiters and waitresses, arguing that the men and women got enough in tips." Yet without fixed wages (which represented usually a third or a fourth of his earnings from tips) the waiter might go entirely penniless during a spell of bad weather.

After hearing many complaints and pondering a great deal over what a union man could do against people who used Thompson submachine guns to settle arguments, the peppery Koenig suddenly decided to go into action.

One day early in 1931, newspaper readers of Detroit rubbed their eyes with astonishment on reading about an uprising of men and women who served food in speakeasies:

THOSE IRRESPONSIBLE BLIND PIG WAITERS

The blind pig waiters of Detroit went on strike last week and just to demonstrate their sincerity and determination threw a picket line around a recalcitrant drinking place Friday night and almost started a riot.

One waiter had not received his weekly wages and refused to go to work. The handling of wages was said to be "unorthodox" or "irregular" in certain drinking stations. The waiter reported the matter to business agent Louis Koenig of the Waiters and Waitresses Local 705 and Koenig took action.

"I decided to picket the place," he stated, "and show those fellows where they belong."

Two men and three women were sent over with orders to keep the public outside. What followed illustrated the serious hazards of such unorthodox union action. The proprietor of the place, embarrassed at having his address advertised, opened the door and called one of the men on picket duty to come inside for a little conference.

Koenig related to reporters:

As soon as he got inside someone hit him in the face; he is now at the dentist's getting his teeth fixed up.

The women screamed . . . a crowd collected. Then the police came along and the joint was closed up.

In commenting on the affair, Koenig said:

"It's all a matter of principle with us. All over town these illegitimate blind pigs are hiring waiters and waitresses without paying them."

"What do you mean by 'illegitimate' blind pigs?" he was asked.

"Well, those fly-by-night places that don't even bother to get restaurant or beverage licenses. They open up in dirty and unsightly places, and serve poisonous beer and liquor. They don't pay fixed wages of any kind." [5]

Louis Koenig, described by the newspapers as "dour and honest," thus helped to bring the whole problem of the ill-treatment of workers by their lawless employers out into the open. It was the police authorities of Detroit who entered the most serious objections to the picketing of speakeasies, holding that the union agents were acting unlawfully in trying to organize persons "engaged in an illegal business." What the police really objected to was the publicity created by the pickets posted in the street before supposedly "secret" resorts that were doing a wide-open business—with the complete tolerance of the police. But Koenig answered stoutly that his union was not concerned with the enforcement or violation of the Prohibition laws, but with protecting its members.[6] At any rate, Mayor Frank Murphy of Detroit (later a Justice of the U. S. Supreme Court) was friendly to labor and did nothing to halt the campaign of Local 705, which continued to grow in membership, despite the demoralizing conditions in its industry.[7]

*

With great zeal Flore from 1925 to 1930 attacked once more the difficult job of organizing New York; he had tried it about twelve years earlier, but had been blocked by Jere L. Sullivan. The great trouble here was that official unionism in this trade, as one local organizer well phrased it, was "a sort of hybrid between employment office and job trust." The long-established Waiters Local 1, which had 2,000 members, a treasury, and prestige, as always refused admission to competent craftsmen coming from out of town with traveling cards. It would not expand for its own part, and would not allow other locals in the city to develop the field. Thus in a city of nearly 7,000,000 souls and some 30,000 eating-places, the existing HRE locals fought each other continually—instead of going after the employers —and had less than 4,000 members in all.

At the end of 1925 the new Local 16 had been chartered with jurisdiction over the restaurants in the mid-town theatre district. Two years later, J. William Knispel, an old-time waiter and local officer, on being elected Secretary, headed an organizing drive in the Broadway mid-town section, but soon came into collision with the officers of Local 1—and quite literally so. His Local 16's members had won an agreement with three large restaurants, but found agents of Local 1 also negotiating agreements with these establishments. When the Local 16 men came to work they were prevented from entering the restaurants, as Knispel said with evident understatement, "through the application of physical force."

Once more, the patient, long-tried President Flore had to come down to New York to settle the matter. He marked out zones on the map of the Borough of Manhattan placing Local 1 east of Fifth Avenue, and Local 16 to the west of it, and bounding both at certain streets to the north and south. But Local 16—after the well-intentioned Knispel was supplanted as Secretary—was to go from bad to worse, since its members and officers operated in the racketeer-ridden night-club center of the city.

A more serious effort was also made by Flore to organize New York's cafeteria workers through Local 302, specially chartered for that purpose in 1925. Here, too, Local 1, under Lehman, powerful in the councils of the New York Joint Board, provided much opposition, claiming the right to expand into the cafeteria business itself, through a branch of its own organization. In 1928, it was arranged that Max Pincus, a former business agent of Local 1, become the Secretary of the Cafeteria Employees Union Local 302; and, with Flore's support, he made some effort to organize the field. But Local 302 had only a few hundred members up to 1929. A much greater number of the cafeteria people were in the independent, left-wing union—now called the Amalgamated Food Workers Union—which for years, under different names and ideological programs, and different leaders also, had stood as a rival of the AFL union in New York.

Finally Flore's revived organizing staff set to work building up a new cooks' local, possessed of a charter, since 1926, which designated it as Cooks Local Union No. 719. In this department there was also a large unorganized field of highly skilled and semi-skilled craftsmen, though here again the dual union of cooks offered serious competition. Local 719 of the HRE had accumulated about 500 members by 1929, when one day a disloyal officer of the local, after having managed to create disaffection among the members, suddenly walked out, taking with him most of the people enrolled in that local into the Amalgamated Food Workers Union.

This unhappy turn of events, which followed the expenditure of much effort and money by the HRE, gives the measure of the troubles besetting those men of good will who hoped to unify the catering trade workers of New York. The left-wing rival, moreover, called a general strike in New York in the spring of 1929 that was featured by mass demonstrations. Their followers among the cafeteria and kitchen workers were by now full of anger and bitterness, for as one of their spokesmen related, wages in cafeterias were still only $12 a week for bus boys; $13 a week for dishwashers; and $25 and $30 for cooks and countermen. He added:

> The rule in the cafeteria is the twelve-hour day. The few who work less than eighty hours a week are the fortunate exceptions. Unsanitary conditions, affecting the health of workers and customers alike are scandalous.[8]

It was during the disturbances of the May, 1929, strike of the Amalgamated Food Workers Union that the HRE's cooks of Local 719 had decamped, convinced that the AFL union moved all too slowly to help them. At this period the independent union offered the most ruthless competition to the Hotel and Restaurant Employees, the members of the rival organizations sometimes slugging it out in the streets of New York.

In the HRE's cafeteria Local, No. 302, several members had gone out on strike without authorization from their local, at the time of the Food Workers' walkout. Charges were filed against these members who, at hearings before President Flore, openly admitted their affiliation with the rival union and with the Communist party, whereupon their expulsion from the International Union was ordered, and later sanctioned by convention vote in 1929.[9]

In 1929, Flore seriously turned his attention to the problem of communism as posing a new threat to the official trade union movement in the catering industry. For some years now, he was informed, communist leaders had taken command of the independent unions formerly sponsored by the old IWW and other groups.

In the forty years of their history members of the AFL-affiliated catering trade union had seen radical, utopian and "revolutionary" groups of all sorts come and go in the labor movement. The "dream" of bringing about some day a state of perfect social justice by organized political and economic action is indigenous to working-class movements. Under Gompers, who expounded his own shrewd brand of "practical idealism," the official trade union movement carefully refrained from such "dreaming," and made the best terms it could, within the existing economic system, for the skilled or steady type of workers. The typical AFL craft union member, it has been observed, really gave up both his "American dream" of winning fortune and his radical "dream" of a great revolution, and asked of his union job security and "pork chops," or good wages and hours.

But where the official labor movement had not done its job well, where it had ignored large masses of the unorganized and exploited workers, these, out of desperation, in regularly recurring cycles would flock to the banners of the radical crusaders who appeared to lead them. Yet when the radicals met with unforeseen obstacles and came to grief, as often happened, the official trade unions, thanks to their powers of endurance, their steady organizations and financial means, usually ended up by taking over the remnants of the distressed radical groups, added them to their own membership and continued steadily on their way, as before. This was to be the destiny of the Hotel and Restaurant Employees, as of other unions of moderate doctrines which, at repeated intervals (as in the case of the IWW branches), absorbed or swallowed up the radically directed unions that appeared for a time to challenge them in their field.

The communists, a quarter of a century ago, were regarded by the "regular" trade unions simply as one more small radical group, rather than as the wicked and traitorous conspirators they are now generally alleged to be. Though they were exponents of industrial unionism and mass action, they differed from the "native Reds" of the IWW in that they gave allegiance to the Soviet-dominated Third International. But Russia seemed much farther away in the 1920's than now. Their labor policy, for several years prior to 1928, under the direction of William Z. Foster, had tended to avoid setting up dual unions and bringing on head-on conflicts with existing organizations of conservative type. The hope was to "bore from within" and, eventually, win control of these AFL unions without destroying them in the process.

In the culinary trade of the great cities such as New York and Chicago, the leaders of the "moderate" AFL unions saw with regret that many ill-educated foreign-born workers knew no better than to join unions that had come under communist sponsorship. These poor dishwashers of New York knew little or nothing about Marxism, but they knew that they were working twelve hours a day for $13 a week —and that International Vice-President William Lehman, head of the rich Waiters Local No. 1, AFL, would do nothing for them. In truth there was for years a sort of armistice between the AFL craftsmen-waiters in New York and the radical union, which confined itself chiefly to organizing the less-skilled employees of cafeterias and hotels.

But in the years 1928-1929 the communists' policy suddenly veered about sharply, as it so often and puzzlingly did, and their followers who had split off from the Amalgamated Food Workers formed dual unions which offered direct competition with the Hotel and Restaurant Employees. They raised money by sale of the Amalgamated's headquarters building on Fifty-first Street, and used it for organizing campaigns and strikes in behalf of the newly formed Food Workers Industrial Union. As related in the book *Growth of a Union*, by two former officers of the FWIU, its organizing efforts

> included cafeteria workers, and in [May] 1929 it had felt strong enough to call a general strike in the cafeteria industry. Local 302, HRE, which had made no effort to organize cafeteria workers up to then, saw opportunities to increase the scope of its influence and promptly got jurisdiction from the International Union (AFL) in this field.[10]

On May Day, 1929, the left-wing group organized a large parade of cafeteria and food workers, in which several thousand persons participated, under the banner of the Food Workers Union. Such an impressive demonstration spread gloom in the Cincinnati headquarters of the Hotel and Restaurant Employees, especially when it was contrasted with the inactivity or apathy of the regular AFL locals in this field.

The Food Workers, under the militant leadership of Michael Obermeier and Samuel Kramberg, called strikes against hundreds of establishments in the mid-town New York area, and in the crowded garment center where there were many union sympathizers. The tactics of "mass action" were used by the left-wing union, creating high excitement in the busy streets and ending up with many arrests by the police. Court injunctions were issued against the radical union, but hundreds of members violated the injunction orders, submitted to mass arrest and were jailed.

In some cases cafeteria employers signed union shop agreements with the FWIU; but in others they were inspired to sign agreements with the Hotel and Restaurant Employees Local 302, which, after doing little or nothing for many years, intervened actively in the 1929 strike as a competitor of the left-wing union. Thus there were frequent street fights between representatives of the two labor groups and some court suits as well.[11] But thousands of the unorganized, lower-grade culinary and hotel workers, whom Flore had hoped to win over, were now joining the left-wing union, and hundreds of members of the HRE were deserting their locals to join the rival group. According to statements made by William Z. Foster, the communist-led unions had several thousand adherents, but a hard core of no more than 1,500 members in good standing; though small in actual numbers, they seemed able to stir up from 5,000 to 10,000 in organizing strikes.*

*

On coming to New York in the spring of 1929 to study the situation, President Flore had become convinced that the communist rivals must be handled with stern measures. Abe Borson, the business agent of Local 302, HRE, had informed him that the executive board of the local had a majority of communists, but that he managed to circumvent them by going over their heads and appealing to the rank and file. Flore had the power to expel union members for unbecoming conduct, but not, as yet, on grounds of their political beliefs or affiliations.

President William Green and the AFL Council were highly aroused over the communist issue at a period when the rest of the country, feeling itself at ease and secure, refused to take it seriously. There had been a very costly internal struggle between left and right factions in the AFL's big Ladies Garment Workers Union, and, in some degree, in the United Mine Workers Union also. Now drastic measures were prepared for the expulsion of the communist partisans, which Flore laid before the 1929 convention of the HRE at Kansas City.

This convention was a relatively small gathering of only 162 delegates representing 96 locals (out of 260 in good standing). A notable change in the composition of the delegates—and of the atmosphere—

---

* From 1921 to 1928, according to W. Z. Foster, the policy of the communists in the labor movement had been to work within established unions. But under the new policy of the so-called Trade Union Unity League, a department of the C. P., vigorous efforts were made to set up new or dual unions where the official union in the field was weak or had failed to bring in the unorganized workers. Some headway was made toward this end in the textile and needle trades, in the mining and maritime industries, and in the "food industry," including restaurants, bakeries and confectionery workers.

Foster's maximum claim is to communist "influence," toward 1929, over about 7 per cent of the going labor movement, though this appears to have been an exaggeration. Actual membership in unions organized by the C. P. in the 1920's has been estimated by others at no more than 1 to 2 per cent of the 4,000,000 union workers in the United States. The communists, however, asserted their influence more effectively after the depression began to be felt in 1930-1933. (*From Bryan to Stalin*, by W. Z. Foster, p. 229 ff. International Publishers, New York, 1937.)

was indicated by the presence of a large minority of forty enthusiastic women local officers. It no longer looked like the old "Bartenders Union."

At this gathering also, a further amendment to Section 112 of the Constitution was adopted, to permit the General President both to appoint and to supervise the organizers, as Flore had long desired. This was not accomplished without the covert resistance of the new Secretary, Hesketh, who had hoped to run things much like Jere L. Sullivan. But the convention's Law Committee, in which John Book-jans and Jack Weinberger played a leading part, strongly recommended an end to the system of divided responsibility, and the convention voted accordingly.

Their difference in 1929 over who was to hold authority over the paid organizers caused ill-feeling between Hesketh and Flore; thus for years, as in the time of Jere Sullivan, the bitter spirit of faction at the top level was a permanent feature of the union. Flore had shown himself on this occasion stubbornly determined to assume full command of the International. Thereafter the two worked separately at their tasks, Hesketh handling the administrative and financial business in Cincinnati, while Flore resided in Buffalo, but cruised all about the country adjusting local union troubles and directing membership campaigns.

The liveliest sessions of the Kansas City convention of 1929 were those given to debate over the disciplining of communists in the union. It was a discussion carried on in much more enlightened and civilized terms than are used nowadays, one that was wholly without the fear and hysteria aroused by this issue in later years.

To deny any worker the right to the protection of membership in a labor union appeared a punishment too drastic to the men of 1929. Therefore, Flore's original proposal of expulsion was amended finally so that it read:

> No member holding office in any dual association, or society that in any way whatsoever seeks to engage in similar functions as our local unions . . . shall be eligible for six months thereafter to hold office within our local unions.

To the idea of expulsion many delegates had expressed vehement opposition, Delegate Michael Wolf of Local 2, Brooklyn, saying he disapproved of it

> not because of sympathy with the Communist party, but because of the danger it may be to our organization. I never favored making a big thing out of nothing. We should not show the Communists

we are afraid of them. We don't want to recognize the Communists, we don't want to bother them and we don't want to make big fellows out of them.

Vice-President Ernst then spoke with an air of deep conviction and with great force. His voice, despite his European accent, had a low and pleasing pitch but could rise to great volume:

DELEGATE ERNST: I am fully in accord with the sentiments expressed by Delegate Wolf in regard to the part of the President's report . . . which recommends that this convention go on record to expel anyone in our International who sees fit to disagree with us on policies and politics.

The right of an individual member to believe as he sees fit is sacred and inviolate. The locals have full autonomy and can deal with any individual who may commit an overt act, but I deny anyone, be it the AFL, or our own International or the courts of this country, the right to punish anyone for his beliefs. This country is based on freedom of thought, freedom of speech and freedom of the press. If you start to abridge any part of these three essential pillars of our democratic institutions you will tear down the whole structure and whether you know it or not . . . bring us back to the dark ages.

I believe with Voltaire, who said: "I disagree with every inch of this matter you have submitted to me, but I will fight to the last drop of my blood to bring it before the people and allow you to express your opinion." I disagree with Communism, but I hate to see this body go on record to deny the Communists the right to their own foolish notions as long as they do not hurt me. When they do hurt, there is ample provision in our laws to deal with them.

In debate Ernst proceeded with strong logic and was quick to seize the weak points or contradictions in his adversary's argument. He called attention to a passage in Flore's report wherein the President remarked that he had finished writing it on July 4, Independence Day, which reminded him that this very nation was conceived in 1776 by an "act of protest." Flore had observed further that

The right to protest is as sacred today as it was in the days of '76. The established order . . . is never so perfectly fashioned that it cannot be improved. And the established order changes only as those who live under it protest against its imperfections, its mistakes, its injustices.

Ernst pointed out that the President's recommendations were not in accord, in this case, with his own excellent statements on the need to preserve the liberty of petition or protest. Any organization that could not withstand criticism was not on a sound footing. He concluded his long speech:

> Today you may disagree with a man you term a Communist; tomorrow you may disagree with me and say that I am a Communist, which I deny. You may point out that I, by reading a certain pamphlet which deals with Communism have injured the organization, and out I go. I don't believe in that. . . .
>
> Local 30 had some Communists. We did not throw them out, but we made loyal citizens of them. We showed them that our organization was preferable to the C. P. and now they are good members. So I beg of you, brothers and sisters, not to be carried away by sentiment, but to be rational, calm and cool in your decision on this matter. You are doing harm by passing . . . legislation of this kind. I want to emphasize to you, lest I be misunderstood, that I have absolutely nothing in common with the Communists. Neither my ideas, nor my ideals jibe with the Communists', but I would "fight to the last drop of my blood" to protect them in their right to their theories and then knock them on the head whenever they did anything to harm our organization.[12]

Kovaleski of Rochester, Flore's old ally, objected, warning the delegates "not to be carried away by the eloquence of Brother Ernst, with whom I have always disagreed on politics." The AFL had already taken drastic action against the communists, holding that there was no room in the labor movement for men who carried the cards of the C. P. Other delegates who asserted that they had been fighting the communists for years argued that it was wiser not to make martyrs of them. Jack Abrams, of Local 25, Chicago, made the interesting reflection that the crusading zeal or "fanaticism" of these latter-day radicals could be turned to account by practical-minded union officers. No one should be punished for being more radical or conservative than his fellows, he held, saying:

> Educate them. See if you cannot prevent them from becoming members of some dual union.
>
> In Chicago we have a member who is an outspoken Communist. I have always felt that on account of the rotten conditions that existed in that city he helped the situation to some extent. Of course I always have my eye on that man, and when I think he is going too far I am ready to step on his neck and squash him.[13]

Others, however, such as Delegate Harry Fox, of Local 337, Wyoming, supported Flore's idea of expulsion, declaring that the communists were "sailing under false colors" and "poisoning" the International Union and other organizations. "I want a clear-cut declaration,

I want the word to go out to the catering industry that we are going to clean our ranks of the members of the Communist party."

It was Vice-President "Jack" Kearney of Boston, however, who helped win the convention delegates to support the amendment narrowing the original resolution. To expel anyone merely because of his "faith" or because he belonged to a communist political organization was "too strong." Though he, like Flore, was a devout Catholic in religion, Kearney tended at this period to speak lightly of the "communist menace."

> Samuel Adams, James Otis, John Hancock and Paul Revere were all Communists years ago, and the British Government came in with its armies to suppress the Communists of those days. . . . Sam Gompers, according to the Chamber of Commerce, was a Communist for forty years. The American Federation of Labor, according to the Manufacturers' Association is a Communistic organization. I remember the time in my state legislature when some fellow of progressive ideas got up and we called him a "Red." That settled him.
>
> Communists have a right in this country and they have a right to disagree with Kovaleski and Flore and others. . . .[14]

This was in 1929, a quarter of a century ago, when Americans of all walks of life believed that issues such as communism should be discussed with common sense and without emotionalism.

President Flore, observing that the liberals in the union were present in force, spoke forth once more in behalf of his resolution. His opponents, he said tactfully, had displayed great eloquence and provided a "wonderful education" for the delegates. They had urged that it was a question to be handled by the local unions. However, he was for taking action at the International Union level. Nobody, he said, was going to molest anyone "who simply says he is a communist or merely expressed some radical thoughts." But, he insisted:

> . . . When it comes down to the trade union movement, when it comes down to the question of protecting the rights of working men and women, I say we have a right to declare here and now whether we want those people who are coming into our organizations to wreck them and for no other purpose.
>
> Let us have a clear and definite action here, so that when press reports of the proceedings go out they will not say that the Hotel and Restaurant Employees International Alliance is either in favor of Communism or that it is straddling the question.
>
> Let us say that we are opposed to Communism, that we are opposed to allowing communists to come into our organizations, and

give the man you will put into office as your General President—
where he finds a man or woman who is trying to destroy our organization and acknowledges affiliation with the Communist party—
the power to expel that man or woman from the organization.

Give us a chance to teach the men and women coming into the
labor movement that Communism does not mean anything for the
advancement of the workers.[15]

The earnestness of Flore's final appeal apparently carried the day;
for the resolution, amended by the committee reporting on it, was
passed—barring the election of union officers who had been affiliated
with "dual organizations" for a period of six months after they had
severed connections with the other union. The debate had been conducted in a highly democratic manner; and the punishment voted
was a moderate one. The union delegates showed awareness of the
complexity of the issue and also the will to deal with it themselves,
without help from the outside.

*

A marked decline in employment in the restaurant and hotel trade
was reported by President Flore in the summer of 1929. With the
bursting of the Wall Street bubble in October of the same year, the
greatest economic depression ever experienced in American history
was formally ushered in (though in the early stages few foresaw the
depths it was to reach). The catering industry is one of the first to
feel the effects of a slump, especially in demand for luxurious service.
The round of banquets stops and the music dies. The dismissal of
culinary workers in first-class hotels and taverns becomes widespread.
As unemployment increased rapidly in 1930 many idle laborers from
factories that had shut down applied, as always before, at the doors
of restaurants and hotels where they hoped they would at least be
assured of food. In many towns where the local unions did not as
yet operate employment bureaus or assign jobs through a labor chief,
even veteran members were forced to wander from door to door looking for work.

Only yesterday our "Grand" or "Splendide" hotels had been the
scene of long-continued carnival. But overnight the scene shifted
and the revelers with money in their pockets were gone. The great
hotels were still serviced, cleaned, lighted and heated, but they were
more or less empty. Bemelmans, the literary waiter, in his book,
Hotel Splendide, recalls how he used to be posted, with a score of
other waiters, in a vast, columned dining-hall, all its tables gleaming
with white linen, and flowers upon them and polished silver. But

nothing happened. There would be no more than three or four lonely guests, in a palatial and mirrored room capable of seating five hundred, who had the wherewithal of a two-dollar breakfast or a three-dollar lunch. A pall of gloom hung over the place while the waiters, with their towels behind their backs, stood and waited, talking or whispering to each other sadly all day long.

There were some hard-working and thrifty waiters who had laid something by and were able to fend for themselves for a time; but great numbers were of the notoriously improvident type. As one experienced hotel supervisor described the old-timers who usually served as "extra men" at banquets:

> They have had good jobs in their time, a lot of them. But they have drunk so much whisky and played the horses all their lives, and they haven't got a dime at their stage of life, when they ought to be resting and taking it easy in a little house of their own somewhere out in the country.[16]

With their heavy maintenance and interest charges, the hotels, in such a season, quickly found themselves under pressure to reduce costs, and they began to lower wages and "stretch" their help. Even where the union was well entrenched hotels and restaurants used all means, in 1930-1933, to break the union.

For twenty years the Cleveland branch of the HRE had been considered one of the "bulwarks" of the union in the area east of the Rocky Mountains. Its veteran members had long enjoyed excellent relations with their employers, had the benefit of written agreements providing for the union shop in the better-class restaurants and hotels, and a better than average wage scale. But 1930 was different. Some weeks before the date when the current agreement with the Cleveland Hotels Association was subject to renewal (July 15), the officers of Locals 106 (waiters), 107 (waitresses) and 167 (cooks) mailed a new contract, as was customary, to the manager of the Cleveland Hotels Association. They assumed that they would soon hear from him and go into conference over its terms. But the date of expiration approached, after two weeks, and no answer was received by the union men. When they telephoned the office of the Association for an appointment they were told merely that the executives were "out." Then, as President Flore related:

> There came from a blue sky a tip that an ultimatum was to come from the Cleveland Hotels Association that all employees had to sign an *individual contract* or lose their jobs. We were unable to

get a hearing and accepted that evasion as confirming the rumor. . . .[17]

The so-called "individual contract," better known among union men as the "Yellow Dog" contract, provided that John Doe as employee was to enter into an agreement with the employer stipulating (in guarded terms) that he was to be hired only on an "open shop" basis. What it meant was that if he stayed in a labor organization, or joined one, he would be denied a job. Such anti-union contracts had aroused the most intense indignation among workers all over the country, who felt that they were clearly being forced thus to abandon their hard-earned right to bargain collectively.

The Cleveland Local Joint Board, then headed by Ed Whissemore of Local 106, barely had time to call a meeting and warn the 1,500 members to prepare for the expected storm. The members voted overwhelmingly to authorize a strike if their agreements were not renewed by July 14.

Two days after the union meeting, W. D. Madlin, Secretary of the Local Joint Board, received a letter from the Hotel Association curtly announcing a rupture of relations:

July 12, 1930

Dear Mr. Madlin:
    Please be advised that the Cleveland Hotels Association, Inc., will not continue, renew or enter into any contract or relations whatsoever with the local Association of Waiters, Waitresses and Cooks Unions.

    The Cleveland Hotels Association, Inc.
    (Signed) W. Stiles Koones, President

On July 14, each hotel in the Association handed its employees individually a letter and open shop contract more or less identical in wording. It declared that such and such a hotel desired to "deal directly" with the employee and that this would be of mutual advantage. Various conditions or work rules imposed for the workers' benefit, in the past, were now declared to have been "unsatisfactory." The employer promised that there would be no reduction in wages so long as the worker rendered courteous and satisfactory service. The letter concluded:

    Some union constitutions contain clauses forbidding their members' entering into individual contracts. We have no information as to whether or not your union has such provisions. Therefore, if and as long as you are a member of the union, we have no desire to cause you to break any such provision if one exists.

If you desire to continue in our employ and are satisfied that no such provision exists, we will be glad to enter into a contract with you individually (form of which we will show to you) to be effective beginning Thursday, July 15, 1930.[18]

Such was the all too clever device by which employers, combined in powerful organized groups, forced the worker, who was desperate for a job, to leave *his* union and negotiate alone, as a helpless individual, with the employers' "union." It was a system of inequity that has been condemned by some of the country's highest judicial authorities, and against which the American Federation of Labor had conducted a ceaseless agitation for ten years before Congress and the state legislatures.

The union members gathered again in an emergency meeting on July 14, 1930, and voted to ignore such individual contracts and return to work as if nothing had happened. That it was a deadly challenge, long prepared, and aimed at destroying the union in Cleveland was grasped at once by President Flore, Secretary Robert Hesketh and the other executive officers of the International. Flore had hurried over from Buffalo to address the meeting of July 14, and cautioned the members about the danger of accepting such a challenge in a season of depression. But he was soon convinced that, despite some minor disagreement, the majority of the members and their officers were utterly determined to resist to the bitter end the concerted campaign to break up their long-established union.

Powerful banking interests, holding mortgages on hotel properties in Ohio, it was learned, were behind this move to cut wages in the Cleveland hotels and break up the union. The HRE, therefore, had "a national fight on their hands," as Flore realized; indeed it was a fight for the entire labor movement. For if the Cleveland locals were destroyed, the same methods would be used against other well-organized city units, and against all labor organizations. The imposition of the Yellow Dog contract would reduce workers morally to the status of the pauper labor of the early nineteenth century.

The union men closed their ranks. Behaving with much self-restraint, the members tried to go back to work quietly, but were told in some instances that the dining rooms were "closed for repairs." In others, men who had worked for seventeen years at the same job were stopped and ordered to take their things out of their lockers and be gone, while crews of non-union white and colored workers moved in to take their places. Picketing began on July 15, 1930, not as a strike, but as a *lockout* contest precipitated by management. In all 300 workers were locked out.

Some forty to fifty pickets were posted before each of the six leading hotels of Cleveland. The hotel workers were promptly given the
unstinted support of the AFL's Central Labor Council, with the
teamsters', electrical workers', engineers', and musicians' unions that
also serviced hotels refusing to cross picket lines. "This is an open
shop fight, attacking all labor. If a wreck is coming we may as well all
go down in the wreck together," said the Secretary of the Cleveland
Central Labor Council.[19]

Flore bestirred himself to win financial support from the Council
of the American Federation of Labor, while Secretary Robert Hesketh
appealed to unions all over America for money. As the strike settled
down to a long endurance contest, the HRE's Executive Board allotted $50,000—and later $25,000 more—almost its entire defense
fund, to provide for pickets and strike relief. Though times were bad,
HRE local unions from Boston to San Francisco made large additional donations of money, with Waiters Local 30, under Hugo
Ernst, and Cooks Local 44 each contributing checks for $1,500.
President Daniel J. Tobin of the International Teamsters sent
Hesketh a sizable money donation from his union though half its
members were also out of work. In all, the sum of $126,000, very large
for such a local affair (raised almost entirely by the International and
its locals), was flung into the contest.

The Hotel and Restaurant Employees had never before appealed
to the AFL or any other unions for financial help. Yet, save for the
Teamsters, other unions seemed indifferent, or overwhelmed by
troubles of their own. Too many failed to understand what this small
affair of 300 locked-out men and women meant for American labor,
as Daniel Tobin said in a letter to Hesketh. But William Green himself came to Cleveland to speak at a rally of the hotel workers, for
the importance of the contest was increasingly evident to leaders of
the AFL.

While unemployment and actual hunger spread that winter, the
300 pickets held their lines solidly in Cleveland. Some of the struck
hotels carried on by serving simplified menus cooked by chambermaids or clerical personnel. But "scabs" and plain clothesmen and
uniformed police faced the union men, and though it was an orderly
affair on the whole, there were some small clashes and fisticuffs such
as flare up naturally in the heat of a tense industrial struggle. At one
lunch-hour fracas 99 union men and women were arrested; in all 300
arrests were instituted, or the total force of those locked out by the
employers.

Flore moved heaven and earth to reach the employers and win a reasonable settlement. In New York he approached the heads of several big hotel chains and urged them to use their good offices toward bringing about a conference between the two parties in Cleveland. But those gentlemen refused to intervene, implying that they were watching the course of events with deep interest. If the Cleveland employers won out, hotel management in other large cities would move at once to liquidate any labor organizations they dealt with.

Secretary Hesketh was a pillar of strength in this struggle, working effectively to gather funds, which was now quite difficult, and exhorting the local leaders to ever stronger effort. "You say you are *marking time?*" he said to one of the International Organizers posted in Cleveland. "I'm telling our folks you are battling like hell." [20] In Cleveland public-spirited citizens, churchmen and all the newspapers were won over as allies in a struggle against what the *Cleveland Citizen* termed "a most hypocritical attack on all labor organizations."

Flore and Hesketh, with the help of Dan Tobin and William Green, did particularly effective work in bringing political pressure to bear upon the hotel managers, both in Washington and in Ohio. In Congress the Norris-La Guardia bill, which, besides restricting the use of labor injunctions, incorporated a clause banning the "Yellow Dog" contract as discriminatory, made steady progress in gaining adherents and was finally enacted in March, 1932. Somewhat earlier, in the autumn of 1931, the Ohio State Legislature passed a similar act designed to discourage the inequitable use of "individual" contracts; other states, such as New York, New Jersey, Wisconsin and Oregon, followed suit. To the AFL must go the glory of having fought unremittingly for the Norris-La Guardia Anti-Injunction Act of 1932; but the Hotel and Restaurant Employees played a strategic role in the final stages of that campaign by arousing public opinion with regard to the ugly lockout situation in Cleveland. As Flore justly said later: "It was largely due to the resistance we offered that Ohio outlawed the 'Yellow Dog' contract."

In the summer of 1931 the appeals of Flore and other AFL leaders led to intervention in the contest by the Secretary of Labor at Washington, the Department of Labor's Conciliation Service being assigned to the task. President Hoover had been calling upon employers everywhere (though with small effect) to avoid actions that would add to the present distress and unemployment. In May and June, 1931, three of the hotels dropped their Yellow Dog contract, and soon the rest followed. Finally, in response to proposals from officials of the Department of Labor, W. S. Koones, head of the Cleveland

Hotels Association, issued a formal statement declaring that the use of "individual labor contracts" would be discontinued; discrimination against former employees would be avoided; and re-employment would be offered them "regardless of their union affiliations . . . whenever opportunity affords." [21]

The Cleveland lockout struggle thus ended quietly in late July, 1931, as what appeared to be a drawn battle. For twelve months the pickets had held their lines. The International Union had used up all its defense funds, and the local unions were broke also, and still no recognition and no union shop conditions were granted. But the attempt to smash the union and enforce the anti-union contract had been stopped at a vital point. For this alone, as the enthusiastic old Dan Tobin said, the battle was worth every cent it cost—the significant thing was that "it was the finest fight that was ever made in the labor movement."

When, a few months later, the Cleveland Hotels Association did not live up to its informal understanding with the Department of Labor's Conciliator, the HRE local unions of waiters, waitresses and cooks were still in business—instead of being extinct—and were able to bring pressure upon the employers to see that the agreement was observed. They are still there today.

*

The sweep of the depression, with unemployment at approximately 15,000,000 by 1932, engulfed whole unions in ruin. Prices of commodities fell steeply; wages were cut in 1931, and then again in 1932. Panic conditions continued, the catering industry being particularly depressed. You could buy a plate of ham and eggs in cheap Chicago lunchrooms for a dime in 1932.

At the 1932 convention of the International, President Flore reported somberly that whole chains of hotels, such as the "Ambassador" group, were bankrupt. "The Stevens Hotel with 2,400 rooms had only nine people staying there on Sunday, last week," another speaker reported.[22]

For union officers a great depression is a nightmare period of lost battles and forced retreats. Employers, in panic, were putting wage cuts into effect without regard to existing union contracts; and the workers, who were demoralized, submitted. Their unions seemed virtually powerless to help them. "Those were really terrible years," Jack Weinberger wrote afterward. "Our locals were crumbling away like everything else."

Weinberger, one of the two International Organizers left on the payroll (out of a staff of twelve to twenty) remembers "running here and there and everywhere" in the spring of 1932, to Duluth and St. Paul and back to Vancouver, B. C., while "trying to hold his thumb in the dyke." Faced with demands for excessive wage cuts the local members sometimes tried to rebel, though there was no chance to carry on a strike for long with whole armies of desperately hungry workers ready to serve as "scabs." Hence the International's officers and organizers worked feverishly to bring about compromise agreements to stave off strikes.[23]

In New York and Chicago one heard of waiters being reduced to $5 a week, or even nothing a week but their meals and such tips as they could garner in these lean times. But even in cities where the union had been powerful, successive wage cuts were accepted in 1931 and 1932. Where the members, as in the case of one large San Francisco cafeteria chain known as the Leighton Corporation, voted to reject such wage cuts, the firm often went into involuntary bankruptcy, with the result that 138 of Leighton's unionized employees went to the soup-lines. Thus the union officers, like Hugo Ernst, caught between two fires—of the employers in funk and the workers in discontent—often struggled against their own union members to prevent actions that, in these critical times, would breed new disasters.[24]

In January, 1932, Vice-President Ernst, reporting from California, wrote:

> Demands for wage cuts are on the daily menu and right here in San Francisco we had to accept an additional cut in wages for all four locals, so that we go down into the new year with wages about ten per cent lower than the ones we had a year ago. And the so-called best houses are as badly hit as the Class B houses and perhaps worse. Two of our largest places where style and refinement were the order of things have closed their doors, one of them reopening subsequently as a dairy lunch, so that the field of employment for waiters has been still further restricted. . . . The dear sisters [waitresses] are also breaking into some of the departments of our catering industry. With unemployment rampant, wage scales trimmed all around, there is nothing of a cheerful tenor to report, except that our membership is standing up in good shape. . . . We are fortifying ourselves so that when times change for the better, we will be ready to swing the machinery into operation and regain lost ground. Let us hope this will come soon.[25]

Local 30, San Francisco, was one of the richest in the union, with reserve funds of about $15,000 in 1930. By 1932, this was all gone, since the members had voted to pay cash relief to the unemployed among them. Elsewhere the plight of the culinary workers was even more desperate than in San Francisco. As usual the San Francisco workers employed more inventiveness in contending with the disaster of unemployment than people elsewhere.

By 1932 public food relief, supplied in part by Federal and municipal government funds and in part by private charity, was organized on a large scale and dispensed through soup-lines at various public buildings in San Francisco as in most other cities in America. But the waiters bethought themselves of schemes for avoiding the soup-lines. At a meeting of Waiters Local 30 in 1932, a rank and file group proposed that their officers petition Mayor Rossi for a direct allotment of cash to the waiters' and cooks' union equal to the sums being expended for the same number of unemployed through public channels. The amount granted then for three simple meals for an unmarried person was reckoned at 35 cents per day and $4.50 per week for a family. Ernst, though skeptical of the success of such a petition, undertook to head a union committee of five that would present it at the City Hall.

At first Mayor Rossi objected that the proposal was improper, holding that "all must be treated alike." But Ernst made his plea with great force, arguing that his union members, who were accustomed to handling food, would feed more people and better than in the public soup-kitchens; and "we will do it in our own headquarters," he said. "It would be better for the dignity and self-respect of my people; they will be helping themselves." In the end the request was granted. The three HRE locals, Nos. 30, 44 and 110, organized "soup-barns" in their headquarters in which, all together, about 500 persons were fed three warm meals each day. In these cooperative kitchens the unemployed cooks and their assistants, who had formerly prepared epicurean repasts at de luxe hotels, devised simpler, though tasty and nourishing meals for their brothers, destitute as themselves —which were served most elegantly by the union's skilled waiters. Many of the idle members contributed to the variety of the union-made cuisine by roving about the produce markets and waterfront of San Francisco to gather in fresh fruit and vegetables, which they solicited as donations. And at night many of the single men who were homeless were given cots so that they might sleep in the union meeting halls. Thus the San Francisco union members fended for themselves, kept their people from being lost in the "jungles" and the "Hoovervilles" that sprang up near our great cities and ports. They managed to come through the years of the great depression better

nourished and with higher morale than most other groups that suffered severely from unemployment.[26]

The International Union was so impoverished in 1931 that the
biennial convention scheduled to be held in Boston that year was
postponed, by referendum vote, to August, 1932. A steady and heavy
fall in membership from 39,694 in January, 1929, to 27,481 in 1932—
and finally to a low point of 24,500 a year later, in 1933—greatly reduced revenues, as Secretary Hesketh reported. Officers' and organizers' salaries were cut by 10 per cent, and the organizing staff was
finally reduced at the end of 1932 to one man, Jack Weinberger.

Yet the Hotel and Restaurant Employees hung on better than
most unions, some of the strongest of which lost from 50 to 75 per
cent of their membership in the same three-year period. At the very
depths of the economic crisis, in which 10,000 banks closed their
doors, there was even some stirring of hope for the end of Prohibition
among the 100 delegates who were able to afford the trip to Boston
in 1932. In gloomy tones the magnates of the AFL, such as William
Green and Daniel J. Tobin, began by addressing the convention on
the fearful economic catastrophe that the whole country endured.
President Green, in an extended analysis of the depression, concluded
that it could only be defined as a "veritable social upheaval" whose
consequences none could foretell. The AFL, though formerly opposed to the "dole" or to welfare legislation by the Federal Government, now called for unemployment compensation, the establishment
of the five-day week by statute and, if need be, the six-hour day, so
that workers displaced by the introduction of labor-saving machinery
(as Green held) might be given employment.

Ed Flore, in a speech of unusual bitterness, declared that employers in the hotel and restaurant trade were violating their contracts
everywhere in defiance of all law and morality. The situation was
becoming a "revolutionary crisis." Like other AFL leaders he opposed
resorting to radical experiments in national planning, or "production
for use," as advocated by various theorists, but called for Federal and
state expenditures for public works. "The solution must come
[through] public money to business and industry that will divert the
same to channels providing work for the unemployed. . . ." This
much was already promised in the Democratic party platform
for 1932.

Tobin, the old ally of the culinary workers, spoke with much feeling of the virtual breakdown of the whole social structure during the
depression:

When men are out of work . . . when men are hungry they are almost impossible to reason with. . . . But the awful conditions that surround us, with almost thirty million human beings dependent upon charity in this glorious country of ours, are unreasonable. . . . Before we are through with this depression those who are responsible for this awful disaster to the industrial life of our nation may be forced to pay a price they did not reckon with when they began.

Law and order are being ignored everywhere; money and power and position are being scoffed at by the masses of the working-people—not by law-breakers but by men who have been forced to break laws to live. . . . I saw farmers in Indiana destroy eggs because they could not get a cent apiece for them while in the city people were starving. About five weeks ago there was a riot because of want of bread in St. Louis, while wheat and corn and vegetables were rotting in Indiana, Illinois, Missouri and Kansas. You do not have to be a mathematician to figure out that there must be something wrong in our present system.[27]

But in the ranks of labor there was now widespread expectation of an impending change in the Administration at Washington, and from this was derived a sense of fresh hope, of seeing at last "a light ahead," which the union's official paper had been announcing to the members in recent months. The HRE had been struggling against a depression not of three years but of thirteen years, since Prohibition had been enacted. But now, as Tobin prophesied in more cheerful tones, "I feel that your time will come in the near future." President Green of the AFL also brought the heartening news that public opinion in every part of the country now favored modification of the Volstead Act enforcing the Eighteenth Amendment. Soon wholesome beer would be sold everywhere in the United States, he predicted. But Democratic Mayor James Curley of Boston, who gave welcome to the union delegation, went even further by promising that the Democratic party would be swept into office in November. "We are going to modify the Volstead Act and we are going to repeal the Eighteenth Amendment." [28]

Throughout the summer of 1932, in many state capitals, officers of the International Union, such as Vice-President John J. Kearney of Boston, Jay Osborn of Denver, and Leslie Sinton of Minneapolis, had been lobbying busily for the early repeal of the Volstead Act. Indeed, Kearney, a member of the Massachusetts State Legislature for many years, helped to write the new enabling act that would restore alcoholic beverages to general use in his state. He and President Flore also bestirred themselves to win from the 1932 International convention an outright endorsement of the Democratic party and its presidential candidate, Governor Franklin D. Roosevelt of New York.

In August, 1932, the country was in the midst of a bitterly fought national political campaign. Ed Flore, arriving in Boston before the opening of the convention, had given an interview to the Boston newspapers that was displayed on their front pages under the title: "HEAD OF HOTEL MEN'S UNION URGES SUPPORT OF ROOSEVELT." He was quoted as saying:

> In the recent political conventions held in Chicago one party proposed a complex plan for solving the liquor and beer problem that none could understand. . . . As to the other party's program no difference of opinion can exist as to its meaning. It is undeniably wet. It favors the repeal of the Eighteenth Amendment.[29]

Though AFL unions traditionally avoided partisan commitments in political contests, Flore's resolution for the outright endorsement of the Democrats was presented before the convention with his enthusiastic support. With his customary verve and eloquence, Kearney championed the resolution. But Vice-President Farrell of Cleveland, who was a Republican now, and the veteran Kovaleski of Rochester stood in opposition. Hugo Ernst was also one of the leaders in the fight on the floor against the endorsement of Roosevelt—whom in later years he so greatly admired. "It would be a fatal mistake," he said, "for our organization to go on record officially for any party." By the narrow margin of 9 votes out of 214 the resolution fathered by Flore was defeated.*

The depression had changed many things. It still was to undergo its darkest hours in the winter of 1933. But the Hotel and Restaurant Employees' delegates ended their sessions in a mood of high hope. A poll of the states conducted that summer by the *Literary Digest* had shown that only two were still left in the "dry" column. The union members, like others, saw their long thirst approaching its end. That winter they would be busily preparing to initiate thousands of barmen.

Secretary Hesketh, who worked diligently and cheerfully during the worst days of the depression, sketched plans for new organizing drives in a report to the GEB of March 16, 1933. All the banks in

* President Flore and Secretary Hesketh were re-elected by unanimous vote. All other officers of the General Executive Board, as of 1929, were re-elected, save for Vice-President Kitty Donnelly of Cleveland, Ohio. The Vice-Presidents named were C. T. Frederick, William Lehman, J. M. Osborn, Hugo Ernst, Thomas S. Farrell, John J. Kearney, Leslie Sinton and Kitty Amsler of St. Louis, who succeeded Kitty Donnelly.

America were closed that week, but Hesketh could see a "gleam of sunshine ahead." He reflected:

> Spring is about here, summer not far off, and Beer to be pretty soon on "tap." Quite a cheerful response from many sections and large locals, saying: "We are with you in the Organizing Campaign."
>
> . . . We slipped a lot in the last three years. Now seems the opportunity to advance, to *come back*, as it were, and we must grab it with both hands.[30]

NINE

Rebirth: 1933-1934

"Continue to organize and collect upon the promissory note the Roosevelt Administration has passed out."—GOV. FLOYD B. OLSON of Minnesota, to 1934 Convention.

Although by 1933 the HRE was forty-two years of age, it was still a "young organization" with its future before it, as some of its members used to say, since it had as yet conquered but a small part of its large industrial domain. It had endured the peculiar misfortune of having a large portion of its membership eliminated by law in 1919; thereafter, promising efforts at its reorganization as a union largely of catering workers had been initiated by President Flore. But the blighting force of depression had followed. The union's "economic power" over the industry, in the sense of being able to impose union shop standards, remained very low, or "spotty," up to the time when Franklin Roosevelt entered the White House in March, 1933.

Now the situation was reversed; and predominantly favorable factors emerged, with the change in our whole social and political climate, that inspired the revitalization of the Hotel and Restaurant Employees, as of many other trade unions. In 1933, out of the miseries of the great depression, the International Union was reborn.

Armed with emergency powers, as in war, President Roosevelt issued sweeping decrees and persuaded Congress to enact, with the rapidity of lightning, laws aimed at economic recovery and reform. Not only did he rouse great hopes and renewed confidence by these

New Deal measures, but he also made the people merry again by giving them beer.

As soon as the decisive Democratic party victory was reported in November, 1932, it was foreseen that the Volstead Act would be modified and beer quickly restored; the repeal of the Eighteenth Amendment and the return of liquor was expected to take longer. But Repeal came sooner than was foreseen. The American people, who had been so determined to improve our drinking habits by statute, were now as firmly convinced that the "noble experiment" should be wholly repudiated as having bred mainly organized crime and corruption. Flore and "Charlie" Sands, the International's Washington representative, who had long labored toward this end, were jubilant as bartenders joined the local unions "in droves." By the end of 1933 the "Beverage Dispensers" could proudly call themselves "Bartenders" once more. At the August, 1934, convention the International resumed its old long name: The Hotel & Restaurant Employees International Alliance & Bartenders International League of America.

One of the most important of the emergency laws enacted in the opening "hundred days" of the Roosevelt Administration was the National Industrial Recovery Act, or NRA, announced with great fanfare on May 22, 1933. If we would speak charitably of it today, we could conclude that it was a well-intentioned scheme to please both the Chamber of Commerce and the American Federation of Labor; on the one hand by allowing management to control production and raise prices, on the other, by promising labor the right to put a floor under wages and shorten hours. Notable in its provisions, as a proclamation of the new Government policy, was the historic NRA 7-A clause, or "charter" for labor, which seemed to assure workers the right to organize into unions of their own choosing, to bargain collectively, to designate their own union representatives, and to be free from interference by their employers in such choice.

Under the terms of the law, manufacturing units and owners of various businesses were induced to enter into trade associations and formulate "codes of fair competition," setting prices, and hours and wages for labor—subject to the approval of the NRA Administrator, General Hugh S. Johnson, as the President's deputy.

By the summer of 1933, Sands reported, Washington was "a madhouse," as thousands of trade association representatives and their lawyers, and the spokesmen of many labor unions, thronged its corridors and offices, eager to help formulate advantageous codes for

Leaders of the San Francisco strike in 1937. Seated, left to right, Joseph Marino, Hugo Ernst, Walter Cowan; standing, John A. St. Peter, Tom Nickola

Relief kitchen where 3,500 striking San Francisco workers were served by expert chefs and waiters in 1937

Hugo Ernst, Seventh General President, 1945–1954

Hugo Ernst in the chair at a convention

every industry under the sun—from diapers and ladies' hats to cinder blocks. Sands, the union's watchdog in the capital, followed closely the progress of the hotel and restaurant codes. Ed Flore now joined him, and, as Sands reported, "On the go every minute, morning and night . . . we pulled every string we could reach to every labor official, every committee." [1] The trouble was that the employers were supposed to submit the terms of a given code, and propose wages and hours as well, while the labor union in the industry was required to wait until these were made public, whereupon the labor spokesmen might demand a hearing and propose revisions.

There was no doubt that Roosevelt and his advisers had wished to strengthen the unions in order to help restore wage levels and mass buying power; a minimum wage of $12 to $15 a week for unskilled workers and shorter hours was declared to be part of the President's policy. Yet the hotel men who wrote the NRA code for their trade attempted to set the minimum of 25¢ an hour as their *maximum!* Taking advantage of special exemptions that were permitted the service trades, the hotel men brought forth a minimum for hotels of $8 a week (!) and a 60- to 70-hour week, with management claiming that tips and meals added to the earnings of workers placed in this low category. Such rates were far below the union scale.

In the autumn of 1933 Flore came to Washington repeatedly to seek revision of the proposed hotel and restaurant codes—accompanied by Secretary Hesketh and Vice-Presidents Hugo Ernst and John Kearney, who served as his most active lieutenants. The fight was on to establish the 40-hour week, or at least 48 hours, as standard, and thus "spread work." Failing that, the union men fought to delay the NRA code, Flore bombarding Administrator Johnson and President Roosevelt with his protests.

The HRE's President reported later

> he had come with his associates to Washington on one day to meet with General Johnson, but they were told that they were to meet with the representatives of the National Restaurant Association later in the day. That meeting never took place for some reason or other best known to the operators. We suspect they were fearful to contact our representatives.

In this manner, without the approval of labor, the first proposed codes were made ready by December, 1933. Flore, in angry statements to the newspapers, declared that the representatives of labor were extremely dissatisfied with the hotel and restaurant code provisions by which waiters, waitresses and bartenders were "treated as slaves." Sec-

retary of Labor Frances Perkins was persuaded to help set aside this
code on the ground that its sanctioning of a ten-hour day violated
some state laws that restricted women's hours of labor. Flore, moreover, made serious moves to prepare the union members for a nationwide demonstration, sending out telegrams to all locals in the
United States with stand-by orders for a twenty-four-hour stoppage
"on a given day to be announced later." [2]

At the threat of "a wave of strikes"—other unions were also forced
to such measures—Administrator Johnson and his staff had the hotel
and restaurant codes revised upward, with minimum wages set at $2
a day, a 54-hour week for men, and a 48-hour week for women, this
to take effect in January, 1934. Where a higher scale was in force by
previous agreements with the union, such contracts were not to be
disturbed. Wretched though its terms, this code represented a decided
improvement over the exceptionally low wages and long hours demanded by the restaurant and hotel keepers as "traditional" in their
trade.

In many cases the establishment of the NRA codes brought reductions below the wage levels ruling in strongly unionized centers. The
minimum pay of 28 cents an hour for waiters in restaurants for a
54-hour week was well below that established long before, in San
Francisco, for bus boys who received 40 cents per hour and worked
the 40-hour week.

How the very "flexible" provisions of the NRA codes were exploited by management is shown by the experience of a first-
class waiter, named Emil Schlitz, at the old Bismarck Hotel in
Chicago, as narrated in the union's journal. After obtaining a job
there in April, 1933, and working to everyone's satisfaction at the low
prevailing fixed wages for eight months, in December he received his
first two-week pay check under the new scale established by the NRA
code. To his disappointment the pay for two weeks, $18.15, was
approximately $10.27 below his regular pay for the same period before
the NRA system came into effect!

As politely as possible, at the roll-call, he asked the maître-d'hôtel
whether the hotel was living up to the NRA code, as the waiters were
promised. He said:

> Since my last pay I have worked 101 hours for $18.15 while
> under the Code rate I should receive $28.42. Furthermore, you
> must have taken out a charge for the use of the uniform, and under
> my interpretation of the code, this is not permissible. Mr. Harding
> interrupted me and asked: "Aren't you making 28 cents an hour?
> Aren't you making any tips?" I proceeded to explain that what he

called tips were not such to me and have nothing to do with the wages. . . .

As I was explaining my interpretation of the word "tipping," Mr. Harding became enraged. He asked: "Haven't you made 28 cents an hour?" To which I replied: "No." Then he said: "Any waiter who cannot make 28 cents an hour can't work for me. Give me your badge."

I gave him my badge which signified my dismissal.

It all went to show, Waiter Schlitz concluded, "how great is the need for organizing the hotel industry." [3]

On one or more occasions, in 1934, Sidney Hillman, President of the Amalgamated Clothing Workers Union, then acting as a labor advisor to the NRA Board, warned Flore that the restaurant keepers were trying to have even this wretched code scrapped. "Without Hillman's help we would *not* have a code today," Sands reported from Washington in November, 1934.[4]

The strong unions launched a series of organizing and wage-raising strikes in 1933 *before* the codes for their industry were set. The so-called "charter" of labor's rights, the NRA 7-A clause, did provide favorable conditions for labor if the union representatives came to the bargaining table at Washington in a strong position to demand satisfactory terms. As Sidney Hillman said at the time:

NRA can be made a great power in the hands of labor, but I know from my training and experience in the labor movement that only labor which is organized can take advantage of the NRA.

As a rule the NRA codes set wages too low and hours too long to spread work and raise buying power in large measure. Where employers' groups faced a weak union or none at all—thanks to legal loopholes in the NRA law—they rigged up company unions, with management paying the members' dues, choosing their officers and doing their "bargaining" for them. The recovery law is said to have benefited only about 20 per cent of the 15,000,000 workers who were idle in the spring of 1933.

It was in view of these unpleasant facts that the Farmer-Labor party's Governor Floyd B. Olson of Minnesota, addressing the convention of the HRE at Minneapolis on August 13, 1934, exhorted the members present to help themselves by going out and organizing everyone. "To take advantage of your legal rights under 7-A *continue to organize*," he urged, "and collect upon the promissory note the Roosevelt Administration has passed out."

Thus, with hope revived, John L. Lewis, whose union had been all but destroyed in the depression, took the field in the spring of 1933 and organized 300,000 soft-coal miners. The working man was now told that the liberal President Roosevelt wanted him to join a union. Everywhere labor raised its head; after union organization had been dormant for so many years, great mass meetings were staged and the union leaders roared: "Organize! Organize!" Even among the unskilled and the long unorganized, who had known desperate hardship in the years of depression, sentiment for unions now spread with powerful momentum as in the days of the Knights of Labor or at the peak period of the AFL in 1917-1920—a form of mass protest at the need and hunger they had known in the land of plenty.

In his large territory in the northwestern states, International Organizer Jack Weinberger, with the same idea in mind, began moving about rapidly day and night and was able to address numerous meetings of culinary workers who were forming new locals immediately after the enactment of the NRA. He felt that a new confidence was showing itself all around him. The trip of six or seven weeks stimulated organizing activities in many towns; the sight of new beer taverns was heartening to the union men, and organizing bartenders was "easy." Virtually every day a new local was chartered; old locals regained their losses, and defunct locals were reorganized. Things were really moving. Now hotel organizing campaigns, never before successful, were carried on in Portland, Seattle, Tacoma, Aberdeen, Everett and other cities. Here the field was vast.[5]

*

Inspired by a new militancy, organized labor, in the early months of the New Deal, invaded the mass-production industries of steel, automobiles and rubber which had long been strictly non-union areas. However, the most dramatic upheaval of the period was undoubtedly the San Francisco general strike of July 16-19, 1934, in which the Hotel and Restaurant Employees' locals, under the leadership of Hugo Ernst, played a very active part.

In May, the longshoremen's union, then affiliated with the AFL, had called a strike, following the collapse of negotiations with the shippers' association of San Francisco. Soon the longshoremen were joined by the other maritime unions, and finally—as strenuous efforts were made by the employers' group to break the strike—by the powerful Teamsters Union. Incidents of violence succeeded each other day by day as police, and later militia, were ordered out in heavy force to protect property and non-union workers, these incidents culminating in the pitched battle of June 5, 1934, which resulted in two unarmed union pickets being killed and scores of others wounded. One of the two men killed was an unemployed member of Cooks Local 44 who, with many other culinary workers, had come out to help their old union allies, the San Francisco longshoremen. The cooks, as it happened, were also involved in a strike against the hotels that ran concurrently with the longshoremen's up to June 1, 1934.

Among the workers in "union shop" San Francisco hot anger blazed up at the employers and at the local government officials who seemed to the union men to have joined in a strike-breaking campaign backed by naked armed force. Sentiment for the declaration of a general strike in the entire city now gained rapidly among all labor groups in the Central Labor Council, the thought being that unless a strong demonstration of labor's solidarity were made now, all trade unions would soon be in danger of destruction. Undoubtedly the workers, embittered by suffering, unemployment and want for years, were exasperated anew on finding that the hoped-for improvements and the new rights of organized labor were to be taken from them by force. The hungry and desperate people of the "Unemployed Councils," formed during the depression, and the "wild men" of the labor movement were quite evidently moving into the battle area of the San Francisco waterfront; while the employers were described by some observers as "maddened" at the "obnoxious" and "undesirable" unionizing movement of labor, as Citizens Alliance spokesmen termed it.[6]

In the directing group of the Central Labor Council of San Francisco, the well-loved George Kidwell, of the Bakery Wagon Drivers, and John Shelley, of the Teamsters (now a Democratic Congressman from California), were the leading spirits, with whom Hugo Ernst, heading the second largest local union group in the city, had been closely associated for many years. These seasoned AFL union officers were now aware that the movement toward a general strike rising throughout the days of June, 1934, could not be turned aside. Their problem, as they saw it, was to take the command of this "spontaneous revolt" away from the extremist groups and direct it as a powerful, but orderly, demonstration of labor's protest at the use of guns, tear gas, and other forms of violence against unarmed union pickets.

Kidwell, who was a lifelong student of labor tactics, had warned everyone—as local officers of the HRE recall—that the general strike was primarily a "revolutionary weapon," and that it might produce untold damage for organized labor. In all earnestness he urged, therefore, that the action be controlled and *limited* at all costs. The AFL unions were to walk out at a given hour upon a given day; but the duration of their stoppage was to be short, with certain vital services continuing in operation.

Hugo Ernst, as a member of the General Strike Committee, gave full support to Kidwell's proposals to limit the scope of the general strike. If all the hotel and restaurant workers walked out, half of San Francisco's population (which ate in restaurants) would starve. "People have to eat—we cannot turn the people who might be with us against us!" Ernst exclaimed at one of the stormy meetings of the Central Labor Council.[7]

On July 16, 1934, to the alarm of the entire country, the general strike of 150,000 workers in San Francisco and Oakland began, though in perfect order. No wheels turned without permission of the General Strike Committee, though electric power and gas service and trucking delivery of medicine, milk and perishable food continued. Diners-out in San Francisco ate only by order of Hugo Ernst and John St. Peter, head of the cooks' local, the culinary unions leaving but nineteen popular-priced eating establishments open out of 2,000. On the second day of the strike, however, the number of eating-places open was increased to fifty-nine. On the third day the general strike came to an end, without violence or disorder, an impressive demonstration intended to administer a sound lesson to the obdurate men of business and the anti-labor politicians of Northern California.

After that strike employers in the Bay Area proceeded with greater moderation; and organized labor, largely by peaceful bargaining, made rapid headway.[8]

The years 1933 and 1934, the years of trade union revival in America, were surely Edward Flore's finest hours. The election of Roosevelt, Repeal, the spirited movement of wage-workers of all sorts into labor organizations kindled him with an enthusiasm that he communicated readily to gatherings of the catering trade people at many mass meetings which he addressed at this period in Boston, New York, Chicago, St. Paul and even in "open shop" Los Angeles.

In Los Angeles a unique Joint Executive Board set-up, which proved to be a medium for a successful organizing campaign, was inaugurated. Seven unions, Waiters Local 17, Bartenders Local 284, Miscellaneous Local 440, Cooks Local 468, Hotel Service Employees Local 435, Waitresses Local 639 and Oriental Hotel and Restaurant Employees Local 646 all occupied the same headquarters and the Secretary of the J.E.B. was also financial secretary for the seven local unions. Under this joint set-up the J.E.B. directed the activities of the affiliated locals. This made it possible for the unions to take quick and effective strike action whenever necessary. The culinary unions in Los Angeles were the first to violate *en masse* an anti-picketing ordinance that was in effect in that city from 1904 to 1933 and were successful in having it repealed. This cleared the way for organizing the hotel and restaurant workers in Los Angeles.

In January, 1933, and, a year later, in January, 1934, President Flore announced "spring membership drives" in the union's journal, declaring: "There never was a greater opportunity for organization than the present . . . with the workers fully protected in their rights." By a special dispensation, per capita taxes of locals gaining 25 per cent or more of membership were to be waived; reinstatement fees, often fairly high, were to be reduced to $3.75, and initiation fees also were to be cut to nominal sums of a dollar or two, during the season allotted to "mass action."

In effect Flore himself seemed determined to finish what he had begun before the economic depression of 1929-1932—the organizing of the unorganized, above all in the great cities of New York and Chicago, where large numbers of catering workers were concentrated and could be approached quickly. To this end it needed a decided shift in policy, from that of the craft union, as championed by the late Jere L. Sullivan, to the industrial union strategy exemplified by John L. Lewis and the United Mine Workers.

For the Hotel and Restaurant Employees, purely craft union methods were really very ill-adapted to successful organization of their field, in which so many unskilled or semi-skilled people constantly reduced the status of the trained craftsmen. Debate over the issue of craft versus industrial union policy had raged within the union for many years, as now throughout the AFL. In the darkest days of 1932, before the International's convention in Boston, a resolution had been brought in proposing that new organizing campaigns be conceived along entirely different lines from those used in the past, and as part of a broad industrial-union program. The HRE stood in danger of missing the bus again when business recovery set in, as the progressive delegates urged. The whole catering trade was in "revolution" thanks to the spread of large popular-priced units and chains of self-service cafeterias. The very attitude of these masses of food workers, hard-driven in their chain cafeterias and skyscraper hotels, was changing. For they were no longer craftsmen who functioned in a personal or individual relationship with their employers, but laborers in the belt-lines of "food factories." Would the old Hotel and Restaurant Employees Union wake up in time to take advantage of their growing militancy?

The "industrial union" resolution introduced by John Bookjans, of Local 237, Pittsburgh, proposed, therefore, that organizing campaigns be extended to cover not only cafeteria workers, but the armies of unskilled hotel workers, bellboys, porters, housemaids, dishwashers and, in fact, "all catering workers who would come under the jurisdiction of our International Union."

To such proposals men like Paul N. Coulcher of Captains and Waiters Local 16, New York—who was already suspected of being the evil genius of the New York locals—replied, as so often before, by claiming that the unskilled people were "floaters" and "riffraff" and should be ignored, while as in the past efforts should be concentrated exclusively upon the trained cooks, waiters and bartenders, who were "the key to the situation."

But Bookjans with much spirit defended his resolution against those who termed it "impractical":

> It has been said that the cooks or the waiters are the key to the industry. I contend that no class is the key to the industry. If everybody . . . is organized, we will have more chances for establishing our union. The chain restaurants and the cafeterias are practically unorganized. There is a reason for that.
>
> When I came into this International over thirty years ago in Toledo, Ohio, . . . there were practically no such things as chain restaurants and very few corporation-owned establishments. In the small saloons and restaurants where we used to work, there were seldom more than two crafts employed, except that once in a while there was a porter. We were able to handle the smaller places through the boycott. We could put pickets in front of a place and the employer would be willing to talk about a settlement.
>
> I predict that in a very short time we will not be able to get anything without a powerful organization. It is not easy to organize those big places *without organizing the crafts outside those now represented in our International.* . . . I believe in organizing everybody in the industry.[9]

Despite the conservatives and the "Philistines," the resolution sanctioning a departure from craft-union methods toward industrial union tactics was adopted by a sizable majority vote at the 1932 convention—a clear reflection of the union's change of temper.

By 1934 the labor world was startled by the spectacular advances of the "industrial unionists" of the type of Lewis and Hillman. Meanwhile the failure of attempts to organize steel and motors along craft lines offered impressive evidence of the need for changing methods, especially in the mass industries, and inspired intense controversy within AFL circles, soon to be split by the 1935 Committee for Industrial Organization.

To go forward two years—while we touch on the question of industrial unionism—the Hotel and Restaurant Employees, like all the rest of the American labor movement, was rent by strong divisions of opinion in the summer of 1936, when the group of AFL unions affiliated together as the Committee for Industrial Organization, or CIO, was suspended by the AFL's Executive Council, and threatened with final expulsion (carried out in January, 1938). The CIO, nevertheless, under John L. Lewis and Sidney Hillman, raising millions of dollars for a vast organizing job, went forward rapidly with the unionization of the mass industries where craft union methods had so grievously failed.

President Green, seeking support for his campaign against the dissident unions, appeared before the HRE convention on August 11, 1936, and delivered himself of a vehement attack upon the Lewis faction, charging that they had behaved in an undemocratic spirit by defying the ruling of a majority of the AFL convention delegates (in 1935) and proceeding upon their independent course toward "dual unionism." In defending the policies of the AFL, incidentally, Green stressed the fact that the official labor federation had long harbored both types of unions, industrial and craft, and left the choice of form of organization to the members of the separate unions in the AFL.

What then was the real bone of contention between the two bitterly divided factions of labor? It was curious that one of the three leading sponsors of the CIO originally, together with Lewis and Hillman, was Charles Howard, President of the International Typographers Union, the oldest and most orthodox craft organization in America. But Howard and the Typographers were highly "liberal" in their outlook, compared with many other AFL groups.

The answer to this question comes out in a very striking speech Vice-President Hugo Ernst made in reply to William Green. He stressed the vital difference in outlook and philosophy between the craft union and the "industrial" faction, between conservatives and —one might say—modernists. The one wanted to organize the "cream of the crop," the skilled and the better-paid people, or wanted them within their old craft union jurisdictions; the others wanted to organize the masses, no matter what they were; and, in view of the advance of technology that was constantly "down-grading" craftsmen, they wanted them in big, new organizations where all classes of workers were equal. For the great majority of semi-skilled or unskilled workers in the mass-industries, Ernst argued, the industrial union plan was the superior method. Yet the old guard in the AFL opposed this course.

The AFL had been created and made stable by highly skilled craftsmen, who struggled to maintain their strategic economic position and protect their jobs—concentrating on the defense of their own craft interest and their rigid craft unions, while excluding the great hordes of unskilled, immigrant laborers who worked at lower wages. But all that came about in the 1880's and 1890's before the arrival of modern labor-saving machinery. Ernst pointed out that

> It was out of those skilled and exclusive unions, that most of the present leaders of the American Federation developed. However successful they may have been as craft leaders, in gaining certain advantages for their own small following, they have been, for the most part, men *without a social vision or understanding* of fundamental economic processes.

The recent attempts to organize the rubber and motor industries by means of "Federal" charters, by connecting them temporarily with the AFL (to be allotted to various crafts afterward) had brought only confusion and failure, he said. For the warring craft unions could not deal by such methods with the "new machine technology" that faced them. Today, out of more than thirty million wage-workers, less than four million were organized in unions. Yet the AFL Council, in the face of this stark fact, had just moved to suspend nearly half of its own membership and the most aggressive and significant half at that. Ernst believed that the CIO might organize the many millions who were without unions of any kind, without setting up competitive groups and without touching a single previously organized field.

> What is industrial unionism? It is the organization of all the workers in a given industry—no matter what type of work they perform, whether they are skilled or unskilled—into a single big union. Wage scales and working conditions for the various skills in that union are decided upon by the union, and the whole union stands behind any group of workers within the industry. The employer does not have to bargain with a dozen sets of union offi-

cials—often with conflicting demands and bitter jurisdictional disputes. He deals with one organization. . . . We have successful and long-standing examples of industrial unionism already existing: the United Mine Workers, to which William Green himself belongs, and the Amalgamated Clothing Workers, which covers every type of worker in the men's clothing industry.

For his part Ernst would never advocate "breaking up" existing craft unions, or transferring their membership to others, holding this "impossible and foolish." There were certain fields where the craft organization was most effective still. "There is a place for *both* craft and industrial unions," he urged. The real issue, then, was not that of "dual unionism" but of "the organization of 25,000,000 workers outside of the ranks of the AFL which the AFL has never been able to organize—largely because of the craft-union setup." The deepest hope of every progressive unionist was that the next AFL convention would reverse the action of the Council in suspending the CIO unions. Labor must remain unified and the present split in the movement must be mended.*

How effective the new methods could be was shown by the Hotel and Restaurant Employees' "drives" of 1934 to 1937.

There had never been, for example, a real union local of miscellaneous and "amalgamated" hotel workers in the great center of Chicago. In 1934 George B. McLane headed a tremendous bartenders' "drive" that brought in thousands of members almost overnight to Local 278. What was more remarkable was that, at the same time, James Blakely, Lucien Kapp and others began to organize dishwashers and busboys in restaurants; and later bellhops and scrub women in the hotels for a new local, No. 593, formed on industrial-union lines. "We started out in the Produce Market section, and the restaurants around there used by union men," Blakely recalls. "The people there were earning $8 a week or $10 a week. We called them to meetings night after night and sometimes, in those days, as many as 99 per cent would sign union pledges."

Blakely, a youth who had been raised in the stockyard district, used to go to hotel managers and propose that everyone "under the roof" be included in the new union. One manager, pointing to a woman scrubbing the floor, exclaimed: "What! You don't mean you are going to organize the *charwomen!*"

* Hugo Ernst: Address before the Commonwealth Club, San Francisco, October 5, 1936; cited in the CIE, November, 1936, pp. 14-15. "The AFL, stimulated by the successes of the CIO in later years adopted industrial union methods wherever practical. The conflict of *personalities,* however, continued."

These people, as Blakely recalled—using President Roosevelt's phrase—had been the "forgotten men" of industry. But now the unskilled workers in restaurants and hotels showed a new will for organization. Thus, under the sign of the NRA, were laid the foundations for what was to be one of the International's giant locals.[10]

The cooks were, in great measure, skilled craftsmen—long accustomed to driving individual bargains with managers for themselves and their kitchen crews—and it needed a somewhat different approach to persuade them to enter (what was to become actually) a union of mixed craft and industrial locals. Their numbers were now enormous, since the U. S. Census report for 1930 indicated that there were 565,392 male and female cooks—approximately 40 per cent, however, being self-employed in small establishments. However, not even one per cent of this great working population had ever been enrolled in the International Union, most of the professional or skilled people being members of "benevolent" associations, such as the Chefs de Cuisine Association of America, Helvetia Association of North America, Inc., International Cooks Association, International Geneva Association, Kadir Society, Inc., Société Culinaire Philanthropique, the Vatel Club, Inc., and the Élite Waiters Association (mixed). Moreover, they were jealously divided, as we have seen, into separate race and language groups. Thus no one had been able to make much headway in unionizing these highly important craftsmen—save the old left-wing union which had long held a small number of the New York cooks, now affiliated with the Food Workers Industrial Union.

In 1933 Miguel Garriga, a cook of Spanish extraction, had done a good job of recruiting the many foreign-born "association" cooks for the union in Chicago; thanks to his initiative, Cooks Local 88 was chartered.

At this period, as Vice-President John Kearney noted, the cooks, once devoted to their various guilds or clubs, and extremely suspicious of American trade unionists, underwent a decided change of heart. Formerly well-paid and prosperous craftsmen, they had suffered greatly during the depression, and, since the NRA, as Kearney said, "They have become more friendly to organized labor. They now feel that their condition, formerly deplorable, will be improved by the union."

Thus, after the cooks had been organized in Chicago, the members of the new cooks' local soon afterward wrote to the several cooks' associations in New York, urging their people to join the Hotel and Restaurant Employees. Garriga, now appointed by Flore an International Organizer, was sent on to New York, and there began a vigorous campaign to bring the cooks into the union.

Flore himself came down to New York in secret at one stage of the spring, 1934, "drive." Together with Organizer Garriga, he approached the heads of the several cooks' societies in the city and invited them to sign applications for a charter from the International Union under which several of the craftsmen's associations would be combined into a new cooks' local, No. 8, New York. The whole situation, as Flore related afterward, was an extremely delicate one. The hotels had lately set up a company union of their own (called the "Hotel and Restaurant Guild"). At the same time the existing New York locals were embroiled in their habitual quarrels over which one was to receive the influx of new membership. Flore said:

> We told the officers of local unions, particularly Local 16, that we were in New York on a secret mission, that we intended to put over a big deal . . . but were not prepared to tell them what it was. In the preliminary stages I do not think even Vice-President Lehman [head of Local 1] knew what we were doing.

Flore's secrecy was also inspired by fear of attempted interference on the part of the left-wing Food Workers Union. Their method, he said, was to "flood their members into the new organization being chartered and then by overnight process take the membership over, and the charter would be a wasteful instrument." Thus in secrecy and stealth, arrangements were made to establish Cooks Local Union No. 8 of the International, with 500 members at the start; by the summer of 1934 it was hoped that 500 members a month would be coming in.[11]

*

The Twenty-Seventh Convention of the International Union at Minneapolis, in August, 1934, was a most cheerful and liquid affair; the delegates were plainly in high spirits, celebrating not only the progress of membership drives, but also the return of the "cup that cheers," brimming with lawful beer, wine and liquor. President Flore, with beaming face, announced that membership was almost at 50,000, as the convention opened, and gaining strongly. The International Union was now nearly twice as large as two years before!

"The fiscal year for 1933-1934," Flore declared, marked truly a turning point, "and was the most significant in the annals of our Union." He added:

I intend to have our union known as one of the leading organizations of the AFL. I may be optimistic, but I expect to report at the next convention that we have the largest membership in our history.[12]

The curious developments attending the NRA codes were reviewed by Flore and Secretary Hesketh. Despite disappointments resulting from the previously weak bargaining position of the union in its industry, prospects were bright because of the striking change in our political climate. "Our salvation," as Robert Hesketh said truly, "lies in our own economic strength, which means *organization.*"

That was now going forward swiftly, and generous sums of money were being disbursed for an expanded staff of International Organizers and Local Special Organizers stationed in scores of cities. At the start, the largest gains for the union were, of course, in the bartending trade, with Local 278, Chicago, reporting 3,000 members, at the end of 1934, under the drive of George B. McLane—as compared with a membership of only 150 before Repeal. In Boston, bartenders were being inducted in crowds into the "amalgamated" Local 34, headed by "Jack" Kearney, the new recruits numbering 1,000. And thus it went throughout the United States, and Canada also.

In 1928 the sale of beer in western Canada had been made lawful and respectable again. Thereafter, Tim Hannafin, aided by Organizer Jack Weinberger, resumed the HRE's unionizing campaign in British Columbia, Alberta and other western provinces. In the more populous cities of eastern Canada, and particularly in Toronto, catering-workers' locals that had been wiped out years ago were revived in 1934 and 1935. In this region an organizing problem made difficult by vast spaces and small population had been further complicated for the unions in the official Trades and Labour Congress of Canada (allied with the AFL) by the opposition of dual union groups, such as the Catholics' in French-speaking Quebec, and the radical One-Big-Union movement, which resembled the IWW. Flore, nevertheless, sent Organizer John J. McDevitt to Toronto to direct the organizing campaign in eastern Canada.

Soon rapid progress, especially among barmen, was reported from this section. There had been formerly seven locals with only 2,000 union members, all told, scattered over the vast expanse of Canada; but after 1936 membership was doubled. The hotel workers were also successful in setting up new locals within the chain of Canada's large railway-owned hotels. Keeping step with the labor union revival going on in the United States, the Canadians built up a sizable organization in Toronto. Numerous catering-workers' locals, though generally quite small in membership, spread themselves from Halifax, Nova Scotia, to Moose Jaw, Saskatchewan, and even to the Yukon in the far north.

In 1934 large-scale organizing strikes were under way in almost every important industrial center of the United States. When the culinary workers' delegates gathered together for their biennial convention in Minneapolis that summer, the city was in the grip of a general strike of the Teamsters Union. In fact, martial law had just been declared in the city, thanks to a rather high-handed mayor. But the morale of the strikers was tremendously high, nevertheless. At one session of the HRE convention in Eagles Hall, 400 of the striking truck drivers, clad in blue overalls, came marching in single-file up to the platform and out of the hall, with Mrs. Sarraine Loewe, of Chicago, an HRE delegate, at their head. The audience of delegates cheered the Teamsters to the roof, and Secretary Hesketh presented them with a check for $1,000 for their strike fund in behalf of the International Union. That meant real money in those lean days, and helped the Teamsters at a critical period, as their local union officers still recall. The officer who accepted the donation declared that, once the Teamsters had won their strike, "No non-union cook, waiter or bartender would be found working in Minneapolis." [13] To be sure, they did win, and Minneapolis thereafter became one of the most strongly unionized centers of the catering trade.

The 1934 convention was surely the most "progressive" ever held by the International up to that date. There had always been a forward-looking, sometimes even a radical, minority in the organization. Now in the liberal dawn of the Rooseveltian Era, the delegates, remembering the great hardships their people had lately suffered, and also inspired with the new hope that had come thereafter, gave themselves to long and tense discussions of such issues as social insurance for all workers—which would have seemed a pipe-dream to the men of Jere Sullivan's generation. The voting of a resolution demanding that a "comprehensive system of unemployment, sickness, and old-age insurance" should be enacted into law, and that the AFL support such a legislative program, was in itself a sign of the reversal of sentiment on welfare laws throughout the labor movement.

Once more the question of industrial unionism engrossed the delegates of 1934, as so often before. Earnest voices were raised in behalf of the "amalgamated" type of local, in which divisions between crafts were suppressed (for collective bargaining purposes), so that the long-trained hotel cook and the skilled waiter stood shoulder to shoulder with the ill-paid dishwashers, bus men, chambermaids and all the other "slaveys" in the solidarity of big, combined local organizations. A resolution authorizing the union's delegates to the next AFL convention to espouse the cause of industrial unionism—in support of the John L. Lewis faction—was defeated by only a narrow margin. But in effect the HRE had already committed itself to industrial union policies since 1932, and was making progress in this direction by turning itself into a "mixed" union made up of both industrial and craft locals. Flore himself related how, in chartering Local 8, New York, he had "amalgamated" ten or more "benevolent associations" including different classes of kitchen workers. The delegates from Detroit's growing Local 705 declared they were using similar industrial union methods, as was being done by Local 237 of Pittsburgh and also, since long years ago, by many West Coast locals.

Before this convention President Flore spoke of the dual union problem with a new breadth of vision. The New Deal for labor had also given a mighty impetus to the independent or dual union groups outside the AFL, notably the Food Workers Industrial Union. In New York, under the leadership of their International Secretary, Jay Rubin, and of Michael J. Obermeier, the FWIU had multiplied their membership several times over in 1933-1934, particularly in the hotel field, where they were conducting large organizing strikes. In Pittsburgh another local of the rival union had done organizing work in the two biggest hotels, and in the winter of 1934 called a strike against them. The HRE's local 237 in Pittsburgh had up to then felt itself not ready to strike against the hotels. But it was significant that when the left-wing union's strike broke out and Secretary Bookjans, of Local 237, wrote President Flore asking what attitude his union was to take toward the rival union, Flore replied, this time, that the HRE must in no case engage in strike-breaking activities or permit their membership to accept employment as 'scabs" in the struck hotels. Bookjans, therefore, treated the FWIU strike "much as if it were our strike. . . ." [14]

At the same period, when reports reached Flore that Local 16, New York, had intervened in a similar situation in that city during a strike of the FWIU locals, and that fighting had broken out between the rival unions, Flore issued a stern rebuke to his own subordinates.

He was now feeling his way carefully toward the absorption of the membership of the left-wing union which was believed to possess about 9,000 adherents. To the delegates of the convention at Minneapolis in August, 1934, he declared his belief that "all the workers in America" should be affiliated with "the legitimate trade union movement" represented by the AFL.

As a matter of fact, the communist faction—which had lately taken control of the rival union—after executing another sudden, about-face maneuver in the spring of 1934, made repeated overtures to President Flore for a merger of their Food Workers' locals with the HRE. Flore reported to the convention at Minneapolis that this proposal was being studied; while aware that officers of the International's Locals 1, 16 and 302, in New York, had expressed bitter opposition to it, he remarked that he favored it, provided that the members of the rival union dissolved their locals and came into the AFL organization "individually."

The 1934 convention, near its close, also dealt in a forthright manner with the extremely serious problem of racketeering that now threatened the existence of a number of important American labor unions. A resolution was passed authorizing the General Executive Board to appoint a committee to investigate all cases of locals where complaints of gangsterism and racketeering were made by members. At the time Vice-President Kearney opposed the resolution on the ground that it would have the opposite effect of what was intended: in other words, "it would convey the impression that the [labor] movement tolerated racketeering." But the majority of the delegates were determined to take strong measures against the gentlemen from the underworld who were reported to have "infiltrated" a number of locals.

About two years earlier, following the election of Roosevelt in November, 1932, when it was known that Prohibition would soon be ended, the newspapers had carried sensational stories of the plans of powerful underworld characters of the type of Al Capone, of Chicago, to "muscle into" the legal brewing and liquor industries— since their illicit rum-running business would soon be halted. It was rumored then that part of the scheme of the so-called "Capone syndicate" was to gain control of the brewery workers, the hotel, restaurant and bartenders' unions and also some teamsters' locals, so that the members would help sell and distribute the brands of beer and whisky produced by firms the racketeers had bought up.

At about that time, the last week of November, 1932, President

Flore had gone to Chicago and conferred with officers of the International Brewery Workers. Their Secretary-Treasurer, Joseph Obergfell, on November 25, 1932, openly declared to newspaper reporters:

> Our union has understood for some time that Chicago's gangland had plans to get its clutches on our industry . . . and we have inklings of the efforts of gangsters to infiltrate into the unions with a view of ultimately controlling the whole industry. We ask the cooperation of all people to keep this industry out of the hands of gangsters . . . who will wreck our industry and our union.

In Chicago there were persistent reports at this time that the Capone Syndicate was "forcing" thousands of workers into the bartenders' local union. In truth, the International's Local 278, Beverage Dispensers (as they were then called), underwent an astonishing mushroomlike growth that aroused suspicion in some quarters. But Flore, on being interviewed for the press, denied rumors that Capone gangsters were taking over HRE locals or "forcing" people into his union by "gorilla methods." The bartenders were simply taking advantage of the change of public sentiment as shown in the election. He added: "We have been careful to keep our business on an honest basis and bar out racketeers. . . ."

This was a correct statement, but it applied to the past. The officers of several AFL unions at the Chicago Conference, with Flore's evident concurrence, as a matter of fact, announced that they were combining their forces to fight efforts of gangsters to get control of the brewing industry.[15]

This was more easily said than done. In less than a year, by the summer of 1933, Flore heard disturbing reports of irregularities on the part of officers of Waiters Local 16 and Cafeteria Employees Local 302, in New York. Other reports, mere rumors as yet, linked George B. McLane, Secretary of Bartenders Local 278, Chicago, with labor union racketeers. Then, in September, 1933, twenty-five persons were indicted and tried in New York County Court on charges of extortion in the restaurant trade, among them several officers of HRE Locals 16 and 302, including Paul Coulcher, Aladar Retek and Abe Borson. Among the witnesses who had come forward to offer the District Attorney evidence against those accused of racketeering was Benny Gottesman, business agent of the old Waiters Local 1—which had been fighting the racketeer-infested locals. But Gottesman was never called to testify at the trial, and the charges were dismissed for lack of evidence. Soon afterward, in November, 1933, Abe Borson, the indicted business agent of Local 302, was found murdered out in a field in Westchester County, New York—a typical gangland incident.[16]

Anxiety for the good repute of the International Union, threatened by a small infiltration of racketeers, had led the majority of union men at the Minneapolis convention in August, 1934, to support measures for trying and punishing local officers who were associated with gangsters. Oddly enough, Paul Nicholas Coulcher, the head of Local 16, New York, who had been indicted and then cleared, supported this resolution, asserting that his local was "not afraid of any inquiry and was willing to open its books for inspection at any time." Men like Coulcher were resourceful fellows; it was not going to be easy to pin them down.

It was significant that at this same convention a sudden, powerful movement showed itself in support of the candidacy of George B. McLane, the popular Chicago bartenders' leader, for International Vice-President. He headed what was then the largest local in the union; his star was rising swiftly. Seeing that it was hopeless to stand against McLane, the veteran Vice-President Carl Frederick of Portland, Oregon, withdrew his candidacy and McLane was elected in his place.

A similar attempt was made to defeat Vice-President William Lehman, of Waiters Local 1, New York—which was reported to have resisted efforts of the gangster leaders of Locals 16 and 302 to take it over. After Lehman was renominated, "Nick" Coulcher, of Local 16, leaped to his feet yelling that he wanted to nominate John J. Williams, then head of Local 302, New York, as a candidate for Vice-President against Lehman.

But Flore, who was in the chair, moving quickly, declared that he had already recognized a motion—among the many motions being shouted at him—to declare Lehman's election unanimous, and that it was ready to be voted on. Coulcher tried to deliver a loud harangue in protest, but Flore, determinedly, gaveled him down, and carried on with the unanimous election of Lehman. It was clear that he had some suspicion or foreknowledge of the scheme of Coulcher and his cronies to eliminate Lehman, an old union wheelhorse and a Flore supporter, and put one of the New York racketeers on the GEB.

At this convention you could already distinguish among the gathering of 146 delegates—ranging in appearance from the plain, honest, working-class types to men of education and sartorial elegance, such as Hugo Ernst—a sprinkling of those hard-faced characters who were the children of the bootleg generation, now muscling into a good many respectable unions. One of the young men actually followed

Flore out to the lobby at the end of the session (in which Coulcher had been ruled out of order), and, after abusing him in foul language, uttered some plain threats. Flore turned pale and appeared greatly troubled, but maintained his dignity and said nothing.[17]

After the repeal of the Eighteenth Amendment as noted earlier, the former rum-runners, acting in combination, had turned up as owners of a number of the once defunct distilleries and breweries. They knew only one way to sell merchandise or "persuade" people to buy their goods—by force and terror. The local unions of the Brewery Workers, of the Teamsters, and of the Hotel and Restaurant Employees seemed to be in a position to help "sell" the underworld syndicate's liquor or beer, and so their agents had "muscled into" these unions.

Then these enterprising bandits discovered that the unions themselves could be turned into profitable "rackets"; soon their mobsters were pushing into unions of the building trades, the motion picture operators, the cleaners and dyers, the garment workers and others still. Threatening or calling "strikes," after their own fancy, the hoodlums destroyed merchandise with acids, or set off stench bombs, and carried out a variety of sinister pleasantries—all in order to maintain themselves in the style to which they were accustomed. It was difficult even for the power of the law to dislodge them. For those who paid tribute to them or did business with them did not care to talk.

Ed Flore had some vague suspicions of what was going on, in three or four locals (out of 400); yet for the time being, he remained close-mouthed as was his habit, saying nothing to his associates of the Executive Board. But on one occasion, after the end of the Minneapolis convention, he did speak out in private and evidently in some emotional distress, to Bookjans, one of the union's "old incorruptibles," saying: "The racketeers are creeping into some of our local unions. I'm very much afraid of what may happen; and I really don't know what we should do. . . ."[18]

A week after the Minneapolis convention closed, on August 25, 1934, Flore and Mrs. Flore departed by steamer for England where he was to serve as a member of an AFL delegation to the British Trades Union Congress at Weymouth. He was very tired and greatly in need of a vacation, and so extended his stay in Europe for two months longer, during which he traveled in France and Italy as well as England. For the period of his absence he had appointed Vice-President Hugo Ernst as Acting President in charge of the Western half of the union, and placed John J. Kearney in a similar temporary role in charge of the Eastern half.

He had hoped to distract his mind; but it was a troubled Europe he journeyed through, then under the sway of those masters of force and terror, Hitler and Mussolini. When, on October 24, 1934, he reached New York harbor again there was more trouble waiting for him at the dock, trouble brewed by home-grown terrorists.

TEN

The New York Racketeers

"We are indeed, Mr. President, living in a strange age, an age of changing social conditions in which the lives of human beings are held so cheap."—
JOHN J. KEARNEY, Speech at 1936 Convention.

The 1920's, the years of Prohibition, were the years of "syndicates" of organized crime, and of "easy money" garnered from the enormous traffic in illicit rum. Nothing contributed more to undermining respect for all law, in the view of local and Federal authorities, than the unpopular statutes enforcing Prohibition. The bribery of police and government officials became a common, everyday occurrence; racketeering spread from the brewing and distilling industry to many other lines of business. Labor unions certainly were not alone in being affected by the growing habit of flouting the laws; our banks and insurance companies and our stock exchanges were also the field of spreading "white collar crime." That gangs of racketeers were forcing their way into legitimate trade, after the repeal of the Eighteenth Amendment in 1933, was undeniable. But it was also true that the American labor movement reflected the declining moral standards and cultural environment of the whole country, whose citizens generally had been violating the law for years by drinking illegal beer and whisky and laughing over it. But stories of regularly defaulting bank cashiers were given back-page treatment in the press; whereas the inveterate enemies of labor, in the press and radio, gave far more space to the tales of crooked union officers, who, in collusion with mobsters, betrayed the interests of their union members or plun-

dered their local treasuries. Meanwhile, the politicians who prose-
cuted them were often so greatly publicized or "glorified" that their
road to high public office became a swift and easy ascent.

As in the instances of grafting office-holders (so numerous at the
local level of our government), so with the cases of crooked local
union officers who robbed their union brothers—detection and punishment was not easy. The infestation of unions by racketeers became a deep-rooted disease, like cancer, difficult to check, deadly
when unchecked. The racketeers had many ways of concealing their
operations. Union members, suspecting, even feeling to their own
loss what was being done, were usually too terrified to give evidence.
Flore, pondering over the problem during long periods, stood in fear
of scandals that might be used by the employers' side for attacks on
labor. He did a great deal of "watchful waiting." But other honest
and well-intentioned labor leaders found this problem no less baffling
than did Flore.

In New York, at this period, the situation was as difficult and even
as paradoxical as possible; culinary unions seemed to be responding,
on the one hand, to a spontaneous sentiment among the workers for
organization, and on the other, they were being held back by the
rising power of gangsters in their midst.

The major portion of the city's catering workers who were union
members were in the independent or left-wing organizations, such
as the Amalgamated Food Workers Union. On January 24, 1934,
some 600 of their people walked out of the dining rooms and kitchens
of the new Waldorf-Astoria Hotel, in protest at attempts to herd
them into a company union. Soon this movement broadened into a
general strike of about 8,000 workers against twenty-five New York
hotels—the third time in fifteen years. Picketing was carried on in
spirited fashion: the appearance of celebrities from the fields of literature, journalism, the theatre and the church, as voluntary pickets—
among them Heywood Broun, Norman Thomas, Fannie Hurst, Susan
Glaspell, and even a poet named Selden Rodman—was an innovation that soon became a permanent feature of the culinary workers'
strikes in the Manhattan theatre and hotel district.[1]

Meanwhile, though the strike fever was gaining rapidly, the HRE's
Local 16 (which made some pretense of trying to organize the hotel
workers) announced that its members would continue on the job.
Shortly afterward, President Charles Baum of Waiters Local 16 applied to Superior Court in New York County for an injunction "to
restrain the Amalgamated Union from destroying the AFL union,

or interfering with its members' employment, or picketing at places where they are employed." [2] It was an action that few union officers would have cared to take even under the circumstances of jurisdictional rivalry.

The organizing strike of the independent faction went forward day by day, until as many as 30,000 were reported out. It was a mixed left-wing group that sponsored this affair, including anti-communists of the "splinter" variety as well as known communist labor leaders. After several weeks, Mayor Fiorello La Guardia succeeded in bringing about a settlement that won for employees better conditions and wage scales than had first been offered under the hotels' NRA code. Another outcome was that the Food Workers Industrial Union, headed by Michael J. Obermeier and Jay Rubin, displaced the old Amalgamated Food Workers as the leading independent organization in the field opposed to the AFL's Hotel and Restaurant Employees.

For several years, members of the dual union group and HRE members had been clashing with each other on occasions when the independents called strikes against certain cafeterias which the HRE's Locals 16 and 302 considered were under their jurisdiction. In some cases, though the Food Workers Union had come in first to organize an establishment, its employer would decide finally to sign an agreement with the AFL cafeteria union—HRE Local 302—rather than with the left-wing organization. There were similar collisions in the Times Square restaurant and night-club center, where the Food Workers' people came to organize various places and the HRE's Local 16 intervened and won "union agreements" of some sort from the employers, even though it had had no union members previously employed in such places. Men claiming to represent Local 16, under Coulcher, or Local 302, under Max Pincus, apparently in connivance with the employers, drove away the independent union's pickets by force. But thereafter workers employed in such places found that nothing resembling a union shop was established; that conditions remained as intolerable as before; and that when workers protested they were beaten up by hoodlums, discharged, and placed on an employers' association blacklist.

It was a most "peculiar situation," as a group of suspended rank-and-file members of Local 16 described it, in a letter of protest addressed to President Flore in the summer of 1934:

> The present leadership of the Local is using the vilest form of intimidation to maintain themselves in office and power: members

have been thrown out of jobs for daring to express their opinion on union affairs. The officials in unholy alliance with the bosses' organizations look on without lifting a finger while we work under miserable conditions, long hours, low wages, indecent treatment. . . .

The uniform racket is blooming. We are forced to spend $22 for uniforms for miserable jobs that don't bring us a living.

. . . There is no auditing committee or trustees to check up on financial affairs. The officials call strikes and settle them without consulting the membership. They remove duly elected shop chairmen at will, replacing them with their henchmen. They keep any member who is opposed to their tactics out of Union Headquarters; they refuse to accept dues from members in good standing.

We are demanding of the International an immediate investigation of the affairs of Local 16.[3]

Numerous reports had reached Flore of the racketeering ways of certain New York local officers, and of the beatings of union members who brought complaints against them. Before the opening of the convention at Minneapolis, the International's Executive Board, on August 9, 1934, held a hearing of charges against Secretary Coulcher and Business Agent Aladar Retek of Local 16, and of President Charles Baum and Business Agent Harry Koenig of Local 302. These gentlemen blandly attested their innocence, denied the accusation of racketeering as "mere rumors" circulated by enemies of their union, and, in proof, submitted copies of union shop agreements signed by various restaurant owners of New York, that appeared to be executed in good faith. Brother Coulcher, in particular, a smooth and clever fellow, appeared as a fine and persuasive talker—though it was also reported he had for long years frequented some of the New York night clubs owned by the notorious Dutch Schultz gang.[4]

Flore had been authorized at that time to conduct further investigations of these people. But at that stage he had gone off to Europe, leaving such affairs temporarily in charge of Vice-President Kearney. During his stay abroad he heard by cable that serious troubles had broken out in New York and that a process server would be waiting to greet him on his return.

In response to an urgent call, Kearney, shortly after Flore's departure, had come down from Boston to New York, in order to help settle a dispute that had arisen between Cafeteria Employees Local 302 and an employers' group called the United Restaurant Association. As he recalled afterward, the terms for wages and hours submitted by the union officers, with Max Pincus then at their head, seemed to him very unsatisfactory, and aroused his suspicions of those officers. He, therefore, according to his own account, rewrote the agreement, setting minimum wages and maximum hours in line with those in force in other cities, and persuaded the employers' group to accept it. But oddly enough, the officers of Local 302 refused to go along with him. The United Restaurant Association demanded a collective agreement covering a sizable group of cafeteria owners, while the Local 302 officers wanted to sign agreements only with employers as individuals.

At this point Kearney was obliged to leave for Boston to attend to other pressing business, after ordering the union officers to complete the job and sign the agreement he had written. When, later, he learned that the union officers and members had absolutely refused to obey his orders, Kearney, who was quick to wrath, ordered the suspension of Local 302 and called for its reorganization under new officers.* He was convinced, he says, that there was something fishy about the behavior of those officers.

What Kearney may not have known at the time was that the officers of Locals 302 and 16, in collusion with a powerful underworld gang, were, at this very time, in October, 1934, secretly preparing to start a new (and "phony") restaurant owners' association which they intended to force the restaurant keepers to join, so that they might levy tribute on them. At any rate the officers of Local 302, resisting suspension, went to court and sued the International Union.

As Flore's ship arrived in the outer harbor, a tender pulled up beside it and the officers of Local 302 and 16, headed by the ineffable Coulcher, appeared as if to give their President a fond welcome home after his long absence. They invited him to come on board the tugboat, land with them, and proceed to a private conference on urgent union business. Flore had never found these people so affectionate before, but went along.

According to Kearney's account:

> The racketeering union officers took Flore off to a hotel in midtown New York, and what happened there was that he may have been intimidated. After coming out of that conference Flore issued an order stating that I had exceeded my authority in revoking the charter of Local 302 and restored the local and its officers to good standing.
> I was greatly surprised at Flore's attitude, and at his action.[5]

* Other accounts of the affair hold that the Kearney agreement was not satisfactory to the union members and that it was improper to *force* it upon them.

Flore indicated that in his belief Kearney's actions had exceeded his authority and that the International might lose such a suit as had been instituted. Meanwhile he had other plans for bringing new blood into the New York organization and changing the picture there.

*

The independent union had been trying to carry on a vigorous organizing campaign in the restaurants as well as the hotels. But it was plain that unless the rival unions in the field quit fighting each other no one would succeed in unionizing the city's vast catering trade. At the time of the rising threat of Hitler and Nazism in Europe the slogan of the "united front" was in fashion. The left-wing group known as the Food Workers Industrial Union, in 1934, made earnest proposals both to the AFL local officers in New York and to President Flore that a merger be effected between the two organizations. The FWIU then claimed about 14,000 members, with the bulk of them in New York and Chicago. Such a combination would end jurisdictional quarrels that favored the non-union employers, increase the HRE's strength by 25 per cent and create one great unified labor organization in the field.

Flore had been studying the problem slowly and carefully as was his wont. On March 28, 1935, a few months after his return from Europe, he wrote Jay Rubin, Secretary of the FWIU, that he was sending Emmanuel Kovaleski as his personal representative, together with Organizer Garriga and Vice-President Lehman, to confer with a committee of the FWIU on the question of a merger. He added: "We are approaching these negotiations with an open mind, hopeful of their success." [6]

Jay Rubin, formerly an organizer for the Upholsterers Union, had worked as a baker and then become an organizer for a bakery union affiliated with the independent hotel and restaurant workers' organization. Lately he had been one of the directors of the recent hotel strike, in which he had shown outstanding abilities. Michael Obermeier, a left-wing leader who had been organizing restaurant labor since World War I, represented Local 119, FWIU, consisting of hotel and restaurant workers, at the conference in New York. At this April, 1935, meeting the problems of a merger were explored in reasonable spirit. At their own suggestion the representatives of the Food Workers Union came to Cincinnati a few weeks later to discuss plans for affiliation with the HRE in greater detail. On their arrival at the International's headquarters, Secretary Hesketh gave them cordial welcome and handed the delegation a printed card, such as might have been found in a hotel room, bearing the legend: WELCOME TO CINCINNATI.

Meanwhile, International Organizer Garriga, who was then highly enthusiastic about combining forces with the left-wing groups, had already worked out a merger with the independent organization of cooks in New York, whereby a new local was chartered as the Cooks Local No. 89. Starting with 700 members, in April, 1935, and Garriga as its President, Local 89 soon began to gather in members in droves.

As for the other independent locals with a numerous membership of cafeteria and hotel workers, their entrance into the AFL's International Union was blocked for a time by the strenuous opposition of the old New York HRE Locals, 16 and 302, to any such agreement. Their chief officers, Coulcher and Pincus, insisted that they would have no truck with the rival unions, despite the added strength and revenue these would bring to the International Union.

But Flore, after his European trip, made further investigations of the New York local officers who had come under suspicion and received reports of their association with the gang of Arthur Flegenheimer, alias "Dutch Schultz"; he also heard that in combination with the Schultz "mob," they had incorporated a dummy employers' organization called the Metropolitan Restaurant Association, through which, it was rumored, they blackmailed restaurant keepers.[7]

Coulcher and his associates appeared in Cincinnati at the same time as the FWIU delegation. On being questioned again, they stoutly denied any connection with "certain people whose names were mentioned," that is, the notorious Dutch Schultz gang. They persisted, meanwhile, in opposing any combination between their locals and those of the militant and ambitious left-wing groups. Without their cooperation the merger seemed blocked.

Yet there was a strong rank-and-file pressure to end the constant brawling between the two unions in New York and get on with the job of organizing the field. Edward Flore, moreover, pressed for the plan of amalgamation. The HRE was expanding very rapidly now in Chicago and on the Pacific Coast, and Flore was ambitious to bring the membership of the union to the greatest figures in its history, as he had predicted at the Minneapolis convention. The elimination of inter-union strife would also pave the way for an irresistible drive to win over the immense armies of catering trade and hotel workers concentrated in New York, estimated now at over 100,000. Flore's determined stand in favor of amalgamation persuaded the General Executive Board to render a favorable decision. The GEB report read:

. . . In principle we favor the application [of the Food Workers Industrial Union] and urge our local unions to give the application of these people, throughout the country, favorable consideration. The acceptance of these applications being from individuals and not as a unit. We believe that all workers of the country should be connected with the legitimate trades union movement represented by the American Federation of Labor.[8]

In the autumn of 1935, following a series of joint meetings between local officers of both unions in New York, an agreement was finally reached between Cafeteria Employees Local 302 and the FWIU's Local 110, which resulted in the creation, overnight, of a local union of 7,000, the largest the HRE had ever had up to that time. Max Pincus was chosen President of the reorganized Local 302, while Sam Kramberg, leader of the FWIU's cafeteria workers, was elected Secretary-Treasurer. Later, Coulcher and his fellow-officers of Local 16 also came to terms, and the long retarded merger of the hotel workers and the waiters of the Times Square establishments was completed in December, 1936, between Local 16, headed by Coulcher, and the FWIU's Local 119.

But it had needed a disastrous turn in the affairs of the racket-infested New York locals, 16 and 302, to bring their officers to yield at last to the demand for labor unity.

*

On March 3, 1935, the body of one Jules Martin had been found in the woods near Troy, New York. Martin was known as the manager of a Broadway cabaret and also, by repute, as the lieutenant of Dutch Schultz, the former big-shot bootlegger who had become more recently the head of various "industrial rackets." A long series of crimes were attributed at this period to the activities of the Schultz gang; early in 1934, he had gone into hiding, leaving Martin and one Sam Krantz as his deputies in charge of his underworld enterprises. After the mysterious murder of Martin, apparently by hired killers who escaped without a trace, Governor Herbert Lehman appointed Thomas E. Dewey, then a young Assistant District Attorney, as a Special Commissioner authorized to prosecute criminal rackets.

Why was Jules Martin killed? Investigation showed that he had been "invited" to come to an upstate resort for a conference with Schultz; also, that before leaving the city he had tried vainly to raise a very large sum of money, some $80,000, apparently owed to Schultz out of the profits of the shady undertakings Martin managed for him.

Martin, presumably, had not been playing straight with Schultz; he had not brought enough cash and so he had been "taken for a one-way ride."

Dewey and his assistants, among them a young New York lawyer named Milton Schillback, who learned much about industrial and labor rackets, worked silently at their investigation for over a year. What they found was that one of the "business interests" Schultz, Martin and company had been drawing profits from was the so-called Metropolitan Restaurant and Cafeteria Owners Association, formed in October, 1934, which was supposed to adjust the labor relations of employers in the restaurant trade. At first the restaurant keepers who were members of this bogus association had all refused to talk, for fear of their lives. The trail then led to two union locals, some of whose officers had quite evidently been acting as confederates of the Metropolitan Association and regularly received payments or fees from it. Some complaints had been made against these men as "fakers," who threatened restaurants with strikes, but called them off when the owners joined the Metropolitan Association and paid fees for "protection." They were also said to have collected "union dues" for workers who never saw a union card.

When he was ready, Dewey called restaurant keepers to testify in Grand Jury proceedings, eventually forcing several of them to speak up; he also haled officers of Locals 16 and 302 of the HRE (who had been indicted in 1933), and of Local 1, which had been fighting the gangsters, for questioning. However, these men, Paul Coulcher, Aladar Retek, Charles Baum, Harry Koenig and Max Pincus, all refused to talk. Those restaurant owners or union men who did tell what they knew did so with the utmost reluctance and fear, sometimes in taxis or crowded public places where none could notice or overhear them. The Metropolitan Association office was also raided by Dewey's men and its books seized.[9]

Reports of Grand Jury proceedings going on in the winter and spring of 1936, though supposedly secret, leaked to the newspapers. President Flore thus learned that the name of Max Pincus, President of the expanded Local 302, Cafeteria Employees, was mentioned in these rumors. Flore, who was in Buffalo, once more asked his old lieutenant and neighbor Emmanuel Kovaleski of Rochester to make some discreet inquiries. Kovaleski, who had long known Pincus as a conscientious union officer—in the old days, when he was in Local 1 —wrote him a letter alluding to the current rumors of his connections with racketeers. To Kovaleski's surprise, Pincus, on receipt of the letter, rode all the way to Rochester and suddenly appeared in Kovaleski's office, protesting angrily that he did not like such loose talk and vowing: "There is nothing in my life, now or in the past, that I am ashamed of. . . ."

Because of the prominence he had achieved by the amalgamation of his huge local, Max Pincus was just then being "boomed" as a candidate for International Vice-President to represent the New York area. When Flore learned of how Pincus had made a 400-mile journey to Rochester to deny the rumors about himself, he felt more doubtful of the man than ever. For Pincus did plainly protest too much. According to Kovaleski, President Flore remarked at the time: "This bears out information I have; now I don't believe any of them will come clean." [10]

While the racketeers and their several accomplices in the union were being regularly "grilled" in secret and subjected to a good deal of mental torment, outwardly everything went on as before. The International Union members, meanwhile, in joyful mood, were preparing for their twenty-eighth convention to be held at Rochester, New York, on August 10-15, 1936. It was to be a gala affair, in honor of the twenty-fifth anniversary of Edward Flore's election as President; also an occasion to "point with pride" to the truly extraordinary achievements of the past two years. When Flore, opening the convention and reading his prepared report, interrupted his reading to remark that the organizing momentum of 1934-1936 had brought the membership up to "nearly 100,000," the large body of delegates gave themselves over to a frenzy of cheers.

The Hotel and Restaurant Employees and Bartenders Union, which had seemed a dying organization only three years earlier, had become at last one of America's major labor unions. In 1935-1936 it exerted its considerable economic power by conducting strikes and organizing drives in 322 cities of 39 states and several provinces of Canada. The change in the character of the union could be seen in the appearance of the delegates with "new faces," many of them youths in their twenties, and from new locals. The old-time barmen of "Bob" Callahan's days also would have rubbed their eyes at the number of women officers present, such as Gertrude Sweet of Portland, Pauline Newman of Seattle, Ida Peterson of Bellingham, Washington, Bee Tumber and Mae Stoneman of Los Angeles, Kitty Amsler of St. Louis, Theresa Peterson of Kansas City and Myra Wolfgang of Detroit. There was less beer in evidence and more flowers, masses of them banking the rostrum in honor of Ed Flore's Silver Jubilee.

Nineteen thirty-six, the year of the great "sit-down" strikes, was the time of labor's renascence, with all unions feeling a tremendous lift and surge. Much had happened in the two years reviewed before this gathering: the NRA had been quashed in May, 1935, by the ruling of the United States Supreme Court, though none regretted this less than the HRE's people; the Wagner Labor Relations Act, truly the high-water mark in our labor legislation, had been enacted by Congress immediately thereafter—though it was not yet sanctioned by the Supreme Court; the CIO, under Lewis, was rolling across the country, organizing millions of Forgotten Men in the mass industries. But though the AFL, in 1936, was rent by the controversy over the "rebellion" of the partisans of industrial unionism, all labor felt the great stimulus of the CIO movement; and the service workers, including hotel and restaurant labor, who occupied less vital or strategic economic positions than workers in heavy industry, were at last coming into their own.

The measures passed at the Rochester convention, almost overnight, amid the excitement and enthusiasm of Roosevelt's campaign for re-election, stamped the HRE as one of the most "liberal" or "progressive" of American unions.

It was at this gathering that President William Green of the AFL spoke on August 11, 1936, in defense of the Executive Council's recent suspension of the several large unions that had combined to form the Committee for Industrial Organization. But the temper of the Hotel and Restaurant Employees now strongly favored the industrial union program, and it needed all of Flore's great influence to defeat resolutions supporting the CIO. "This is no time for our union to become involved in this maelstrom of labor politics," Flore exclaimed, "either by subscribing to or against the policy of the AFL."

But inspired, as so often before, by the eloquence of Hugo Ernst, the "New Deal" delegates passed a resolution calling upon the AFL Executive Council to refrain from expelling the CIO unions, until they had been granted an opportunity to present their case at the next AFL convention in November, 1936.

It was again Ernst who led the fight to have the International Union make a generous donation to the defense of Tom Mooney and Warren Billings, the San Francisco labor leaders, who still languished in a California penitentiary after twenty years. The convention voted its donation and was rewarded, not long afterward, by seeing Mooney pardoned and released from jail.

Long efforts to have the International Union remove all vestiges of the "color line" and make an all-out drive to organize workers of the Negro race, were crowned with success in 1936. The existing rules

Action against the world's most famous hotel, in January, 1934, with 3,000 waiters, busboys and cooks protesting at wages of $7.50 a week and tips

Start of the New York City Hotel Trades Council. Signing of the first union wage-hour contract with the Hotel Association, January 18, 1939. Seated: Jay Rubin, Director of the Council; Father John P. Boland, for the New York State Labor Relations Board; Martin J. Sweeney, President of the New York Hotel Association. Among the standing: City Councilmen Stanley M. Isaacs and Newbold Morris; Mrs. Anna Rosenberg; Edward Flore; Mrs. Elinore Herrick

The General Executive Board, 1939. Seated, left to right, Bee Tumber, Gertrude Sweet, Hugo Ernst, Edward Flore, Olivia Moore, Ed S. Miller; standing, A. J. Kilday, James McNamara, John J. Kearney, Edward W. Burns, Miguel Garriga, J. M. Osborn, Fred H. Rasser

Scene of organizing activity against chain restaurants, New York City, 1936; many HRE demonstrations were festive occasions, with pickets wearing theatrical costumes or performing skits on floats

Industrial unionism comes to Broadway—Secretary David Siegal directing action of Local 16 against a "name" restaurant while a policeman behind him observes the proceedings

stipulated that qualified colored workers *might* be accepted as members of any local in a city where there was no (segregated) colored local. This provision was now stricken out and it was ruled that, henceforth, any local union that prohibited the admission of "any competent person working in the allied crafts" was acting contrary to the laws of the International Union. The feeling of the convention was now overwhelmingly in favor of ending racial discrimination.[11]

The delegates also voted to admit Orientals as union members, this measure having special bearing upon Chinese workers on the Pacific Coast. They had long been excluded as non-citizens; but as in the case of Negroes, exclusion led to their competing with white workers at low wages. Henceforth Oriental workers were to be admitted to union locals on giving evidence that they were competent craftsmen.

The convention went on record as endorsing President Roosevelt for re-election and enthusiastically voted $2,000 for his campaign fund. It also found occasion to condemn Fascism in Spain, then plunged in civil war, following the Franco insurrection, and voted a small donation of money to aid the Loyalists.

President Flore was now able to report a tremendous improvement in the union's treasury position, its total assets having risen to more than $467,000, about 40 per cent of which was available for general organizing purposes. A highly interesting report was then laid before the convention by its Committee on Organization, headed by Jack Weinberger of San Francisco, and including among its members Ed S. Miller, the youthful Kansas City leader who was attending his first HRE convention. This report presented plans for an ambitious campaign to unionize nation-wide chain systems of hotels and restaurants (such as Childs'). The idea of working out national agreements with such chains, through the office of the International President, rather than at the local level, and of attempting to bring about a standardization of the highly variable wage scales used in different sections of the country, was also thoroughly explored. These projects aiming at bringing some order into the most chaotic of industries encountered many difficult problems of adjustment between different sections of the country; their completion was to be deferred during a period of further study. Yet the serious, well-informed discussion of such complex industrial questions was an index of the very constructive and even idealistic spirit ruling the Rochester convention of 1936.

On the one hand the International Union seemed all zeal and hope and enthusiasm for progress in this "heroic age" of the labor movement; but on the other hand, as some knew, the shadow of scandal and tragedy overhung this cheerful gathering.

It was in awareness of the sinister elements lurking behind scenes that President Flore in his opening speech had observed in guarded language:

> We are today, I believe, confronted with the most serious situation in the American labor movement that has existed during your day and my day as active representatives of the workers in our industry. We are very hopeful that before this convention adjourns to at least give expression to the things that are now occurring that will both safeguard and protect the future of our International Union.[12]

What he desired of the convention delegates was that they invest him with greater authority than before to intervene in the affairs of local unions, adjust disputes, or to discipline officers and members guilty of dishonest practices or of "disturbances." Flore had often intervened in the affairs of local unions, sometimes to save them from destruction. But actually the union's constitution gave locals such great autonomy, or "home rule," that he had no real authority to interfere in their workings; and where this had been done, such action had sometimes been challenged successfully in the courts. What the convention granted, after the report of its Law Committee had been rendered, was a vague amendment stating that the General President "shall have authority to enforce discipline upon Local Unions and members thereof." [13]

*

Among this happy throng, notable, as veterans remarked, "for its many new and young delegates," there were some who felt older than their years and with little reason for joy or hope.

Paul Coulcher, Secretary of Local 16, a knowledgeable and well-spoken man, made what was to be his last appearance at these biennial meetings and uttered fine phrases upon the prospects before the International Union, "still in its infancy," as he said, but entering upon a magnificent future in which, he may have already sensed, he was not to share. Near him sat his associate, Labor Chief Harry Koenig of Local 16, described as a "big, hulking, rather homely person, careless and sloppy of dress and uncouth in speech." [14]

Max Pincus, President of Local 302, was also there among the New York delegation, a high-strung man with keen, dark eyes. Much glory had come to him for having helped to unite rival left- and right-wing organizations into a giant "industrial" local; and with it a powerful support for his candidacy against Vice-President Lehman of New York.

On the sessions of the fourth day, set aside for elections, all incumbent officers were re-elected, with the exception of the aging Lehman. He was defeated by Pincus in a sharp contest—thus, as one of the younger delegates wrote at the time, "bringing about the election of one who was considered more representative of the new industrial union element in New York." [15] But those who were better informed thought that it was an evil omen that a local officer about whom there had been very unpleasant rumors should be moved up to the General Executive Board. Some even felt that Flore should have attempted to check the movement for Pincus; but he stood aside. Thus the GEB now had two members (including George B. McLane of Chicago) who were said to be on more than nodding terms with the underworld.

Where would it all end? The answer to that came sooner than one would have expected.

On the day after the elections, Friday, August 15, the convention, occupied with its many reports and resolutions, adjourned for dinner, and returned for a night session scheduled for 7:30 P.M.

A delegate was droning through the report of a committee, while Vice-President Ernst pressed him with numerous questions, when suddenly two members from New York were seen making their way hurriedly down the aisle toward the rostrum. They called for President Flore and whispered news to him at which his face, quite visibly, turned very pale and grave.

He interrupted the proceedings and, apparently laboring under great emotional stress, began to address the audience. A great hush fell over the hall.

PRESIDENT FLORE: It becomes the sad duty of the Chairman to announce that three of our delegates were shot this evening when coming out of a restaurant. They are in a serious condition and there is a necessity for some young men to contribute blood for a transfusion to save their lives.

A large number of younger delegates immediately prepared to go to the hospital.

PRESIDENT FLORE: Because of this thing occurring as it did I think it would be rather unfair to go through with our program . . . because some of those people who are going to the hospital are interested in that report. We can take it up first thing in the morning.[16]

The convention hall by now was in an uproar. People began moving about or leaving; a vague terror gripped everyone. Delegate Nat Messing of Local 2, Brooklyn, who had reported the shooting, announced that Harry Koenig, labor chief of Local 16, one of the three persons shot, was in a serious condition and sinking fast. Messing moved for adjournment, and the evening's business was halted. Everyone present understood that the shooting was caused by a falling out of some sort among the racketeers in New York.

According to eyewitnesses of this murderous assault, Harry Koenig, who had been in a very genial mood, had invited two fellow delegates and their wives to dine with him at a restaurant in Rochester. As they left the place and stood for a moment in a group in its doorway, a car drew up to the curb and a man with a submachine gun stepped out and sprayed the whole group of five persons with shot, Koenig receiving the brunt of the fire, the two men beside him also being wounded. The professional killers then made off without being followed. The persons who had joined Koenig at dinner were but slightly acquainted with him and had no knowledge of anything that might have caused the shooting.

The Rochester police, after bringing the victims to the hospital, called Emmanuel Kovaleski, a man of mark in Rochester and sometime President of the New York State Federation of Labor. Koenig had been questioned by the police in vain. Kovaleski, who was permitted to see him, also begged him to name his assailants or enemies. The man had not long to live; but though he was in great agony, he smiled at Kovaleski and kept his lips sealed. Soon he lost consciousness and died during the night.

Something led the Rochester detectives to proceed to the Powers Hotel, where "Nick" Coulcher, Koenig's superior in Local 16, had been stopping. They found him hurriedly packing his bag for a quick departure (though the convention was not over), but learned nothing from him.

In New York, Special Rackets Commissioner Dewey picked up the trail marked for him by the Koenig murder, and resumed questioning of Coulcher and other New York local officers. Moving into the open at last, Dewey began now to secure indictments and carry out numerous arrests of persons charged with conspiracy or extortion in various industries.[17]

Mr. Dewey was young but not innocent of political ambition. The rackets inquiry made sensational newspaper stories touching organized crime in the trucking, building, baking, garment, cleaning and dyeing trades and many other lines besides restaurants. The newspapers were filled with hints or rumors of where the prosecution would turn next, which kept the racketeers on the anxious seat, as was intended.

In Rochester, on the night of the assassination, Flore, in a state of great mental distress, had called the Executive Board for an emergency meeting at his hotel rooms and proposed adjourning the convention, putting all unfinished business in the hands of the Executive Board, in accordance with usual procedure for such an emergency. But Kearney made most vehement protests, urging that the convention must go on. "This is war, war with the racketeers," he recalls saying. He was for "going on with the show" by continuing the convention to its close at the next morning's session.[18]

As his associates advised, Flore slept on it. He said the next day in a calmer vein:

> After having a good night's rest, this morning I concluded that the best interests of the organization would be served by this convention carrying on its work, assuming its responsibilities and doing the job we came here to do. . . .

In his parting words, as if still shaken by the events of the night before and fearful of their effect upon the good name of the union, he said that he was fully aware of "the seriousness of his position this morning." The organization might be growing swiftly, but the difficulties and responsibilities were also increasingly heavy though he was determined to face them with courage and with his best judgment. "Be patient with me," he pleaded, "give me your cooperation and loyalty and we will carry on." [19]

The twenty-eighth convention concluded its business in sober mood. A feature of the last hour was a long and strange discourse by the union's irrepressible orator Vice-President Kearney, of Boston, who had demanded special permission to take the rostrum. On this occasion, Kearney evidently felt that Ed Flore had seemed "rattled," or, at any rate, not equal to the emergency, and that some fitting words must be pronounced upon this tragic affair that had cast such a pall over their proud gathering. Their meeting must close with the International's morale upheld as high as ever. He, Kearney, would step to the platform and "hurl defiance" at the miserable racketeers, some of whom would be sitting right here before him. Conceivably, he might steal the show? He said:

> Since we assembled in this convention one of the delegates has passed away. There are various reasons expressed for the killing

of one of our delegates and the shooting of two others. We . . . have no right to pass judgment upon this dastardly affair. None of us is equipped with sufficient knowledge of its cause, reason and consummation.

We are, indeed, Mr. President, living in a strange age, an age of changing social, economic and industrial conditions; an age where the lives of human beings are held so cheap; an age that appears to be drifting away from God, church and faith; an age where we are forgetting the principles of the brotherhood of man and the Fatherhood of God as predicated by this International Union.

It is a new system that is injected into our industrial lives and our labor movement of which we know nothing. This convention does not consider that this unfortunate death of one of our delegates has any direct relationship to this International Union as a whole. . . . We deplore the use of firearms to remove from our midst any of our delegates by hired assassins. . . . There has been taken a splendid young man whom I liked personally. He leaves a good wife and five children . . . but he was taken by some agency which we know not and whose existence we deplore.

I now move that this convention rise and remain in silent prayer and that the Secretary-Treasurer be instructed to send to the widow and family our deepest sympathy and our expression of grief.[20]

On the preceding night, after having seen the dying Koenig, Emmanuel Kovaleski had returned to the Powers Hotel, where the union men stayed. The hour was late; most of the guests had retired and the lobby was deserted, save for one man sitting alone in a corner. It was Max Pincus, just elected Vice-President, but the very picture of despair. Kovaleski approached him and, after reporting that Koenig was done for, asked him if he knew anything about it.

"I don't know a thing," he replied, and there were tears in his eyes. "It's terrible . . . I don't know what will happen." [21]

But everyone knew that Pincus had worked hand in glove with Coulcher and with the murdered Koenig. For months after the shooting he seemed to his associates extremely nervous and depressed. One high union officer, who had formerly thought him an able and likable citizen, met Pincus in New York at this time and said: "Why don't you get out, go away somewhere?"

"I'm scared," Pincus said.[22]

The murdered Harry Koenig, who had been the confederate of the Schultz gang, had been repeatedly "grilled" by Dewey and before a Grand Jury. Yet, according to well-informed sources close to Dewey, he had told nothing. But his criminal associates *thought* that he had squealed. And they had taken action.

In New York, on October 20, 1936, Prosecutor Dewey, with his case prepared, indicted fourteen persons connected with the Metropolitan Association on charges of extortion and took nine of them under arrest. Of these, five were officers of Local 16 and Local 302, among them Pincus; the others were notorious gangsters or disbarred lawyers acting as agents for Schultz's bogus restaurant association. The prisoners were released under very heavy bail and faced trial. Now the scandal was out.

Max Pincus, then fifty-six years of age, whom everyone had thought of as "a nice fellow," while out on bail, was repeatedly examined by Dewey and his aides, but did not talk, according to reliable sources. However calm he appeared on the surface, he lived in a state of unending dread or torment.

One night in December, 1936, he returned to his home in the Bronx after a union meeting, but apparently, after sleeping poorly or not at all, arose at dawn and went to the window of his fourth-floor apartment, where he stood for a while smoking many cigarettes. In a few more days he was to stand trial and face, if convicted on the full count, a possible sentence of 670 years all told. There was no way out. As the newspapers reported, he "either jumped or fell" from his bedroom window, toward 7:30 A.M., and was found dead. According to reliable sources, no one pushed him out of that window; no one threatened him. It was simply that he knew he would be going to the penitentiary for a long time.[23]

ELEVEN

"The Man Who Would

Be King"

"A business man, who permits theft, extortion and murder to take place on his property and business because in spite of these malpractices he is making an annual profit, likewise is to blame. . . . The fact that the same profit could be theirs under an honest system seems to have no effect on the thinking of these men."—MALCOLM JOHNSON: *Crime on the Labor Front.*

On January 18, 1937, Special Rackets Commissioner Dewey, amid the fanfare of the New York press, opened a sort of mass trial of sixteen persons associated with the Dutch Schultz restaurant rackets through which, Dewey charged, "a $2,000,000 shakedown" had been engineered in the New York area alone. This was to be but one of a series of successful prosecutions of rackets of all sorts that would spread Mr. Dewey's fame far and wide and lead him, within a few years, to the Governor's Mansion at Albany.

In his brief, Dewey stated:

> Notorious underworld characters were the dominant figures in the [restaurant] racket, namely, "Dutch" Schultz, his lawyer, J. Richard ("Dixie") Davis, and two henchmen, Jules Martin and Sam Krantz. The defendants performed their bidding and received

a share of the payments they extorted from restaurant and cafeteria owners throughout the city. Strikes, picket lines, stench
bombs, violence and threats of violence were the instruments employed. The victims faced with business ruin and in terror of what
might happen to themselves or their families met the racketeers'
demands and paid the "shakedown" money. . . . Under the guise
of legality fabricated by astute lawyers the racket grew until a
whole industry . . . became subject to their extortions.[1]

So "nearly legal" had been the operations of the gang that preparations for the trial had required sixteen months, during which evidence had been gathered from honest union members, victimized
restaurant keepers and, finally, from one of the principal figures in
the gang who had decided to turn state's witness. Setting up a big
chart in the courtroom, Dewey placed the late Dutch Schultz (also
murdered in October, 1935) at the head of it, and the names of his
co-conspirators below, eight of whom were agents of the Metropolitan Association, the others being officers of Locals 16 and 302.

Dewey charged that the union officers involved drew a share of
the underworld's take; and that they embezzled union funds supplied
by their hard-working, ill-paid members. The vast majority of the
workers, who were innocent of wrongdoing, had been terrorized and
plundered by a few corrupt officers. In no sense, the prosecutor em-
phasized, was it his intention to discredit labor unions as such, but
only to pave the way for decent officers to clean house and do their
duty by the members.

What emerged also was that some of the biggest New York café
owners, some of whom were nationally known celebrities, such as
former heavyweight prize-fighting champion Jack Dempsey, regularly paid tribute and as members lent their prestige to the bogus
Metropolitan Association—though one would have thought that a
Dempsey need not have feared the threats of mere hoodlums. The
truth was that many of the restaurant keepers found it highly
profitable to cooperate with the racketeers in "adjusting" their relations with what was the "second lowest-paid labor group" in the
country. To this aspect of the affair reflecting lax business ethics at
the management side of the industry, Mr. Dewey gave less emphasis.
Actually, the restaurant-owning "victims," were far less "terrified"
or victimized than Mr. Dewey believed.

The restaurant rackets trial of 1937, and the subsequent appeals
trials of 1939, afforded the public a clear picture of a criminal "empire" that had flourished rankly for four years. Schultz and his part-

ner Martin at one time owned a bootleg establishment on West 48th Street, New York, where Paul N. Coulcher, a founding member of Waiters Local 16, had worked for some years after 1926. There Coulcher and his associate Aladar Retek used to come to take meals toward 1932, and, in conferences with Jules Martin and Sam Krantz, another henchman of Schultz, worked out the scheme to gain control of all the restaurant and cafeteria labor unions in New York as a preliminary step to launching their racketeering organization.

In December, 1932, Coulcher was elected Secretary-Treasurer of Local 16 and Retek became its business agent. Harry Koenig, labor chief of the local, was also drawn into their conspiracy. Then, early in 1933, the chief officers of the cafeteria workers' local, No. 302, Max Pincus and Abraham Borson, were induced to join forces with the Schultz mob; later the racketeers also made approaches to the officers of the large and long-established Waiters Local 1, who, however, steadfastly refused their proposals.

At periods there were some ugly fights between agents of Local 16 and the pickets of Local 1 for the jurisdiction over certain restaurants or sections of the restaurant trade in New York. Then Martin came to President Max Gottfried, of Local 1, and offered to end their war, saying: "Listen, Pop, I don't want to harm you personally, but if you want to get along with me, you will have to change your methods, you will have to be friendly with Local 16." Another agent of the "boys uptown" came to Benny Gottesman, Secretary of Local 1, with the threat: "We have all the unions in your line. You are the one that is the missing link. . . . The boys have decided to take you over. Better make up your mind and listen to us!" If they did, they would make "big money." Or the Local 1 officers who, as heads of a legitimate union, persisted in rejecting propositions of this sort, would be warned that the racketeers would "get them," that "they have the police, the D.A., everything." [2]

At any rate, with two locals and approximately 1,500 union members under their control, racketeers Martin and Krantz proceeded to organize an employers' association called the Metropolitan Restaurant and Cafeteria Owners Association, and endowed it with a proper office, officers, and a clerical staff. Like any trade association it solicited employers as members, but its dues were extremely high, and people "invited" to join seldom refused the invitation. Those who joined, paying fees of from $250 to as much as $25,000 a year, would be given a bronze plaque which they placed, for their protection, in a prominent position in their restaurant or show window. The professional artist who was engaged by the racketeers to design the plaque was one of those who later gave evidence concerning their curious business activities.[3]

The "cash shakedown" and the "joining shakedown" were at the heart of the business. One of the crooked officers, such as Koenig of Local 16, or Williams of Local 302, would call on some restaurant owner and make demands on him in the name of his union members for an increase of wages which was sometimes as much as 100 per cent. If the man refused to yield, a line of pickets would be thrown around his establishment. Or Jules Martin's chauffeur, who in his spare time functioned as a bomb expert, would drive by the place and deliver a stench bomb during the lunch hour, with effects scarcely encouraging to business volume. After that the Metropolitan Association's "collector," one Louis Beitscher, would call on the harassed employer and strike a bargain with him whereby the "strike" would be settled on a much lower wage basis than the union officers had demanded, provided that the café owner joined and paid annual fees to the Metropolitan, the sum varying according to the size of the firm. After it was paid the "victim" enjoyed peace and a continued low wage scale.

One large restaurant proprietor in the Broadway district at first refused to believe, when approached in this manner during a strike, that the gangster's agent could really induce the union members to come to terms. The man said to him: "Come back to your place tomorrow, and you will see that the pickets will go off at one-thirty o'clock sharp. If you have not settled with us by three o'clock, they will go on again right at that hour." And surely enough the schedule was kept as promised. Whereupon the restaurant man paid $2,000 to join the Metropolitan Association.

In the case of one large chain system, having over thirty branches, which had been struck by the independent union in the trade, the proprietor paid Beitscher $25,000 in cash, handing it to him in the basement lavatory of his restaurant so that none might witness the transaction. Then President Pincus of Local 302—which had not even tried to organize the employees of this big concern—ordered up a banquet to celebrate the signing of such an important "union shop" contract, the banquet being attended by notables of the city's labor movement who, of course, knew nothing of what was going on. The wage scale established, without pretense of consulting the workers at any meeting, was low enough to allow the proprietor of that big cafeteria chain to pay not only the enormous initiation fee, but $11,000 in annual fees additionally, the sum being figured at a stipulated rate of "protection" for each branch of the concern.

The crooked local officers, such as Pincus, Coulcher, Retek and company, had good reason, moreover, to celebrate such an affair, for it was declared by witnesses that they usually received 15 per cent of the money extorted by the racketeers.

By another ingenious device, the restaurant proprietors were forced to sign a "non-coercion" affidavit certifying that "no compulsion or threat whatsoever" had induced them to join the Metropolitan Association; and that no money or other consideration had been paid to any officer of the union involved. Thus when President Flore tried to investigate Pincus and Coulcher they could produce, when needed, copies of such affidavits as evidence of their good conduct. Nor was it surprising that the waiters', cooks' and cafeteria workers' unions made so little progress in the huge New York market. Some workers who protested at what they saw of this system were fired from their jobs: others who walked out in spontaneous strikes were beaten up by hired hoodlums.

That the whole system depended upon the ready cooperation of most of the 103 café owners who were members of the Metropolitan—for the sake of the "insurance" they received against the entrance of legitimate unions into their field—was fully borne out by detailed evidence furnished at the trial. The typical pattern of those "deals" was exposed in the testimony of one employer who described how the crooked union officers had threatened him with wage increases that would have added $18,200 a year to his payroll. Then Beitscher appeared to collect for the Metropolitan Association, and put the bite on him. The threatened strike would be called off if he paid Beitscher $3,500, or about 25 per cent of the added wage bill. He paid, and was advised that he could now tell the union officials that things were all "straightened out."

But where the racketeers demanded too much money, or asked for more than the profit picture would allow, the employers—pictured as in very fear of their lives—proved to be not at all afraid to go to the District Attorney or to Special Rackets Prosecutor Dewey with bitter complaints of the extortion being practiced upon them. Where a restaurant owner calculated that his business could afford to pay only a given sum, such as $3,500 a year, but *not* $5,000, then no threats could change his mind. For example, Krantz, head of the Metropolitan (after Martin's death), in one case demanded $40,000 a year of the owner of a large restaurant chain, but was told flatly that he would be given only $2,400 a year—"or nothing." In such cases, as the Dewey Commission showed, the racketeers ended by accepting the best terms they could get, usually by a prolonged process of haggling.

On the other hand there were such instances as that of one courageous and honest restaurant operator who stubbornly refused to pay any tribute to the underworld. His establishment in midtown Manhattan was harassed by "phony" strikes, given the stench-bomb treatment, and as a result incurred serious financial losses. But he himself in person was never molested in any way. This suggests perhaps that the restaurant keepers' compliance with the racketeers' demands was motivated less by fear of the loss of life and limb than of loss of profits.

As in the New York waterfront rackets, described in Malcolm Johnson's book, *Crime on the Labor Front*, as a case of collusion, so in the restaurant and hotel trade do we find that the costs of this system were levied against the wages of the workers and prices charged the public. Thus racketeering, and the corrupt practices of union officers who became partners of the underworld "mobs," are not "caused" by the advance of labor unions, but instead labor unions and their members are among the chief victims of conditions and tendencies encouraging or condoning "business crime" and racketeering.

The trial of the restaurant racketeers figured in the front pages of the newspapers for many weeks and ended in the conviction of three of the four accused union officers and of the professional criminals involved, who were sentenced to long prison terms running from seven to fifteen years. The very exposure of the extortion ring destroyed the usefulness of the Metropolitan Restaurant Association. These developments came at a period when the Hotel and Restaurant Employees and Bartenders were being thoroughly reorganized and expanded. At the same time the rising independent union groups in New York—with whom the racketeer-dominated Locals 16 and 302 had been engaged in intermittent strife—were pressing the International Union to agree to a merger of the two organizations.

At the beginning of the trial, in January, 1937, Locals 16 and 302 were suspended by the International Union. Meetings and elections of new officers were called for; at the same time arrangements for bringing over waiters and cafeteria workers from the independent FWIU locals that were at last being merged with the AFL organization into Locals 16 and 302 were completed. Under the impetus of a powerful rank and file movement, all local officers who were associated with the plunderers in any way were expelled and honest men elected in their place.

Only the two locals had been involved in the scandal of the racketeers' trial; their treasury funds, amounting to about $100,000, were gone, and they were laden with debts. The trustee appointed by President Flore to reorganize their affairs reported that the "dissatisfied and exploited membership had lost all faith in their officers; that they had no wages and no working conditions." [4] It was not surprising, therefore, that the disillusioned and demoralized members turned now to left-wing leaders of the type of Michael J. Obermeier, men untouched by any scandal, who had struggled for long years to unionize the culinary workers of New York.

In truth the near-catastrophe of 1936-1937 led to a great rallying movement of the New York organization that gained for it tremendous labor victories in the next two years. With the rascals turned out, and the quarreling left- and right-wing groups united, a vigorous campaign was launched to dispel the cloud of suspicion that had fallen over some of the HRE locals. The organizing movement of 1937 and 1938, financed equally by the International Union and by assessments upon the local members, was the largest ever known in this field. The general public were shown that these locals were now run by honest officers, who soon gained the respect of all the catering trade employers and hotel managers with whom they did business.

New contracts were drawn up calling for improved wage scales, and submitted to meetings of the union members for their approval. The restaurant and hotel keepers, many of whom had grown weary of being plundered by underworld elements, also found themselves benefited by the housecleaning process. Thus the New York workers, recovering from their misfortunes, were imbued with a new hope and a new élan. The fivefold expansion of their (formerly so backward) local unions in the next four years, up to the beginning of World War II, was to be one of the great exploits recorded in the annals of the International.

The real story of the years from 1936 to 1938 is not of a few knavish local officers or their gangster friends, but of the triumphant upsurge of the old International Union throughout the United States, with tens upon tens of thousands of workers pouring into its locals, while the wage-workers' payroll increased progressively and more sanitary working conditions and shorter hours were established in ever-wider areas of the industry. It was the time when the sweeping electoral victory of Roosevelt opened a new phase of labor's advancing movement. It was the time of the "sit-down" strikes staged by CIO union members in the mass production industries, with the same methods being adapted in spontaneous strike actions of the Hotel and Restaurant Employees in Detroit and other cities. The old locals mushroomed in size; almost 250 new locals were chartered during those two years up to the 1938 convention, during which the total membership was actually doubled. The augmented importance of the HRE as one of the country's big unions and its greatly increased economic power were recognized when President Flore was elected as a Vice-President and member of the AFL Executive Council.

Yet as this splendid chapter of achievement was about to unfold, a still greater threat was directed at the International Union from a new quarter. It was nothing less than a final, desperate effort by underworld groups to seize control of the entire organization at the top. For, as was all too evident, the job of clearing out crooks and racketeers already begun in New York was still to be completed in certain other centers.

*

At the very time when Flore was busy reconstructing the New York branch reports came to him that troubles of a similar nature were brewing in Chicago. There also the bartenders and other locals had been expanding in amazing fashion. But rumor associated the leader of the Chicago organization, George B. McLane, with notorious racketeers of the so-called Capone Syndicate. The former rumrunners, after the passing of Prohibition in 1933, had acquired a number of breweries and distilling plants in their own right, as well as taverns and night clubs. Thereafter, it was reported, they had "muscled in" on the HRE's Chicago locals, formed an alliance with McLane, and soon had the union bartenders pushing the sales of brands of beer and whisky they manufactured to the exclusion of other brands.

What was worse, the Chicago "mobsters" seemed not only to have taken over McLane and his organization but, with unexampled effrontery, were busily plotting still greater mischief. It was widely rumored that they were backing the campaign launched in the spring of 1938 to place McLane in the presidency of the International Union itself; newspaper articles in Chicago, reflecting "grapevine" gossip, described him as the "front man" for the Capone Syndicate. At this time the bold-handed ring of racketeers stemming from Chicago was also said to have gained control of more than one international union, among them the Motion Picture Operators and Building Service Employees.

At the May, 1938, Executive Board meeting, held in Cleveland, an incident occurred that gave Flore quite a turn. It began with his old friend Emmanuel Kovaleski coming to him in private and appealing for Flore's support of his candidacy for the office of Vice-President. Flore, though very fond of the Rochester labor leader, sought to discourage him from running, holding that in the best interests of the union, Organizer Miguel Garriga was the logical man for that office. Kovaleski took all this in good part; but as soon as he had left Ed Flore, he was approached by McLane and General Secretary Hesketh, who urged that he now lend support in his upstate New York district to the "McLane-for-President" movement. Once elected President, McLane promised that he would see to it that Kovaleski was appointed to fill the next vacancy on the Executive Board. What was most surprising, however, was that Hesketh strongly seconded the proposals of a man like McLane, who was by now gathering for himself considerable ill-repute.

The Rochester man indignantly rejected this bargain offer, declaring that he was loyal to Flore and "didn't play the game that way." Then, as he related afterward, he returned to Flore's hotel room and reported the whole incident.[5]

The two men now realized that Hesketh, who had been a staunch old trade unionist, was in league with the McLane faction. They now understood why Hesketh, as editor of the union's official journal, *The Catering Industry Employee*, had been publishing articles month by month on the "brilliant" progress of the Chicago local headed by McLane. He had been "building up" McLane for over a year.

What was more, there was a passage in Secretary Hesketh's report to the 1936 convention which, in the light of recent rumors, strengthened their suspicion of his behavior. It was known that some distillers and brewers in the Middle West were trying to advertise and promote their own special brands by having the bartenders ordered to "push" certain products while saying they were temporarily "out" of others. That such methods were employed in certain sections of the country through collusion with some local officers was a bad business that would have to be stopped. But that Hesketh should be a party to them was a distinct shock to his old associates. Yet Hesketh had said before the 1936 convention, as the record showed:

It is our job to maintain the business in which we make our livelihood . . . in such a manner that it shall command the respect of the general public whom we serve. And how can we do that? While we don't have all the say, like in the old days that many remember, in the purchase of supplies in the catering and beverage lines, *we can do a lot in an advisory capacity*. . . . Immediately after Repeal, some poor goods in the Beverage line was put on the market. They have improved considerable since, but there remains in evidence products that are far from up to standard. The largest Bartenders Local in our International Union, Local 278 in Chicago, and, by the way, conducted in a manner that is a credit to the labor movement, is showing a very keen interest in the quality of the beverages they serve, and will continue to do that; and in their conferences with the distillers and wholesale liquor dealers they keep important matters before them, i.e., good goods and better goods to serve the people.[6]

These seemingly well-intentioned phrases—about pushing certain choice liquor products "in an advisory capacity" when examined by the well-informed were far from innocent in purpose. They hinted clearly at some form of collusion or conspiracy that might bring millions in revenue to some of the shady elements now engaged in the liquor business. Flore, usually slow to act, this time grasped the whole scheme of his adversaries well in advance; he saw at once the peril to which the International Union was exposed.

During the 1920's Chicago was acknowledged to be the bootleg capital of America and "Scarface" Al Capone was chief magistrate of its underworld. As George McLane himself in repentant mood was to testify in court:

Capone surrounded himself with men of . . . most vicious habits. Innumerable acts of violence, murders, assassination . . . were attributed to them. It was thought by the public generally that the gang's leaders ordered the execution of persons who had incurred their ill-will, or interfered with their designs. The entire community was terror-stricken. . . .

Members of the gang were reputedly armed with machine-guns, and drove over the city and countryside in high-powered cars so armed. . . .[7]

McLane, a thick-set, two-hundred-pound man, with the genial manner of a "good mixer" and an impressive appearance sometimes described as "hard-boiled," had made good headway for a time in organizing the bartenders of Chicago's blind pigs. After Repeal, he had gone to work with a will on the taverns and night clubs and began to cut quite a figure as Secretary of the growing Bartenders Local No. 278.

But probably at some time in 1934—though he has placed the time a year later—the agents and pickets who helped organize bars in the Loop district ran into very serious trouble. There were certain bars and night clubs that were reputedly owned by the Capone gang. Although peaceful union activities were entirely permissible by law, these places evidently were ruled by a quite different "government" from the elective one in Chicago. Pickets stationed before the Syndicate-owned bars were repeatedly slugged into insensibility and there seemed to be nothing that the police or courts could do about it.

McLane was much puzzled about how to proceed with his organizing drive when one day, as he places it in the affidavit he gave later, "early in March, 1935," a rough voice called him on the telephone at his union office and represented itself as belonging to a member of "the Syndicate." The voice demanded that the sum of $500 be paid over by the bartenders' union. McLane replied that such an action would be irregular, and that he had no authority to honor such a demand. Whereupon the unknown informed him that "they would come and take over the organization."

A week later he received another message from the same quarter inviting him to appear at a certain restaurant on North Clark Street, an invitation he hardly cared to refuse—though he was a man of stout loins. There he met Frank Nitti, known to fame as "the Enforcer" of the Capone Syndicate, and two other equally sinister characters. The three men then ordered him to put one of their associates, a Mr. Louis Romano, on the payroll of the bartenders' union —"or else." Romano was to serve as a contact man or "adjuster." Again, as McLane recalls, he demurred. Whereupon the three strange gentlemen politely inquired if he thought the color black would be becoming for Mrs. McLane. He was not sure on this point, but, as he declares, he was certainly frightened out of his wits. He was then assured that once Romano went on the union's payroll, the slugging of pickets would stop and McLane could go ahead and organize all the saloons and restaurants in Chicago. Mr. Romano got the job.

So well did Romano do his "adjusting" that within a year or two, Local 278 boasted 4,800 members and became the largest barmen's union in the country. Its members paid initiation fees of $150, dues of $3 a month (a high rate then), and reinstatement fees of $65.

Annual revenues of the local were estimated at over $200,000, making it, in itself, a rich plum for the Syndicate.

A breezy, sociable, free-spending individual, George McLane was a popular figure during the middle 1930's in Chicago labor circles. Though there were rumors about his unorthodox methods of taking members into his union, willy-nilly, the HRE's official journal published many effusive articles about his good works, and he was elected to the office of International Vice-President in charge of the Middle-Western district in 1934 and re-elected in 1936.

Later on, in May, 1938, as he recollects, he was suddenly called to a conference with five persons prominent in the underworld. George Browne, President of the Motion Picture Operators Union (who was sent to prison later) and "Willie" Bioff, the West Coast "Czar" of movie labor, were there and so were the formidable Nitti and Louis Romano. These gentlemen now made the bold proposal that McLane enter the race as candidate for President of his International Union at its forthcoming convention to be held in August, 1938.

McLane, astonished at the whole idea, expressed some doubts that he would be able to capture control of such a large and long-established organization, with branches all over the country. But he was assured that the Chicago group would take their own measures to persuade the HRE delegates to support him; and that they had known how to capture other labor organizations "through the same channels." They wanted him, as they said, to rule as President of his union for only two years during which they would be able to "parcel out different parts of the country" among their agents. When McLane made new objections that it might become known that he was acting as a "front man," the Enforcer, motioning with his revolver, brought forth his most decisive argument—"Either I would run, or I would be found in an alley." [8]

*

The big racketeers of the 1930's certainly showed no lack of imagination and audacity. They had flown in by airplane from Los Angeles and New York to meet privately in Chicago and coolly plotted the conquest of several of the country's important labor unions. In trying to carve out new "empires" of industry and labor, they were but emulating the more ruthless type of American business leaders who, in former times, were called "robber barons."

Once he had cast the die, George McLane (who was perhaps not as shy and reluctant as he later claimed to be), like a bold and merry pirate, began to wage a nationwide campaign for the leadership of the International Union. The convention, whose site was to be San Francisco, lay some three months ahead in time. Accompanied by agents of the Syndicate and bodyguards and provided also with fat bundles of cash, McLane and his troupe journeyed to Boston, New York, St. Louis, Denver, Los Angeles, Seattle and even stopped at small-town branch unions, in order to reach influential officers of the union or gather the pledges of delegates.

Wherever McLane or his agents appeared they displayed all the signs of their affluence and power. They wined and dined and dazzled the local union officers; and, in one way or another, conveyed hints of the practical favors they would perform for those who would enlist themselves in their cause. Many small local unions were too poor to send delegates all the way to San Francisco; the McLane group was reported to have advanced money to some of them so that their delegates arrived at the convention looking very well heeled.[9]

Indeed, one delegate from a waitresses' local appeared at the convention in a stunning afternoon dress, decorated with a large "McLane-for-President" badge. When approached by one of the Flore supporters who tried to change her mind, she pointed to her clothes and exclaimed: "Everything I am wearing I owe to George McLane!"

McLane was like "The Man Who Would be King," in the story by Rudyard Kipling bearing that title. His was really a madcap venture. Under the delusion that the large funds raised for his campaign by the Chicago underworld interests—estimated at roundly $100,000—would grease the wheels for his drive to the throne, believing also that his sinister partners would manage to influence or terrify enough of the union people to assure him of success, he carried on with supreme confidence, circulating advance reports that the strength gathered by the Chicago contingent was overwhelming.

On his visit to New York he met with the active new local officers who were then directing the movement to unionize the city's hotel industry. These were the men who had courageously helped to fight the Dutch Schultz gang and bring about sweeping reforms in the New York organization. McLane made his appeal to this group on the ground that he was bent upon "revitalizing" the "old-fashioned" International Union. Ed Flore, he asserted, had no "guts," as shown by his behavior at the 1936 convention; he was unaggressive and "ran away from trouble." But when McLane was asked to specify just how he would reform or revitalize the organization, he was extremely vague, saying nothing about the help he may have counted upon from such peculiarly aggressive individuals as Frank Nitti, the Enforcer.

The New York union leaders had had their experience with the racketeer types and could judge very well what kind of men Mc-Lane's confederates were. In New York, a number of their erring brethren had died violent deaths, or had just been sentenced to long prison terms. The rank and file members were now up in arms over the issue of "machine-gun unionism." So far as McLane was concerned the vote of the big block of delegates from New York was lost to him and committed to Flore.[10]

Although the racketeering faction drew its strength mostly from the Middle West, one growing union center which they gave a wide berth was Kansas City, where Ed S. Miller, a rising young local leader and protégé of Flore's, had assumed great influence over the union members during a successful hotel strike in 1937 (described in the following chapter). Miller, who was devoted to President Flore, made it known to all comers that he and the other Kansas City members would give but poor welcome to those who hoped to overthrow the union's administration.

Nevertheless McLane and his band—some members of which were armed with blackjacks and revolvers—arrived in San Francisco ten days ahead of the convention's opening session, full of hope and good cheer. His agents set up their headquarters at the Whitcomb Hotel (which was to be the residence of most of the union's out-of-town delegates), opened a bar of their own and invited all and sundry to eat and drink "on the house." The Chicago contingent also donated gifts of all sorts to the delegates and their wives, and entertained them at theatres, night clubs and luxurious restaurants —all of which had some effect on people with weak heads.

In more than a quarter of a century no one had yet succeeded in supplanting Ed Flore as President. But then he had never faced such dangerous opposition since 1911. Worst of all was the defection of the veteran General-Secretary Hesketh, who had always hitherto enjoyed the respect of many union members.

Hesketh, in truth, had been estranged from Flore for many years, since the day in 1929 when it was made plain to him that Flore, as President, was resolved to run the staff of organizers himself and not delegate that task to the Secretary or the Board. Hesketh was thereby reduced to playing second-fiddle to a man whom he, doubtless, regarded as less clever and deserving than himself. This able union officer, who had handled the union's financial affairs skillfully during the depression years, had aged a good deal and was a "changed man," as his old friend felt. His wife had died in 1932, and shortly thereafter, though he was almost sixty-five, he had married a much younger woman. Then he and his wife had formed very close social ties with the George McLanes, and soon Hesketh appeared to be under the spell of the Chicago bartender. After remarrying, Hesketh, the once thrifty Scotsman, it was noticed, seemed to change his whole way of life: he threw out the shabby old pieces of furniture he had long kept in his Cincinnati home, bought new things, and stepped out a good deal with the free-spending McLane.

Political and labor-union life often generates suppressed, long-smoldering jealous passions between men who, though incompatible, have long been forced by circumstances to work together. Secretly obsessed with the idea that Flore must somehow be supplanted as President, believing that he himself would never be happy again unless his association with the man from Buffalo was ended, "Bob" Hesketh, from an early date, had given his covert support to McLane's aspirations.

His old West Coast friends pleaded with him to reconsider his decision to support McLane, warning him that such a man would be the first to cast off Hesketh as unsuitable to his ulterior purposes. But Hesketh simply drank more whisky and swore great oaths at Flore—whom he now accused of being in league with "New York communists." Flore must go, at all costs. Yet, oddly enough, Hesketh himself had long been familiar with "Wobblies" and radicals of all sorts in the Northwest and had never worried about them.[11]

Flore's position was stronger than was supposed, but he badly needed friends. The California Vice-President, Hugo Ernst, was to play a leading part as official host at the convention ceremonies in San Francisco. Though Flore had never before opened his heart to Ernst—or to anyone, for that matter—he now turned to the California leader in his time of trouble and imparted his knowledge of what was going on behind the scenes.

Ernst said later that he had never really known much about McLane, except "rumors, such as you hear about almost anybody." But now he was made fully aware of the danger facing their organization. The elections at the San Francisco convention of 1938, he felt, would be "a turning-point for the International Union." [12]

Ernst, who often seemed a banterer and jester, taking all troubles lightly, was apparently without fear of anything. But on this occasion he prepared to give the unwelcome visitors among the Chicago contingent a hearty, old-fashioned Western reception. He took counsel with his San Francisco union colleagues and with his old friends who headed the AFL's labor body in San Francisco, John Shelley, John O'Connell and George Kidwell, and with their help made arrangements for staunch union men to be ready to handle any disturbances that might arise. He also called on Mayor Angelo Rossi to provide special police protection for the convention and to have undesirable characters arriving in the city's air and railway terminals searched for arms and warned to behave themselves. A detective was assigned to act as bodyguard for President Flore; but his services were politely refused. Instead, Organizer John J. Mc-Devitt, a man of large and powerful frame, remained watchfully at Flore's side throughout the proceedings. Hugo Ernst would open the convention formally and was to preside over several of its sessions.

*

The twenty-ninth biennial convention began on August 15, 1938, at the Civic Auditorium in San Francisco with a record-breaking attendance of 649 delegates. The newspapers followed the sessions with unusual interest, for the Hotel and Restaurant Employees were then described as the fifth largest and "the fastest growing organization" in the AFL. In the past two years alone, it was reported, the union had gained 112,000 new members, and was carrying on large campaigns and organizing strikes in the principal cities of the country. The region of the Hotel Whitcomb, for four days before the convention opened, was the scene of "hot campaigning" by adherents of Flore and McLane, and the atmosphere was described in the press as "extremely tense." [13]

Over the week-end there had been strenuous caucusing by both sides. The large West Coast contingent shepherded by Ernst produced a flood of pro-Flore signs, placards and leaflets, in which the McLane faction was stigmatized as the accomplices of "racketeers." The opposition's canvassers and pamphlets assailed the usually conservative Flore as the "ally of communists." But the size and enthusiasm of the demonstrations in behalf of Flore, whose supporters seemed to spring up at every street-corner of the city, made a strong impression on delegates arriving at the week-end and somewhat depressed the followers of McLane.

On the one side were the loyal element of sound trade unionists, (mainly from New York and California) and the younger leaders typified by Ed Miller of Kansas City; on the other side were the most reactionary elements in the organization, as well as a number of delegates from scattered locals that were dissatisfied with the current leadership for one reason or another

A breakdown of the roll-call showed that the New York delegation, once abnormally small, had come to San Francisco with all of 95 delegates commanding 282 convention votes; the California bloc was larger than ever, with 179 delegates and a voting strength of 424. Illinois was now the third largest group, having 74 delegates and 200 votes. What had not been foreseen by the opposition was that without the support of the unexpectedly large New York delegation and the Californians the outlook for McLane was hopeless.

The union had now reached a phase of healthy and progressive organizational growth and had before it much serious business to transact in order to pave the way for future expansion. Yet at this time the menace of "machine-gun unionism" offered the most terrible threat, and this became the issue around which the forces here were divided. The California section had been free of racketeers and would have none of them. The New York group, together with many new and large delegations, such as that from Detroit, were no less determined to root out the gangster element.

The McLane agents had started out by entertaining and cajoling people. But everything went wrong. Even at the hotel where they were giving away free drinks with free meals, serious trouble broke out when a considerable number of Negro delegates who had come to town were excluded by the hotel managers and had to be quartered elsewhere.* This was at the climax of the New Deal era and such racial discrimination did not go down well. Following a storm of protest at the Whitcomb management on the first day of the convention, most of the union's white delegates also moved out of the hotel, and the hospitable bar set up by the Chicago contingent was deserted by all—save for a few faithful and thirsty McLane followers.

On the first day, Monday, Vice-President Hugo Ernst, very much the dandy, with a colored vest, a carnation in his lapel, and elegant spats on his feet, opened the convention cheerily before an audience of 5,000 persons, including numerous members of the HRE's San Francisco locals and other AFL unions, as well as the delegates and their wives. Ernst had Mayor Rossi on hand as a guest speaker; also, as if by coincidence, the Sheriff of San Francisco County; and some of the local AFL leaders, such as John Shelley, head of the Teamsters

---

* The Chicago delegation itself included twenty-one Negro delegates who were refused accommodations at the Whitcomb. Removal of the convention headquarters from this hotel followed and led to a suit for damages filed by both sides and later settled out of court.

Union in the city. Shelley, an old hand in union affairs, evidently knew his lines well, for he said:

I hope that during the sessions of your convention you will think clearly and act calmly. Don't allow yourselves at any time to lose your balance and your good judgment. . . . Your International is one of the most outstanding in the AFL. I am sure you are going to build on that reputation at this gathering.

Ernst then handed various gifts and verbal bouquets to President Flore and turned over the gavel to him. Flore's customary "Report of the President," usually read as a routine affair, began on this occasion with a fairly emotional appeal for order and sanity, reflecting the tension everyone felt among the delegates: "As your presiding officer, I ask and plead with you to be tolerant in your dealings and your discussions."

With pride he pictured the remarkable recovery of the International Union from the near-wreck of Prohibition days; and declared that:

. . . now one could roll in the glamor of success . . . and boast, not alone that our union has reached a membership of approximately 200,000, but that it occupies an outstanding position in the industry as the bargaining agency for the larger majority of the workers in that industry. . . . Growing as rapidly as it has grown in the past few years, our International has become one of the most, if not the most, progressive trade union in the American Federation of Labor.

It must continue to organize the unorganized, he went on, "regardless of race, nationality or creed." There must be no racial discrimination of any kind against Negroes or Asiatics qualified for membership. Flore also advocated unity in the labor movement and a reconciliation between the AFL and the CIO.

This, in short, was a Flore in fighting mood, as he had seldom been seen before, making his appeal as a liberal or "progressive" of the labor movement. His closing words were spoken with great force and, plainly enough, constituted a strong challenge to the opposition:

Two years have passed; two years of accomplishment unknown in the annals of our International Union. We have met every opposition and conquered every foe. We propose to keep our flag flying to the wind. There must and will be no surrender.[14]

At these words the whole audience seemed to stand up and burst into mad applause. Hugo Ernst, leaving his place on the platform by the side of Flore, descended to the floor and promptly yelled for all Flore men to follow him. Many delegates jumped from their seats to form a column behind him and were led by Ernst back to the platform where they hoisted the President to their shoulders and then paraded about the aisles of the auditorium. The demonstration lasted for some thirty minutes, while the McLane men looked on with angry or gloomy faces.

At the close of the first day's sessions, Secretary Hesketh also made his biennial report. In doing this he managed to direct some thrusts, in scarcely concealed language, at Flore, and to convey hints of his sympathy for McLane. For the large expansion of the union in recent years, he declared, "no one person can claim the honor." Yet if the recent organizing drives had been a failure, President Flore would have borne most of the responsibility. One of the resolutions introduced at this convention (but not adopted) had proposed moving the union's general offices to Chicago. And Hesketh said meaningfully:

> I hope to see the day, during my tenure of office, when the General President and the General Secretary will be located in the same Headquarters' city, working in and out of the same office. It would be more satisfactory in every way. . . .[15]

None could miss the implications of these words. Some of Hesketh's former associates in his Seattle local were so disgusted at what appeared to them as a betrayal of his own principles that they were now prepared even to oppose his re-election as Secretary.

Despite the excitement engendered by the group of racketeers in its midst, this convention passed a series of important measures designed to facilitate the swift expansion of the union. The General Executive Board was reshuffled so that henceforth it would be made up of fourteen Vice-Presidents, eleven of them being placed in positions of executive authority in separate geographic zones or districts covering the entire country.* In addition to these officers, two women were to be elected as Vice-Presidents-at-Large, and one Vice-President-at-Large was to represent the Railway Dining Car Employees on the Board.

The union's treasury funds now approached $1,000,000, but approximately half of this was reserved for death benefits. To provide

* Hereafter the members of the GEB were designated as: Vice-President, First District (New England states); Vice-President, Second District (New York and New Jersey); and so on, with California in charge of the Tenth District Vice-President, and Canada designated as the Eleventh District.

additional money for the greatly increased organizing drives going on throughout the country it was voted to raise the per capita tax from twenty-five to thirty cents per member each month.

This convention also strengthened the power of the President to discipline locals and their officers or members and regulate their affairs, where conduct injurious or disgraceful to the union was complained of. Provisions for fair hearings and appeals were made for such cases, the new ruling being clearly aimed to check the activities of racketeers or grafters.

An illustration of the temper of this convention was seen in the debate on a special tax levied by the AFL in 1938 of one cent monthly per member of each constituent union, the money being intended to supply a "war chest" for the struggle being waged by the AFL against the CIO. The HRE delegates, however, though loyal to the AFL, were strongly opposed to contributing to the "war" between the two wings of American labor. A resolution flatly rejecting such a levy and urging that the AFL Council reopen negotiations for peace with the CIO was adopted by a decisive vote. Highly instrumental in shaping the sentiment of the delegates on the issue of the industrial unionists was the ardent speech of Myra Wolfgang, delegate from Detroit's big "industrial" local, No. 705. The Detroit waitresses had also been involved lately in a number of "sit-in" or "sit-down" strikes, their victory, as Mrs. Wolfgang reported, having been gained "mainly because of the fine support given by pickets of the United Automobile Workers, CIO." Raising money to fight the CIO was unthinkable; it would be better to send out more organizing crews and "establish a research and educational department as well." [16] Flore and Hugo Ernst, however, prudently opposed the demands of a minority of the delegates to take their union into the CIO, since cooperative relations with the Teamsters, Building Service Employees and other AFL unions were extremely important for the development of the culinary workers' organization.

The first test between the two warring groups within the International came on Tuesday, August 16, in the report of the Rules Committee (dominated by McLane men), which brought in the recommendation that elections of general officers be held on Friday, the last day of the convention—instead of on the fourth day, Thursday, as was traditional. The motive here was to filibuster the convention into a second week, so that many anti-McLane delegates—who could not afford or had not allowance enough to stay beyond the normal five-day convention period—would go home while the McLane men stayed on; thus Flore's support would be weakened. But this motion was defeated by a decisive vote of the delegates on the floor of the convention.

Balked in one maneuver, the lawless element then resorted to their old-time system of intimidation and brought out their "goon-squad."

International Organizer Miguel Garriga of the New York delegation, who had taken an active part in the proceedings as a partisan of Flore, and who had openly denounced the McLane faction, left the convention hall before noon to take his wife and small son for an hour or so to an early motion picture performance. Apparently he was trailed there by some of the strong-arm boys who surrounded McLane, and, at 12:30 P.M. in broad daylight, they set upon him and beat him brutally. Only the cries of his six-year-old boy caused the thugs to take flight and saved Garriga from more serious injury.

News of this assault came to the convention that Tuesday afternoon at the same time that a telephone message was received from St. Louis, from Harvey Fox, delegate of Local 51, St. Louis, and an active Flore supporter, who had mysteriously "disappeared" from San Francisco late Sunday night. Fox now reported that he had been forcibly taken by a number of McLane's henchmen to a tavern in Oakland, across the Bay, and that they had threatened to kill him. Their threats had seemed so convincing to Fox that he bestirred himself to escape in a taxi, and took the train back to his home in St. Louis.[17]

On Wednesday the McLane faction issued a slanderous leaflet assailing Flore's supporters as "Reds" who were playing "communist tricks to capture the union"; they also announced that the veteran Secretary Hesketh had joined with McLane in the movement to form a new administration. A pro-McLane caucus was called for that night, just preceding the election of general officers scheduled for the next afternoon.

But the loyal element, made up largely of the big California and New York delegations and of the Detroit and Kansas City contingents, quickly called together a caucus of their own on that same night. At this much larger gathering Hugo Ernst presided and spoke with good effect, exposing the attempt of the opposition party to fashion a "Red scare," so that the delegates might be frightened into voting for McLane. He, for his part, as he said, was unconcerned about the political beliefs of the members of the union in New York or elsewhere, so long as they worked zealously to organize the unorganized.

Numerous speakers who had had their experiences with racketeers warned the delegates of the disaster that faced the union. Indignation at the violence done to Garriga and Fox ran high. Far from being intimidated, the caucus that night obtained firm pledges of more than 1,000 votes for Flore (out of a total of 1,709 for the full convention), or more than enough to assure his re-election. Thus far the sound core of the union stood up more and more staunchly as the threats and assaults of the underworld element in their midst grew more vicious.[18]

The convention that day had also moved swiftly to condemn, by resolution, the violent incidents inspired by the lawless faction. In a statement given to the press, Hugo Ernst said: "Labor in San Francisco resents the introduction in this city of methods alien to our trade union movement." [19] By urgent appeals to the Mayor, Ernst obtained stronger police guards for the critical day that was to follow. The next day numerous plain-clothes men, stationed at the entrances of the convention hall, intercepted persons whom they recognized by their police records and "frisked" them of some twenty-six revolvers and an assortment of knives and blackjacks, on the eve of the presidential poll.

On Thursday afternoon, August 18, as the election of officers was about to begin, Vice-President Ernst calmly took the chair. The whole place seemed to be on the verge of a riot; Ernst, nevertheless, appeared debonair as always. The Chicago men were described as shifting threateningly in their seats as if preparing for action, while the San Francisco, New York, and other pro-Flore delegations also shifted and made ready for their adversaries.

As at many previous conventions, Delegate Kovaleski, of Rochester, jumped to his feet to make the nominating speech for Edward Flore. The genial Kovaleski, in his plain, old-fashioned union man's oratory, spoke for tradition, experience and order. "In all those years," he exclaimed, "no persons living can say that your General President has not been true to his trust!" Again there was a long demonstration and parade of Flore supporters.

Big John Staggenberg, a veteran of Bartenders Local 278, Chicago, then rose to his feet and said:

> I am presenting a *man* as a candidate for the General Presidency of this organization who comes from the Middle West, one who has proven his worth . . . *he is a man with real guts.* . . .
>
> If it could be written into the records—and it is not—what this man has done in the last four years since he has been Vice-President, it would make fine reading for you delegates here who at the present time have ridiculed this man.

Many of the delegates booed the speaker and cried, "Racketeer!" But Staggenberg went on to declare belligerently that his candidate had "the audacity and the right to run," and none should dare ridicule his supporters or call them "everything under the sun." He suggested also that those who had made accusations against the McLane following without proof might be called to account:

I carried my first card in 1892 and have carried it continuously, and I am no racketeer and I don't associate with them, and I think it is cowardly, dastardly and malicious infamy to make those remarks in an attempt to break down a man's character. We come in here with clean hands. Remember, especially, a lot of you delegates in this convention, remember you will find out in time the way to deal with this International. . . . But we have a man here that we think can do the job just a little better than the man we have. . . . Therefore I propose a real man for the presidency of this International Union, George B. McLane.[20]

After a tumultuous ovation for McLane, Delegate Ben Parker of Local 25, Chicago, rose to second the nomination. He was in a venomous mood toward those who had made reflections on his candidate, and shouted angrily words which (though not officially recorded), ran as follows, according to one account:

I have worked in every millionaire's house in Chicago; I have worked in every silk-stocking club and every political club because I am a waiter, and I am a caterer, and while I have worked there I have studied them. I used to wait on Sam Insull. And they talk about gangsters. I worked in Cicero . . . and came in contact with a wonderful character by the name of Al Brown, afterwards they hung on him the name of Al Capone. And what crime did he commit? They used him to boost the word "gangster." Well, if he is on the Rock [Alcatraz, in San Francisco Harbor, at the time] the other gentleman I used to wait on, Mr. Insull—I liked him too, because he was a wonderful character, but no more than Scarface Al Brown. He was a gentleman, and he wasn't a thug; he is a victim of the bankers' racket.

CHAIRMAN ERNST: The gentleman who is now addressing the convention is evidently seconding the nomination of Al Capone. The nomination of Al Capone is not before the convention and I would like to have the Brother confine himself to seconding the nomination already made.

DELEGATE PARKER: If I lived in San Francisco, I would start a movement to move that disgraceful rock from this community.

CHAIRMAN ERNST: I do not think that Alcatraz Island is before the convention. If you desire to second the nomination of a candidate, all right. (Laughter)

Troubled by the mockery of Ernst, Parker floundered about and lost the thread of his seconding speech.

The tabulation of the votes by roll call proceeded amid a growing uproar. When the polling was half done it became clear that President Flore was to be the victor by a two-to-one margin—he received in all 1,095-1/6 votes compared with 611-5/6 votes for McLane. The men of the Chicago delegation sat as if stunned for the moment, the stout McLane utterly deflated, Hesketh in tears.

Then, after the tally was completed and the result announced, as one eyewitness related:

> The Chicago delegation as a whole rose from their seats, milled around and called upon other delegations to leave the Convention with them and hold a "real Convention." The tension was high and the air electric, for it looked for a moment that our International Union was in danger of being split. This move, again, proved to be a boomerang, for no other delegation moved. It was a shock even to those who sincerely and honestly voted for McLane, thinking a change would be for the better.[21]

The lack of real sympathy or mass support for the Chicago "movement" was in glaring evidence at the climax of that convention.

*

The vivacious Ernst emerged from that storm-tossed gathering at San Francisco as the proverbial "man of the hour." In the thick of the fight he had shown himself cool, good-humored and yet fearless. He wound up with a display of generosity and nobility of character that the crowd of union delegates would never forget.

On the occasion of the Wednesday night caucus of the pro-Flore men, just preceding the elections, the whole gathering as with one voice demanded that Ernst be nominated for General Secretary in place of Hesketh. His San Francisco colleagues, as well as delegates from all over the country, pressed him to accept the nomination which would have meant his certain election, as over 1,000 votes would have gone to him.

But Ernst firmly said: "No." Hesketh, by his folly, had virtually destroyed his own usefulness to the organization; yet Ernst did not want to be the "instrumentality" by which the older man was to be driven from the labor movement. To have done that, in his view, would also have meant continuing the struggle between the factions in the union.

Ernst was a proud man and extremely sensitive to the spirit of intolerance or religious and racial prejudice shown by many persons, in and out of the labor movement, against Jews, a sentiment which appears to have grown weaker in recent years. In the city that he had made his home for a third of a century he had overcome all such prejudice in his own case by the sheer force of his personality and by his integrity of character. What was more, he hated the thought of leaving San Francisco, where "everybody knew him" and where he had formed lifelong friendships and passed as a man of mark in the city's labor movement. His present duties as an International Vice-President and Secretary of Local 30 only occasionally took him away from San Francisco or California. "Put it that I'm not ambitious," he used to say to his friends. Higher office and salaries counted for little in his book, as against the maddening vexations of big-time union politics, or the possible difficulties of going along with a President with whom he might disagree on almost every subject. An intense individualist at heart, Hugo Ernst would never give up his sacred "right to disagree."

To be sure, on the Friday morning before the balloting for the General Secretary was to begin, Hesketh came tottering over to see Ernst and begged him not to run against him. He spoke of himself as a ruined old man who had nothing left but his job. All his hopes of winning added power through association with the McLane group were now crushed, and he felt he had not long to live in the face of such misfortune.

Ernst gave him his hand and promised he would not oppose his re-election.

Hesketh had also gone the night before to beg the forgiveness of Flore, shedding tears of repentance as he said over and over again: "Ed, I don't know why I did it." Ed Flore forgave him, knowing that henceforth he would have his hand over the man. The renomination of Hesketh, with Flore's approval, would be, at any rate, a means of restoring harmony in the organization.

But the movement to nominate Ernst by "drafting" him went forward; cards presenting his name formally were printed up quickly, and delegate Grover Tracy of Local 33, Seattle, Hesketh's old stronghold, made the nominating speech for Ernst. "There is nobody can deny there has been a breach," he argued, "and that breach is going to widen. . . ." The years of intense activity that lay before them would require, above all, that the rank and file trust its leaders im-

In 1937, imbroglios with famous Broadway hostelries won prompt publicity for the union and were supported by many theater and movie celebrities

The "Brass Rail" strike in New York City, one of the longest in American history (1941–1947), which ended in victory for Local 16 (now merged with Local 1)

(opposite) An iron robot intervenes in the hotel workers strike of 1941; one of a number of surprise plays used by the alert San Francisco members

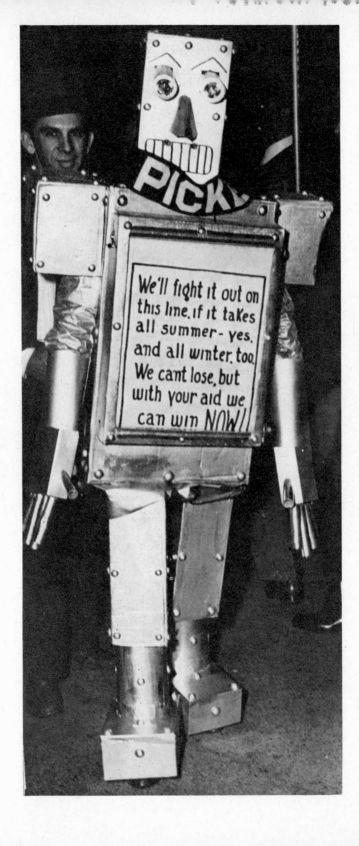

President Hugo Ernst and Secretary-Treasurer Ed S. Miller at the White
House presenting to President Harry Truman the first union pledge for
support of his 1948 re-election campaign

plicitly. To elect Hugo Ernst would "give us all assurance that . . .
we would be starting off with a clean slate . . . and that President
Flore would have his general officers, not fifty per cent but one hundred per cent with him."[22]

After a long ovation, Hugo Ernst took the floor:

> May I, at this time, say a few words in declining the nomination.
> I am deeply grateful to the delegates who have seen fit to propose
> my name, and I want to assure them that it was much against my
> wishes and against my desire to accept it for several reasons. I
> would regret very much, were I elected to any position at all, to
> disagree with my superiors and co-workers; and second, I do not
> feel that I can justifiably transplant myself from the environment
> of San Francisco, where I have been for thirty-five years, and do
> justice to the job of secretary-treasurer, as has been done by Bob
> Hesketh. I have disagreed with him in this instance, but I can say
> without fear of contradiction that Bob is a good secretary.
>
> I think Bob now realizes that the overwhelming sentiment of the
> convention is with the leadership of President Flore. I believe the
> next two years will show a closer cooperation between Hesketh and
> Flore so that our organization will grow. I thank you for the con-
> fidence you have placed in me, and I most respectfully decline.[23]

This gallant gesture, the magnanimity of Ernst, caught the eye of
all that gathering and the applause for the San Francisco leader was
even greater than before. Certainly no man in the organization, that
day, looked "bigger" than Hugo Ernst.

To run ahead of our story, Robert B. Hesketh fell ill after the 1938
convention and was never able to return to his duties as General
Secretary Treasurer. He died July 3, 1939. After Hesketh's death,
changes were made in the International headquarters staff. W. R.
Wasson, a member of Cooks Local 468, Los Angeles, and formerly Secretary of the Los Angeles Joint Executive Board, was
designated Director of the new Department of Education and Research, but the press of other assignments prevented him from establishing the new department. Harry W. Fox, an active member of
the Culinary Workers Alliance, Local 337, Cheyenne, Wyoming, and
for more than a quarter of a century a cook by trade, was designated
managing editor of the *Catering Industry Employee*.

At the International's first General Executive Board meeting
after Hesketh's decease, held in Cincinnati on October 4, 1939, Hugo
Ernst was elected Secretary-Treasurer without opposition. Though
he made strenuous efforts to have the union move its headquarters
all the way to his beloved San Francisco, this was not easily arranged,

and so he came, with some reluctance at first, to take up his residence in Cincinnati. He was then in his sixty-third year.

But to return to the convention, McLane's bitter cup was filled to the brim. The only important elective office remaining to be contested was for that of Vice-President for the Fifth District (Illinois and the neighboring states) then filled by McLane who was, of course, standing for re-election. But this time Flore was determined to show no mercy. A majority of the delegates also were resolved to eliminate McLane from the GEB.

For a year or more President Flore had had his eye upon the rising young local officer Ed S. Miller, who now headed the delegation from Kansas City. The union had been more or less extinct in that Middle-Western center prior to 1935, when Miller, a recent member of Bartenders Local 420, was elected as its Secretary-Treasurer. After organizing the barmen with much zeal, then, as head of the Local Joint Board, he had helped rebuild the old waiters' and waitresses' locals. Almost overnight a union structure of about 3,000 culinary workers had been created in Kansas City. Miller and his compatriots, moreover, had acted as stalwart supporters of Flore.

Ed Miller recalls how Flore sent for him and talked to him privately in his hotel room. He appeared to be laboring under great tension and "his manner was very stern." Very abruptly Flore asked Miller to stand against McLane for the office of Fifth District Vice-President. It was perhaps not the pleasantest or easiest of assignments just then, but it was "an order," and the tall Missourian, a veteran of World War I, accepted it without question. From that day on, Flore and Ed Miller worked very closely together.

With the Flore supporters mobilized for him, Miller defeated McLane, though in a close contest, by a vote of 904-5/6 to 726-1/6. It was a crowning misfortune for McLane, who, after having failed in his bid for supreme control of the union, could not even serve his lawless confederates any longer as a Vice-President and member of the Executive Board. No less humiliating was the election of a full slate of five AFL delegates with not a single Chicago man on it. When this result was announced it brought forth another stormy demonstration from the defeated faction. On the final day, Saturday, the McLane delegation were beaten again on the question of a site for the next convention. At which one of their members, Louis Romano, jumped up, seized the microphone near his table and threw it on the floor, while yelling for all the McLane people to leave the convention, which they did. After that was over, the majority of the delegates who remained there were able to get down to the serious busi-

ness of enacting measures of union policy without further interference.

There was a final sequel to the series of disasters that befell The
Man Who Would be King. He returned to Chicago counting, at
least, upon holding his $275-a-week job as boss of Local 278. But
according to the sorrowful account given later in his own sworn affidavit, when the President of the local died, the group of racketeers
called McLane again to a conference and gave him his orders. One
of them, in a rather bored tone, simply informed him that there need
be no special elections for a new local president, and that Business
Agent Louis Romano would henceforth fill that office. Though he had
little trade union experience, Romano, thereafter, would be given the
sole power to sign checks and draw funds. McLane, a useless in-
cumbrance to the racketeers, would be allowed to draw a salary as a
business agent, at Romano's pleasure. But he was told "it would be
much safer if he took a long vacation outside the State of Illinois
for the next few months."

McLane departed for Hot Springs, Arkansas; but on his return,
three months later, in January, 1940, Romano told him that he and
all the other officers (except for two or three he retained) were
through. They could "get the hell out!" Some of the persons who
replaced the ousted local officers were men of unsavory reputation.
It was truly a tale of woe. George McLane had yielded to every demand of the mobsters. He had, so to speak, opened the door and
invited these wolves inside; and now after eating everything up they
had ended—financially speaking—by eating him too. It was then
that McLane brought suit against the racketeers in the union for the
restoration of his office and salary, and that he wrote and signed the
affidavit containing his version of life with members of the Capone
Syndicate. But when the time came for the trial, he himself was
threatened with—among other things—a libel suit. At which juncture
he suffered a sudden loss of memory, revoked his affidavit and
dropped his suit. By then the once mighty George B. McLane, who
had risen like a meteor over the firmament of the International
Union, was back where he had started from: tending bar in an ob-
scure tavern in Chicago.

TWELVE

Triumph of the
Service Workers: 1937-1941

"We rejoice in the right to picket . . . !"

The strenuous defense of the union against the incursions of racketeers from New York and Chicago was, after all, but a distracting interlude. During those years the real task of the men and women who had the interests of the catering trade workers at heart was to organize their people and win collective bargaining power in their growing industry. In the successful battle to drive the "mobsters" out of the union the veritable heroes were the average, or cross-section, local officers who served as delegates at the San Francisco gathering. Once that was over they resumed the less romantic, everyday job of organizing the unorganized that had been carried on with a rising tempo since the winter of 1937.

Everything now seemed auspicious for the growing mass-movement of the armies of cooks, waiters, bartenders, waitresses, dishwashers, chambermaids and bellhops into the union. As Edward Flore said at this period, more had been accomplished for labor in the few short years of Franklin Roosevelt's first term than in all the previous administrations at Washington. What had happened under the New Deal was equivalent to a peaceful revolution in which the legal rights of organized labor had been fully recognized. After the landslide victory of Roosevelt in the 1936 election, to which union

labor contributed so greatly, there followed the President's strenuous attempts to "pack" the Supreme Court—which up to now
had refused to sanction the principal New Deal reform measures. In
April, 1937, the Court finally yielded and sustained the legality of
the Wagner Labor Relations Act of 1935. Now the log-jam was
broken. "Unfair labor practice" was sharply defined in this historic
act; company unions were virtually banned; no member of a union
might be discharged for the reason of such membership; and an impartial National Labor Relations Board was empowered to oversee
workers' polls in their shops for the purpose of assuring their right
to choose bona fide labor organizations. Many employers who had
tenaciously resisted unions in their industries by every means, now
gave up the fight.

A very important development for the hotel and restaurant workers was the passage of so-called "baby" Wagner Acts in many states
which revised local or state laws in line with Federal labor legislation. For many employers in this trade had previously set up the
legal defense that their local restaurant or hotel business did not
enter into interstate commerce, and so did not fall under Federal
regulation. This barrier also gave way.

The service workers generally were late in winning a real collective
bargaining position in their industries, as compared with more
skilled labor groups, or people in more concentrated industries or big
factories. This was as true of the retail clerks' unions or the laundry
workers' unions as of the HRE. Though the catering-workers' organization was actually one of the older unions, it had been run for too
long a period as a small "job trust" affair in chosen localities.

But from the year 1937 on, the powerful momentum of the
CIO's campaigns in the heavy industries opened the road for almost
all other less strategically placed labor groups. Where Lewis' miners
and steel workers organized new towns that had never before known
any real unions, as in many localities of Pennsylvania formerly ruled
by the "Coal-and-Iron Police," the AFL's Teamsters unions followed closely on their heels. After them came the service workers of
various categories, all "the butchers and bakers and candlestick makers," and, notably, the Hotel and Restaurant Employees and Bartenders. Previously, in this region, the mere appearance on the street
of a union picket bearing a sign had meant his immediate arrest
and severe punishment. But now the Secretary of HRE's Local 237
wrote in jubilant spirit: "We rejoice in the right to picket in Pittsburgh!" [1]

At the back doors of hotels and restaurants in America from Boston to San Diego people were talking of the union "drives" in progress. Organizing strikes for "recognition" were under way in Pittsburgh, Detroit, Cincinnati, St. Louis, Kansas City, Los Angeles, San Francisco and many other towns. This "crusade"—rather than the exploits of a few gangsters—was the real story of the International Union in the late 1930's.

The San Francisco organization of 8,600 workers, with its many seasoned members and Hugo Ernst at its head, was for years the bellwether of the rest of the flock. Since 1934 a tight Joint Board control over the separate craft locals had been worked out, so that thereafter their teamwork was fairly complete, having the effect of one big unit. One advanced feature of the San Francisco branch was the "industrial" local, No. 110, that had been created out of the "miscellaneous workers" who were dishwashers, kitchen-assistants, bus boys and scullery maids, now grown to a strong body of 1,900 people, with Walter Cowan as secretary. A newer development, in March, 1937, was the chartering of Hotel Service Workers Local 283, the idea being to complete the job in the city's hotel trade by unionizing janitors, doormen, bellhops, housekeepers, chambermaids, and even the clerical staff of the hotels, who had never, up to now, been organized.*

The time seemed well chosen to establish the union shop in the hotels, as had been done in most of the city's restaurants, and "from the roof down," not merely for the kitchen and dining-room staffs. While negotiations were opened with the hotel men's association, funds were gathered and careful arrangements were made in advance for a possible conflict. The San Francisco Local Joint Board was the first branch of the International Union to engage the service of a team of economists, the Pacific Coast Labor Bureau, headed by Henry Melnikow and Samuel Kagel, for the purpose of surveying conditions in their industry prior to making proposals for new contracts. The International itself had, as yet, no research department at Cincinnati.

---

* Here there was some overlapping of jurisdiction with the International Building Service Employees, AFL, who organized various service workers stationed in apartment houses and hotels, including elevator operators. But the dispute was eventually settled by a ruling of the AFL Council providing that all workers in apartment and hotel buildings that maintained eating places were to go to the HRE, the rest to go to the Building Service Employees. Later, also, all points at issue were adjusted by the signing, on October 12, 1943, of the so-called Flore-McFetridge jurisdictional agreement. (William McFetridge was President of the Building Service Employees.)

The employers' association, meanwhile, complained bitterly of the "exorbitant" demands of the union in San Francisco, which, for various reasons, was able to maintain a higher wage scale than other cities. Strong objections were also made to the union's proposal that Local 283 include in its membership hotel personnel designated as clerical or desk workers associated with management. But the union members were now determined that all the remaining unorganized groups in the hotels, always a threat (as potential "scabs") to the other workers, should at last be brought under the tent. At a large mass meeting held early in April, Hugo Ernst gave a report of the employers' counter-proposals which, though making numerous concessions to the workers, were still unsatisfactory, inasmuch as they insisted upon straight-time pay instead of time-and-a-half for overtime work and still refused to hire "extra help" through the union. The rank and file, by an overwhelming vote of 3,173 to 35, authorized a strike in the event that the union's demands were not granted, and a deadline was set for April, 1937.

A peaceful settlement seemed to be "in the bag," as the union officers believed, when almost all their demands for preferential union hiring, the eight-hour day and the forty-four-hour week, the establishment of a joint arbitration board to handle grievances, and other improvements were granted. The one stumbling block remained the refusal of the employers to accord similar union shop conditions to the new Hotel Service Workers Local 283. A final conference on the last day of April continued until 2 A.M., then the negotiants parted company on this one issue. C. W. Pilgrim, an officer of Cooks Local 44, related:

At 5 P.M. on May 1, 1937, the union business agents walked into the [15 Class "A"] hotels in the city and gave the signal: "That's all, boys and girls," and the parade started. Bartenders took off their coats and aprons; waiters and bus boys put down their trays, stenographers left their desks; clerks put on their hats; in fact, every worker just simply walked off. It was the most complete strike this scribe has ever witnessed. . . .

At first some of the guests treated it as a joke and took it upon themselves to show how good waiters and bartenders they were, but that did not last long. When it was time to retire and they found the elevators were not running, it was not so good. . . . A movie star named Oliver Hardy, weighing 230 pounds, staged a "sit-down" of his own in a hotel lobby rather than walk up twenty floors. . . .

We have a hundred per cent strike. The hotels are practically in a stage of siege.[2]

Some 3,200 hotel workers were out at the start; later 1,500 more workers struck several more hotels and about 1,000 employees who were in other unions serving hotels, such as the musicians and engineers, joined them. In all about 10,000 were affected by the stoppage, and this at a time when San Francisco's famous hotels, such as the Fairmount and Mark Hopkins on Nob Hill and the Palace and St. Francis, were expecting floods of tourists for the Golden Gate Fiesta a few weeks later. But the union avoided calling out the many small "Class B" hotels.

Mayor Angelo Rossi tried to mediate between the two parties, but this failed. Tradespeople were furious at the prospect of heavy business loss and the newspapers reflected their anger. Some of the hotel keepers were emboldened to attempt to bring in "scabs." In one case, that of the Manx Hotel, some sharp clashes took place. The hotel owner, a former football star, and also president of the San Francisco Hotel Association, had set up a banner proclaiming that he believed in a "Free America," and that as the grandson of California Vigilantes he would have no truck with the unions. This brought him much newspaper publicity, large crowds of pickets and onlookers, and a riot—for thousands of workers, filling the streets approaching the hotel, demonstrated angrily against the idea of a return to nineteenth-century conditions under the Vigilantes. With the result that the hotel was closed up tight and nobody would patronize it.[3]

The strike continued through June and into July, when efforts at mediation by the Governor of California and by a conciliator from the U. S. Department of Labor also failed. The employers had hardened in their attitude and appeared to offer less than before.

The rigors of industrial warfare would have borne heavily upon the 4,700 idle union members had it not been for 4,000 of their union brothers who remained busily at work in the city's restaurants, and paid assessments each week so that the strikers might be fed. Cash relief payments of $10 a week were provided for married men on strike, while single persons were provided with two warm meals each day—cooked by the finest of chefs—and small sums of cash. To maintain morale, strike meetings were held at union halls each afternoon, a daily bulletin was published and the strikers were sent out en masse for picket duty.

At first Hugo Ernst had been highly optimistic, saying cheerily: "We'll have the employers on their knees in twenty-four hours." But the weeks stretched into months and the cost became increasingly heavy—ultimately over $193,000, most of which was raised by the San Francisco local unions.

Ernst worked harder than ever before, staying at his job for what he estimated was a "twenty-three-hour day." All day long his door at Local 30 headquarters was open to "hardship cases," and when the union till was bare, as his friends recall, he would give freely of whatever money of his own he had in his pocket. Night after night he addressed meetings at which funds were raised. And at the lunch hour he would often take his homburg hat and cane and go strutting along at the head of his band of pickets, very distinguished in appearance, as the press described him, "always meticulously dressed to the point of dandyism . . . and looking as much unlike a union officer as anyone could imagine." [4]

A feature of the 1937 strike was the great militancy of the rank and file and the active participation of women workers, mainly waitresses of Local 48 led to the picket lines by the inspiring Margaret Werth. It was she, also, according to her own union colleagues, who organized a series of parades with San Francisco's prettiest waitresses appearing in costume on "floats" mounted on trucks, thus effectively advertising the strike. Such parades, thereafter, lent a festive air to HRE strikes in other cities as well. The bartenders, usually a conservative element in the union, also supported this action with great ardor under the leadership of William McCabe, who, not long afterward, became secretary of their union. When the time came to bring about a settlement, the moderate leaders, Ernst, St. Peter and Walter Cowan, had their hands full holding down the militant groups that had become prominent in their locals.

Travelers by the tens of thousands shunned the city that summer, and business losses for the hotels alone were estimated at $6,500,000. At length, after eighty-nine days' stoppage, President John Shelley of the San Francisco Central Labor Council was able to arrange for a new conference between representatives of both parties at which compromise terms were agreed upon. These, unfortunately, were less satisfactory than the agreement almost accepted on the night preceding the strike. Yet they included the basic demands for the preferential union shop, the eight-hour day, and recognition of all but 150 union members whom the Hotel Men's Association regarded as attached to management. An elaborate set of work-rules was now drawn up for the first time and a joint arbitration committee empowered to adjust grievances and wage disputes. This first comprehensive agreement, a veritable "trade treaty," helped stabilize the industry during most of the next seventeen years—for the employers had learned that the HRE's members in San Francisco were not to be beaten down by force or economic pressure.

The problem now, however, was to win acceptance of this compromise agreement by the rank and file, which had become greatly wrought up during the three months' struggle. At a large mass meeting on July 28, 1937, Walter Cowan, who was then President of the Local Joint Board, announced the terms of the new contract, but was met with an explosion of angry protests and boos. Cowan interrupted his reading to shout that he also was not happy over all of the terms proposed, and said: "Now let's boo all together, and I'll boo with you!" And so they all let off steam by booing together, his humorous sally helping to calm the crowd. Then Ernst spoke in behalf of the agreement, declaring that the unions' essential demands had been won, the "preferential shop" clause providing for effective control of hiring, with non-union workers to be engaged only when the union list was insufficient. The agreement with nineteen "Class A" hotels was presented by him as part of a continuing process, a long stride toward full control of labor in the city's big hotel trade. A similar agreement was also to be established with forty "Class B" hotels.

Following long debate, in which the malcontents had full opportunity to speak, a decisive majority voted by secret ballot in favor of the proposed agreement, by which the strike was ended the next day, July 29, 1937. The 1937 strike, called by Ernst the "most successful hotel strike" up to that time, was, in the opinion of students of West Coast labor, a "key strike" that established the permanent labor power of the six HRE locals in their industry. It was also the most completely planned strike action ever carried out by the Hotel and Restaurant Employees and Bartenders and marks the union's "coming of age" as a modern labor organization. Previously industrial contests with employers in this trade had been small or casual affairs involving a few hundred workers, or sometimes even spontaneous "mob movements," with the International's executive leadership playing little part in them. This time, in recognition of the importance of the contest, Cincinnati headquarters gave powerful support, contributing over $52,500 in cash. Indeed, all San Francisco labor was lined up behind this strike.

It was said at the time that the whole strike could have been avoided if the union had been less rigid and the Hotel Association had not been frightened by certain unyielding demands (made in April). But Ernst and his associates wisely yielded to the ardor of the rank and file sentiment during this season of labor militancy instead of trying to impose unwanted terms at the wrong time—and permitting themselves to be swept aside by extremist leaders. Meanwhile the San Francisco employers were given another lesson in the advantages of peaceful industrial relations by the hardest-hitting group in the International Union. Their establishment in a still poorly unionized field of a true collective bargaining position equal to that of the most advanced unions also served as an inspiring example to other sections of the HRE that still lagged in the rear.

In the ten years that followed, membership of the San Francisco locals was more than doubled, attaining a number of over 20,000; and wage scales were the highest for the country in their trade.

*

The effect of the San Francisco hotel strike was quickly reflected in favorable developments for the union up and down the West Coast; its repercussions reached even New York. It was the signal to start organizing the (mainly non-union) hotels, which employed about 30 per cent of all catering workers.

While the struggle still raged in San Francisco in mid-July, 1937, the Local Joint Boards of the HRE in Seattle and Portland, Oregon, were also involved in negotiations for a union shop agreement with the hotel men's associations in their cities. The bargaining process might have been long-drawn-out, but the Seattle employers were fully informed of how much the San Francisco strike was costing the hotels there, and they quickly came to terms with International Organizer Weinberger, chief spokesman for the Seattle locals. On the next day Weinberger was off to Portland where the hotel owners also surrendered and "handed over on a platter" an agreement granting improved hours and conditions and the union shop. As Weinberger related:

> The San Francisco strike unquestionably helped Portland and Seattle obtain their first hotel contracts without any serious dispute, strikes or lockout. The hotel men, having made up their minds about the handwriting on the wall, decided it would be wisest to go along with our organizations on a reasonable and friendly basis.[5]

It also may have occurred to them that they would do better to deal with the long-established AFL unions than with some of the newly formed and less disciplined groups affiliated then with the CIO. Thus a very rich and important area of the hotel and restaurant industry's labor in Washington and Oregon fell to the union almost without a fight. In Seattle alone the Waitresses Local No. 240 began to expand until it reached a membership of 3,700 at its peak. City-wide agreements were also won from associations representing drug-store lunch-counters and large department-store restaurants, as well as from the regular restaurant and tavern proprietors. And what was equally important was that wage scales and conditions, ranking close to the highest in the trade, were made standard for the Seattle culinary workers in all these different types of establishments at about this period.

Waitresses Union Local 240 had been led for a quarter of a century by a famous champion of working women, Alice Lord; and after her death, by Pauline Newman, who was also imbued with Miss Lord's qualities of idealism and courage. In friendly competition with the San Francisco branch, another Seattle local, largely of women workers, Hotel Service Employees No. 551, became the first in the industry to win a straight five-day week for its members—this piece of negotiation being managed by Organizer Jack Weinberger. What was more, an effective system of peaceful arbitration was established under the Seattle Local Joint Board which, while avoiding dislocations in the industry and loss of work for the members, brought about a steady improvement of conditions. The healthy effect of such advances in labor's status was also shown in the "one hundred per cent" unionization of hotels and restaurants even in smaller towns of the Northwest, where Jack Weinberger, himself a product of the San Francisco movement, trained many able local officers during the years he spent in this section.

Indeed, the San Francisco unions for years "exported" talented union leaders to other areas that the International had long struggled in vain to organize. Walter Cowan, for example, after being appointed an International Representative and stationed in Southern California, directed a vigorous drive that led to the rapid development of HRE locals in an immense market that had been for long years anti-union. Soon Waitresses Local No. 639, Los Angeles, with Mae Stoneman at its head, emerged as one of the two largest in the whole organization. John Sargent, secretary of the cooks' local in this city, and later an International Vice-President, also contributed greatly to the growth of the culinary workers' locals in this area—which expanded from a membership of 4,600 in 1938 to about 20,000 ten years later. Miscellaneous Restaurant Employees Local 440, under the leadership of Harvey Lundschen and John Cooper, was one of the most progressive unions in Los Angeles and did a lot to establish the culinary unions.

Meanwhile Thomas J. Meehan, who had worked with Walt Cowan in Los Angeles, moved on to the resort towns of Nevada at the end of World War II, when Las Vegas became a rich oasis of legalized gambling. Here, too, a strong local organization of 3,000 grew up in the very heart of the Western Desert, and Las Vegas became "one hundred per cent union."

Moving eastward to view the action along the far-spreading panorama of the International Union's "front" in 1937 we find, as on the Pacific Coast, virtually all the local branches in the Middle-Western cities on the march, effort being centered particularly on winning over the big hotels.

Even earlier than the San Franciscans, in the winter of 1937, the culinary workers of Detroit had caught the fever from the epidemic "sit-down" strikes in the Automobile City. Almost overnight this open-shop stronghold had become a union town. Early in March, workers in drug stores and "five-and-tens" serving quick lunches began to "sit-down" and made demands for wage increases and an eight-hour day. At this period the veteran Louis Koenig, Secretary of Local 705, had as his chief assistant Myra Wolfgang, a young woman possessed of both brains and energy. Day by day the calls came to them to send help, food and cot beds or mattresses to groups of girl workers who had shut themselves in at "Camp Woolworth" for eight days and nights, or at the units of chain drug stores. The whole movement appears to have been spontaneous. As Mrs. Wolfgang recalls:

> I would be in the local union office and a girl would call up suddenly, saying: "Say, is this Myra? Someone told me to call you. I'm Mamie, over in Liggett's Drug Store. We threw out the manager, chased out the customers and closed up the place. We are 'sitting in.' What should we do *now*?" [6]

Koenig, Myra Wolfgang and Floyd Lowe, officers of Local 705, with the aid of Lou Walters of Cooks Local 234, directed the union's main efforts toward organizing Detroit's big downtown hotels, such as the Statler and Book-Cadillac. There workers began their "stay-in" during the second week of March, 1937. Waiters, cooks and other service workers pitched their camps in the spacious banquet halls and ballrooms of the hotels and, as always in such cases, silence and gloom fell over these great edifices. Guests were marooned on high floors, or forced to carry out their luggage themselves, among them, as it happened, Miss Sonja Henie and Tyrone Power. The union officers gladly arranged to have such celebrities pose for newspaper photographers, so that their strike was well advertised, and few persons cared to lodge at such places. By March 16 the big downtown hotels capitulated; agreements were reached for arbitration of all union demands and for a poll of the workers, under the National Labor Relations Board, to determine their entrance into the union.[7] Thus thousands of employees poured into the HRE's amalgamated Local 705 which, though allotting part of its numbers to form cooks' and bartenders' locals, soon grew to an astonishing membership of over 11,000.

Pittsburgh, three years earlier, had been the scene of an ill-fated hotel strike by the independent Food Workers Industrial Union, most of whose members later joined the Hotel and Restaurant Employees Local 237. Now, in the fall of 1937, following long preparation and recruiting of members, and with liberal financial support from Cincinnati, vigorous organizing strikes were directed at the city's leading hotels, such as the William Penn, the Fort Pitt, the Pittsburgher and the Roosevelt, until some 2,300 employees were out. The result of this contest was a first hotel agreement for a union shop that included in its provisions the categories of unskilled workers who had never known the benefits of a union before. Here, too, the HRE's units virtually trebled in size as a result of the 1937 action.

In Kansas City, Missouri, the years of Prohibition and depression had seen an old waiters' local, No. 19, reduced to a membership of 150, while the old bartenders' local had lost its charter during Prohibition. But by 1934 Organizer Frank Johnston, who had been sent out to reactivate the union in Kansas City, succeeded in reorganizing Bartenders Local 420. Among the charter members who helped revive this local as soon as beer and liquor vending had been made legal was Ed S. Miller, a native of Kansas City, then thirty years of age. It happened that his father, John Miller, had once been a member of the Cigarmakers Union and later, toward 1903, of the Bartenders Union in Kansas City. Ed Flore himself had been acquainted with the elder Miller, who had been well known in the town's labor circles. The younger Miller seemed to have come naturally by his interest in union activities. With the friendly encouragement of both Flore and Organizer Johnston, Miller, at the beginning of 1935, became a candidate for the secretaryship of Local 420, was elected to the office, and a year later also became head of the Local Joint Board. Thereafter things began to move in Kansas City, the union men organizing most of the bars and some of the leading restaurants.

In all of Kansas City's hotels, however, there were only sixteen employees who were members of the HRE at the beginning of 1937 when Miller launched a vigorous hotel organizing campaign. As almost everywhere else in that season of labor revival, the action spread as if by spontaneous combustion. In the last week of May, when the union was recruiting the waitresses, two hotel maids who had taken out union cards were discharged by their employer, and one of them began picketing the establishment, one of the city's leading hotels, all by herself.

Miller promptly demanded the reinstatement of the two women; this was refused and he called a strike meeting of 800 hotel employees. The city's Hotel Association refused to consider the union's demands, and the next thing that happened was a swift walkout of some 1,800 workers, almost the full personnel of Kansas City's six leading hotels. The hitherto unorganized waiters, bellhops, kitchen assistants and housemaids rushed to the picket lines in high spirits and stayed on guard twenty-four hours a day. Ed Miller strove to keep them in order, saying: "Don't block traffic, avoid arguments, be peaceful. Be ready to relieve your brothers and sisters on picket duty."

Here, too, as in many cities all over the country, guests tussled with their luggage, and with elevators dead, went panting up endless stairways, while skeleton staffs of desk clerks and office employees cooked breakfasts in the partly deserted hotels. After two weeks of this, efforts by hotel managers to bring in scab crews precipitated violence. On June 15, 1937, about 2,000 striking workers, led by an eighty-piece band (provided with the compliments of the Musicians Union), filled the downtown streets in the vicinity of the struck hotels and tried to bring out the non-union crews. Guards were lined up before the hotels, and strong police units charged the crowd, crying: "Break it up! This is tear gas." Everyone clutched at his eyes and ran; then brickbats flew and plate-glass windows went crashing to the street. The union people, rallying their forces, soon returned to surround the Muehlebach and other downtown hotels with masses of pickets.[8]

Amid the intense excitement of the struggle, Ed Miller fell sick and was hospitalized. The city at this period lay under the complete political control of "Boss" Pendergast, who, according to Miller, whatever his sins, was always friendly to labor. In this almost

"Southern" city, organized labor had been very weak prior to the Roosevelt era. Now, however, the Mayor and Police Commissioner (who were, of course, the henchmen of Pendergast) called on Bernard Allis, owner of the Muehlebach, and firmly recommended that he come to terms at once with the union. "We'll go over to see Ed Miller at the hospital and settle it all now," the Mayor said. Otherwise, it was implied, the police might not be able to maintain order and protect the hotels.

Pendergast, it was reported at the time, had known Ed Miller years ago when he was a youth and had the job of helping the local Democratic organization watch the polls on election days. The powerful Democratic boss seemed determined in this instance to support the union.

Allis, wealthy operator of the Muehlebach, was the head of the Kansas City Hotel Association. At first he objected vehemently to such advice, but changed his mind and within twenty-four hours had yielded, and was negotiating with Miller—who, by then, had bounced up out of his sick bed to help wind up the strike. The other members of the Hotel Association followed suit, and a blanket agreement, bringing 3,000 workers under the union shop, granting them the six-day week, and gaining for them wage increases averaging 25 per cent, was accepted by both sides.

After a brief struggle of nineteen days, Kansas City had a going union, and the hotels were solidly organized. Ed Miller, a new union officer, had thus won his spurs in his first strike, a very rough-and-tumble affair. President Flore, who had watched over the proceedings in Kansas City closely, was much impressed with the behavior of the tall young Missourian, and in his mind marked him for future leadership in the organization.

Miller, following the settlement, addressed the meeting of the union members in his usual jovial manner:

> The strike is all settled. When you go back to work in the morning, don't go looking for trouble. Walk in with a smile. Do your work better. You're getting more money and shorter hours.[9]

Cincinnati, site of the union's headquarters, and boasting some of its oldest locals, had fallen on evil days after World War I. The city's famous beer gardens, once manned by staunch trade unionists, were devastated by Prohibition; an employers' blacklist and the use of the "yellow dog" contract served to eliminate labor organization from the city's hotel and restaurant trade. Yet here, too, revival came: in 1936 a Hotel Employees' Council was formed and worked thereafter in close liaison with Cincinnati's central labor body. A year later, a twenty-four-hour strike by the HRE locals against the city's biggest hotel, the Netherland Plaza, was supported solidly by the walkout of all carpenters, painters and engineers, and paved the way for an industry-wide collective bargaining agreement with eight leading hotels. In the years that followed, master contracts were also negotiated with employers' associations representing over 800 restaurants and retail liquor dealers in Cincinnati and in the neighboring Kentucky towns of Newport and Covington. Cincinnati's six locals, which had formerly been reduced to a total membership of about 500, expanded until they embraced, eventually, over 6,500; wages, once abnormally low in this area, moved up to the level of other important Middle-Western cities.

Likewise, in Milwaukee, whose local organization had become moribund, being reduced to about 350 union members during the 1930's, a change for the better came at the end of 1936, when Phil Valley was elected Secretary of Local 122. During the year that followed, energetic unionizing promptly brought membership up to 2,800.

In St. Louis a strike of 5,000 hotel workers broke forth in the spring of 1937, headed by Kitty Amsler, the veteran leader of the waitresses, and Jess Keller, head of the cooks' local. Within a few days the union forces managed to regain all the ground that had been lost seventeen years before in the disastrous lockout struggle of 1920. Thus the International's local units were on the move almost everywhere, breaking new ground.

*

This season of swift growth was also featured by the large numbers of Negro workers entering the union's ranks. The International, as noted before, had had colored union officers present at its founding convention in 1892, and ever since then had tried, from time to time, to organize Negro labor in its industry, although too often in segregated locals. Colored cooks working in railway dining cars and at the terminal station restaurants of Washington, D.C., had formed a part of a "mixed" local, No. 767, as long ago as 1904. Thereafter small groups of railway-dining-car cooks and waiters in other regions had also been attached to the International. At the beginning of World War I there were several small locals in the HRE made up both of railway-dining-car employees and sleeping-car attendants, for their jobs at that period were more or less interchangeable.

In the 1920's the movement of the colored service workers on the railroads—long a backward group, through no fault of their own, to be sure—went forward in earnest. Under the spirited leadership of A. Philip Randolph, a former newspaper editor, the Brotherhood of Sleeping Car Porters was solidly organized in 1925 and acquired an international charter of its own from the AFL. When this union, however, tried to add the dining-car employees to its ranks, a conflict developed with the HRE, which claimed jurisdiction over both the dining-car workers and Pullman porters. By a decision of the AFL Council in 1928, the HRE was awarded the charge of the dining-car people, while the Sleeping Car Porters, under Randolph, continued as a separate union affiliated with the AFL.

The great depression beginning in 1929 halted efforts of HRE organizers to build up a strong Dining Car Employees Division. The colored dining-car employees had been too long ill-paid and ill-used: their fixed wages in 1929 averaged twenty-six cents an hour; they had no specified lay-over periods or relief days, nor vacations, nor job security. Little wonder that their locals had remained weak, and that all but two collapsed during the depression years.

After 1934, however, active organizing was resumed—following passage of the Railway Labor Act in that year. Ten new dining-car locals were chartered, the largest of these being No. 370, New York, headed by George E. Brown; No. 465, Omaha; and No. 351, Chicago.

An important step in the development program for this division of the HRE was the formation of the Dining Car Employees Joint Council, in October, 1937. At that time also, George E. Brown, the resourceful leader of the dining-car men based at New York's railway terminals, was chosen as an International Vice-President representing the growing numbers of colored dining-car workers.

Strong progress was registered by the dining-car employees up to the eve of World War II, unremitting efforts being made by the members to win improved wages and conditions from forty-seven of the country's principal railway systems. Organizing of these migratory workers, seldom at home, ever on the move, was an arduous task. Yet by 1941 a solid strike vote of 9,000 dining-car employees— though no strike followed—was an important factor in bringing railway management to acceptance of higher wage scales.

For how many long years the union's officers had been saying that organizing the catering trade of New York was "an impossibility." And yet upward of 200,000 were employed in this market alone. As one of the local leaders said at this period:

New York is the key to all our work. Break through here and our International would grow by leaps and bounds.[10]

But the conflict between rival unions and jurisdictional quarrels among the locals of the International itself had retarded the advance of unionism in this huge center. The cutthroat competition of many thousands of small concerns in Greater New York, moreover, made the problem far from easy; and there had been the reign of terror under the racketeers.

In the winter of 1937, however, the whole picture changed. The International's largest New York locals, 1, 16, 89 and 302, greatly reinforced by the new members who came over as a result of the merger with the Food Workers Industrial Union, held meetings and elected new officers. Left-wing leaders were placed in the saddle: Salvatore Gentili, formerly of the FWIU, became Secretary of Local 1; Michael J. Obermeier and William Albertson, who also came from the independent union, now headed Waiters Local 16, with jurisdiction over the Times Square restaurants; Samuel Kramberg assumed charge of the Cafeteria Employees Local No. 302; and Harry Reich became Secretary of the Cooks Local 89. Combining their forces in a new body called the New York Hotel, Restaurant and Cafeteria Employees Organizing Committee, made up of representatives of eleven locals in the city, the New York union officers chose International Organizer Miguel Garriga and Jay Rubin, former General Secretary of the FWIU, as co-directors of the Committee, which carried on a "whirlwind campaign" to unionize their industry.

On June 2, 1937, a delegation of fifteen, in behalf of the Committee, headed by Rubin and Garriga, appeared before the General Executive Board of the International, sitting in Cleveland, and reported that all jurisdictional differences between the New York locals had finally been ironed out. They outlined a plan for the most intensive organizing campaign ever undertaken in their industry and petitioned the International for a donation of $25,000 to meet the expense of the drive. The local unions joined in the movement pledged themselves to raise an equivalent sum in addition by assessing their membership.

Flore, on learning of their plans, expressed himself as highly enthusiastic. The blessings of the GEB and the funds requested were both given. Garriga, Rubin and the others then returned to New York and proceeded to raise more cash by assessments of 25 cents a month throughout 1937 upon approximately 14,000 union members.

That summer and autumn in New York were taken up entirely with mass meetings, drives and organizing forays led by men and women of the crusading type who had experience in organizing the unorganized under the most adverse conditions. Now under a favoring political climate—for Fiorello La Guardia, an old friend of labor, was Mayor of New York—armed with adequate funds and supported by AFL unions in allied industries, the new leaders carried on with a tremendous zeal that shook up the whole industry.

Their methods had been developed from careful study of the field and of its working population. Intensive efforts were made to approach workers of different minority races, such as the Puerto Ricans, now very numerous in the industry, by assigning organizers to visit them in their homes and converse with them in their own language. At first, pressure was directed against certain of the big chain restaurant systems, such as Childs and the Waldorf Cafeterias, where the workers were concentrated in great numbers and could be organized with some economy of means. Blueprints, in fact, were made of the large open-shop strongholds and active "colonizers" were planted in them.

Upon the passage of New York's "baby" Wagner Act in July, 1937, the Organizing Committee put in the first petition received by the new State Labor Board, requesting the certification of their union as representing the Childs Restaurant chain, with fifty-two branches and 3,200 members. Their spadework had been well done, for the election held among the Childs workers was won by the union overwhelmingly, and with it a union contract providing for a betterment of hours and wages; also improved meals and sanitary conditions for workers.

Another great coup, at about the same time, followed negotiations with a body of ninety-seven independent cafeterias who entered into a "blanket agreement" bringing 4,000 new members under the protection of Local 302. Numerous other large restaurants or chains were unionized—though in one important strike against the Horn & Hardart system the union men suffered a setback. Nevertheless the movement was carried on at a fairly breathless pace; soon the eating-places in the central sections of the city were organized and the long-sweated culinary workers began to enjoy the eight-hour day and wages and conditions more nearly approaching parity with labor in other trades. During this "great push" Local 302 reached a membership of more than 10,000, while Waiters Local 16 also mushroomed in size, so that it was arranged to divide up its membership and allot part of it to a new local that was to specialize in the hotel industry.

Under a rejuvenated leadership and free of racketeers, the New York organization, within sixteen months ending in May, 1938, reported a membership gain of 80 per cent, the total rising from 14,000 to 25,000.[11]

By now the New York group felt strong enough to take on the formidable job of unionizing the city's 350 hotels and clubs which employed over 80,000 people, only an insignificant fraction of whom were organized. Early in February, 1938, a new local, the Hotel and Club Employees Local Union No. 6, was chartered as an "industrial union," with exclusive jurisdiction over the hotel field and designed to include a great army of service workers of the most varied type. Michael Obermeier, then one of the popular rank-and-file leaders of the New York catering workers, was moved over from Local 16 to serve as Secretary of Local 6, while Gertrude Lane (Mrs. Jay Rubin), the ablest of the new women organizers in the movement, became General Organizer of Local 6—which began business with an allotment of a portion of the membership of Waiters Local 16.

It was Jay Rubin who mapped out the broad strategy for the hotel organizing campaign. His hope was to bring all labor elements into one solid, collective bargaining agency, and at the same time eliminate friction between the different AFL International Unions holding jurisdiction over the many and varied crafts employed in hotels. To this end, early in 1938, a new body, called the New York Hotel Trades Council, was created, and, by dint of much patient persuasion, the several different unions, including the HRE's Local 6, Hotel and Club Employees, were eventually brought together to act as a single cooperative unit. It was a wholly new idea, born of the experience of Rubin and his associates in the 1937 drive.

A big modern hotel is, in truth, a "factory" processing food and shelter, sometimes for many thousands of people, and using the most varied forms of labor: not only lobby, bedroom and dining-room attendants, but carpenters, painters, electricians and engineers who constantly see to the repair, maintenance and heating of the hotel, and "housemen" who set the stage for banquets and balls. If the hotel manager were forced to deal with demands for adjustments of the grievances of eight or ten different AFL unions all through the year, then his headaches might be unending. Analysis of this complex industrial situation led Rubin to go outside the Hotel and Restaurant Employees and Bartenders Union and seek firm agreements with the other unions in the field, such as the Building Service Employees, the Electricians, the Operating Engineers, the Firemen and Oilers, the Brotherhood of Painters and the Upholstery Workers. By establishing a unified council, with its cost to be borne by them in ratio to the membership involved, Rubin hoped the disruptive effect of craft divisions would be overcome and the whole group would act together, for collective bargaining purposes, as "one big union."

It was a scheme whose difficulties might have daunted the boldest of organizers. But Rubin and his associates showed themselves most persistent as well as planful. Father John P. Boland, chairman of New York State's first Labor Relations Board and an old friend of Edward Flore, is also given much credit for having encouraged the different AFL unions to join with each other in the proposed Hotel Trades Council.

At the start of the hotel "drive" a very dangerous stumbling block appeared in the form of the Building Service Employees International Union, AFL, many of whose New York local members were employed in apartment buildings and hotels. This union was one of those that had lately been infiltrated with racketeers, one of whom, named George Scalise—said to have been connected with the Capone Syndicate in Chicago—had become its International President. Thus when Rubin's organizers tried to approach certain New York hotels, they were driven off or beaten by gangsters. The officers of the Building Service Employees were able to claim that they had contracts with these hotels. Actually (as was later revealed) these crooked officers received "protection fees" from those hotels, usually running to $3,000 a year. At every step the BSE refused to go along either with the Hotel and Restaurant Employees Local 6 or with the proposed Hotel Trades Council, the BSE claiming sole jurisdiction in this field. The rival union, under Scalise, not only entered suit against Rubin and Local No. 6, but also carried the dispute to the AFL Executive Council, which, in the spring of 1938, rendered a verdict favorable to the Hotel and Restaurant Employees' locals.

It was the obstructive action of the gangster-ridden union that had led Rubin to his idea of a "consortium" of the other unions in the field, thus bringing stronger public pressure to bear upon the racketeer element.

The BSE's Locals 144 and 32-A (whose members were employed in many hotels and apartment buildings) were then notorious for their low wage standards, failure to hold any meetings and lack of any financial records. Scalise's hoodlums also directed many threats against the persons of the HRE local leaders.[12] But the indictment of Scalise—who was eventually tried and sentenced in 1940—led to an upheaval among the rank and file of his local union members. In December, 1938, they voted to join with the other AFL unions who had combined forces in the Hotel Trades Council. The road was now clear so that agreements could be written with the New York Hotel Association.

An Executive Board, representing the eight different union locals, was now established; Jay Rubin was elected President and Director, and John J. MacDonald, of the Operating Engineers Union, Secretary-Treasurer. In this new body, the HRE's Local 6 was, however, the largest single unit. The Council then set up its own research department, newspaper and legal staff.[13]

At this period the hotels called themselves a public service industry working around the clock, and still kept their personnel laboring at three split shifts running ten to eleven hours or more.

As the New York State Labor Department characterized these workers:

They were the lowest paid of any service industry, their job security was practically zero and working conditions . . . universally bad. Sunrise to sunset marked their working hours for generations. Many never saw their families for days and days because they arose at such an early hour and worked such long hours for meager wages paid once a month, which drove them into the clutches of loan sharks.[14]

Yet New York's giant hotel industry in 1937 was one of the largest industries in the country and was valued at a billion dollars in assets. Hotel and Club Employees Local 6 led the big organizing drive of the several combined unions, starting off with the signed membership pledges of 7,000 hotel workers. Early in the 1938 campaign one non-union hotel that had instituted pay cuts of 10 per cent was picketed and the case brought before the State Labor Relations Board by the union. The result was that a reduction of wages of 700 workers was canceled, which made a most favorable impression on the hitherto unorganized hotel employees. An answer had been given to the working man's eternal question: "What can the union do for me?"

In this lively campaign one hotel after another was engaged in rapid succession, yet few strikes of long duration resulted. Much inventiveness was employed by the organizers, as shown in one placard displayed by pickets before a luxurious Fifth Avenue establishment:

HIGHEST PRICES CHARGED—LOWEST WAGES PAID

In May, 1938, Rubin was able to report:

Part of our success so far is undoubtedly due to the fact that we have made a special appeal to women workers through women organizers, and established a Negro council under the auspices of a Negro organizer to unionize the large bloc of Negro hotel workers.[15]

A prime factor in the organizing of the women workers was Gertrude Lane, an eloquent and courageous young woman, who contributed as much as anyone to the spectacular growth of Local 6 as a giant industrial union (of 27,000 members). To its multitudes of women workers, white and colored, Gertrude Lane, who filled top executive positions in the local, was for fifteen years the most beloved of their leaders.*

At the outset a group of large, popular mid-town hotels, such as the Pennsylvania, the McAlpin, the Vanderbilt and the Park Central were organized, following the recruitment of their employees and elections held under the supervision of the State Labor Relations Board. By the end of 1938, the local unions cooperating through the Hotel Trades Council had maneuvered themselves into a position from which they could direct new organizing strikes against the other important hotels in the city, and these were mapped carefully for 1939. At this time the New York merchants were hopefully preparing for the forthcoming World's Fair of 1939, which was expected then to draw millions of visitors and much profitable trade to the metropolis. The hotel managers were, therefore, extremely eager to establish labor peace in their industry.

On December 23, 1938, the New York Hotel Association, representing sixty-two large hotels, accepted terms for a comprehensive agreement with the eleven local unions comprising the New York Hotel Trades Council. Under this agreement former New York City Police Commissioner William E. Mulrooney was chosen as impartial chairman of a joint management-labor committee that was to dispose of all questions of wages and grievances. This notable trade treaty ushered in a "new era of industrial democracy," as George Meany said at the time, for over 20,000 "notoriously underpaid workers," providing for average wage increases of 10 per cent (or a $2,300,000 addition to payroll), the union shop, the forty-eight-hour week and other improvements.

For the unions in the great catering trade of New York it was but a beginning, since wage scales as set in the December, 1938, contract

* The early death of Gertrude Lane, following illness induced by much overwork, occurred in November, 1953, when she was but forty-four years of age.

were low in comparison with other trades and with rates prevailing on the Pacific Coast. But with a permanent machinery for adjustment and peaceful negotiation now in force, the work rules established at the start were bettered year by year, and the unions embraced under this agreement expanded rapidly. Men and women workers, such as bellhops, porters and waitresses, whose fixed wages—apart from tips received—had formerly been $7 to $9 a week, or less, were being paid approximately twice as much in fixed wages at the beginning of World War II on the basis of a forty-hour week. By 1947 the union workers' numbers in the hotel trade approached 70,000.

The beneficial effects of the hotel trade agreement were also felt by the HRE's other catering industry locals in New York, whose membership, by 1941, reached a total of 45,000.

For the hotel workers in particular the benefits of added security and stabilization that flowed from the "treaty" of December, 1938, were so remarkable that, as the New York State Department of Labor reported in 1951:

> In the twelve years of the Hotel Council's existence, New York City hotel workers' hourly wage rates have risen by a larger percentage than the pay of workers in most other industries, service or non-service.*

* Examples: Waiters, from 17 cents an hour in January, 1939, to 55 cents, in June, 1950—an increase of 223%. Hotel maids, in the same period, from 26 cents to 78 cents, or 200%; service bartenders from 52 cents to $1.33, or 155%; elevator operators from 35 to 99 cents, or 183%. During this same period of twelve years, increase of wages in the retail trade was 105%, and in all manufacturing, 120%. (New York Department of Labor Bulletin, February, 1951.)

THIRTEEN

World War II

The fiftieth anniversary of the founding of the Hotel and Restaurant
Employees and Bartenders Union was celebrated in the week of May
21, 1941, at Cincinnati, Ohio. Eight hundred and twenty-five delegates were in attendance at this Golden Jubilee and, with their guests,
made up an audience of 1,500 gathered in the very plush Hall of
Mirrors of the Hotel Netherland Plaza, to review the activities of
their union and legislate for its future. By referendum vote the convention had been postponed six months beyond its regular biennial
date so that the meeting might coincide in time with the date of
the chartering of the original International Union in 1891. How different a scene from that of half a century earlier, when fifteen men
had met in the small shabby office of a local union in a New York
side street to found the HRE.

For the veteran union members it was an occasion to "point with
pride." There were a few present who had served as convention delegates since the 1890's, but all honors went to the bald, sixty-three-
year-old Edward Flore, who had worked as a union officer for forty
years and as President for three decades. He had seen his union
almost wiped out in 1932, then grow to tenfold its size of that period,
until it was the fourth largest in the American Federation.* What

* In 1941 the HRE ranked as seventh largest union in America, giving allowance
also to the three leading CIO unions.

was more, he had seen it win, at last, a real collective bargaining position in its industry. In the great cities of the East, the Middle West and the Pacific Coast the leading hotels of America were operating under the union shop. Much credit was owing to Flore himself for having executed a sharp turn in the International Union's whole policy—at an early stage of the Roosevelt Administration—that made it truly one of the most progressive of unions. Instead of continuing as an old-fashioned craft union and limiting itself mainly to the better-paid bartenders and craftsmen in the trade, it had adapted in its own field the methods of the industrial unions and begun to marshal together the masses of semi-skilled or unskilled people in the hotels and the great "food-factories."

As Flore summed it up in his report to the convention:

> In these fifty years that have passed we have had to learn a great deal.
> We have had to fight for the right to organize and then we have had to learn to live in an organization.[1]

It was significant also, as Flore reported, with evident warmth of feeling, that he and the new Secretary-Treasurer, Hugo Ernst, worked in complete harmony. For the first time the report to the convention was given as signed by both executive officers. They were, as Flore said, "for the first time, a General Secretary-Treasurer and General President who act as one."

At the beginning of its second half-century the International showed not the slightest signs of age, but rather of rejuvenation. Its Executive Board was enlivened by the recent entrance of a number of younger members, such as Ed Miller, who worked in close cooperation with President Flore, and also C. T. McDonough, of Local 44, San Francisco, a diligent organizer who was elected by the Board in 1939 to fill the vacancy caused by Ernst's election as Secretary. Ernst himself, a sprightly figure in his sixty-fourth year, brought more actual trade union experience to his office than any of those who had gone before him. As one of his younger San Francisco colleagues, McCabe of Local 41, said in nominating him for re-election as General Secretary:

> We who have worked intimately with him for many, many years know that there is not a better-informed man in the labor movement within or without this International. We know that his actions and the policies that he advocates come from a broad background of knowledge that is not always visible upon the surface. . . . In fact, we don't think you could do better than to come to

San Francisco and study the structure of the organization that Hugo Ernst was primarily responsible for molding and that has brought to us unquestionably the finest wages, working hours and conditions. . . .[2]

Flore and Ernst, so different from each other, had both feared that they would not get on well together. But Flore found Hugo Ernst, as San Francisco had known him, the most honest and kindly of men in his dealings with others. Moreover Ernst was very staunch in his view that the interests of the organization must be held above that of the individual: though he clung to his sacred "right to disagree" with the other GEB members, once disagreements were resolved in a democratic way, by vote of the majority, he would loyally carry out actions authorized as organization policy, even though he had opposed them to the very last.

At the start Ernst gave much attention to the improvement of the official journal, *The Catering Industry Employee,* and wrote many articles for it on union questions. He showed also a lively interest in gathering information on business and economic conditions that would be of help to the union, and took steps leading to the establishment (several years later) of a Research and Education Department at the Cincinnati general office.

Another innovation that was close to Ernst's heart was the campaign to unionize hotels and restaurants in the South, a field as yet virtually untouched. For Ernst the elimination of the color bar and of all racial discrimination—through the changing of segregated locals into locals of mixed membership, black and white—was to be one of the great goals of the International in its modern phase.

From all sections of this sprawling union great activity was reported to the convention at Cincinnati. In San Francisco the group of culinary workers' locals had brought 237 hotels, large and small, under the union shop by means of signed agreements. In New York the huge Local 6, together with the other AFL unions represented in the New York Hotel Trades Council, extended the union shop to ninety of the large mid-town hotels in the spring of 1941. From Chicago, where Vice-President James Blakely headed the operations of the hotel service workers, came news that ninety-seven hotels had recently been brought under union shop agreement. And from the somewhat smaller center of Seattle came news that as many as seventy-eight hotels, virtually 100 per cent of the trade, had accepted the union contract. The distinguishing feature of the International's achievements in its fifth decade was clearly the unionizing of hotel workers and of chains of low-priced restaurants, particularly in

New York, Chicago and other big cities. In New York the growth
of the new Hotel and Club Employees' union was so rapid that Local 6 became as large as many international unions in the AFL,
holding conventions of its own and electing an Executive Board that
was like a legislative assembly, each member representing 500 union
men or women.[3]

In such a time it would have been easy and agreeable, as the report signed by both Flore and Ernst observed, to indulge in senti-
mental recapitulation of hardships suffered in the past and achievements recorded in more recent days. But these were no normal times,
the report warned:

> Today, as we observe this great anniversary, our nation stands on
> the verge of either possible or probable participation in the greatest
> of human struggles. In every sense except armed fighting we are in
> that struggle now. The issue before the world is: to be free or to
> be herded slaves.

After the spring of 1940, when France had fallen, the United States
moved at a rapid tempo, to arm itself and to furnish arms for the
Western democracies. To the International Union the possibility of
foreign war suggested severe disruptions of its industry. Food would
be rationed; workers would be drafted into the armed services or
drawn off into war industries. Many large hotels in cities strategically
placed for defense activities would be sequestrated for the use of the
armed forces. Nevertheless the sentiment of Flore, Ernst and the
great mass of the union members favored all-out support of President
Roosevelt's program of aid to Britain and the resistance movement
in Western Europe. "Under Hitlerism there are no free unions" was
the slogan repeatedly used in the official journal and other publications of the HRE in 1940 and 1941. The concluding passage of the
report of the President and Secretary (said to have been written by
Ernst) stated:

> What we have known as normal times will never return. What
> lies ahead will be new and very different. But however different it
> may be, and whatever may be the sacrifices called for, the future
> will be better than it could have been had not unions such as ours
> fought day in and day out for a great program of human rights. . . .
>
> Down the backward trail of fifty years, splotched with mingled
> joy and sadness, with depression and prosperity, we see a procession
> out of which we have forged this union and its solidarity. So we
> celebrate fifty years, not as bringing us to a goal, not as something
> finished, but as something that has fitted us for the greatest and
> most important trials of all civilized life.

From the beginning of the war in Europe in 1939, from the time of the "pact of friendship" between Nazi Germany and Soviet Russia and the invasion of Poland, to the Battle of France and the inauguration of Lend-Lease for Britain, there was political conflict within certain sections of the International Union, as in other unions. The HRE membership was an amalgam of different races, many of which, such as the Poles, the Jews, the Greeks, the French, the Jugoslavs, one after another, became victims of Nazi-Fascist aggression, while other members, Italians and Germans, had kin within the camp of the totalitarian powers. A sizable group in the union, made up of Spanish refugees who had fought in the civil war against Franco and later migrated to America, also acted as a militant anti-Fascist bloc. Flore, a devout Catholic, part French, part German, by descent, "with the human sense of a priest," as his friend Kovaleski said, was fully aware of all these tangled threads of emotion and moved prudently in dealing with them.

An added problem was the influx of radical and left-wing groups into some sections of the union during the 1930's, among them a minority of communists. Like other labor organizations in those liberal years the International, though condemning the tactics and doctrines of the communists, had at first avoided imposing harsh measures that would deprive them of the right to the protection of a legitimate trade union. Many labor leaders said then, like John L. Lewis, that the communists were fanatics who made "superb organizers." In sections such as New York and Chicago they had also served as a counterpoise to the racketeers in several locals; for several years, after 1933, there had been no real rivalry or conflict between the moderate and radical trade unionists regarding the need to organize the unorganized. But after August, 1939, in the light of the Nazi-Soviet pact, ideological conflicts had been stirred up again. During the two-year interval preceding the sudden invasion of Russia in the summer of 1941, the attachment of the small communist minority in the labor movement to the sudden shifts of Moscow's policy rendered them suspect and placed them at a disadvantage. Jewish and other foreign-born workers, whose relatives in Europe were being enslaved or exterminated, were deeply angered at assertions from this quarter that the war in Europe was merely another "imperialist struggle." Moreover, the Roosevelt Administration, following the elections of November, 1940, was thoroughly committed to giving armed aid under the Lend-Lease plan to the Western democracies.

Within the International Union the clash of ideologies was reflected in internal quarrels within several locals, as in Local 16 in

New York, where an avowedly anti-communist slate, headed by the popular and energetic David Siegal, was elected late in 1939. A similar change of leadership took place not long afterward in Local 1 and also Local 302, where Joseph Fox, a "moderate," defeated the head of the left-wing faction in the race for the secretaryship. Meanwhile Local 1 and Local 60, New York, brought in a resolution before the Cincinnati convention proposing that the President appoint a "commission on subversive activities" empowered to investigate and expel members who were "Communists, Fascists and Nazis."

Vice-President Garriga, official head of the New York organization, also was embroiled in a sharp fight with alleged pro-communist elements in the Cooks Local 89 and in the big Hotel and Club Employees Local 6. He, too, brought the whole issue to the floor of the convention in Cincinnati, denouncing those whom he described as wicked and subversive local leaders who threatened to undermine the entire organization.

In vehement reply to Garriga, the left-wing leaders called attention to all that they had accomplished in saving the New York organization from the racketeers in the years when "the name of this International Union was being dragged in the mud." And as a demonstration of protest the left-wing faction in New York ran Michael J. Obermeier, Secretary of Local 6, as a candidate for International Vice-President in opposition to Garriga. But after the dust of battle had cleared, Miguel Garriga, with the support of the administration, was the victor by an overwhelming margin of four to one. His re-election as Second District Vice-President (covering New York, New Jersey and Pennsylvania), according to the union's official journal, "showed the determination of the delegates at the April, 1941, Convention to sustain those officers who had been opposing 'isms' and had won enemies thereby." [4]

In the course of the elections that year even that unregenerate liberal Hugo Ernst was subjected to some censure by left-wing members of the home delegation from San Francisco who considered him nowadays less virtuous or at least less radical than he ought to be. One of their spokesmen before the convention at Cincinnati said: ". . . We find it difficult to reconcile some of the policies before this convention with the Hugo Ernst whom we knew of many years ago." [5]

Ernst, for his part, had made clear to all and sundry that he was an ardent supporter of President Roosevelt's policy of aid for the Western democracies. His democratic convictions did not wait upon the *realpolitik* or opportunistic maneuvers of any foreign power. On the emotional side he was, of course, deeply aroused by the invasion of his native Jugoslavia at this very time by the Nazi armies and by the fearful sufferings of his Jewish kin.

In this babel of voices, amid this strife of factions, Flore, ever the impartial magistrate, moved prudently. In any case, the ideological conflict was not yet as serious as it would become after the war was over. A resolution had been brought in authorizing the President to investigate and discipline

> any member who associates himself with any organization or group that expounds or promotes any doctrine or philosophy inimical and subversive to the principles and institutions of the United States Government, the American Federation of Labor and this International Union.

Ernst, however, despite criticism now directed against him from the left, generously threw his influence against the "needless persecution and witch-hunting" of so-called "subversives."

He recalled the hysteria of the "Palmer raids" of 1919-1920, after the preceding World War, and declared:

> I do not subscribe to any theory that everyone who may differ with me is either a Communist, a Fascist or a Nazi—although we have all these in our ranks, many of them unidentified and indistinguishable. . . . Let us hope that even our most radical protagonists may continue with us, as they have in the past, in the onward progressive march of this great organization. . . .[6]

Even John J. Kearney of Boston, who delivered himself of an hour-long harangue upon the totalitarian and communist movements, cast doubt upon the efficacy of measures of repression against those who embraced a fanatical faith. A believing Catholic, he had repeatedly said in the past before this union's conventions that there was too much tendency to call anyone who didn't "belong to the old gang" or didn't agree with one's views a "Red." Kearney was against all conspiratorial and subversive creeds, but seemed to offer no easy antidote for them.[7]

Flore judiciously agreed to modification of the more drastic proposals for eliminating the alleged heretics. In somewhat softened form an amendment to the union's constitution was passed by the delegates enlarging the President's power to investigate and discipline "subversives" or other members shown to have jeopardized the interests of their local or of the International Union.[8]

In any case, four weeks after this convention, on June 22, 1941, the

A typical union-management training school class for cooks, sponsored by Local 88, Chicago

Ed S. Miller, Eighth General President (since July, 1954)

General President Ed S. Miller and General Secretary-Treasurer Jack Weinberger confer with President George Meany, AFL-CIO, in 1955

Jack Weinberger, General Secretary-Treasurer (since July, 1954)

Germans invaded Russia, and the American devotees of the "Socialist Fatherland," who the day before were pacifists, once more reversed themselves, becoming impassioned partisans of Roosevelt's defense program. The communist heresy, as a problem, was thus bypassed for the next five years.

The executive officers on the administration's slate were all elected.* Flore, much feted and adulated on this occasion, received the greatest ovation of his long career. At the banquet that followed his re-election he unbosomed himself and shed tears while recalling the long and arduous years that he had traversed as head of the International, to arrive at last in what seemed the safe harbor of prosperity. As he alluded also to "the next fifty years," he remarked feelingly, as if with a premonition of his own end, that "some of us will, some day, have to lay aside the tools of leadership and give way to others." It was, in truth, the last convention at which the International's delegates saw Edward Flore preside.

At the General Executive Board meeting following the 1941 convention, Flore announced that for the first time the General President was going to have an office outside his home. This would be located in the Sidway Building in Buffalo. W. R. Wasson, a member of the staff in Cincinnati, would move to Buffalo and also assume the duties of assistant to the General President.

That other grizzled veteran, Hugo Ernst, was also elected by acclamation, and with the full support of those delegates who identified themselves as being in the "so-called opposition." As Flore observed at this time, the choice of Ernst as Secretary seemed to be a popular one in all sections of the union.

As was customary, the General Secretary spoke the parting words at the hour of adjournment. Once on a platform Ernst could be one of the most interesting and graceful of public speakers, his voice strong and low-pitched, his manner of address very simple, very human, and conveying all the sincerity of his feeling. He was mindful of the fact that the convention just closed had been the scene of

---

* The members of the General Executive Board elected in 1941, in addition to the President and Secretary-Treasurer, were: Vice-President, First District, John J. Kearney; Second District, Miguel Garriga; Third District, Fred H. Rasser, Local 177, Cincinnati; Fourth District, Clyde Foster, Local 133, Miami, Fla.; Fifth District, Ed S. Miller; Sixth District, J. M. Osborn, Local 14, Denver; Seventh District, A. J. Kilday, Local 152, Minneapolis; Eighth District, Gertrude Sweet, Local 305, Portland, Oregon; Ninth District, C. T. McDonough, Local 44, San Francisco; Tenth District (Canada), A. R. Johnstone, Local 280, Toronto; Woman Vice-President-at-Large, Bee Tumber, Local 498, Santa Barbara, Cal.; Vice-President for Hotel Service Workers, James Blakely, Local 593, Chicago.

some ugly clashes, and that strong feelings of faction or partisanship, even race prejudice, had come to the surface. The thought he desired to leave with the delegates was of the paramount need for maintaining, at all costs, a spirit of democratic tolerance within the union—it was virtually his favorite theme all his life:

> At times we may differ, but I am satisfied that, no matter what the differences may be, there is no difference in anyone's heart as to the purpose of our legislating, of our gathering together and trying to improve our conditions.
> I want to warn the delegates, if I may, not to be carried away by hate and prejudice. We cannot all be alike; we *should* not all be alike, because if that were the case it would be a very sorry existence . . . and when we find that a man or a woman differs with us in strategy or in tactics we should not shove them aside and say to them they should do this, that, or the other thing, just because they honestly disagree.
> . . . This is an entirely different world than it was in 1938. The problems that are facing us now are problems of self-preservation, of the preservation of our democracies, our unions, our liberties and our very lives; and it ill behooves anyone to give way to hysteria. . . . We are commencing to hate people . . . not because they have done something that is wrong, but because they happen to have been born somewhere under circumstances over which they had no control. We have to eradicate that idea from our minds lest we become undemocratic ourselves. I ask you to be patient with propaganda, and with hatred particularly. I ask you to be tolerant in your acts and in your deeds, and not to judge others as you yourself would not want to be judged.
> Mr. President, and Brothers and Sisters, so far as I am concerned, I am not going to change—I cannot change, I am too much steeped in trade unionism, in liberality, to do something I might regret. . . .[9]

Many who were present, and who had listened to so many dull and long-winded tirades of the old-style union officers, were moved by the natural grace and even the nobility of expression that Hugo Ernst achieved. As one of them wrote afterward in admiration of the Secretary's speech, the International Union had at last "found a voice," a voice that spoke for humanity, tolerance and democratic order in a time of danger, rife with divisive passions.[10]

*

During the transitional period of "national defense," lasting about a year and a half, from the time of the Battle of France to the day of Pearl Harbor, December 7, 1941, the Government brought powerful pressure to bear upon all unions to the end that stoppages of production might be banned by voluntary no-strike pledges. The restaurant and hotel trade, however, was less affected by such pressure (exerted through the National Defense Mediation Board) than were the vital war industries—except for instances where hotels were leased by the armed services as quarters for Army and Navy personnel.

With the country involved in war, after December, 1941, the War Labor Board, armed with full wartime powers, prohibited all strikes while efforts were made to stabilize both prices and wages. In compensation, President Roosevelt's deputies, who were charged with war production activities, showed themselves considerate of the claims of organized labor, which generally, in patriotic spirit, practiced great self-denial. To avoid strikes an authoritative adjustment machinery was set up to deal with grievances of labor unions; with the result that, despite the "freezing" of wages, legitimate union activities continued unchecked and steady gains were registered in establishing union shop conditions by labor organizations in a position to demand them under the existing rules.

The experiences of the San Francisco locals of the HRE, during the eve-of-war phase and the early months of actual warfare, furnish an excellent illustration of the peculiar conditions encountered at this time. Here a strike broke out in the restaurant trade, in the summer of 1941, that was unquestionably instigated by the employers. The strike (which was in fact a lockout) lasted up to the time when actual warfare began in the Pacific, then spread to some of the large hotels in San Francisco—at which point the War Labor Board entered the scene and assumed jurisdiction over the dispute. San Francisco, by then, was almost in the front line of the Pacific theatre of war.

Since the struggle of 1937 the catering-industry unions in San Francisco, which reached a membership of over 15,000 by 1941, held a strong position in their trade and made it their policy to discourage the appearance of a unified employers' organization in the field. The restaurant keepers, for their part, made frequent and loud complaint of the unions' allegedly "high-handed" procedure in posting higher wage scales in the different eating establishments, whenever the workers seemed to feel improvements were warranted.

On the employers' side new leadership appeared in the person of a Mr. Almon Roth, who assumed charge of labor relations for the newly created San Francisco Employers Council, a city-wide combination of the different trade bodies, including restaurant keepers.

In the spring of 1941, Mr. Roth called on the culinary workers' unions
for a blanket or master contract covering the group of restaurant
owners he represented. He had promised that he would "crack down"
on the too-aggressive labor force, and issued statements to the press
charging that "the unions are denying the right of collective bargaining to the restaurant owners . . . and trying to break them up
into small groups." [11]

When the HRE's Joint Board in San Francisco ignored these remarks, the restaurant operators, under the direction of Mr. Roth,
announced that they proposed to cut wages by 25 to 33 per cent, but
would cancel such reductions the moment the unions began to negotiate with the new Employers Council. At this period prices of all
goods and services were rising rapidly. A sizable group of first-class
restaurants, nevertheless, announced pay-cuts in July, 1941, and the
union men walked out. It was in effect a "strike" of the employers
against the union, certainly a novel development in industrial relations.

This time the unions employed guerrilla tactics, closing down a
few restaurants at a time (those connected with the Employers Council) and keeping their competitors across the street open. After several months of such harrying tactics, a compromise agreement was
reached with an association of 121 restaurant keepers whom the
union henceforth agreed to "recognize." But instead of cutting wages
the employers were persuaded to grant further pay increases of 5 to
10 per cent above recent levels, and also the forty-hour week and
other improved conditions.[12]

The unions, for their part, promised to stabilize employment conditions through their Local Joint Executive Board which, as a unified
collective bargaining agency, assumed, hereafter, greater authority
over the six culinary workers' locals in San Francisco. In 1941, the
San Francisco Joint Board of the HRE opened an office of its own
and employed a paid staff—at a time when the HRE's Local Joint
Boards in other cities were little more than paper organizations.

The restaurant labor contract of 1941 also provided for impartial
arbitration of disputes between both parties and has been renewed
ever since by peaceful negotiation, so that there have been no strikes
of any consequence in the restaurant trade of San Francisco for
nearly fourteen years. Negotiations for all the different locals have
been handled by the executives of the Joint Board. In the early 1940's
the meetings of the Joint Board executives, then including such high-
voltaged personalities as John St. Peter, Margaret Werth, and others,
were so animated that discussions of union strategy often ran into

the early hours of the morning and the sounds that came from the room suggested that the people inside might be "murdering each other"—though the officers usually presented a solid enough front when they came out to deal with employers.[13]

Even while the unions were embroiled with the restaurant keepers the hotel operators chose this favorable moment—in August, 1941— to attack them again. The hotel men, aligning themselves in the newly organized San Francisco Hotel Employers Association, made up of thirty-three leading operators, refused to grant the preferential hiring conditions that the local unions' Joint Board demanded for hotel service workers. This point had never been cleared up satisfactorily since the strike of 1937. Matters were further complicated by internal dissensions which had broken out within the HRE's Hotel Service Workers Local 283. Thus the San Francisco union leadership struggled both to hold the hotel owners in line and to control a "breakaway" faction among the hotel workers' local. Meanwhile non-union labor was being brought into the hotels once more.

This time the sharp-witted union organization avoided a general engagement with their adversaries and used "war-of-nerves" tactics. While one hotel was struck, another adjacent to it would be merely threatened with a walkout. The transport of food by truck was cut drastically by the union's "spotters" and with the help of the teamsters and longshoremen. The style of picketing, as in 1937, was designed as a dramatic, eye-filling spectacle: before the luxurious St. Francis Hotel, in the social hub of the city, a huge, terrifying figure of a robot, clad in iron armor, was posted and displayed a large sign reading:

WE DON'T WANT TO BE TURNED INTO MACHINES!

The real break for the union came at the end of October when one of the biggest of the hoteliers, Conrad Hilton, owner of the nation-wide hotel chain bearing his name, including the Sir Francis Drake in San Francisco, was persuaded to leave the Hotel Employers Association and sign a separate agreement with the unions' Joint Board. By good intelligence work the union officers had learned that Hilton, having recently made a heavy investment in the Drake, was pressed for cash and hence extremely eager to keep his hotel in operation. The union men had avoided picketing this place and offered Hilton strong inducements to sign a contract.

Hilton's defection caused a great uproar of protest among the other members of the Hotel Association—who were still subject to intermittent stoppages—and he was denounced in large paid newspaper advertisements by the Employers Council as a "traitor" to his class. Hilton, in reply, declared publicly that his withdrawal was caused by "loss of faith in the intentions and ability of the Association to settle the dispute." The Hotel Employers Association actually instituted a suit for damages against the Hilton company, which was eventually dropped—but all this strife among the large employers was as grist to the unions' mill.[14]

The "guerrilla struggle" dragged on for about three months, to December, 1941—when the sudden Japanese attack on Pearl Harbor was made. The Navy Department then moved large forces into the Naval Station at San Francisco and leased a number of large hotels in which its administrative and military personnel were to be housed. Those hotels used by the Navy, when involved in labor disputes, were promptly "certified" by Secretary of Labor Frances Perkins as requiring emergency treatment by the conciliation agents of the War Labor Board. The outcome, after a period of delay in which the labor-management conflicts were submitted to arbitration, was most favorable for the union side: the plan of "maintenance of union membership" was applied; adjustment machinery for the handling of grievances was established for the duration of the war; and wage awards were granted by the Government's conciliator allowing an increase of 15 per cent above the 1939 rates in recognition of the sharp rise in the cost of living during 1941.[15]

The San Francisco hotel workers had managed to "get the elephant's trunk through the door" in 1937. Through the arbitration machinery set up for wartime emergencies, they were enabled to complete the job of unionizing the industry "one hundred per cent."

Since 1941 hotel management and labor in San Francisco have renewed their agreements by peaceful negotiation, the contracts being worked out in great detail before a permanent joint arbitration committee. The result has been a high degree of stabilization in the industry and a relatively well-paid and productive labor force. The spirit of responsibility shown on both sides and the cohesiveness of HRE's Joint Board have contributed a great deal to this good result.

*

The great war caused drastic readjustments of the labor force in many industries and localities, but also produced unexpected gains for labor. As a member of the AFL's Executive Council, Flore participated in its decisions by which the voluntary no-strike pledge was put into effect (with but few exceptions), so that organized labor yielded up its strongest weapon at a time of high employment. There was, meanwhile, much anxiety felt in labor circles lest employers use the emergencies of war, when organizing was "frozen" more or less, to check legitimate union activities. Fortunately unions were by now not only deeply entrenched but contributed to the great rise in production; the War Labor Board showed itself fair in determining labor's just claims, and membership in unions steadily advanced during the four years of war.

Out of the ranks of the Hotel and Restaurant Employees and Bartenders, 25,000 men and women entered the armed forces and fought at the front or served behind the lines of battle in two hemispheres. Another 25,000, approximately, left their trade, and, under the direction of the War Manpower Commission, entered war industries. Yet, amid these immense dislocations in their industry, the International Union maintained and gradually increased its membership; that is, more than enough new workers, especially women, were brought into the trade and into the union to offset losses of the working force. The sturdy bartenders marched off to war, and barmaids often replaced them. It is also notable that those who remained in restaurants and hotels worked much harder during the war.[16]

Food was rationed, meat was scarce, as was good liquor, and the coffee was bad, while hotel accommodations were extremely scarce during those busy years. As one authority has written:

> The Second World War put extraordinary demands upon the restaurant industry. As hundreds of thousands of workers flocked into industrial centers, the existing food facilities were taxed to the utmost. . . . Throughout this period the restaurant industry suffered from a chronic manpower shortage . . . and in addition to food shortages, difficult new problems in the form of rations regulation.[17]

The nation had to be fed during the emergency; restaurant operators and employees (many of whom were inexperienced) struggled to solve each problem as it arose. Meanwhile, though wages were frozen, union workers obtained a gradual betterment of work rules, earned more money by tips in dining rooms, and also gained various "fringe benefits" in the form of contributions by employers to workers' health and welfare funds.

One important innovation of this period was the tremendous expansion of "in-plant" cafeterias and restaurants, since armaments manufacturers generally discovered that they could not maintain a stable labor force on the job without providing cafeterias to serve meals right within the walls of the factories. Many of the war industry plants or military stations employing thousands of workers were often located at considerable distances from city centers, or were placed in remote or semi-inaccessible regions of the Western Desert, and in Alaska. These new wartime restaurant "facilities" were set up by groups of supervisors and experienced workers who organized things rapidly at plant sites in cooperation with agents of the War Production Board or officers of the armed services. Oftentimes the in-plant restaurants functioned on a three-shift-a-day basis in busy munitions factories; here the contribution of the culinary workers in maintaining labor morale and so speeding up wartime output was of no small importance in itself.

The catering industry workers themselves also became considerably more productive per man—though theirs is an industry still involving much labor of hand and foot. One Government estimate of the output of hotel workers showed an increase of 12.8 per cent in their productivity between the years 1941 and 1948.[18]

The International Union's report, following the war, claimed that without the service of many thousands of its skilled members who left their regular jobs in hotels and restaurants to serve food at war plants or military stations, many of these war plants "could not have been operated. Owing to the shortage of help, our members were compelled to work long hours or overtime; some had no vacation during the war."

One defense sector where the HRE members played an important, though unpublicized, role was Alaska, where union officers furnished employees (who were sent out from Seattle) for Army and Navy installations extending from the southern part of the vast Alaska territory to the Bering Sea and the Aleutian Islands. As related by Organizer Weinberger, who, from his headquarters in Seattle, helped in this undertaking:

> As early as 1939, when war clouds were gathering over Europe and Asia . . . preparations were made to protect Alaska and the Pacific Coast from attacks. Bases of operation for our Army and Navy were badly needed. This was the job for the building trades craftsmen. However, before these could go to work in those bleak regions, comfort and food had to be prepared for them. This was our job, and in due course, union shop agreements were arranged with construction firms charged with the Alaskan operations.[19]

In 1938 the International had had one local branch at Juneau, with a few dozen members. At the end of World War II there were twelve local unions established in towns such as Sitka, Fairbanks, Kodiak and Anchorage, with approximately 2,450 members. Wherever the Army Transport Command flew in union mechanics for construction projects, there the HRE local officers arranged also for union-shop commissaries. Those who contributed most to the spread of trade unionism in our remote frontier territory, where the HRE became one of the two or three largest labor organizations, were Miss Lillie Angerman of Fairbanks, Alaska, and Nicholas McLeod, the veteran Secretary of Local 239, Seattle, who was himself a native of Alaska. Jack Weinberger, who served during the war as an alternate member of the Twelfth Regional Labor Board, in the state of Washington, helped direct negotiations for union contracts establishing the five-day week, with time and a half and double time for additional labor, at all mess halls and commissaries throughout the Pacific Northwest and Alaska. Weinberger's conclusions were that the War Labor Board "did nothing to hurt" the HRE's locals, but on the contrary helped inaugurate the five-day week and union-shop standards generally in his region, as in most others except for the South. He said further:

> We shall always regard this as a bright chapter in the history of our International. The catering workers made it possible for the construction workers in the Far North to do their work more quickly.[20]

When the war was over a new and permanent feature of the industrial landscape was the in-plant cafeteria. Another was the ultra-modern, streamlined airport restaurant which the union's organizers also penetrated rapidly.

*

On September 2, 1945, World War II came to an end in the Pacific theatre with the capitulation of Japan. The International Union had come through the upheavals of wartime in excellent shape: though organizing was limited during this period the extraordinary expansion of the restaurant and hotel industry, which grew to be America's second largest service trade, was accompanied by a steady growth of the great union in the field, especially in the closing months of the war, when it reached a membership of approximately 300,000.

On many distant battlefronts, as at many war-industry locations, tens of thousands of the union's members now prepared to return to their old occupation. What would peace bring? Would there be jobs? Would we experience again the painful readjustments of deflation, as after the last war?

At this historic turning point, on September 27, 1945, news came of the death of Edward Flore at his home in Buffalo, New York, following an illness of two months, during which he had undergone an operation at the Buffalo General Hospital. To members and local officers at branches of the union from New England to California and from British Columbia to Florida, the news came as a severe shock; it was well-nigh impossible to think of the International Union without Flore, who had guided its destinies for over a third of a century.

Secretary Ernst called a meeting of the General Executive Board in Buffalo for October 2, on the day following the funeral of Flore. The vice-presidents, the general office staff at Cincinnati and the leaders of many local union organizations had foregathered in Buffalo for a memorial meeting on Sunday night, September 30, the funeral taking place on Monday. The GEB's minutes for the meeting that began on the morning after the services state:

> It was with a great feeling of sorrow that we announced to the members of our International Union the death of our departed chief. . . . The GEB meeting was called to order by Secretary-Treasurer Hugo Ernst at 10 A.M. in the Hotel Statler, Buffalo, October 2. All members of the Board were present.
>
> After a brief eulogy of our late General President the members stood in silence for one minute out of respect for the memory of our departed chief.

The union's journal, the *Catering Industry Employee* (edited then by John Bookjans), said in homage to Edward Flore:

> Because of his agreeable disposition and the impartial and sound judgment exercised by him in handing down decisions in controversies between local unions or between local unions and members, President Flore was liked and respected throughout the entire International. He had no enemies.
>
> He was an outstanding parliamentarian. Not even under the most trying circumstances did he ever lose his composure and presence of mind. He was remarkably even-tempered and quick at seeing through a complicated question. Nearly always he had a ready answer to questions from the floor. . . .
>
> His death is a cause of deep and lasting sorrow among his numerous friends and acquaintances not only within our union, but throughout the entire labor movement in both the United States and Canada.

And Hugo Ernst wrote, after describing the ceremony in Buffalo, at which hundreds of union men paid their last respects to the dead:

Thus the chapter of President Flore comes to a close. His work is done, and judged by human standards it is well done, for all his life was centered in improving the lot of the workers in our industry. . . .

According to the union's laws, the President having died in office, in the interim between regular convention elections, his successor must be elected by the members of the General Executive Board, then consisting of thirteen vice-presidents and the General Secretary-Treasurer, Ernst, who presided over the Board.

During the five days that had elapsed since Flore's death, Vice-President John J. Kearney of Boston had lost no time in launching an active campaign to have himself chosen as President. Nor was it the first time that "Jack" Kearney had acted under the belief that both the interests of his union and his own qualities of mind and character required that he rise to a higher office in the organization. In the late 1920's he had engaged in many a rousing brawl with the aging Secretary Sullivan; in 1939 he had also contended with Ernst for the secretary-treasurership; he had sometimes even had his differences with the tactful Flore—but nevertheless delivered himself of a fervent and tearful eulogy at the bier of the dead president. That "Jack" Kearney was a most colorful and eloquent man everyone granted. And as a politician, who had long served in the Massachusetts legislature, he had known how to be both liberal and conservative at different times. But the Boston branch of the union, once the most powerful of all, had made poor progress in late years, as his critics pointed out, and this at a period when an administration friendly to labor ruled in Washington. The Boston waitresses and hotel service workers were ill-paid and ill-organized in comparison with other sections.

Meanwhile, this unpredictable man had recently become embroiled in public controversy with important groups in the union, especially the leaders of the big New York locals, whom he had attacked as "Reds" in an open letter published in Boston and New York newspapers.[21] It was a form of argument that Kearney himself, in earlier, liberal days, had described as a base expedient, unworthy of reasonable men. He was paid back in kind by being assailed as an intemperate man who exhibited, as Hugo Ernst said at the time, views calculated to arouse factious strife within the union.

In the hours that followed the funeral services for Flore on Sunday, prevailing sentiment among the gathering of many local leaders who seriously discussed the future of their organization favored not Kearney, but Hugo Ernst. There was some talk, also, of nominating

Vice-President Ed S. Miller (sometimes called Flore's "crown prince"), who had managed things very well in his Middle-Western district. But the likable and attractive Miller was young in the service, and he himself urged that Ernst would be the best choice at the time. A large group representing the New York delegation—in fear that Ernst might refuse the office—joined with the West Coast and Middle-Western leaders in "insisting" that he accept the nomination and, as he relates, gave him "most compelling reasons." These groups alone represented the majority of the union members.

"Much against my own wishes, I allowed my name to be presented at the last moment," Hugo Ernst wrote shortly after the meeting in Buffalo.[22] The statement was quite true, according to persons who remember the incidents of that day. While others might aspire, he, by instinct, did not want to be "King." The head of a great union in modern times occupies, in effect, a high political-economic position in the public service, in many ways more vital than that of mere politicians. As in public life, the ambitions of lesser office-holders, all the intrigues and passions of rivals swirl about the head of the man in the topmost office. At heart Hugo Ernst shrank from the "miseries" as well as the "grandeurs" of life as a big union president. It was very much in his character that, in the old days in San Francisco, when the question of elevating him to some higher post in the AFL's central labor bodies had arisen, he had usually preferred to serve as the counselor of others, or

> to have some member of one of our other locals in San Francisco serve in my place. . . . I had honors enough and work enough, and I thought that by having some other officers elected to such positions it might strengthen our union's influence in the labor movement and give the members of our other locals added incentive to cooperate, which turned out to be correct.[23]

Besides, he was sixty-nine years of age, a time to shun heavy responsibilities and wearisome administrative tasks—which he had never liked. Perhaps it was the strong bid of Kearney for the presidency, suggesting to Ernst the possible dangers of factional division in the union, that made him determined to run.

At the meeting of the GEB October 2, 1945, the first order of business was the election of a General President. Vice-President McDonough nominated Secretary Hugo Ernst, and Clyde Foster, of Miami, Florida, nominated John J. Kearney. A vote was taken with the following results:

For Vice-President Kearney, in addition to himself, votes were cast by Osborn, Johnstone, Kilday, Foster, Rasser and Blakely; for Secretary-Treasurer Ernst, in addition to himself, votes were cast by Miller, Garriga, Brown, Tumber, Sweet and McDonough.

Since the voting resulted in a tie of seven to seven, Ernst, who was presiding, called for another vote, which produced the same deadlock. The union's law had provided for such a contingency: in accordance with Section 96-A of the constitution, Ernst, following the second tied vote, declared that he, as Secretary-Treasurer, would also assume the duties of the General President for the interim preceding the next Executive Board meeting or convention.[24]

There was some bitterness expressed at this outcome by the partisans of Kearney, one of whom wrote in this spirit to Ernst. He replied with his characteristic magnanimity:

> In the final analysis, the rank and file will have an opportunity to have their say as to who shall be their General President at the next convention, which I hope will be held as soon as arrangements for it can be made.
>
> Let me say that as far as John J. Kearney is concerned, I have only the highest regard for him personally—though I disagree with some of his policies and ideologies. . . . For the same reason I hold an admiration for you for your loyalty to the man with whom you have lived and worked for a great many years.[25]

Hugo Ernst was almost three-score and ten when he assumed the leadership of the International Union—under circumstances suggesting considerable discord within the organization. Yet within the first year of his stewardship the progress of the union, rapid though it had been in late years, surpassed all that had gone before.

FOURTEEN

The Presidency of Ernst:

"The Miracle Year"

"I have grown up with this International Union. It is my life. I have worked at the trade under very deplorable conditions . . . that prompted me to devote the rest of my life to the betterment of those who work in our industry."—HUGO ERNST, at 1947 Convention.

In sober mood Hugo Ernst returned to Cincinnati in the early autumn of 1945 to take up the heavy responsibilities of office as Acting President at what seemed a most difficult turning point in the International Union's history: the transition from war to peace. At sixty-nine, he had lived a year longer than Flore, was in the October of his life and in delicate health. Yet he threw himself into the task of reshuffling and reorganizing the union's administrative structure with the utmost zeal.

The general office in Cincinnati even in recent years had been run by a modest staff of about a dozen persons. Flore, of late, had also maintained a small office in the Sidway Building in Buffalo, with W. R. Wasson, formerly an officer of Cooks Local 468, Los Angeles, serving as his assistant during several years. But the organization had grown immensely; it needed a larger staff and bigger headquarters. After Ernst took over, all general office activities were centered in

Cincinnati where the union headquarters had been maintained at the same address, 528 Walnut Street, for almost half a century. (In October, 1950, the office was finally moved across the street, to the modern Keith Building at 525 Walnut Street, where it occupies virtually the entire tenth floor.) Following the death of Flore, Wasson, who in earlier years had done effective organizing work as a local union officer in Colorado, Texas, and Southern California, and knew the union's business thoroughly, was assigned to work there as President Ernst's assistant.

Two years earlier, in June, 1943, upon the death of Harry W. Fox, editor of the *Catering Industry Employee*, Ernst, who had charge of the union's monthly publication, appointed John Bookjans, of Pittsburgh, in his place. A veteran union officer, Bookjans had for many years contributed articles on the problems of the catering workers to the union's journal and to other labor publications. His views on the labor question, moreover, were most congenial to Ernst.

One of the first and most important steps taken by Ernst in December, 1945, while overhauling the International Organization, was the appointment of his old brother-in-arms of San Francisco days, the sixty-two-year-old Jack Weinberger, as Director of Organization for the entire union. In this newly created post, working under the Acting President, Weinberger was to assume full command of the growing staff of organizers.

Organizers had come and gone during these many years of the Hotel and Restaurant Employees' campaigns, but Jack Weinberger had remained a landmark of the union. Moreover, he was a lifelong student of the labor movement and of his own industry. In earlier years when he had shared with Ernst the leadership of the forward-looking Waiters Local Union No. 30 of San Francisco, he had been an ardent exponent of the industrial union philosophy and one of the group of San Francisco "rebels" who had fought against the old-fashioned craft union policies of Jere L. Sullivan. In those days he had even had dreams of seeing union labor, by virtue of its progress both in organizational power and productive efficiency, win "an increasing share of the responsibility and management of industry." In 1920 he had even persuaded the California State Labor Federation to pass a resolution favoring this idea—which was then in fashion among the intellectuals of the labor movement and which was to be advocated again with much enthusiasm a generation later, during World War II, by men like Philip Murray and Walter Reuther.

Close observation of the IWW movement and experience of other radical groups, however, had long ago led Weinberger to lose faith in the extremists and the doctrinaires. That the labor movement in America had begun as a movement of protest, political and social, he believed to be true. But by 1929, Weinberger was writing articles in his union's journal suggesting that labor in the United States was undergoing a phase of evolution, during which its exclusively "protest" characteristics were diminishing and its program was being directed to a more "inclusive trade unionism, working for a better life for all the people."

Indifferent though he was to current political sects or crusades, he never ceased to believe in the long-term value of labor's day-by-day struggle for increased economic power and betterment of conditions. He had discovered that what he disliked was the talkfests of the labor world; what he liked was being a "doer." A prodigious worker and extremely methodical, he used to rise very early and walk to the post office downtown to collect his mail, then proceed to his office—"with such regularity that you could set your watch by his movements," one of his Seattle colleagues recalled.[1] When he was local secretary in San Francisco, his annual reports were models of good business sense and also included very keen and painstaking analyses of the union's problems. Flore had "discovered" him in 1927 and soon promoted him to the post of General Organizer. In Seattle this indefatigable man, under the favorable climate of the late 1930's, took infinite pains in planning and carrying on the work of the organization.

One of his coworkers in Seattle, Secretary Eudora Wellander of Local 551, recalls:

> Jack Weinberger really drove us very hard. We went into the back alleys, we went to the small hotels, we went everywhere, and really began organizing all the clubs and hotels.

Another woman organizer, Beatrice Rice, of Vancouver, Washington, relates that after her first week of study under the "severe" Weinberger, she suffered a nervous breakdown. Recovering quickly, however, she proceeded to compile an impressive record by organizing "one hundred percent" of the catering workers in her district.

In developing new local unions and expanding the scope of existing ones in his territory, Weinberger not only helped impose sound union standards but also perfected new or improved tactics of organization. When planning a campaign he would study carefully the character, record, and business methods of the different employers he encountered; then, in soft-spoken manner, he would gain approach to them and offer peaceful proposals for collective bargaining agreements without any hint of hostilities. Normally he was very composed; but once engaged in a fight, he could be fierce enough: some still remember him on such occasions as "the mad Hungarian."

One of his ruling ideas was that it was wasteful and stupid for different unions to engage in separate organizing efforts against the same groups of employers at different times. He therefore devoted himself to bringing about the closest cooperation of allied unions, such as those of the building trades' and the teamsters' unions, when there was some important membership campaign or organizing strike from which they could commonly benefit. Under Weinberger's plan the representatives of three or four AFL unions would simultaneously approach the owner of a large hotel, or the trade association representing a number of such establishments, and negotiate for a union-shop agreement. Thus a contract worked out in 1937 with the Seattle Hotel Association covered the Electricians Union, the Building Service Employees and other crafts, as well as the cooks, waiters, bartenders and hotel workers of the HRE. Examination of this contract, however, shows that the HRE members gained the five-day week, strict union hiring terms, and other conditions superior to those provided for the other unions—which then still retained the six-day week.[2]

Weinberger, more than any other man, had studied the special problem of covering for the International Union a very wide, sparsely populated area where the workers to be organized were to be found only in small groups. He had just negotiated a new contract for the Seattle hotel workers in January, 1946—the first to provide for overtime pay at time-and-a-half on the sixth day, and double time for the seventh—when he arrived in Cincinnati to take up his new post.

The organizing department had become the union's principal business, its "engine room," toward 1937, though it could hardly be said to have been run by Flore in a very systematic fashion. Now, with the full support of his old-time associate, Ernst, Jack Weinberger proceeded to "streamline" the staff. Seven International Organizers were appointed with authority over different subdivisions of the United States and Canada; in addition to these, thirteen state organizers and eleven special organizers were engaged, who were to be moved from place to place as need for them arose. Weinberger, thereafter, stayed at the "end of a telephone wire" in Cincinnati, in contact at almost any hour of the day and night with these men who were stationed in all parts of the continent.

In 1946 a large number of AFL unions launched a cooperative campaign to organize workers in the Deep South—a project postponed during the recent war—and the HRE allotted the sum of $100,000 for this drive. Its industrial standards retarded by racial divisions between white and black workers, the South had long been the graveyard of trade unions. But now the HRE, like other unions, sent some of its younger men, such as Organizers Charles A. Paulsen and Bert H. Ross, to do missionary work in the manufacturing cities of Tennessee, Georgia, Alabama and Texas. Renewed efforts were made to organize catering-trade people in the huge resort center of Miami, Florida.

With the return of peace in 1946, a new "wave of strikes," like that of 1936-1937, swept over the country. Prices had been much inflated, the dollar had fallen to about fifty-eight cents of its 1939 purchasing power, and wages had lagged far behind. Strikes for wages and conditions or for the union shop were large and very numerous, but during the spiral of inflation employers furnished much less resistance than in the early 1920's to pay raises, and the union advanced everywhere.

The hotel and restaurant trade, partially restricted during the war, underwent a spectacular growth, for the eating habits of Americans, now provided with a larger buying power, were changing rapidly. Expansion of the catering industry to the stature of a "$12 billion business" favored the union at the time when Weinberger launched the greatest organizing movement in its history.

"No particularly new methods were used," he has stated, "but our momentum was going up after the war." Everywhere workers seemed eager to hear the message of the union agent or organizer. In centers where labor had been established in strong force before the war, such as San Francisco, growth of membership was moderate. But in Los Angeles, Chicago, Detroit, Philadelphia, St. Louis, the Twin Cities and Miami, Florida, membership gains were sensational.

In the calendar year 1946 the International Union disbursed approximately $1,095,000 of its treasury funds for general expenses and organizing work, which was about twice the budget figure of the year before, under Flore. At the Cincinnati headquarters the staff could scarcely keep up with the task of chartering scores of new locals and reinstating as many more that had been defunct.

Fortunately help was provided by the arrival in Cincinnati of Ed S. Miller, who at the General Executive Board meeting of October 13, 1946, was elected as Acting Secretary-Treasurer.

Just before the elections of the general officers at that Board meeting, held in Chicago, Kearney had privately appealed to Ernst to support him, Kearney, for the office of Secretary-Treasurer, promising that he, in return, would back Ernst for President. But Ernst had replied that "he would have to talk the matter over with his people." There had been up to now a sort of gentleman's agreement by which Ernst was to fill both offices until the delegates at the forthcoming convention had an opportunity to vote on the succession. The Executive Board members, on learning of Kearney's maneuver, decided that if it was fair for one man to seek election at this time then it was honorable for another to do so. The upshot was that the GEB, by a decisive majority, voted for Ernst as President and Ed Miller as Secretary-Treasurer. At the same time James Blakely was chosen Fifth District Vice-President to succeed Miller, and Harry Scott, of St. Louis, Vice-President-at-Large (for Hotel Service Employees) to succeed Blakely.[3] Miller was then in his early forties and brought strong support to the executive team gathered around Hugo Ernst during the eventful days of the 1946 movement.

The total of membership gains recorded day by day at the Cincinnati office astonished even old-timers like Ernst and Weinberger. In Chicago, where Ed Miller, as Fifth District Vice-President, had recently headed organizing operations, the number of union members rose about 33 per cent to nearly 30,000, making it the second largest union center in the International. In the two years following the end of the war the city of Los Angeles increased its membership from 10,207 to 16,775; its large "satellite" towns, such as Long Beach and Hollywood, grew almost as rapidly. Detroit, whose locals listed 10,859 members in 1945, jumped to a number of 18,082 in the same period.

Altogether, during the fifteen months between the death of Edward Flore and the beginning of 1947, an army of 101,000 men and women had poured into the locals of the International Union. When Ernst had taken office the membership had stood at 301,205; on January 1, 1947, it reached 402,000.

A breakdown of membership statistics of the 1946-1947 campaign in six cities, Chicago, Pittsburgh, Detroit, Cleveland, St. Louis, and Los Angeles, shows that the heaviest influx of new members came from: 1) waitresses; 2) cooks and kitchen assistants; and 3) hotel and service workers—thus from the groups that had had least union protection previously.

The prevailing increases of pay instituted during this first postwar readjustment raised wages, on the average, about 20 per cent. However, the scales varied greatly; there were enormous differences between various sections, with a San Francisco hotel maid receiving then $34.40 for a forty-hour week, while a hotel maid in unorganized Atlanta, Georgia, might be earning only $11.60 a week for the same labor. To be sure a very large portion of the workers, including waiters, waitresses and bellhops, had their fixed wages set at relatively low rates, reflecting the established usage of tipping, earnings from which amounted usually to several times more than fixed wages. Nevertheless, the rise of fixed wages for those counting on tips added to the sense of security of these workers. During the war, also, varying "fringe" benefits had been introduced into union agreements— in lieu of cash wage increases—providing for paid vacations, employer-paid sickness and accident insurance and, in some cases, modest life insurance payments. In the postwar period the five-day, forty-hour week became standard in most large cities, and many union agreements tended to eliminate, or at least modify, the wearisome "split shift," by which culinary and service workers went on and off duty intermittently during twelve or more hours of the day.

The cooks, who were such a numerous army of workers, were the last group to enter the union in force. But after World War II strong cooks' unions arose in the large cities, the biggest and most advanced of these being New York's Local 89 (with 9,000 members), headed by the extremely able young Secretary Arduilio Susi.

By 1948 over 1,700,000 persons were reported as employed in America's eating and drinking places and hotels. Of this number about 41 per cent, or roundly 700,000, were estimated as being either self-employed or working in tiny "hole-in-the-wall" establishments. In the Deep South, moreover, the catering workers, who were mostly colored, had only a dozen small locals (of less than 100 members, as a rule) despite a heavy expenditure of effort and personnel to organize them. Here it would take much time to overcome the long-rooted political opposition to unions. There was, indeed, a great deal to be done. Nevertheless, at the beginning of the postwar period the International Union could claim to have organized almost half the workers in the thirty-five Northern states who were available as union members and to exercise effective control of the job in the more concentrated centers of its industry north of the Mason and Dixon line. The 1946 drive, headed by Director of Organization Weinberger, gained for this once "backward" union the plaudits of the entire American labor movement.

*

Almost six years had passed since the last convention, when the union's delegates met again at Milwaukee, Wisconsin, in the week of April 4-11, 1947. Owing to the war, the conventions scheduled for 1943 and 1945 had been cancelled.

Beaming with joy, President Ernst opened the sessions by announcing to the 1,138 delegates present:

This is the largest convention in the history of our International Union, and rightfully so, because we now have the largest number of members in our history.

The account of the stewardship of Ernst and Miller, and the report of the record-breaking membership campaign of the past year left no room for doubt that the new leadership would carry on.

Before this big and animated convention the gray-headed Hugo Ernst, now in his seventieth year, appeared as the union's "elder statesman," a mellow and paternal figure who had at last come into his own. He was less the parliamentarian and more vigorous and forthright in speaking from the chair than Flore. Traditionally a staunch liberal, he had grown older and, if anything, more prudent. As one of the California delegates had said in reference to him:

. . . When a man is young and not a liberal there is something the matter with his heart, but as he grows older, if he is not more conservative, there is something the matter with his head.[4]

An aging philosopher, he had learned, as he had written in one of his reports to the union some years before:

There is good and bad in everything. One cannot hope for the pleasure of life without meeting up with some saddened hour. . . . We recognize the weakness of man, but the desire to be good is infinitely present in every soul. To condemn is arrogant; to forgive is human.[5]

Though peace had come, these were times of great tension once more; fear and suspicion were spreading at home, as abroad. In the United States the demonstrations of union labor's militancy had been followed by the victory of conservative Republicans in the November, 1946, congressional elections and in various states. New laws to restrict trade union activities—"to redress the balance between employer and worker," as it was alleged, were being rushed through Congress and state legislatures. President William Green of the AFL, in his address before the HRE convention at Milwaukee, declared that there were 105 anti-labor bills pending in Congress then, one of them the Taft-Hartley Bill—and its various restrictive provisions safeguarding the interests of employers largely—which was to become law a few weeks later, in June, 1947. These were so many danger signals that the pendulum was swinging back, that the New Deal-Fair Deal cycle was coming to an end. And within the mushrooming Hotel and

Restaurant Employees Union there was also factious strife. In such a time it was good that the experienced Hugo Ernst headed the organization. This frail old man embodied in himself the hope of unity and mutual tolerance felt by the best elements in the organization. On this the union delegates were in general agreement; and they proceeded, with customary demonstrations of enthusiasm, to elect him by acclamation as their General President.

His acceptance speech (like his own temperament) verged from sallies of humor to serious expressions of anxiety concerning the prospects of the union:

> I have a very bright future *behind me,* as you know, but whatever the good God will give me over the three-score years and ten I will do my best to serve you.
>
> Composed as it is of 400,000 people of various races, creeds, nationalities and political beliefs, it is hardly to be expected that one can please everybody. But I do give you my pledge that, as I have done in the past thirty-five years . . . I will meet every problem with an open mind and with the sole purpose of doing justice as I see it. Should I make mistakes, as I no doubt will, I beg your indulgence.
>
> I have grown up with this International Union. It is my life. I have worked at the trade under very deplorable conditions, and it was those conditions that prompted me to devote the rest of my life to the betterment of those who work in our industry.
>
> . . . When we leave this convention hall let us not leave it with rancor in our hearts. Let us understand that there must be differences and when the majority has decided, as good Americans, let us abide by that will and expression of the majority and put our shoulders to the wheel. . . .[6]

But the meetings were stormy with dissension, which at moments reached such a pitch of intensity that it needed all of Ernst's skill and courage to avert disorder.

The "ideological" conflict, frozen for the duration of the war, raged again in this union as in many other unions. Yesterday the communists, Russian or home-grown, were in Winston Churchill's words, "our noble allies"; but today, with Germany and Japan prostrate, what many had foreseen at the end of the war came to pass: the "inevitable" conflict between the United States and Communist Russia, shown in a complete deadlock within the United Nations over the settlement of the peace. By 1946 the "cold war" was upon us; many Americans were utterly convinced that Russia's intransigence derived from her ulterior intentions of eventual aggression against the free capitalist world; and the tiny minority of pro-Soviet partisans at home (about one tenth of one per cent of our voting population) came under the severe ban of all who considered themselves patriots. Thus the Taft-Hartley Bill, drastically amending the Wagner Act, included among its provisions the non-communist oath, exacted of union officers whose organizations sought the benefits of Federal supervision of industrial disputes under the National Labor Relations Board. The AFL Executive Council at first considered refusing to comply with this discriminatory provision, but later yielded. At this period the great labor unions began to clear their decks in anticipation of stormy weather.

There were by now cases of "atomic spies" exciting the public, and investigative committees of Congress and local governments were in full cry after reputedly "disloyal" or "subversive" citizens. Rumors and charges, circulated in the press and radio by the inveterate opponents of labor, now pointed at various unions as "infiltrated" or "controlled" by communists, among them two or three of the International Union's locals in New York.

That the left-wing group in New York had made a large contribution to the successful organizing of the hotel and restaurant trade in the late 1930's was well known to both Flore and Ernst. As late as 1946 the huge Local 6 (frequently mentioned as being "controlled" by communists) had completed a ten-year struggle to unionize the famous Waldorf-Astoria Hotel, and gained a union shop contract covering 2,000 employees. Various AFL as well as CIO unions had benefited from the militancy of communist groups or leaders in industrial disputes; but now it became expedient in both great federations to remove these objectionable elements, as far as possible, without weakening the structure of the locals in which they had assumed active leadership.

Many employers who were anti-labor tended to exaggerate the prevalence of alleged communists in the unions; hence Edward Flore had been prudent in prosecuting such cases. Hugo Ernst, though he had had many differences in former years with the communists, firmly believed that workers of all creeds were entitled to the protection of a labor union. As he said before the 1947 convention:

> I have stated time and again that I do not care what political belief any person has, as long as they devote their time and energy to the betterment of our labor movement and the union of which they are members and officers. I have paid compliments to the officers of Local 6 for the splendid work they have done in the

hotels of New York, which we tried unsuccessfully to organize a good many years ago. After these boys and girls came into our organization we were able to organize, practically speaking, every large hotel in New York. These people have not accomplished that because they were Communists, or accused of being Communists —probably in spite of that. And had these people refrained from using their official position for other than trade union [activities] probably we would not be confronted with this issue that is before us now.[7]

Nevertheless, factional strife raged again in the Local Joint Board of New York between left and right wings.

In the winter of 1946, a few months after he had become President, Hugo Ernst had appointed an investigating committee composed of himself, Ed Miller and Vice-President Clyde Foster, of Miami, Florida, to go to New York and examine the affairs of three of the locals charged with being communist-dominated. Under the union laws, as amended in 1941, he was empowered to investigate, hold hearings, and discipline officers of locals who promoted doctrines "inimical and subversive" to the principles of our Government, the AFL and the HRE. The committee's findings showed that in three New York locals some of the officers who were reputed to be communists had grown careless and carried on communist propaganda, circulated pamphlets and newspapers and solicited funds for Communist party auxiliaries in the local union premises or union halls, which was improper.

Ernst said at the time that this was merely a fact-gathering investigation and in no sense a "witch-hunt." He for his part "did not want to be a boss, or a Mussolini, or a Hitler." But nevertheless the committee ruled that in the three locals, 1, 6 and 89, "all Communist influence, contact and affiliation must be severed at once," and they must "clean house themselves," on pain of being suspended by the International Union.[8]

The investigation had been conducted in cooperation with high officials of the AFL's New York body. It was realized at this time that the wording of the International Union's constitution on this point was not clear enough, and disciplinary action begun by the General President of the union might lead to long court contests. For this reason, an amendment to the constitution was prepared by Ernst and the GEB, explicitly barring from office in the union all persons who were members of the Ku Klux Klan, the Communist party or the Columbians, or who were Fascists or Nazis. Presented to the thirty-first convention at Milwaukee on the last day, this proposed amendment precipitated some of the stormiest incidents witnessed that week.

The underlying conflict between the factions showed itself also in spirited fights over the election of various executive officers. Like a true liberal, Ernst fought to discipline the communists on the one hand and at the same time worked to eliminate certain reactionary, or too opportunistic officers and members of the Executive Board.

*

As part of this program Ernst wished to make sure of the election of the former Kansas City bartender, Ed Miller. Miller had been chosen in 1946 as Secretary-Treasurer with the support of Ernst, and by a strong majority of the Executive Board. The bartenders' locals had undergone a great revival and Miller, as their spokesman in the International's high councils, helped to bring about a better and more unitary feeling between the crafts.

But on the West Coast a vigorous movement for the election of Vice-President C. T. McDonough, of Cooks' Local 44, San Francisco, as Secretary-Treasurer, was initiated at the beginning of 1947. The McDonough campaign was sponsored, to Ernst's embarrassment, by some of his old San Francisco associates, among them the veteran John St. Peter, who helped raise funds for electioneering and also helped organize a special conference of HRE local union officers from nine Western states, which committed itself to support McDonough. McDonough himself was an officer who in 1939 had succeeded to Ernst's position as Vice-President in charge of the California district, where he had shown himself one of the most diligent of organizers.

On a tour of inspection to California in January, 1947, Ernst had paid a call on McDonough, whom he had originally sponsored for membership of the GEB. He now used his best offices to persuade him not to run against Miller for the secretaryship, urging that the election of Miller would help preserve unity in the organization. The whole affair was an embarrassment to Ernst and constituted a sort of uprising against him in his home district. Besides it seemed improper to him that both general officers of the International Union should come from California.

McDonough, however, clung to his decision to stand as a candidate before the 1947 convention, declaring that he considered he had been "drafted." The left-wing factions in New York and California, up in arms that year against the Ernst-Miller administration, had also announced that they would join with the West Coast group supporting McDonough. At any rate, McDonough said that in the event he did not win he "could always go back to working as a cook," since he had been a very successful one. Ernst, usually so tolerant in spirit, grew extremely angry and resolved that McDonough would, indeed, have to go back to his old job in the kitchen.[9]

Another faction that joined in the movement to defeat Miller by supporting McDonough stemmed from Chicago and was headed by James T. Crowley, Secretary of Bartenders Local 278—the successor of the unlamented George McLane. Crowley, it was said, had some grievances against the present International Union's administration and also aspired to become Vice-President for the Fifth District. A rough-hewn type of labor leader, Crowley had lived in the thick of Chicago's labor politics for twenty years, had given and received blows, and had not only friends, but enemies as well, some of them connected with the racketeers who still occasionally hovered about the unions.[10]

In the early morning hours of March 18, 1947, three weeks before the convention was to open, James Crowley drove to his home with his wife by car from a late supper in downtown Chicago. On his reaching the driveway, an unknown assailant hidden near the house in the dark fired several blasts at the occupants of the car from a sawed-off shotgun and made his escape. Mrs. Crowley, who happened then to be in the driver's seat, was instantly killed, while her husband (for whom she had been mistaken) was sorely wounded. For several weeks thereafter Crowley lay in the hospital, recovering from very heavy wounds in his shoulder and side.

Once more the Chicago branch of the International Union figured in lurid newspaper reports of this mysterious and horrible affair, generally attributed to underworld figures who had sought to "rub out" Crowley. He himself had declared at the time that he did not know who his assailants were or why they had tried to kill him. In any case the killer was never apprehended.

Hugo Ernst, then in Cincinnati, had flown to Chicago to appear at the bedside of Crowley. He later issued statements to newspaper reporters declaring that, after investigation, he had satisfied himself that the local unions and their officers were not this time involved in the affairs of racketeers.

The union convention had opened soon afterward in Milwaukee. On its fourth day, April 8, 1947, when elections of the general officers were to be held, James Crowley determinedly rose from his sick bed in Chicago and rode to nearby Milwaukee. There, looking very pale and drawn, he made an unexpected and dramatic appearance on the floor as a delegate for his local. The whole gathering of about 2,000 persons stood up and cheered the wounded man as if he were a hero, though none really knew what the shooting was about.

Nominating speeches and seconding addresses for Miller and C. T. McDonough as candidates for Secretary-Treasurer were going on and the place was in an uproar.

> PRESIDENT ERNST: I see that Brother Crowley of Chicago has arrived and is with us today. I desire to express my personal gratification and, I am sure, the sentiments of our whole International Union, of utter contempt for that dastardly attempt on his life. I am sorrowful that his charming wife became a victim of this attempt.
>
> I would like to assure Brother Crowley that he will receive all the protection that we can give him and all the recognition that we can give him.
>
> Welcome, Brother Crowley! [11]

Emotion among the union members over the Crowley affair at this time undoubtedly added strength to the McDonough candidacy, which was evident when Crowley rose to nominate the Californian. All sorts of charges and counter-charges were flung about, one side accusing the other of being "communists," and being called in return "racketeers." Passion ran so high that Ernst, presiding, managed only with difficulty to maintain order. On one occasion the pro-McDonough factions loudly booed the chairman's ruling that nominating and seconding speeches were to be limited to five minutes. "Well boo and be damned," Ernst cried wrathfully. "I've been booed by better men than you!" [12]

Even John Kearney, who seconded the nomination of McDonough, said, in an effort to calm the crowd: "Let us be mindful of the fact that pinning appellations on courageous trade unionists, because they aspire to high office, is unjust."

It was a strange group of bedfellows that supported the excellent McDonough: many of the big West Coast locals; the left-wing faction among the delegates from New York; and the opposition group in Chicago, under Crowley, as well as the conservative, Kearney, of Boston. McDonough received an unusually large vote, though the result was as foreseen, with Miller elected by 2,446 to 1,744. (In the two subsequent conventions, however, Ed Miller was to be re-elected by a unanimous vote of the delegates.)

The Executive Board of thirteen Vice-Presidents was now thoroughly reshuffled at this convention, so that Ernst might have associates he could work with, as he phrased it. Some were to be replaced by younger and abler men; McDonough was to be replaced as a Vice-President mainly because of the intense heat engendered by his campaign. At an evening caucus of the delegates who had supported Ernst and Miller, Ernst in forgiving mood appealed to the majority group to "forget the bitterness that was engendered by . . . the lousy propaganda" of their opponents and agree to re-elect McDonough to the post he had filled so ably in California. But the breach was too wide, and the pro-administration leaders seemed determined that McDonough should not now be put back on the Board. They took the position that the new administration at the outset needed solid support by all members of the GEB. James D'Arcy, of Local 31, Oakland, California, was therefore nominated and elected in his place.*

Another casualty of the 1947 elections was John J. Kearney. On learning, the night before balloting for vice-presidents was to begin, that official support for his re-election would be withheld, and that another candidate, Marcel Kenney, of Springfield, Massachusetts, would be run against him, Kearney made loud lament at the injustice that was being done him. "If I am purged then there won't be much difference between Stalin and some others at this convention," he exclaimed in one of his thrusts at Ernst.[13]

Meanwhile, counting upon his own wit and fluent tongue, he made audacious plans to take the platform himself when nominations for his office were to be made and "stampede" the convention. What followed was a scene of mingled pathos and farce.

Kearney began by asking for permission to replace the speaker from his Boston local who was to have nominated him.

PRESIDENT ERNST: Whom do you wish to put in his place?

VICE-PRESIDENT KEARNEY: Brother Kearney.

PRESIDENT ERNST: Well we will dispense with decorum and permit you to do so.

VICE-PRESIDENT KEARNEY: Mr. President, in the short remarks I made to you today I anticipated that for the first time in twenty years the Vice-President in the First District must be purged. This, to me, is a sorrowful moment, and, oh, I hope that Brother Hugo Ernst will be no party to such a program.

* D'Arcy, after one term of two years, however, was replaced by John Sargent of Local 468, Los Angeles, one of the ablest of the California leaders. But Sargent very soon thereafter, in 1950, died of cancer, and C. T. McDonough was brought back to his old post as Vice-President for the Ninth District.

In all, five new members of the GEB were elected at the 1947 convention; namely, Marcel Kenney, of Springfield, Massachusetts, for District No. 1; Carl Hacker for District No. 4; Phil Valley for District No. 7; D. A. Baldwin for District No. 6 and James D'Arcy, District No. 9.

He was being "purged," he claimed, because he had dared to vote for candidates who did not have the approval of Ernst and his "machine"; and because he had never been a "yes man" for any president, or a "subservient tool for the autocrats who will now read me out." If the delegates tolerated such proceedings then the "steam roller" would triumph. He exclaimed:

> Oh, Lord forbid that we must be fearful of Stalin. The Lord forbid that we must agree with you, though I hate these things. . . .
> I will go out, but not you. I will go out not by those who are leading me out. I want to go out by the vote of the convention. (Cries, interrupting the speaker: "*You will, you will!*") [14]

Kearney turned wrathfully upon those who derided him, recalled his forty years of service to the union and then nominated himself.

It was a fantastic scene. Ernst had surrendered the chair and come forward to answer his old adversary—who in the morning session had himself joined with the left-wing faction supporting McDonough, and then in the afternoon accused Hugo Ernst of being a "Stalin"! Recovering from his amazement, Ernst replied by denouncing Kearney's baseless insinuations. He, Ernst, was merely trying to perform the work and duties assigned to him by virtue of his office, and felt it but natural to surround himself with people who would cooperate with him and not those "who are ipso facto antagonistic to me."

By a vote of 2,379 to 1,745, a younger man, Marcel Kenney, Secretary of Local 67, Springfield, Massachusetts, was elected as First District Vice-President and Kearney relegated to the role of a local union officer.

This was a fairly tumultuous convention, swept by gusts of passion from the rank and file. The opposition was made up of a numerous minority; and its spokesmen were all allowed ample opportunity to take the floor. It was thus a far less "steam-roller" affair than many that had been witnessed under Flore. Ernst, from the chair, presided in aggressive fashion, making no effort to appease anyone who didn't like him. On the other hand the California delegation which had made an angry demonstration over the McDonough candidacy and marched out of the hall during the morning session was induced by Ernst to return peacefully in the afternoon. The upshot was that stubborn opponents of Ernst were eliminated at this convention from the Executive Board, and its new members, as the union's journal reported, gave it a more "progressive" slant. [15]

*

In its closing session the convention took up the resolution for an amendment to the union's constitution, designated as Section 20(c), which would debar any member of the "Nazi, Fascist, Communist, Ku Klux Klan, or the Columbians groups" from holding office in locals or in the International Union. By this amendment, moreover, the President was given power to take prompt action in such cases and remove from office any person found to be associated with such groups.

The move was undoubtedly dictated by the intensification of the "cold war" and the increasing pressure brought by the Un-American Activities Committee of Congress against unions or other organizations accused of harboring alleged subversive characters.

The HRE, as one delegate remarked, included in its ranks both extreme reactionaries and extreme radicals. The consensus clearly condemned the actions of officers who used the union's name or facilities in connection with outside political organizations, or as a medium of propaganda, or to solicit funds for such organizations as were now styled "un-American." The convention's Law Committee which reported on the proposed amendment declared that its desire was to dispose of the issue of communism without turning the union "into an instrument to perpetuate a witchhunt."

Kearney, who helped write this amendment, now appeared far more determined than before (as if reflecting the changed political climate) to show no mercy and allow no democratic privileges in the union to its small minority of communists, said to be entrenched in only two or three locals out of the 713 making up the International Union. Where formerly he had spoken for the tolerance of a radical minority, Kearney now condemned the communists in fairly emotional terms as "double-crossers" and "conspirators" who were in no sense members of a legitimate political movement.* They were to him but agents of a "diabolical plot to wreck the American way of life," destroy our cherished liberties and conquer the country for "the godless communist way of life." The International Union, he held, reserved the right to regulate its locals and "make sure that our membership is not exploited by those who believe in communism."

Vice-President Clyde Foster's prepared statement on this question went even further than Kearney's in calling for the outright expulsion of the communists who had placed themselves in strategic positions in some local unions as presidents, secretaries, organizers or committeemen. Yet, he held, the majority of the members of such locals were good folk who knew little or nothing of the objectives or meth-

* See p. 179.

ods of their leaders. The communists, Clyde Foster charged, "have now become the agents of a great nationalistic foreign power"; they were accustomed to "lie, cheat, deceive, forge, make fools of liberals, betray friendships, make united fronts only to subvert them. . . ." It was wrong, he argued, to think of theirs as a "philanthropic movement to improve the condition of the poor. . . . Communism is the opposite of democracy." [16]

The opponents of this anti-communist measure argued, with no less vehemence than men like Foster, that it constituted, as Jay Rubin said, "a most dangerous and disastrous step toward the rule of hysteria," such as was experienced during the fierce anti-Red campaign after World War I. The amendment involved the restriction of the members' individual rights to hold such political beliefs as they chose. It would lend strength to the campaign of the chain-hotel managers to force wage cuts and break up the union. Nothing could be more to their advantage, he argued, than to use the issue of "communism" in order to create a breach in the International Union. The New York locals, he recalled with pride, had made a most impressive record since they had elected new leaders and expelled the men with unclean hands. "I tell you, you are forgetting yourselves," he wound up, "you are losing yourselves, and the workers in the industry will not let you destroy the union."

Gertrude Lane, Secretary of Local 6, New York, added her warning voice to her husband's, saying:

How easy it will be for the employers, the labor baiters, to break down what we have built up. . . . I urge you, fellow delegates, to get rid of the spirit of frenzy that has been mounting steadily throughout this week. Don't do anything that you will regret on behalf of our International Union.

One spokesman from New York's Local 1 declared that while he was unalterably opposed to communist doctrine, and had never marched in a May Day parade—as had certain recent converts to anticommunism—he wished to safeguard the rights of union members who had formerly been moved to take some actions (now held "subversive") only out of innocent or humanitarian motives:

I dread the day when some member of our Local, for reasons best known to him, will go to the District Vice-President or our International Union stating that he knows you or I might have attended a meeting that wasn't to his liking, and, upon investigation, you may be removed from office or expelled.[17]

During the debate tumult had arisen in the hall, many of the delegates singing national hymns, waving American flags, and shouting
down the speakers for the minority faction. At this point a left-wing
delegate for one of the San Francisco locals, who had come back from
the Pacific war theatre as a disabled veteran, arose before the convention and inserted into the proceedings a statement that created
some new wrinkles for the members to worry over. For that very day
the convention had scheduled a ceremony in honor of the many
union people who had died in the war. Declaring himself bitterly
opposed to any measure that would deprive a minority of the members, no matter what their political beliefs, of their "freedom of
thought and expression," the speaker said:

> This afternoon in this same hall we will be bowing our heads
> and paying homage to those of our brothers who made the supreme
> sacrifice for their country. I ask the proponent of this amendment:
> is he going to separate our dead buddies by political philosophy? [18]

Here, certainly, was a grim illustration of the old problem of "the
tyranny of the majority," which has never been easy for the most
democratic bodies to solve, except by way of reasoned discussion
and self-restraint. But most of the delegates were in a great hullaba-
loo, determined to strike at the advocates of a detested and subversive creed, while Hugo Ernst, the gray-headed old liberal in the
chair, fought steadily to keep order and shouted to make himself
heard. He would not have the delegates act upon such an important
measure while in a state of "hysteria." Let them be guided by good
sense and not by passion and hatred. He, too, was opposed to communism; but, he urged, by trying to stamp out the dissident minority, would not the union be sacrificing its own established principles
of equal rights and democratic process? Under this head he cited
the famous saying of Benjamin Franklin: "They who give up essential liberty to obtain temporary safety deserve neither liberty nor
safety."

Ernst, in truth, had had many bitter clashes with the communists himself, especially when, in 1939-1940, they had condoned the
German-Russian "pact of friendship." A foreign-born citizen, he
had devoted himself for many years to humanitarian movements for
the protection of the foreign-born and the minority races. His heart
had been torn by the slaughter of the Jews and other peoples by the
Nazi genocides. But though he had been fighting communists in
the union even that very week of the convention, he still clung, then
as before, to his convictions about the preservation of the rights of

the minority. The other way, of imposing conformity or loyalty by force or by law, in his view, led back to the methods of inquisition and proscription used by tyrants for thousands of years to suppress those they feared as heretics. In the religious struggles of the past they had filled the world with blood. The orthodox had always called the non-conformists agents of the devil and placed them beyond the law. And once free Americans began suppressing people who embraced heretical ideas, where would it all end?

Proposals had been made by those who resisted the anti-communist resolution that the rules be left as they were before, with the General President retaining considerable authority to regulate the affairs of local unions whose members or officers had committed actions "inimical" to the International Union or the AFL. In summing up the debate, Ernst for a moment leaned to the view that this was the best solution for their problem. Of the proposed amendment he said: "I feel that too much power may be given to one individual and that he may abuse it if he is not liberal or broad-minded enough." He had repeatedly warned the people who had used the organization's name and its local union headquarters for "out and out Communist purposes," and told them "in a friendly manner, what they should do to eliminate the friction bound to arise from such conduct." But now the whole issue was being settled amid an outburst of emotion on both sides.

> It seems to me the sane thing would be to refer this matter to the Executive Board and let's establish a commission to investigate, as a means of abating all these nuisances . . . not for the purpose of driving the members of the Communist party underground and thus doing more damage—but I am fearful that we might do our organization more harm if we again let passion instead of reason rule our behavior.
>
> . . . I am not a Communist. Everybody knows that, and I am going to carry out the instructions of this convention to the best of my ability. But I plead with you, when you vote, do not let hatred or prejudice be your guide, but think soberly and then tell me what you want me to do.[19]

But in spite of these cautionary words the ayes voting for the presumably drastic amendment carried the day by a wide margin. The Hotel and Restaurant Employees and Bartenders had shown that they were as sound in their Americanism as any others and were ready to play their part in the cold-war crisis.

*

Shortly after the convention ended, Ernst went to New York and opened hearings of various witnesses for and against the locals combined in the New York City Joint Board of the HRE (excluding Brooklyn). Although only three of the eleven New York City locals were accused of having pro-communist officers at their head, namely Locals 1, 6 and 89, Local 6 alone, the club and hotel workers union, with about 28,000 members, was as big as many an international union, and was said to dominate the New York Joint Board by the sheer weight of its numbers. When the hearings were over, the International's GEB authorized President Ernst to place the New York Joint Board in trusteeship and reorganize it. But before he could move, the Joint Board's President, Sam Spitzer, of Local 1, with the support of six of the eleven New York locals, on May 1, 1947, obtained an order from Superior Court in New York, enjoining the International Union from placing a trustee in charge of the Joint Board.[20]

The new clauses of the union's constitution applying in such cases were evidently not legally strong enough to avoid a lengthy court process which, in this case, lasted six months. But the injunction suit was, at length, withdrawn by the plaintiffs, and Ernst was enabled to place the New York Joint Board in trusteeship, as of November 17, 1947, and reorganize its affairs in friendly cooperation with the local unions represented in the Board. The left-right quarrel was thus patched up for the time being. In 1948, Jack Townsend, Secretary of the Bartenders Local 15, and a fierce anti-communist, agreed to head a compromise slate as President of the New York Joint Board, while the leftist Harry Reich, of Cooks Local 89, served as its Secretary.

However, the reorganization of the affairs of big local unions, involving cash funds, investments, property and all sorts of legal rights, remained a highly complex problem. On finding that its constitutional amendment regarding "inimical" activities, as drafted in 1947, had been too weak in the legal sense, the Executive Board, two years later, framed another and more explicit amendment, which was presented before the April, 1949, convention, held at Chicago, and passed by the delegates with comparatively little opposition. As Article XI, Section 18, the amendment ruled that

> No person shall be eligible for, or continue to hold office in the International Union or any of its subordinate affiliates, or serve as a convention delegate, if such person associates himself with Communist, Fascist or similar organizations, or the Ku Klux Klan or the Columbians. Such eligibility shall likewise be denied where

THE PRESIDENCY OF ERNST 325

a person associates himself with . . . or subscribes to the subversive doctrines of the organizations enumerated herein. . . .

Here also, the authority of the President to take action against violators and to determine where cases of violation had occurred, as well as procedures for declaring a state of emergency in a local, and for hearings and appeals, were clearly written. The new amendment was devised with the aid of J. W. Brown of Cincinnati, the new General Counsel to the International Union, who had succeeded Joseph Padway, deceased in 1947.[21]

Hugo Ernst was always a "loyal organization man." If the majority had spoken, even though he disagreed, he must obey their wishes. He now moved vigorously to rid the union of local officers still associated with leftist organizations, and to do this, as he said, while "being mindful of the rights of individuals under charges, and of the duties of the International Union." In such affairs caution was imperative; for in trying to reorganize an important local, under a trustee, one ran the danger of disrupting its members' relations with their business agents and employers and causing great loss to thousands of workers.

While these gradual steps were being taken, serious dissension broke out late in 1949 within the leftist-controlled Hotel and Club Employees Local 6, with its President Martin Cody, and business agent Charles Collins, heading the left-wing faction, and Secretary Gertrude Lane and Jay Rubin, who was the President of the New York Hotel Trades Council, now heading the opposition. An explanation of the power-struggle within this big local was given in a pamphlet published several years later, in 1952, by the moderate faction, who had apparently renounced their left-wing ideas:

> Some [of the New York] locals were said to have leftists and Communists among their leadership in the early days of hotel organization. The best of these leaders discovered what AFL President William Green has seen: *A trade unionist will come to realize there can be only one boss—the union and its members. These rejected disruptive orders, and for the good of the union helped clean house.*[22]

Meanwhile, in July, 1950, the Korean War broke forth; soon American armed forces were fighting in a distant theatre of war to "contain communism" and the cry was on, louder than ever, against communists at home. Ernst then sent the International's General Counsel, J. W. Brown, to New York, to carry out a quiet investigation of the reported conflict within Local 6. It was now learned that the right- and left-wing factions in the local were actually up in arms against each other and were preparing for an election of officers in the autumn. At a conference held in Cincinnati early in September, 1950, with Ernst, Ed Miller, Jack Weinberger and J. W. Brown present, plans were laid for swift intervention by the International Union, thanks to the added powers vested in the President since 1949. In moving to place the local under a trustee, Ernst and his associates at the general office would hereafter have the friendly cooperation of Jay Rubin, Gertrude Lane and Michael Obermeier— all of whom had parted company with their former left-wing associates of Local 6.

For Obermeier, incidentally, it was almost the end of his career in the union; an order for his deportation had been issued by the Immigration authorities, and was now being tested in a long court process, at the end of which, in 1952, he was to leave voluntarily for his native Germany.

Although the International's representative in New York was Vice-President Miguel Garriga, he had been engaged in such bitter controversies with the various factions in the New York organization that Ernst decided to send in another and younger man, International Organizer Bert H. Ross, to act as trustee of Local 6. A former bartender, who had joined the union in Boston, Ross had done some organizing in the Eastern states of late years and was considered impartial in attitude.

Ross arrived in New York on September 20, 1950, and appeared at the headquarters of Local 6, armed with a letter from President Ernst designating him as his deputy and authorizing him to assume complete trusteeship over Local 6. The letter declared that substantial evidence of communist influence and of factional strife being waged in Local 6, at the expense of the rank and file, had reached Ernst, and he had therefore, under the authority of Article XI, Section 18, of the union's constitution, appointed Ross as trustee of the local. The proposed supervision was to last only as long as was necessary to restore harmony and secure compliance with the International Union's laws, after which a fair election of new officers was to be held.

Ross promptly called a meeting of the Executive Board of the giant local—which had sixty-seven members—and it was held on September 27, in a long meeting-room at the union's headquarters on Eighth Avenue and 44th Street. General Counsel J. W. Brown was also present. Ross began by announcing that the local was hereby placed in trusteeship and that all its offices were declared vacant;

then, adding that he had no intention of changing or injuring the structure of the local, he reappointed the same officers, who were thereafter to act under the International Union's orders. The assumption of control by Trustee Ross was approved by a unanimous vote of the members of the Executive Board.

The fight among the top officers of the big local had flared up a few weeks earlier, at the end of July, 1950, after President Michael Obermeier, faced with deportation, had announced his intention of resigning. At a meeting of the local's Shop Delegates Council, Martin Cody, of the left-wing faction, ran against David Herman, "moderate," for the office of Acting President, with the result that Cody, as he subsequently claimed in court, had been elected by an overwhelming majority. The Herman-Rubin group had called the election irregular, and prepared to fight it in court. The regular election of officers was scheduled for October 2, 1950, when Trustee Ross stepped in and canceled the election.[23]

One of Ross's first steps was to fire the editor of the local's weekly newspaper, *The Voice*, whom he charged with being a member of the Communist party. This action inspired an indignation meeting on the part of the Cody-Collins faction, where leaflets were circulated denouncing Ross, Jay Rubin and others as being the agents of a "plot" to break up and parcel out the local's membership. Whereupon Ross called another Executive Board meeting for the purpose of disciplining the officers who had been party to the protest demonstration.

This was expected to be a stormy affair. Ross angrily preferred charges against thirteen Board members, including Cody, for "slandering" him, as Trustee, and thereby impugning the integrity of their International Union, and disqualified them from holding office. But nobody assaulted him. His action was upheld by a vote of a majority (forty-two) of the Executive Board, and thus, as he said: "Everything I did was done regularly." [24]

Cody appealed this decision to President Ernst and at the same time instituted court action in New York State Supreme Court to enjoin the trusteeship process. Ernst thereupon sent another representative, Walter Cowan, to New York to conduct proper hearings of the appeal of the ousted officers, eventually ruling that their dismissal was justified. He concluded in his ruling: "You have acted in an open and notorious manner in your furtherance of Communist party activities. I am loath, however, to deprive you of the means of earning a livelihood, and will therefore not order you expelled from the International Union." [25]

In court the Cody faction won delays granted through a temporary injunction, while a referee appointed by New York Supreme Court Judge Nathan took testimony from witnesses during January, 1951. J. W. Brown, counsel for the International Union, came on to New York to help direct the legal contest. Although the United States Department of Justice at that time had instituted a suit against national officers of the Communist party on the ground of "conspiracy to advocate the overthrow of the government," it was, legally speaking, not yet a crime to be a member of that party. The New York Court in the Local 6 case, therefore, did not rule on the propriety of suspending members or officers accused of being communists. But the final recommendation of the court's referee in February, 1952, indicated that sufficient evidence had been found for holding that the Hotel and Restaurant Employees and Bartenders Union had been injured in various ways by those officers' actions. Thus the International's trusteeship was sustained in court, which, as Secretary-Treasurer Miller declared, was an important and precedent-making legal victory. The new clauses of the Union's constitution touching pro-communist activities and its disciplinary measures had stood up in court. It was important also that the approval of the change of control by the Local 6 Board, and the dismissal of officers, had been arranged for at the outset.

At the International's GEB meeting held in San Diego, California, in April, J. W. Brown's report was received with great satisfaction. Ernst then declared that measures would be taken at an early date to end the trusteeship of Local 6, elect new officers and restore their democratic privileges to the rank and file members. The July, 1951, issue of the *Catering Industry Employee* was able to announce that "autonomy is restored to Local 6"—after only nine months of trusteeship. Ross, in his own account of the affair, paid tribute to Secretary Gertrude Lane, popular leader of the New York hotel workers, who used all her great personal influence to keep them loyal to the International Union.

The whole affair was closed with the election of an "administration ticket" at a special convention of Local 6 on June 13, 1951. David Herman was elected President; Gertrude Lane, Secretary-Treasurer; and James Marley, General Organizer.

In two other important New York local union elections, moderate officers supplanted left-wing leaders at this same period, and factional strife subsided. On June 20, 1951, Trustee Bert Ross withdrew from the scene and handed over the reins of office to the Local 6 administration.

Ernst had not particularly enjoyed the task of "purging" the New York local; it was justified, to his mind, chiefly by the need to resolve promptly the dangerous factional strife that had arisen there. In three other cases, of much smaller scope, developing from complaints of "subversive activities" in local unions, he gave his personal attention to the work of investigating accused officers, and taking evidence, and, with the added authority vested in his office, declaring such officers ineligible, suspending them and reorganizing their locals. In view of the hysterical fear of communists being propagated throughout the country by statesmen of the demagogic type, these affairs were managed by Ernst in a spirit of moderation. "We very definitely avoided any witch-hunts," he declared in his report for the 1953 convention, adding:

> In these times of disturbance, politically, as well as physically and morally . . . we are Americans first and partisans afterward. If you translate that a little, we are working people first and everything else afterward. The interest of the working class is paramount, and even if we have disagreed once in a while with something sent down to us from above, either from our own union or the Government, as true trade unionists, believing in democracy and majority rule, we have to carry on until we are able to change things in a democratic way.[26]

FIFTEEN

The Modern
International Union

"You have had a difficult industry to organize . . . and those of us who have seen the struggles waged in the past to get recognition for this union realize what a splendid job has been done."—GEORGE MEANY, Address at 1953 Convention.

The era of swift advance for the Hotel and Restaurant Employees and Bartenders had come in 1933-1934 with the sharp turn of President Edward Flore toward a "New Deal" for the union, under which the organization was rebuilt along semi-industrial union lines, and began to bring into its ranks masses of the unskilled or semi-skilled. The influence of the militant West Coast leaders, among them Ernst and Weinberger, had also counted for much in the process of *modernizing* what had been once a somewhat select, old-fashioned, craft-union affair. Finally, the absorption of independent or dual union groups in New York and other large city centers in the late 1930's had helped to lift the International Union to a place in the ranks of the country's most progressive labor organizations. After World War II, under the leadership of Hugo Ernst, the same process had continued with increasing momentum for several years, then reached a phase of consolidation.

It was at this period of postwar readjustment that the International's Canadian branch also experienced a phase of rapid growth under a group of younger leaders typified by Archer L. Johnston, of Local 280, Toronto. Local 299, Toronto, alone by 1954 attained a membership of 2,174, which was greater than the entire Canadian Department's membership prior to 1936. The HRE members in Canada were much stimulated also by the nation-wide railway strike of August, 1950, in which many of their local unions (those servicing the big railway-owned hotels) participated actively. Following this brief, tense contest the catering workers registered sharp gains in working conditions and in the establishment of union shop agreements, with the result that the Canadian Department rose to a membership, as of January, 1954, of 12,423. The locals in the northern sector of the International thenceforth appeared to be in a position to expand with the dynamic economy of modern Canada.

The progress of the Dining Car Employees was also noteworthy in the years following the end of World War II. Under the existing Railway Labor Act unusual difficulties had stood in the way of organizing these workers (prior to the war), since the law forbade the functioning of a complete union shop. In other words employees in the nation's dining cars did not have to belong to the union in order to work, and wage-and-hour conditions granted non-members were the same as those granted to union members. A favorable development for the dining-car men was the affiliation of their organization with the Railway Labor Executives Association in 1943, a step long sought by them, and as long denied, which now allowed the colored dining-car men to act in solidarity with the independent Railway Brotherhoods and the AFL railway unions. Thanks to the pressure of all railway labor in the United States, the union shop amendment to the Railway Labor Act was passed by Congress in January, 1951. Henceforth the task of completing the unionization of the dining-car workers went forward; a total of seventeen locals were chartered as of April 1, 1954, the largest units being in Chicago, New York, Omaha, St. Paul and Oakland, California, and the combined membership reaching 9,398 workers. The movement of these workers like that of other labor groups had not been lacking in dissensions over ideology, the split-offs of factions, and the clashes of ambitious officers. But after a campaign of fifteen years, as their veteran leader, George E. Brown, declared, the dining-car workers could boast of having raised their average wages approximately 400 per cent, from a basis of 26 cents to one of $1.43 an hour. Also, in paid vacations, job security and welfare benefits, dining-car workers now enjoyed conditions that at last approached parity with that of the rest of railway labor.*

Membership tended to become stabilized, after the "great push" of 1946, at a level of 400,000 to 415,000. But in the years preceding the Korean War, in 1950, many powerful unions which had also grown swiftly failed to hold their ground and lost from 10 to 20 per cent of their membership, this development being due, in part, to adverse labor legislation by both Federal and state legislatures. In the catering industry, moreover, many employers still had to be weaned from their fixed idea that success could come to them only through the acquisition of a corps of cheap labor. It was still an industry in which "many people could take jobs without prior training and skill." [1] The turnover of labor was high; the turnover or lapsation of membership within the union was unusually high: in the calendar year 1952 it was over 153,000, and the ranks of the union were solidly maintained only by arduous and unremitting efforts of the organizing staff under Weinberger to initiate an equivalent number of new members and reinstate many former members.

The industry also was being transformed by a huge influx of women workers, who nowadays account for approximately 45 per cent of the labor force. Young women (to whom the trade union was but a recent development) took up jobs in the industry for brief periods, left them when they were married, and often returned after marriage or when they were divorced. Fortunately, the problem of educating women workers in trade union principles was met by the exertions of outstanding women union officers.†

But while growth in numbers appeared to be stabilized for a period of several years after World War II, important gains were steadily made in other sectors: the reduction of hours, the gradual increase of take-home pay; and the introduction of health and welfare, or "fringe" benefits.

The eight-hour work-day had become the standard by 1947. There-

* Following the death of Vice-President George E. Brown, in November, 1952, Richard W. Smith, of Dining Car Employees Local 351, Chicago, succeeded to his place as head of this division.

† The contribution of various women leaders in different sections of the country to the success of the union would require an extended study in itself. Officers who have distinguished themselves in dealing with the particular problems of women in industry (several have been mentioned earlier) are: former Vice-President Bee Tumber, Los Angeles; Ethel Taylor, St. Louis; Fay Rothring, Cincinnati; Vice-President Gertrude Sweet, Portland, Oregon; Alice Wesling, also of Portland; Lena Mattausch, Butte, Mont.; Reva Walterskirchen, Missoula, Mont.; Ida Peterson, Bellingham, Wash.; Beatrice Rice, Vancouver, Wash.; Margaret Leishman, Spokane, Wash.; Anne Rimington, Peoria, Ill.; Mary Dempsey, Chicago, Ill.; and Beulah Compton, Seattle, Wash.

after the trend to the shorter work-week, the "basic forty hours," continued. On the Pacific Slope from Vancouver, B.C., to San Diego, California, the forty-hour, five-day week was almost universal in all the many local unions of the International. The same five-day week was widely adopted by union agreements in the large cities of the East Coast and in the Middle-Western centers of St. Paul, Minneapolis and Cincinnati. In Chicago and Detroit the work-week was gradually reduced from a six-day basis to a forty-five- and forty-four-hour week by means of agreements usually providing also for premium pay of time-and-a-half for the sixth and seventh days.

As Director of Organization Weinberger estimated (as of April, 1953), "one third of the entire membership is now covered by agreements that provide for the forty-hour week, of five days." [2]

At the outset of the United Nations' "police action" in Korea—whose sudden advent seriously dislocated the American economy—there was a rapid spiral of price inflation that continued for about six months before it was checked by Government control measures early in 1951. When the unions began fighting for another round of wage increases a formula permitting up to 10 per cent increases above the January, 1950, level was established by the Government's Wage Stabilization Board (though it was not always observed). Many of the HRE local unions which acted energetically to reopen wage negotiations were able to improve their members' position before wages were "frozen." But others which had lagged behind, prior to the stabilization order, found themselves limited to a maximum 10 per cent raise above what were still sub-standard pay levels—which was generally insufficient to compensate workers in low wage groups, such as the catering industry, for the sharp rise in the cost of living in 1950-1951.

Nevertheless, the HRE unions, which conducted collective bargaining on a local basis usually, exerted a far stronger economic pressure than in former years toward bringing wage standards in the trade up to equality with pay levels in manufacturing fields. Station cooks and assistant cooks reached a rate of $9 to $15 a day, the higher rates being paid in the Far West and East Coast sections; service bartenders were up to $11 to $16 a day; while waiters, waitresses and hotel maids (their rates partially based on added earnings from tips) were up to $4 to $8 per day on the average. (To these rates the value of meals, and sometimes lodgings also, were to be added for purposes of comparison with wages in manufacturing industries, estimated at an average of $13.75 a day in 1952.) At any rate, skilled craftsmen in the organized centers of the industry, such as the cooks, who were very numerous, approached parity with factory workers.*

The freezing of wage levels during the Korean War, as in World War II, led many unions to bring pressure upon employers for "fringe benefits" in the form of health and welfare insurance plans, in order to gain for their members all the advantages possible under stabilization. Between 1944 and 1949 employer-financed welfare plans were adopted in the New York, Minnesota and Wisconsin locals of the union. After 1950 similar health and welfare plans were introduced in the West Coast and Middle West areas. These varied widely in scope of benefits and methods of financing: some were underwritten entirely by insurance companies; others combined insurance company underwriting of life policies with Blue Cross hospitalization insurance. Most of the plans laid emphasis on life insurance coverage, sickness and accident payments, and hospitalization; some provided a minimal income when members were too sick to work. In a few cases, such as those of Local 6, New York; Local 84, Duluth, Minnesota; and Local 681, Long Beach, California, comprehensive and continuous health care was provided for union members at union health centers. The New York plan, for example, set up an $800,000 medical center for 35,000 eligible workers (including members of other AFL unions affiliated with Local 6 through the New York Hotel Trades Council).

Thus a new concept of the labor movement's goal—pioneered originally by the International Ladies Garment Workers—involving active promotion of the health and physical welfare of the workers came into being, and was embraced with enthusiasm in many important local centers of the HRE. The further hopes of union members and their leaders, who pursued the grand objective of truly comprehensive medical care, were thereafter directed to extending the original plans so that they made provision for the health of workers' dependents also—for it is the worker's family that accounts for the heaviest share of his medical bill.†

* A brief summary of contract rates in the industry, as of 1952, varying from section to section, was compiled by the union's Research Department:

Job	Far West	Middle West	East
Station Cooks	$12–15	$ 9 –14	$10–15
Dishwashers	7– 9	5 – 7	6– 8
Waiters/Waitresses	6– 8	4 – 6	4– 5
Service Bartenders	14–16	11 –14	11–14
Maids	6– 9	5½– 7	5– 7

† Up to the time of writing the most complete plan put into effect is that of Cooks Local Union 89, New York, directed by Secretary Arduilio Susi, which furnishes life

The worker was thus secured against the financial disaster of illness, hospitalization or maternity confinement; the effect upon the worker's morale of such an important change of status has been decidedly visible in recent years. Employers themselves have become thoroughly convinced that such welfare plans, based on regularity of employment, help to cut down absenteeism and turnover, and increase efficiency.

"It's a wonderful feeling when you're laid up sick to see some money coming into the house," one worker wrote to his local officers. A Chicago worker reports: "Recently I had a very serious operation and was confined to the hospital for three months. Without my union insurance and benefits I would have been in debt for years, the total assistance being $1,100." Another, a New York hotel worker, relates that his wife has received payments for maternity hospitalization three times since the Fund was started. "It almost seems as if the Insurance Fund has brought us luck. We had three boys formerly, but wanted to balance the family. Since the Fund started, all three of the babies born to us have been girls!"

The International Union of the 1950's, in comparison with its structure of ten or twenty years earlier, was a far more *centralized* organization than before. This was evident in the added power exercised by the President after 1949, in disciplining officers or regulating the affairs of locals, not only in cases of "subversive activities," but in all other instances of proved malpractice. Formerly, intervention by the International officers in the affairs of the loosely federated organization of widely separated local unions had been rather rare. The locals then not only lived under a system of "home rule" with little interference by the men at the Cincinnati headquarters, but, in the old days, could scarcely ever count upon financial aid when they were faced with the crisis of a strike. Today, on the other hand, the International Union, armed with a treasury of over $5,000,000, not only directs a wide-ranging organizing staff, but can move promptly and with powerful effect in local strike actions that may develop anywhere on the North American continent. It also carries

---

insurance, substantial disability payments, maternity care, hospitalization for *both* members and dependents, and complete medical care under group health service (HIP) for its 9,000 members. This program is financed by a charge of 4 per cent on a relatively high payroll (for cooks), and is union-administered. In comparison, the program of the N. Y. Hotel Trades Council, which is under joint employer-union administration, is more limited in coverage, and is financed by a 3 per cent charge on payroll of workers receiving lower average pay. (1953 Convention Proceedings, pp. 59-60.)

on a variety of educational, research and political activities that were initiated after 1947, under the Ernst-Miller administration.

One reflection of the increased centralizing of authority at the executive level of the union was the passage, at the 1949 convention, of an amendment to the constitution changing the frequency of conventions from once every two years to once every four years. The committee of delegates then reporting in favor of this amendment urged that biennial conventions were very costly and that the money spent for them could better be directed into other channels, particularly organizational work and strike relief. A minority group in the reporting committee, however, headed by the Brooklyn leaders John Kelly of Local 70, and Nat Messing of Local 2, handed in a dissenting report in which they argued that more frequent conventions would permit the members of locals in different parts of the country to maintain closer contact both with each other and with the general officers of the International. Other speakers held that under the plan of quadrennial meetings and elections, power was delegated to the General Executive Board members for too long a period between elections. But still others answered that during the recent World War no convention had been held for six years, yet the union had made the greatest progress in its history without any members being deprived, thereby, of their democratic privileges. The amendment, in any case, was adopted at the 1949 legislative gathering, and the next convention was not held until 1953.

From the start of his administration in October, 1945, Hugo Ernst had felt the urgent need for a strong department of education and research, such as advanced trade unions had introduced twenty or more years ago. The HRE's Joint Board in San Francisco, in 1936, under the leadership of Ernst, had been the first in this union to engage the services of a professional labor research bureau, which furnished important aid in the general hotel strike of 1937. But at the union's headquarters in Cincinnati no records of the different contracts negotiated by the local unions had ever been compiled. Efforts to approach some standardization of wages in this industry would be impossible without such vital information.

At the 1947 convention the establishment of a Department of Research and Education was authorized.* Through this department, thereafter, a store of information about hotel and restaurant chains, and about wages and working conditions in the industry was gathered together, as well as a file of hundreds of local union contracts

* For several years, Robert L. Davis, formerly Director of Research of the Brotherhood of Railway Clerks, AFL, headed the department, resigning in 1953.

and other useful data which were made available thereafter to all locals. Information bearing upon every phase of collective bargaining practice was also compiled and supplied to the branch unions.

Other activities sponsored by Hugo Ernst aimed at establishing numerous vocational training facilities for hotel and restaurant labor. As the war had shown, the country could no longer depend upon a supply of trained apprentices from Europe. The first industry-wide steps toward training culinary workers were taken by the union in 1946, in cooperation with the American Hotel Association, the National Restaurant Association, and the U.S. Office of Education, the representatives of which gathered to exchange ideas in Chicago and created a National Council on Hotel and Restaurant Education. Thereafter, courses in the training of apprentice cooks and other culinary workers were established, through the sponsorship of the Council, at technical high schools and colleges located in Detroit, Seattle, Long Beach, California, Minneapolis, Milwaukee, Chicago and Cincinnati. In addition, advanced training programs for apprentice cooks, under French and Italian chefs, were initiated—usually as part of public or trade and technical school courses—at San Francisco, Los Angeles, Long Beach, Seattle, Chicago, Detroit and New York.

The International had more than doubled its membership within a decade, making it one of the country's ten largest labor unions. But tens of thousands of members had come in who were relatively new to unionism. Hundreds of local officers had to assume leadership without prior training for such responsibilities, without knowledge of the history and principles of the trade union movement. Hence one of the first tasks of the new department was to launch an educational program; this took the form of regional "institutes" at which newcomers among the local officers and members benefited from the teachings of experts familiar with the work and duties of a trade union. The coming of the Korean War and the new Wage Stabilization Board provided new problems, which the Research Department helped to meet. An instance of this, and also of the increased resourcefulness of the more centralized International Union structure, was given in the case of a serious dispute over wages that occurred in Seattle early in 1951.

Here the Local Joint Board officers had reached a deadlock in negotiations with representatives of the Seattle hotel and restaurant associations. Strong rank-and-file pressure for wage increases had accumulated during the recent period of price inflation, especially among the hotel service workers and the big waitresses' Local No.

240, headed by Secretary Beulah Compton. The members authorized demands for not less than 15 per cent increases, failing which they voted to go on strike, the deadline being set for midnight May 31, 1951. But the employers remained adamant, holding that no raise above 10 per cent would be allowed under Wage Stabilization Board rulings.

In late May the Seattle union officers appealed to President Ernst for advice and aid, and he sent the union's Director of Research, who flew to Seattle at once to help negotiate terms with the employers. The employers' representatives were urged by him to accept the 15 per cent increase and assured that the higher rate of pay would be given special approval by the WSB in Washington, as was being done in cases where sub-standard wage levels had prevailed. While the two parties conferring in the union hall at Seattle wrestled with their problems up to the last hours of May 31, and then at the midnight deadline "set the clock back," a great crowd of workers were gathered outside holding demonstrations. At this point, thanks to the intervention of Director of Organization Weinberger, via long distance, the employers were persuaded to accept the union's full terms and peace broke forth. The pay increases granted amounted to $1.30 a day on the average, plus $5.60 a month for health and welfare benefits—bringing the waitresses' scale up to $8 a day and the hotel maids' to $9. This contract, establishing a major industry agreement affecting 11,000 employees, "bent" the 10 per cent wage increase limit, but was, in this case, approved by the Federal Government Board.[3]

Another educational project launched by President Ernst was the Anti-Prohibition Division, which Secretary Miller was asked to take under his charge. Frederick B. Sweet, a former newspaperman, was engaged to help Miller, subsequently assuming as well editorial management of the union's journal. After World War I the International Union had been all but ruined by the Prohibition Amendment. Now, as Sweet said in a speech before the 1949 convention, the continuing Prohibition movement was "everybody's business."

The anti-Prohibition program developed under the direction of Secretary Miller was oriented toward labor-industry partnership. The figures showed that everyone in the industry, not merely bartenders, had a big stake in maintaining sensible liquor controls under a system of legal sales: in the case of hotels up to 15 per cent of their total revenues derived from their bar business. Another growing problem in the industry, thanks to sharp tax increases, was the increasing percentage of distilled spirits sold by the package, instead of over the bar, reaching 65 per cent by 1950.

The HRE, accordingly, joined with other unions and with a number of interested business groups and trade associations to establish the National Coordinating Committee of the Beverage Industry, which soon became the recognized medium for cooperation between labor and business interests in this field. The object was to disseminate information on the Prohibition issue at the community level, when elections took place, and to present the views of the trade unions and business groups at state legislative and congressional hearings.[4]

For Hugo Ernst the most important aspect of the union's educational job was that of preparing its members for citizenship and participation in the country's political life. He had always a passion for social justice that led him to defend the rights not only of working men and women, but of the Negroes and all the foreign-born of minority races who were so often ill-used. An ardent admirer of President Franklin D. Roosevelt and of the New Deal—which he believed approached many of the social goals he had fought for in his early days—Ernst during the 1940's strongly urged his union followers to support the Roosevelt and later the Truman Administration.

The CIO-Political Action Committee performed great service in the campaign for the re-election of Roosevelt in 1944. Three years later, aroused by the Eightieth Congress's passage of the Taft-Hartley Act, the AFL also organized a political instrument, called Labor's League for Political Education, with Joseph Keenan as its first director, and helped in the campaign for the election of Truman in 1948. The LLPE was financed by voluntary contributions of $1 each by members of AFL unions, and made efforts to set up local union officers as precinct captains throughout the United States to help get out the vote in their districts. Hugo Ernst was one of the founders of the LLPE and served as one of its Vice-Presidents. It was Ed Miller, however, a Kansas City neighbor and friend of Harry Truman, who had the idea of going with Hugo Ernst to Washington in May, 1948, and bringing to President Truman their union's forthright endorsement of his candidacy, theirs being the first labor organization to take this step. Truman and the Democratic party, to be sure, surprised all the political experts by emerging as victors in the 1948 contest.

"Political education must be a major concern of our International

Union, as well as of every local, joint board and state council," Ernst said at the opening of the 1953 convention in Atlantic City. The task of labor's new political arm must be to bring all workers to the polls and also to see to it that they arrived there "armed with the facts." Once they had the facts, he held, the common people of America could be depended upon to make wise decisions in the polling booths.[5]

*

During World War II and the years that followed, Ernst traveled widely along his far-flung union front, visiting locals at the most remote points in the Territories and Canada as well as the United States. Thus he became, as Frederick Sweet wrote in the *Catering Industry Employee,* "a familiar and paternal figure to thousands of the members from Fairbanks, Alaska to Honolulu, and from Halifax, Canada to Miami, Florida." Very outgoing and vivacious and a born raconteur—some of whose best stories, unfortunately, cannot be printed—he could discourse in informal manner not only upon the craft standards of their trade, or the proper conduct of a local union, but also upon the merits of different Italian operas.

During his travels, or at the general office in Cincinnati, he constantly performed the traditional services of the union's President as arbiter, handing down decisions in cases of local union disputes or disciplining members and local officers. He could be unforgiving to those who misappropriated even petty sums of money, usually visiting upon them the punishment of expulsion from the union. (To be sure, local officers are nowadays bonded by insurance companies.) But he was very tolerant and humane toward those who were guilty of the common human frailties. One of his last decisions reads:

To * * *

. . . We can see no reason, after investigation of the facts in this case, to set aside the action of Local 15 and the findings of the Joint Executive Board of New York. Your appeal is denied.

We are modifying the penalty placed upon you, however, to provide that the six-month suspension shall not interfere with your rights and ability to earn a living. . . . The above decision shall not prohibit you from securing employment in any establishment where your services are desired by the employer.

In 1944 he had gone, during wartime, as one of the delegates of the American Federation of Labor to attend the British Trades Union Congress at Blackpool, England. One of his special interests thereafter lay in international movements or organizations that would strengthen the ties of American labor with labor bodies in foreign lands and encourage a constant interchange of ideas. In Europe he found that the culinary workers' unions were relatively small, while his own was the "largest culinary union in the world." On later visits to Europe after the war, in 1949 and 1950, he attended conferences of catering workers' unions in Vienna and Copenhagen. It was in Copenhagen that he helped to establish an international secretariat of hotel, restaurant and bar unions, which was afterward to become a part of the International Confederation of Free Trade Unions.

One of his missions abroad, in 1950, took him to Jugoslavia, and to his birthplace in Varazdin, Croatia, which he discovered, to his sorrow, had seen "the last vestiges of culture obliterated" during the recent occupation by the Nazis. On his arrival in Belgrade he was entertained by Premier Tito.

The problem of race had haunted him all his life. Though proud of his own Jewish heritage, he had not been, in principle, a Jewish nationalist, or Zionist, but had been prompted by his own early experience of anti-Semitism to generalize his protest and help all movements opposing race prejudice or racial discrimination of every sort. Thus he had been an active champion of the cause of the Negroes in America, and for many years had as his close friend Walter F. White, director of the Association for the Advancement of Colored People. In his own union Ernst habitually took a very strong position on the matter of excluding Negro workers from membership in various locals, as occurred in the autumn of 1953 in the case of one bartenders' organization on the Pacific Coast. Here Ernst publicly rebuked the officers and took steps to punish them under recent regulations of the International's constitution, saying, "We cannot tolerate the misguided and misbegotten views of some among us who hold that others who work at our crafts may not join with us in trade union brotherhood."

In the early days of World War II, Ernst had brought his brothers and their families out in safety from Jugoslavia. His parents had long since been dead. The fearful disasters which had overtaken the Jewish communities of Europe, and the heroic efforts of the survivors to establish a Jewish state in Palestine, led him in later years to join in organized efforts to aid Israel. Under his inspiration, members of the Hotel and Restaurant Employees and Bartenders Union undertook to raise a fund of $75,000 by voluntary contributions—to which the International Union added $25,000 more—for the construction of much needed workers' housing in the new Jewish state. Ernst, to whom was entrusted the task of conveying this sum to Israel, journeyed there and presented it in the name of his union members at ceremonies for the dedication of a site for a new housing development near Tel-Aviv.

At its 1949 convention the International Union voted unanimous support of a resolution providing that the local unions and the International together contribute $300,000 for construction of a hospital wing at the City of Hope, Duarte, Cal., hospital for the treatment of cancer and diseases of the chest and heart. The City of Hope is a free, non-sectarian medical center which has since its inception been supported in large measure by trade union groups. In recent years pavilions and wings have been built by a number of trade unions. The Hotel and Restaurant Employees and Bartenders International Union Wing was dedicated by the late General President Ernst in December, 1953, only six months before his death. By the time the wing was constructed, the International Union had raised more than $300,000 for this purpose, much of it through a series of dinners held in various cities.

In the winter of 1953, Ernst, then seventy-six years of age, fell ill and was confined to a hospital for many weeks, while Ed Miller and Weinberger ran the union's business. He had suffered from a heart condition for years, had given up all forms of tobacco and lived very abstemiously in order to conserve his strength.

But as the spring came on he was up and about again, in time to appear at the International's thirty-third convention in Atlantic City, a sprightly figure, with sparse, snow-white hair and wearing as usual a brightly colored vest of brocade, which his admirers in the union had recently presented to him. Despite his failing strength he insisted upon presiding at a good many of the convention sessions— and held the chair in his usual lively fashion.

The Ernst-Miller slate had been re-elected without opposition in 1949; the same mandate was given again by the delegates at the 1953 convention and as unreservedly. The factional strife seen in 1947 had completely subsided. It was a serious-minded legislative gathering that reviewed the activities of the organization over the past four years, and passed new regulations touching the present and future plans of the International. As he looked about him with a vision that grew dim, Ernst could remember the half-century of storm and stress through which the union had passed; there were but few members left who had cards dating back forty and fifty years, and he called out a welcome to some of those he saw. How very large this union had become, which was once so difficult to organize; and how much its whole complexion had changed! All about him the accent was assuredly on youth; the local leaders here were young men and women still in their thirties or forties, who would have been successful administrators of large business ventures anywhere and ran their locals or joint boards in that spirit.*

For the young leaders of the union the whole concept of organized labor's program had been transformed. They were absorbed now in providing for the security and welfare of the union members. They sought to determine which were the best forms of life insurance, health insurance and even retirement pensions for their members. The workers must be protected against the periodic depressions that demoralized and destroyed human lives; they demanded security against old age, illness and unemployment. They wanted new housing and slum clearance projects to provide 810,000 units of low-rent dwelling places so that their children might grow up in the sun. And Ernst could remember when waiters and bus men were "slaves" forced to give up their fixed wages of a few dollars a week to the waiter-captains, and when they worked twelve or fourteen hours a day, and were assured that even one day off in seven was "impossible."

"I'm not a youngster any more; I don't know how much longer I'll be able to carry on. . . . " he said.

Ernst's last speech before a convention of his union, which he had served for fifty years, was a moving plea for the unification of the labor movement in America, divided for years into two great federations of the AFL and CIO, but now clearly showing the will to be reunited.

> Labor unity is an urgent goal for working people. Without it we waste our time, strength and money fighting each other instead of pooling those resources to win new gains for all who work.
> Our divisions remain an open invitation to employers to pit some working people against others by playing one organization off against the other.
> We may be sure that the bosses are not divided on the important questions surrounding labor relations policy—just as they work together on all matters affecting their profits. . . .

* Upon the death of Fred Rasser in 1952, Myra Wolfgang was elected Third District Vice-President by the GEB and re-elected in 1953. In that year Bert H. Ross was elected as Second District Vice-President to replace Miguel Garriga. C. T. McDonough, of San Francisco, following the death of John Sargent, in 1951, also returned to the Board as Ninth District Vice-President.

Any efforts to organize new political movements in behalf of the liberal element in the country, he stressed, would be ineffectual without organic unity among the trade unionists. The announcement of the "cease-fire" between the AFL and CIO, in June, 1954, ending almost all jurisdictional strife between their unions, gave Hugo Ernst the highest satisfaction.

One interesting thought he threw off at the Atlantic City convention was the proposal for a "congress" made up of representatives of diverse interest groups in the American community, which was to meet at stated intervals and endeavor to guide enlightened opinion.

> Let me express to you my support for the idea already being discussed widely in labor and liberal circles [of] a broad coalition, not a party, but a great congress of like-minded people, farmers, unions, consumer groups, cooperatives, which will throw its weight behind able and honest candidates pledged to a liberal course in public affairs.[6]

The summer of 1954 found him working as usual in his office in Cincinnati. On July 13, during one of the season's most fearful heat waves, he returned to his home feeling poorly. That evening he suffered a severe heart attack. Almost immediately an oxygen tank was brought for him, and he was rushed to a hospital, but there he lay for more than a week without regaining consciousness. Early in the afternoon of July 22, 1954, he passed away peacefully. Thus the old union waiter "turned in his traveling card" for the last time.

A lifelong bachelor, Hugo Ernst left no surviving family. At the end his brothers Paul and Bruno Ernst, his nearest kin, were at his bedside.

Three days later, on a fine Sunday afternoon, 600 of Hugo Ernst's friends and union associates gathered together on a quiet hillside of Cincinnati, the site of the city's crematory, to pay their last respects to the dead union leader. Many local officers from all parts of the country were there, among them several of his coworkers of the old days in San Francisco. The International's Executive Board members were all present, as were also notables of the AFL, including President Scott Milne and Secretary Joseph Keenan, of the Brotherhood of Electrical Workers, and William Schnitzler, Secretary of the AFL. Secretary-Treasurer Miller had worked closely with Hugo Ernst since 1939 and a truly affectionate relationship had grown up between the older and the younger man. For Jack Weinberger and his wife it meant the breaking of a warm friendship of forty-three years. In the little crematory chapel a simple and dignified funeral service was rendered for Hugo Ernst in Hebrew and English by a rabbi of the Cincinnati community.

On the following morning the GEB gathered together at the council room of the International Union headquarters in Cincinnati and unanimously elected Ed Miller as President and Jack Weinberger as Secretary-Treasurer. Miller had shown a marked capacity to grow up to ever higher responsibilities in the organization. Jack Weinberger, self-effacing and dedicated worker, was less known to the world outside, but for long years had been considered the "soul" of the union's organizational activities, and one of the country's great labor organizers. Hugo Ernst on many occasions before his death had clearly indicated his wish that Ed Miller might be his successor. As for Weinberger, Ernst took great pride in having appointed him to his post in Cincinnati. At the same Board meeting of July, 1954, Charles Paulsen, of Detroit, was appointed Director of Organization to succeed Weinberger.

On taking up the burden that Ernst had laid down, Ed Miller's statement of policy was simple and clear. He had served for almost two decades under the tutelage of both Flore and Ernst, who had been "teachers to him and creative leaders for the union"; he would endeavor to carry on in the same spirit. Hugo, he said, would have liked those who remained to get on with the job. "Surely," he said, "we could build no finer memorial to such men as Hugo Ernst and Edward Flore than to broaden the ranks and deepen the roots of the union."

Reference Notes

1 THE NOT-SO-GAY NINETIES

[1] "Fifty Years of Progress," pamphlet issued by the HRE, 1941, p. 9.
[2] Hugo Ernst to author, interview, November, 1953.
[3] Joel Seidman: *Leadership in a Local Union*, p. 231. University of Chicago Press, 1941.
[4] 1923 Convention Proceedings: Speech of J. L. Sullivan, pp. 27-28.
[5] W. E. McEwen: "Reminiscences," in *The Labor World*, Duluth, Minn.; cited in *Mixer & Server*, November 15, 1928.
[6] *Mixer & Server*, April 15, 1904.
[7] Lewis Lorwin: *The American Federation of Labor*, p. 22. The Brooking Institution, Washington, 1933.
[8] HRE Files; W. E. Horne Papers.
[9] John Assel: "Culinary Mass Meeting: 50 Years Ago." HRE Files; W. E. Horne Papers.
[10] Article in the "Waiters' Journal," 1892. HRE Files; W. E. Horne Papers.
[11] *Mixer & Server*, April 15, 1904.
[12] John Assel: "Culinary Mass Meeting: 50 Years Ago," HRE Files; W. E. Horne Papers.
[13] Max Becker: "Report of the 1892 Convention."
[14] William Lehman to author, April, 1954.
[15] *The National Purveyor*, September, 1898, p. 4.
[16] Max Becker, *op. cit.*
[17] W. E. McEwen, *op. cit.*
[18] W. E. McEwen, *op. cit.*
[19] J. L. Sullivan: "Résumé of Nine Conventions"; *Mixer & Server*, May 15, 1902, pp. 21-36.
[20] *Ibid.*
[21] W. E. McEwen, *op. cit.*
[22] *National Purveyor*, September, 1898, p. 4.
[23] *Ibid.*, p. 5.
[24] J. L. Sullivan, *op. cit.*
[25] *The American Caterer*, July, 1896.
[26] 8th Convention Report: 1900, p. 17.
[27] Minutes of the GEB Meeting, Brevoort House, Chicago, August 1-2, 1899.
[28] 1923 Convention Proceedings, p. 140.

2 JERE L. SULLIVAN: THE EARLY YEARS

[1] 1907 Convention: Report of the Secretary.
[2] Paul Brissenden: *The Industrial Workers of the World*, p. 36. New York, 1919.
[3] *Mixer & Server*, April 15, 1912.
[4] Letter of J. C. Hickey, *Mixer & Server*, January 15, 1904.
[5] Hugo Ernst to author, interview, March 15, 1954.
[6] Letter of W. H. Pierce, Local 76, Syracuse, May 23, 1904; W. E. Horne Papers.
[7] J. Rubin and M. J. Obermeier: *Growth of a Union*, p. 58. New York, 1943.
[8] Memorandum of J. Bookjans.
[9] 1902 Convention Proceedings, p. 55.
[10] Letter of Charles Ikenberry, July 10, 1953.
[11] *Growth of a Union*, pp. 33-35.
[12] Letter of W. H. Pierce, May 23, 1904. HRE Files.
[13] HRE Files.
[14] *Mixer & Server*, November 15, 1901.
[15] *Ibid.*, August 15, 1901; January 15, 1903.
[16] Speech of Michael Goldsmith, 1917 (twentieth anniversary of Local 108); pamphlet.
[17] Report of M. J. Mattimore, *Mixer & Server*, November 15, 1905.
[18] *Mixer & Server*, April 15, 1901.
[19] *Ibid.*
[20] *Ibid.*, March 15, 1901
[21] Ira Cross: A *History of the Labor Movement in California*, pp. 35, 177, 182. Berkeley, 1935.
[22] Ira Cross, *op. cit.*, pp. 239, 243-245.
[23] *Mixer & Server*, December 12, 1903.
[24] L. Lorwin, *op. cit.*, p. 85.
[25] P. F. Brissenden, *op. cit.*, p. 49.
[26] Memorandum of R. E. Croskey to W. E. Horne, 1941. HRE Files.
[27] *Mixer & Server*, June 15, 1901, p. 2.
[28] *Ibid.*, March 15, 1914.
[29] *Ibid.*, January 15, 1904.
[30] *Cleveland Citizen*, January 24, 1903.
[31] R. E. Croskey: Article in the *Catering Industry Employee*, April, 1941.
[32] Report of U. S. Committee on Industrial Relations, 1914, Washington, D. C., pp. 3244-3249. Testimony of Elizabeth Maloney.
[33] 1904 Convention: President's Report, pp. 10-11.
[34] 1907 Convention Proceedings, p. 77.
[35] Charles Sands: Memorandum, 1941.
[36] *Cleveland Citizen*, June 13, 1903.
[37] *Mixer & Server*, September 15, 1903.
[38] César Lesino to author.
[39] Article by J. L. Sullivan, *Mixer & Server*, October 15, 1904.
[40] John J. Kearney to author.
[41] J. P. Franc, Local 504; letter to *Mixer & Server*, May 12, 1904.
[42] *Mixer & Server*, August 15, 1904.
[43] *Ibid.*, p. 9.

3 SHAKE-UP

[1] 1905 Convention Proceedings, pp. 49-50; *Mixer & Server*, August 15, 1904.
[2] *Mixer & Server*, August 15, 1905.
[3] 1907 Convention: Report of the Secretary.

[4] J. M. Osborn, former International Vice-President, to author.
[5] *Growth of a Union*, p. 83; 1907 Convention Proceedings, p. 78.
[6] 1907 Convention Proceedings, pp. 60-61, 110-115.
[7] *Ibid.*, pp. 114-115.
[8] Letter of Paul Winkel, Local 266; *Mixer & Server*, February 15, 1904.
[9] Otto Schatz, Secretary of the International Geneva Association, to author.
[10] J. M. Osborn to author.
[11] *Mixer & Server*, June 15, 1911.
[12] 1911 Convention Proceedings, pp. 77-78.
[13] 1947 Convention Proceedings: Memorial Speech by Emmanuel Kovaleski, pp. 88-90.
[14] *Growth of a Union*, pp. 35-36.
[15] *Mixer & Server*, March 15, 1901.
[16] *Growth of a Union*, pp. 99-100.
[17] 1909 Convention Proceedings, pp. 110-111.
[18] *Growth of a Union*, pp. 106-107.
[19] J. J. Kearney to author.
[20] *Mixer & Server*, June, 1915. p. 2.
[21] J. E. McCracken, President of Local 300, Spokane, to author; also, 1911 Convention Proceedings, pp. 162-163.
[22] Ed H. Horne: "Brief History of the International"; memorandum.

4 THE DUAL UNION MOVEMENT: 1912

[1] *Growth of a Union, The Life of Edward Flore*, pp. 125-129.
[2] Ed Miller to author.
[3] J. E. McCracken to author.
[4] John Bookjans: "The 1912 Movement"; memorandum.
[5] *Mixer & Server*, February 15, 1912, p. 12.
[6] *Ibid.*, March 15, 1912.
[7] *Ibid.*, October 15, 1911.
[8] *Growth of a Union*, pp. 138-139.
[9] John Bookjans: "You Can't Organize New York," *Catering Industry Employee*, January 15, 1953, p. 9.
[10] *Ibid.*
[11] John Bookjans: "The 1912 Movement"; memorandum (in manuscript).
[12] Mary Alden Hopkins: "The Hotel Workers' Strike," *Collier's*, June 1, 1912.
[13] W. F. Whyte: *Human Relations in the Restaurant Industry*, New York, 1948, pp. 94-95.
[14] George Orwell: *Down and Out in Paris and London*, pp. 71, 73-75. Quoted by permission of Harcourt, Brace & Company. New York, 1950.
[15] César Lesino to author.
[16] A bartender of St. Paul, Minnesota, to author.
[17] W. F. Whyte, *op. cit.*, pp. 94, 370.
[18] John Bookjans: "The Tipping System," CIE, January 17, 1949.
[19] W. F. Whyte, *op. cit.*, p. 372.
[20] Report of U. S. Commission on Industrial Relations, 1914, Washington, D.C., pp. 3244-3249, 3257-3258. Testimony of Elizabeth Maloney.
[21] *Mixer & Server*, February 15, 1913.
[22] Article by Jack Weinberger, *Mixer & Server*, February, 1919, p. 57.
[23] John Bookjans, *Mixer & Server*, July 15, 1915, pp. 24-26.
[24] 1913 Convention, GEB Commission Report.
[25] Otto Schatz to author, letter of January 8, 1954.
[26] Memorandum of Charles Sands, February 18, 1954.

27 Letter of former Vice-President J. J. Kearney to J. Bookjans, March 23, 1954.
28 *New York Herald*, January 11, 1913.
29 *Mixer & Server*, February 15, 1913.
30 John Bookjans: "The 1912 Movement"; memorandum.
31 Report of U.S. Commission on Industrial Relations, 1914, Washington, D.C., pp. 3244-3245, 3251-3252. Testimony of July 22, 1914.
32 1913 Convention Proceedings, p. 122 ff.
33 David Saposs: *Left-Wing Unionism*, p. 122. New York, 1928.
34 1913 Convention Proceedings, p. 28 ff.

5 THE "WESTERN MOVEMENT"

1 Hugo Ernst to author.
2 Henry B. Lister to author; letter of Hugo Ernst, June 2, 1954.
3 Hugo Ernst: "35 Years in San Francisco Labor"; interview in *San Francisco Chronicle*, August 20, 1938.
4 Alfred Armstrong to author.
5 *San Francisco Chronicle*, August 12, 1917.
6 Address at Berkeley, Cal., in 1917.
7 Hugo Ernst: "Survey Tour," *Mixer & Server*, July 15, 1923.
8 Jack Weinberger: Memorandum on the History of the International, 1953.
9 *Mixer & Server*, January 15, 1915, pp. 41-42.
10 William Lehman to author, interview, March 6, 1954.
11 *Growth of a Union*, p. 148.
12 L. G. Harter: "The San Francisco Culinary Workers," *op. cit.*, pp. 23-24.
13 Henry B. Lister to author.
14 Jack Weinberger: Memorandum, 1953; and Report of Local 30, *Mixer & Server*, February 15, 1921.
15 *San Francisco Chronicle*, July 20, 1919.
16 George Mowry: *The California Progressives*, p. 265. Berkeley, Cal., 1936.
17 George Mowry, *op. cit.*, p. 264; and letter of Ed Gammons in *San Francisco Daily News*, July 14, 1936.
18 Hugo Ernst: Address before Students of the University of California, Berkeley, 1917; HRE Files.
19 Ida Peterson to author, interview, April 12, 1954.

6 THE "GREAT DROUTH"

1 1917 Convention Proceedings, p. 14 ff.
2 1919 Convention Proceedings, p. 15 ff.
3 *Growth of a Union*, p. 164.
4 L. G. Harter, *op. cit.*, p. 36; J. Weinberger, "Memorandum," p. 6.
5 Mrs. Kitty Amsler to author, January 8, 1954.
6 Mrs. Kitty Amsler to author, January 8, 1954.
7 *Mixer & Server*, July, 1923, p. 37.
8 *Mixer & Server*, July, 1923, p. 31.
9 Report of the GEB for 1926; 1927 Convention Proceedings, pp. 123-124.
10 1923 Convention Proceedings, p. 192.
11 *Ibid.*, pp. 138-141.
12 *Ibid.*, p. 43.
13 1921 Convention Proceedings, pp. 177-178.
14 1925 Convention Proceedings, p. 191.
15 *Ibid.*, p. 192.

7 THE PASSING OF JERE SULLIVAN

[1] L. G. Harter, *op. cit.*, p. 35.
[2] Jack Weinberger: Memorandum, 1953.
[3] 1927 Convention Proceedings, p. 153.
[4] J. M. Osborn to author.
[5] 1923 Convention Proceedings, p. 157.
[6] 1927 Convention Proceedings, p. 199.
[7] *Ibid.*, p. 189.
[8] J. M. Osborn to author.
[9] 1927 Convention Proceedings, pp. 254-255.
[10] *Ibid.*, pp. 230-231.
[11] Hugo Ernst to author, letter of June 2, 1954.

8 THE GREAT DEPRESSION

[1] J. Weinberger to author.
[2] Ludwig Bemelmans: *Hotel Splendide*, pp. 47-48. Quoted by permission of the Viking Press. New York, 1941.
[3] 1929 Convention: Report of the President, p. 13.
[4] *Growth of a Union*, p. 152.
[5] *Detroit Free Press*, April 25, 1931.
[6] *Detroit Daily News*, May 24, 1931; also, Louis Koenig to author.
[7] Letter of J. W. Knispel, June 15, 1929, CIE, p. 42.
[8] *New York Times*, May 9, 1929.
[9] 1929 Convention: Report of the President, p. 13.
[10] *Growth of a Union*, p. 226.
[11] *New York Times*, April 8, 1929; May 9, 1929.
[12] 1929 Convention Proceedings, pp. 107-108.
[13] *Ibid.*, p. 110.
[14] *Ibid.*, pp. 111-113.
[15] *Ibid.*, pp. 113-115.
[16] Rufus Jarman: *A Bed for the Night*, p. 266. Harper's, New York, 1953.
[17] 1932 Convention Proceedings, pp. 21-22.
[18] CIE, September 15, 1930.
[19] Cleveland Joint Committee File for 1931.
[20] Letter of R. Hesketh to A. J. Van Bebber, March 18, 1931; Cleveland Joint Committee File for 1931.
[21] Letter of W. S. Koones to Charles Bendheim, U. S. Department of Labor, July 23, 1931.
[22] 1932 Convention: Speech of Daniel J. Tobin, pp. 3-4.
[23] J. Weinberger: Memorandum, 1953.
[24] L. G. Harter, *op. cit.*, pp. 38-41.
[25] CIE, January 15, 1932, p. 13.
[26] Walter Cowan to author; James G. Manus, Secretary, Local 30, to author.
[27] 1932 Convention Proceedings, pp. 3-4.
[28] *Ibid.*, pp. 23-24.
[29] *Boston Globe*, August 10, 1932.
[30] Confidential Report to the GEB, by Secretary-Treasurer Hesketh, March 16, 1933.

9 REBIRTH: 1933–1934

[1] 1934 Convention: Report of the GEB, p. 255.
[2] 1934 Convention: Report of President, pp. 23-24.
[3] Letter of Emil Schlitz, CIE, March 15, 1934, p. 17.
[4] CIE, December 15, 1934, p. 7.
[5] J. Weinberger: Memorandum, 1953.
[6] Samuel Yellen: *Great American Labor Struggles*, pp. 279-280. New York, 1938.
[7] Walter Cowan to author.
[8] Hugo Ernst to author, letter of June 18, 1954; Henry Melnikow, Pacific Coast Labor Bureau, to author.
[9] 1932 Convention Proceedings, pp. 131-132.
[10] James Blakely to author.
[11] 1934 Convention Proceedings, p. 149.
[12] *Ibid.*, pp. 20, 129.
[13] John Bookjans: "Report on the 1934 Convention to Local 237."
[14] CIE, April 15, 1934, pp. 18-19.
[15] *New York Times*, November 26, 1932.
[16] Speech of Thomas E. Dewey at Buffalo, N.Y. *New York Times*, November 2, 1938.
[17] Walter Cowan to author.
[18] John Bookjans to author.

10 THE NEW YORK RACKETEERS

[1] *New York Times*, January 25, 1934; January 27, 1934.
[2] *Ibid.*, January 26, 1934.
[3] *Growth of a Union*, pp. 235-236.
[4] 1934 Convention Proceedings, p. 93.
[5] John J. Kearney to author.
[6] *Growth of a Union*, p. 238.
[7] 1936 Convention Proceedings, p. 39.
[8] *Ibid.*, p. 40.
[9] *New York Times*, September 24, 1935.
[10] *Growth of a Union*, p. 241.
[11] 1936 Convention Proceedings, pp. 117-118.
[12] *Ibid.*, p. 2.
[13] John Bookjans: "Report of the 1936 Convention to Local 237."
[14] *Growth of a Union*, p. 247.
[15] "The 1936 Convention," article by David Herman, CIE, September 15, 1936.
[16] *Growth of a Union*, pp. 124-126.
[17] *New York Times*, August 16, 1936; October 21, 1936.
[18] J. J. Kearney to author.
[19] 1936 Convention Proceedings, p. 148.
[20] *Ibid.*, p. 147.
[21] *Growth of a Union*, pp. 248-249.
[22] Walter Cowan to author.
[23] *New York Times*, December 31, 1936.

11 "THE MAN WHO WOULD BE KING"

[1] *People* vs. *Cohen* et al., brief of Thomas E. Dewey, New York Court of Appeals, July 11, 1939.

[2] *New York Times*, January 30, 1937.
[3] *People* vs. *Cohen* et al., New York Court of Appeals, Vol. 107.
[4] CIE, March 15, 1938.
[5] *Growth of a Union*, pp. 276-277.
[6] 1936 Convention Proceedings, p. 34.
[7] Affidavit of G. B. McLane, text in *Chicago Times*, March 31, 1940; December 4, 1940.
[8] *Ibid.*
[9] J. M. Osborn to author.
[10] *Growth of a Union*, pp. 282-283.
[11] J. E. McCracken to author.
[12] Hugo Ernst to author.
[13] *San Francisco Chronicle*, August 15, 1938.
[14] 1938 Convention Proceedings, pp. 23, 25, 29.
[15] *Ibid.*, p. 64.
[16] *Ibid.*, p. 158.
[17] *San Francisco Chronicle*, August 18, 1938; August 26, 1938.
[18] Report of the 1938 Convention, by M. W. Cantu, Local 110, San Francisco, August 29, 1938. Ernst Papers.
[19] *San Francisco Chronicle*, August 18, 1938.
[20] 1938 Convention Proceedings, pp. 139-140.
[21] M. W. Cantu, *op. cit.*
[22] 1938 Convention Proceedings, p. 142.
[23] *Ibid.*, pp. 142-143.

12 TRIUMPH OF THE SERVICE WORKERS:
1937-1941

[1] CIE, March 15, 1937.
[2] C. W. Pilgrim, article in CIE, June 12, 1937, p. 11.
[3] Letter of C. W. Pilgrim, July 21, 1937, in CIE, August 12, 1937.
[4] *San Francisco Chronicle*, August 20, 1938.
[5] J. Weinberger: "Memorandum on the History of the HRE," 1953; manuscript.
[6] Myra Wolfgang to author.
[7] *Detroit News*, March 17, 1937.
[8] *Kansas City Star-Times*, May 30, 1937; June 16, 1937.
[9] *Ibid.*, June 17, 1937.
[10] CIE, January, 1937, p. 7.
[11] CIE, June 12, 1938, p. 10.
[12] *Hy Eisenberger* vs. *Jay Rubin*, et al. Affidavit of Rubin, N.Y. County Supreme Court, May 16, 1940.
[13] *Growth of a Union*, pp. 308-311.
[14] New York Department of Labor Bulletin, February, 1951.
[15] CIE, May 16, 1938.

13 WORLD WAR II

[1] 1941 Convention Proceedings, p. 20.
[2] *Ibid.*, p. 180.
[3] CIE, July 12, 1941.
[4] CIE, May 12, 1941, p. 23.
[5] 1941 Convention Proceedings, p. 179.
[6] CIE, June 12, 1941, p. 9.
[7] 1941 Convention Proceedings, pp. 190-191.

[8] *Ibid.*, p. 201.
[9] *Ibid.*, p. 209.
[10] Letter of George Young, CIE, July, 1941, p. 27.
[11] *San Francisco Examiner*, July 3, 1941; July 9, 1941.
[12] Van Dusen Kennedy, *Arbitration in the San Francisco Hotel and Restaurant Industry*, pp. 46-47. Berkeley, California, 1952.
[13] William McCabe, former President of the San Francisco L.J.E.B., to author.
[14] *San Francisco Chronicle*, November 6, 1941; November 9, 1941.
[15] Van Dusen Kennedy, *op. cit.*, pp. 32-33.
[16] 1947 Convention Proceedings, p. 33.
[17] W. F. Whyte, *op. cit.*, pp. 5-6.
[18] 1949 Convention Proceedings: Speech of Robert L. Davis, p. 77.
[19] 1947 Convention Proceedings, p. 33.
[20] *Ibid.*
[21] *New York World-Telegram*, June 26, 1944; also, letter of J. Rubin and M. J. Obermeier to J. J. Kearney, April 29, 1944.
[22] Hugo Ernst to Charles Yates, letter of October 16, 1945.
[23] Hugo Ernst to author, letter of June 18, 1954.
[24] CIE, November 12, 1945; GEB Minutes, October 2, 1945.
[25] Hugo Ernst to Charles Yates, letter of October 16, 1945.

14 THE PRESIDENCY OF ERNST: "THE MIRACLE YEAR"

[1] Nicholas McLeod to author.
[2] Agreement between HRE and Hotel Association of Seattle, June 16, 1937.
[3] Ed S. Miller to author.
[4] 1941 Convention Proceedings, p. 180.
[5] *Ibid.* (Biennial Report), p. 36.
[6] 1947 Convention Proceedings, p. 116.
[7] *Ibid.*, p. 196.
[8] *Ibid.*, pp. 44-45.
[9] Walter Cowan to author.
[10] *Chicago Sun-Times*, March 20, 1947.
[11] 1947 Convention Proceedings, p. 115.
[12] Walter Cowan to author.
[13] 1947 Convention Proceedings, p. 117.
[14] *Ibid.*, pp. 122-123.
[15] CIE, May 12, 1947, p. 2.
[16] 1947 Convention Proceedings, pp. 194, 196.
[17] *Ibid.*, p. 197.
[18] *Ibid.*, p. 274.
[19] *Ibid.*, pp. 188, 196-197.
[20] *New York Times*, May 7, 1947.
[21] 1949 Convention Report, pp. 170-171.
[22] *A Union of Unions*, p. 20, issued by New York Hotel Trades Council, 1952.
[23] *Garcia* vs. *Ernst* et al., New York Supreme Court, January, 1951.
[24] B. H. Ross to author.
[25] Letter of Hugo Ernst to Martin Cody, C. Collins, Lee Candea, *et al.*, CIE, February, 1951.
[26] 1953 Convention Proceedings: Closing Remarks of President Ernst, p. 267.

15 THE MODERN INTERNATIONAL UNION

[1] 1953 Convention: Officers' Reports, p. 51.
[2] *Ibid.*, p. 57.
[3] *Ibid.*, pp. 56-57.
[4] 1949 Convention Proceedings, pp. 55-56.
[5] 1953 Convention Proceedings, pp. 78-79.
[6] *Ibid.*, p. 79.

Index

ABOUT THE AUTHOR

MATTHEW JOSEPHSON was born in Brooklyn, New York, and was graduated from Columbia University in 1920. In the years just after his graduation he served on the editorial staffs of *transition* and other "little magazines" in Europe and America. Then, after a brief interval in a Wall Street job, he returned to literature and in 1926 began his first major book, a biography of Zola, which was published two years later. This was followed by *Rousseau*, and in 1934 by *The Robber Barons*, the first volume of a trilogy on American business and political history since the Civil War. The subsequent volumes were *The Politicos* and *The President Makers*. The publication of *Victor Hugo* and *Stendhal*, in 1942 and 1946 respectively, showed his continuing interest in the lives of the great French writers in the democratic tradition. *Sidney Hillman: Statesman of American Labor*—published in 1952—and this present book are evidence of his equal concern with the American democratic tradition.

In addition to writing these histories and biographies, Mr. Josephson has continued to contribute to magazines. His articles have appeared frequently in the *Saturday Evening Post*, the *New Republic*, the *New Yorker* and the *Nation*.

Mr. Josephson was elected a member of the National Institute of Arts and Letters in 1948. He and his wife, an editor and translator, now live on a farm near Sherman, Connecticut.